COFFEE WITH HITLER

The British Amateurs
Who Tried to Civilise the Nazis

CHARLES SPICER

ONEWORLD

A Oneworld Book

First published in Great Britain, the Republic of Ireland and Australia by Oneworld Publications, 2022
This paperback edition published 2023

ISBN 978-0-86154-617-6
eISBN 978-0-86154-378-6

Frontispieces: Prologue © Fremantle/Alamy, Ch. 1 © Ullstein Bild/Getty, Ch. 2 courtesy of Library
of Congress, Ch. 3 from author's collection, Ch. 4 © Keystone France/Getty, Ch. 5 © Hulton
Archive/Getty, Ch. 6 © Ullstein Bild/Getty, Ch. 7, 8 © Süddeutsche Zeitung Photo/Alamy, Ch. 9
by Heinrich Hoffmann/public domain, Ch. 10 © World History Archive/Alamy, Ch. 11 © Ullstein
Bild/Getty, Ch. 12 © AP/Shutterstock, Ch. 13 © Süddeutsche Zeitung Photo/Alamy, Ch. 14 ©
Ullstein Bild/Getty, Ch. 15 courtesy of Wikimedia Commons, Ch. 16, 17 from author's collection,
Ch. 18 © Popperphoto/Getty, Ch. 19 © Süddeutsche Zeitung Photo/Alamy, Ch. 20 licensed under
CC-BY-SA 3.0 from Bundesarchiv Deutschland, Ch. 21 © Everett Collection/Shutterstock, Ch. 22
Sueddeutsche Zeitung Photo/Alamy, Ch. 23 © Footage Clips/Shutterstock, Ch. 24 by Ministry of
Health (public domain), Ch. 25 © Popperphoto/Getty, Ch. 26 © Keystone/Getty, Ch. 27 © Trinity
Mirror/Alamy, Epilogue © Everett Collection/Alamy, Conclusion courtesy of Wikimedia Commons

Plate section: Ernest Tennant from *True Account* by Ernest Tennant, Ribbentrop and Kordt
© Ullstein Bild/Getty, Leopold von Hoesch © Mansell Collection/Shutterstock, Duke of
Saxe-Coburg-Gotha © akg-images/TT News Agency, Duke and Duchess of Brunswick
dinner, Kim Philby © Tallandier/Bridgeman Images, von Hoesch funeral © Süddeutsche
Zeitung Photo/Alamy, the Mitford family © Central Press/Getty, Lloyd George with
Ribbentrop © Ullstein Bild/Getty, Haus Wyleberg, Marie and Alice Schuster, Alice Schuster
and Christie from a private collection, Gertrud Scholtz-Klink © AP/Shutterstock, Douglas
Douglas-Hamilton © Hulton Archive/Getty, stills from Lloyd George's tea with Hitler ©
Screen and Sound Archive, The National Library of Wales, Ribbentrop with Halifax ©
Ray Illingworth/AP/Shutterstock, Graham Christie in plane from author's collection

Typeset by Tetragon, London
Printed and bound in Great Britain by Clays Ltd, Elcograf S.p.A.

Oneworld Publications
10 Bloomsbury Street
London WC1B 3SR
England

'If ever there was a case of the road to hell being paved with good intentions, it is surely the story that Charles Spicer tells so brilliantly and empathetically in this exceptionally well-written book.'

David Cannadine

'This is a complex tale, but as skillfully narrated by Spicer, it moves along briskly.'

Washington Post

'In this very well-researched and well-written work of historical revisionism, Charles Spicer reminds us of the important fact that not every Briton who wanted better relations with Nazi Germany did so from malign motives.'

Andrew Roberts, author of
Churchill: Walking with Destiny

'Spicer, who has given close, neutral and unerring scrutiny of the sources, proves to be a brisk, fair-minded and authoritative revisionist… *Coffee with Hitler* should make it impossible to continue to lampoon the Fellowship as an unsavoury gang.'

TLS

'Spicer's book is a resounding success, retelling the fascinating history of the Anglo-German Fellowship.'

History Today

'Charles Spicer tells the chilling story of how otherwise respectable men and women became pawns in a game of international intrigue with a reprehensible regime. The outstanding narrative reads like a thriller.'

…rican Friends

014491457 0

CHARLES SPICER is an independent historian based in London and Suffolk. *Coffee With Hitler* is his debut and was a *Spectator* and *Telegraph* history book of the year. His research is based on his recent doctorate, which was examined by leading historians including David Cannadine, Julie Gottlieb and Richard Overy.

For my parents,
Julian (1934–2019), who taught me to read,
and Sarah (1940–1999), who challenged me to think.

CONTENTS

INTRODUCTION

COFFEE WITH HITLER TELLS THE STORY, FOR THE FIRST TIME, of a handful of amateur British intelligence agents who wined, dined and charmed the leading National Socialists in Germany in the 1930s. They hoped to avert a second war in Europe by building rapport with the Third Reich politically, economically and socially. In parallel, they gathered intelligence on this startlingly vulgar and maverick new regime which they used to educate the aloof British government. By exploiting German admiration for British culture, they hoped to entice Germany back into the fold of civilised European nations and to welcome her alarmingly ambitious leader Adolf Hitler into the pantheon of respectable international statesmen. In short, they wanted to civilise the Nazis.

The vehicle for this unusual mix of amateur diplomacy and intelligence gathering was the then and still controversial Anglo-German Fellowship. Funded by leading industrialists and the City of London, anxious to nurture business with Germany, this exclusive friendship society recruited (to a degree never fully acknowledged) distinguished supporters from both English and German royalty, the British aristocracy, the three fighting forces, and politicians from all parties and both Houses of Parliament. Set up two years after Hitler came to power, the new Fellowship followed in the wake of highly cultured predecessor societies dating back to the nineteenth century and sat comfortably in the traditional cousinhood and mutual admiration of the English and the Germans.

The protagonists were a left-wing, pacifist Welsh political secretary, a conservative, butterfly-collecting Old Etonian businessman and a pioneering Great War fighter ace. Each was fluent in German and expert on the country's politics and economy, but otherwise they made unlikely colleagues. Between them, they befriended Adolf Hitler's most Anglophile and socially aspirational paladins: Joachim Ribbentrop, the 'champagne salesman' who rose to become foreign minister; Hermann Göring, president of the Reichstag,

1

commander of the Luftwaffe, art collector and field sports enthusiast; and Rudolf Hess, scribe for Hitler's *Mein Kampf* and his internationalist deputy führer. Though only minor players in the terrible drama of Europe's descent into total war, the three Britons operated at the heart of the British Establishment. They infiltrated the Nazi high command deeper than any of their countrymen to pass back better intelligence to both their government and its domestic critics. Straddling this porous border between hard and soft diplomacy, their exploits fuelled tensions between the amateurs and the professionals.

The tasteful settings for their efforts ranged from tea parties in Downing Street, banquets at London's best hotels and the coronation of George VI to coffee and cakes at Hitler's Bavarian mountain home, champagne galas at the Berlin Olympics and elegant afternoon receptions at the Nuremberg rallies. More private encounters between the elites of both countries were nurtured at shooting weekends at English stately homes, whisky drinking sessions at German estates, discreet meetings in London flats and whispered exchanges in the corridors of embassies and foreign ministries.

These unlikely heroes witnessed at first hand key landmarks in the seemingly unstoppable rise of the Third Reich: dinner with Heinrich Himmler before the Night of the Long Knives; white tie celebrations for the anniversary of Hitler's release from prison; alerting Whitehall to the remilitarisation of the Rhineland; riding in the Führer's cavalcade at the Nuremberg rally; escorting David Lloyd George to meet the German leader; inviting their host to visit London; warning the British foreign secretary of the invasion of Czechoslovakia; walking through Kensington Gardens with the conspirators plotting to overthrow Hitler; greeting Neville Chamberlain on his return from Munich; briefing Winston Churchill and Anthony Eden on the eve of war; and then negotiating between the British government and the German resistance once war was declared. Drawing on newly discovered primary sources, their story also sheds light on Winston Churchill's approach to appeasement, the US's entry into the war, the early career of the infamous Soviet spy, Kim Philby, and the quixotic peace mission of the deputy führer Rudolf Hess to an aristocrat's estate in Scotland.

Their hands-on engagement with this brutal and apparently uncultured new Germany was in sharp contrast with the head-in-the-sand attitude taken by the British coalition governments led by Ramsay MacDonald and

Stanley Baldwin. Guided by a patrician and Francophile Foreign Office, Downing Street preferred to ignore the perturbing rise of National Socialism and cold shoulder the new German government in the hope it would fade away like a bad smell.

This is not another book about appeasement. By consciously taking *civilising* rather than *appeasing* as its central theme, it seeks to move beyond the often-fevered debate around appeasement that has rumbled on for eight decades. Though a respectable diplomatic strategy prior to 1938, it is now so polarising a term as to risk alienating all but the most specialised of history readers. While respected scholars continue to paint Neville Chamberlain's appeasement of Hitler's Germany in a more sympathetic light, the 'Guilty Men' interpretation of the build-up to the Second World War has captured the public imagination. (Winston Churchill has been the subject of around one thousand biographies while those about his immediate predecessor can be counted on one hand.) More dangerously, post-war politicians have 'weaponised' the term appeasement to justify military incursions from Suez and Vietnam to Iraq and Afghanistan and used it as a brickbat to condemn recent diplomatic compromises such as the ceasefire between the Turks and the Kurds and the Western democracies' dealings with President Putin's Russia and President Xi's China.

Appeasement, in the sense of one nation making concessions to the demands of another to prevent an escalation of hostilities, is essentially reactive and passive. The civilising mission of the leaders of the Anglo-German Fellowship – to charm, cultivate and connect with the new regime – was pro-active and dynamic. This path was smoothed by both the National Socialists' ideological veneration of Britain and her Empire (expertly observed by Gerwin Strobl in *The Germanic Isle: Nazi Perceptions of Britain*) and their deep-seated anxiety to avenge the patronising sneers of the old German elites and international critics. On a practical level, the Fellowship's first principle was to make trade not war – the far from novel capitalist peace theory. Despite progress in Germany's post-war reconstruction, debt and rampant inflation had hobbled her economy; the Fellowship's ambitious programme to promote trade between Europe's two largest economies aimed to redress this. Its leadership advocated a return to well-financed trade rather than barter, favoured some restoration of former African colonies and the cancellation of war debts. In return, Germany should rejoin the League of

Nations, engage with disarmament negotiations and, critically, abandon her anti-Semitic programme. Any territorial expansion in Europe should be subject to negotiations, plebiscites and the blessing of the League. For all this to work, political friendships had to be nurtured through frequent consultations between senior ministers and other political opinion formers. This should be enhanced by tourism and softer social activities designed to build amity between the two nations: the sponsorship of touring choirs, orchestras and art exhibitions as well as cultural exchanges between university students, youth movements and military veterans back and forth across the North Sea.

As Albert Camus said in 1947, 'It is always possible to record the social conversation that takes place on the benches of the amphitheatre while the lion is crunching the victim.'[1] The chapter titles and recurring food and drink motifs in this book are not intended to seem flippant and in no way seek to trivialise the horrors of Hitler's regime. While it is easy to accuse those who broke bread with the Nazis of supping with the Devil, food is the oldest diplomatic tool, and these social interactions offer intriguing glimpses into the belly of the beast. Woven into this narrative is how proudly the socially gauche National Socialists wanted to be civilised as they admired and aped the British elites. But while they took themselves deadly seriously, the British struggled to ignore the frequent social absurdities and black comedy that ensued.

To date, the Anglo-German Fellowship and its champions have had a mostly bad press. One writer painted a picture of a 'knot of peers adrift in an uncongenial world, united by paranoia, pessimism and panic', who blamed the 'misfortunes of their times and class on an immensely powerful but clandestine Judaeo-Bolshevik global conspiracy which could be thwarted only by Fascism and Nazism'.[2] Another dismissed the organisation's members as a 'mixture of English Fascists, appeasers, anti-Semites, hard-headed businessmen, fanatical anti-Bolsheviks, eccentric aristocrats and neurotic Mayfair society women'.[3] At best, these men and women have been lumped together with the 'Guilty Men of Munich'; at worst, roundly condemned as 'Fellow Travellers of the Right'. Such powerful stereotypes have been perpetuated in literature, most famously in Kazuo Ishiguro's *The Remains of the Day*, as well as popular films and television drama ever since.[4]

While a small minority deserve these pigeonholes, the mainstream was culturally Germanophile rather than explicitly Hitlerite. As well as some die-hard conservatives, their number included leading liberals, academics and writers. Many were fluent in the language, having studied in German universities in the late nineteenth century. Most were appalled by the needless loss of life in the Great War. Several had helped to rebuild shattered Germany following the Treaty of Versailles. Typically, they had a deep admiration for the German *Kultur* of Goethe, Schiller and Beethoven and acknowledged the contribution made to British culture dating back to Holbein and Handel.

By charting Europe's descent into war from a new perspective, *Coffee with Hitler* challenges conventional interpretations and popular tropes around British dealings with the Nazis – 'Munich, Mosley and the Mitfords' – to ask whether the Anglo-German Fellowship and its champions have been examined in the wrong context, or tried in the wrong court, and therefore damned by association from the outset. This is a story told from the worm's eye view, from the perspective of three well-intentioned obscure middle-aged men who, while right at the heart of the unfolding tragedy, struggled to pacify, accommodate and negotiate with the Third Reich in the years before and during the Second World War. It allows us to look at this fraught and frightening period of history from a different angle and ask the fundamental question as to whether there were alternatives to Chamberlain's appeasement of Germany other than total war.

Winston Churchill and Anthony Eden on their way to the House of Commons following the recall of parliament, 29 August 1939, on or about the day they met with T. P. Conwell-Evans and David Lloyd George.

PROLOGUE

LLOYD GEORGE'S NAZI

In the last week of the gloriously warm August of 1939, just days before Adolf Hitler's army marched into Poland, Thomas Philip Conwell-Evans, a little-known Welsh historian, political secretary and sometime intelligence agent, received a telephone call at his modest flat in Kensington. The caller was A. J. Sylvester, the principal private secretary to David Lloyd George, summoning his friend to the House of Commons for an urgent meeting with his master. Three years before, the three men had visited Germany together and been warmly received by Adolf Hitler on a trip arranged by Conwell-Evans. He remained Lloyd George's favoured adviser on matters German.

Conwell-Evans had made friends easily in the corridors of power, in both London and Berlin. All four of the British prime ministers who had held office in Hitler's dozen years of power had sought his assessment of the National Socialist government. Their faith in his intelligence and connections with the German political leadership was well placed. Working with colleagues including a leading businessman, a former air attaché and the head of the British Foreign Office, he had penetrated the upper ranks of National Socialism, right up to the Führer himself, more deeply than any other Briton. Though closest to Joachim Ribbentrop, the foreign minister, he was also well connected with Hitler's two deputies, Hermann Göring and Rudolf Hess. At the same time as he was ingratiating himself with the senior Nazis, Conwell-Evans was befriending the cabal of civil servants within the German foreign ministry whose sustained efforts to remove Hitler from office came closest to success. He had dedicated the previous five years to preventing a second armed conflict between Great Britain and Germany.

Conwell-Evans was a perfect foil for Lloyd George. Honoured as Father of the House of Commons, the seventy-six-year-old former Liberal prime minister was still celebrated, especially by Hitler, for having led Britain to victory in the Great War two decades previously. Now a backbencher excluded from the Cabinet, he had both failed to revive his fractured Liberal Party and to persuade the National Government to adopt his economic reforms. Instead, he was deploying his formidable oratorical skills in the Commons to attack the prime minister, Neville Chamberlain, and his failing policy of appeasing Hitler's Germany.

Conwell-Evans was a committed pacifist and a published historian. The second son of a master tailor from Carmarthen in Wales, he excelled at the local grammar school. A natural linguist, he studied in France and Germany before taking his place at Jesus College, where he was secretary of the French Club and immersed himself in left-wing politics, joining the socialist Fabian Society. From there he came up to London to pursue his political ambitions, joining the 1917 Club in Soho, popular with socialists, pacifists and the Bloomsbury Set, and infamous for its awful food. He worked with Francis Hirst, the pacifist Liberal journalist, who had resigned as editor of the *Economist* in protest at the Great War and founded the journal *Common Sense*. In the early 1920s he went to work as political secretary to Noel Buxton, the Labour MP and minister of agriculture and fisheries.

Habitually short of money, Philip Conwell-Evans lived a frugal life as a bachelor. Shorter than average and averagely plump, he was bespectacled, with neatly combed hair, both receding and thinning, and a respectable three-piece suit that seemed never quite to fit – whether the fault of an inadequate tailor or a body shape from which no suit however well cut will hang elegantly, is unclear. His overcoat of thick black broadcloth was likely an essential investment for a man of slender means for whom the weather was often bad and central heating a luxury. Bursting from this unpromising package of a man, film footage shows a constant smile that wins friends, a smile that makes people happy, a smile that engenders trust.

His paid work for Noel Buxton, his patron and mentor, funded a doctorate at the London School of Economics. His thesis on the League of Nations (later published by the Oxford University Press as *The League Council in Action*) drove him to his first nervous collapse but earned him patronage from other leading lights on the political left. These included his supervisor, Philip Noel-Baker, and the LSE's director, Sir William Beveridge. Noel-Baker was a Quaker pacifist, Olympic silver medallist, and later Nobel Peace Prize winner, who had driven ambulances during the war. Beveridge was the social reformer best known for his eponymous report which paved the way for today's welfare state and National Health Service. Both would later be elevated to the House of Lords.

Pacifism, France and writing were Conwell-Evans's early focus. He published his first book, an English translation of *Civilisation*, an important novel set in the trenches, by Georges Duhamel, a French army surgeon and celebrated pacifist author, in 1919. In the early twenties, Buxton had shifted his protégé's attention away from France, appointing him secretary to the British Armenian Committee, which raised awareness of the massacre of Armenians by Turks. They co-authored a book, *Oppressed Peoples and the League of Nations*, and Conwell-Evans also took on the secretaryship of the House of Commons' Balkan Committee. Later Buxton, who preferred the Germans to the French, persuaded Conwell-Evans (to his bitter regret) to embrace 'German questions', sponsoring a 1930 visit to East Prussia, the enclave created under the Treaty of Versailles and separated from mainland Germany by the Polish Corridor. The trip seeded Conwell-Evans's growing conviction that the Allies had treated Germany harshly after the Great War.

Two years later, he returned to East Prussia to start a two-year lectureship at the University of Königsberg (now Kaliningrad), the region's medieval capital and once home to the philosopher Immanuel Kant. Returning for his last term at the university, he met and charmed Joachim Ribbentrop, the businessman who would become ambassador to the Court of St James's in London, and later the Reich foreign minister. Initially unimpressed, he described his new acquaintance as very 'lightweight' to his students.[1]

History has treated Conwell-Evans with suspicion. He has puzzled most historians and been dismissed by many; confusion has reigned over where he came from, what he did and where his loyalties lay. In his seminal study of the British far right, Richard Griffiths called him a 'rather shadowy figure'. Lloyd George's biographer agreed he was 'somewhat mysterious'; Hitler's biographer saw him as a 'great admirer of the new Germany'; while Lord Halifax's dismissed him as a 'German sympathiser'.[2] A recent wide-ranging survey of appeasement dubbed him 'wildly pro-German' and condemned him, alongside his joint secretary at the Fellowship, as 'unofficial travel agents for the regime.'[3] When they first met in the 1960s, Martin Gilbert, then immersed in his study of appeasement, admitted he had initially thought Conwell-Evans had 'betrayed his country'.[4] In her recent groundbreaking book on Hitler's aristocratic go-betweens, the historian Karina Urbach has gone the furthest, citing a 1947 allegation by a captured German officer that Conwell-Evans had carried out 'intelligence work' for Ribbentrop and concluding consequently it is 'not clear to this day what Conwell-Evans actually was'.[5]

The reasons for such suspicions around Conwell-Evans's loyalties stem at least partly from his own self-spun web of mystery but also, it seems, from some degree of British government collusion in blackening his name after the Second World War.

The small group of Britons who founded the Anglo-German Fellowship witnessed, and reported back to the British government, the pivotal decisions in Hitler's mercurial and opportunistic diplomatic strategy – from remilitarising the Rhineland and sending the hapless Ribbentrop to London as ambassador to invading first Austria, then Czechoslovakia, and finally Poland. Throughout those tumultuous years leading up to the Second World War, they were welcome guests at landmark events of the Nazi era – white tie parties hosted by Hitler, the annual National Socialist rally at Nuremberg, the Berlin Olympics, as well as intimate dinners and lunches with Ribbentrop in his garden, at his office and on his train. Despite their extraordinary achievement in securing such privileged ringside seats at Hitler's consolidation of power, the story of *how* Conwell-Evans and his small group of compatriots achieved this intimate access and how they tried to civilise the now semi-mythical monsters to save the peace has never been told. The questions of *why* they tried, and whether they had *any* chance of succeeding, have never really been asked. By telling their story and tackling such questions, *Coffee with Hitler* will weigh up the widespread suspicions and slurs and address the charges laid against the protagonists.

Arriving in the last week of August 1939, as instructed, at David Lloyd George's room in the Commons, Conwell-Evans was surprised to find his former client accompanied by two of the prime minister's other most vocal

critics, Winston Churchill and Anthony Eden. Eden was then the leader
of the 'glamour boys' of youngish MPs critical of appeasement. Appointed
foreign secretary in 1934, at the tender age of thirty-eight, he had resigned
four years later having profoundly disagreed with Chamberlain over foreign
policy. Though each was confined to the backbenches, all three had ambitions to succeed Chamberlain, especially in the event of war. After a decade
in the 'wilderness', Churchill would indeed return to the Cabinet within
days as First Lord of the Admiralty, while Eden would be made dominions
secretary. Within eight months, Churchill would replace Chamberlain as
prime minister and would promote Eden to secretary of state for war and
then foreign secretary.

On the day Ribbentrop and Vyacheslav Molotov signed the non-
aggression pact between Nazi Germany and the Soviet Union, Winston
Churchill, Lloyd George's good friend and rival of many years, had finally
abandoned his working holiday in France where he had combined meeting French generals and inspecting the Maginot Line with painting. As he
was being driven through the Normandy countryside the previous day, he
predicted to his fellow passenger, 'before the harvest is gathered in – we
shall be at war.'[6] He flew back to London, having decided to 'find out what
was going on'. There, wasting no time in preparing for what he feared now
inevitable, he embarked on a series of clandestine meetings to gather the
latest intelligence on Germany.

'This is my Nazi,' Lloyd George announced with mock solemnity as
Conwell-Evans entered the room.

The former prime minister then introduced his fellow Welshman properly to the two future prime ministers. Soon, the conversation turned to
whether any chance remained of averting armed conflict on the Continent.
Perhaps surprisingly, these three ardent critics of Chamberlain's foreign
policy and, in Eden and Churchill, long-standing anti-appeasers (war-
mongers to their critics) were evidently still seeking to preserve the
peace only days before the declaration of war. It shows Churchill in a
far less bellicose light than his 'Fight them on the beaches' tradition so
loved by film-makers and popular historians. As Conwell-Evans later
explained, Churchill had not believed war inevitable, but rather thought it
could only have been avoided by 'organising overwhelming force against
Germany's aggressive activities'.[7] When several years later, President

Roosevelt asked him what the conflict should be called, Churchill had replied, 'The Unnecessary War'.[8]

'Could we avert war by buying them off?' asked Churchill. 'Could anything be done to postpone war?' he added, with perhaps a hint of desperation.

'They are determined on war. You might buy them off for six months, but you cannot avert war,' responded Conwell-Evans.

That Churchill could still consider compromising with Hitler so late in the day is similarly at odds with his well-known opposition to any talk of a negotiated peace less than a year later. At some point in the conversation, Churchill remarked to Lloyd George, 'Well, we cannot quarrel with Chamberlain now he's doing all he can.'

Then, seemingly open to the possibility of preserving peace with a different leader at the Nazi helm, he asked for the Welshman's personal assessment of the other leading Nazis.

'They are all a bad lot – except perhaps Göring…' Conwell-Evans answered, 'he is the nearest thing to a gent'. At this point, despite the gravity of the circumstances, Churchill and Lloyd George both burst out laughing.

As they left the House of Commons together, apparently sharing a bag of fruit, Conwell-Evans asked his companion if he thought Eden was a great man.

'Have another plum,' Lloyd George replied.[9]

Within a day or two, the Cabinet, fearing an imminent and devastating attack by German bombers, gave the order to launch Operation Pied Piper. This was the plan to evacuate, over three days, nearly 1.5 million children away from London and other major cities to the relative safety of the British countryside. Each child had to bring a gas mask, their identity card, a change of underclothes, night clothes, a pullover, a pair of plimsolls and a warm coat. While those under five were accompanied by their mothers, older children were separated from their parents and, in many cases, would not see them for months. Despite moments of chaos, their departure was generally orderly and cheerful, with one 'vaccy' later recalling it as a 'rather larky business altogether'.[10]

Meanwhile, in Berlin, fevered last-minute negotiations between the British embassy and Hitler's chancellery continued. The diplomats snatched sleep on camp beds set up in their offices. Virginia Cowles, the American journalist and correspondent for London's *Sunday Times*, watched their toing and froing with mounting pessimism. 'Poor Peace', she noted sadly, 'nothing could bring the colour back into her cheeks or warm her cold hands now.'[11]

According to one member, the recalled House of Commons was 'calm, bored, even irritated, at having its holiday cut short by Hitler'.[12] Another wrote in his diary, 'today when war seems a matter of hours, the absolute despair of a week ago seems to have changed into determination, the gloom of anticipation melting into a gaiety of courage.'[13] MPs were drifting away from the capital. By Thursday, even Churchill was back at Chartwell, his country house in Kent, working on his *History of the English-Speaking Peoples*. That night, the Russian ambassador, exhausted from justifying his master's new-found friendship with Hitler to his many English friends, and thus in need of light relief, took his wife to see Oscar Wilde's *The Importance of Being Earnest*. They laughed for two hours.

On Friday morning, Churchill was woken by a call to Chartwell from the Polish ambassador to say Hitler's tanks were rolling across the border into Poland. As Conwell-Evans later summarised, the 'German armies… swept across the Polish frontiers and with excessive savagery laid the country waste.'[14]

At a quarter past eleven on Sunday morning, church congregations around the country learned Hitler had ignored British and French ultimatums and so, Neville Chamberlain had finally declared war on Germany. Five days later, Conwell-Evans wrote to Lloyd George, 'well the worst has happened, as I feared, I only regret that we did not take a stronger line last year, as I begged the government to do.' Grimly, he concluded, 'now we have to work to defeat the enemy.'[15]

PART ONE

June 1934–September 1936

Joachim Ribbentrop's villa in Dahlem, Berlin, where he hosted dinner for Heinrich Himmler and Ernest Tennant.

1

DINNER ON THE TERRACE
WITH HIMMLER

FIVE YEARS EARLIER, IN JUNE 1934, WHEN A WAR WITH GERMANY
seemed a remote prospect, one of Conwell-Evans's English colleagues found
himself in a Berlin suburban garden having dinner with Heinrich Himmler.
Reichsführer of the Schutzstaffel (SS), the elite unit created as Hitler's body-
guard, and already one of the most powerful men in Germany, Himmler
would later be responsible for the conception, direction and execution of the
Holocaust. The English colleague was Ernest Tennant OBE, a businessman,
decorated Great War veteran and amateur butterfly collector.

Their host was Tennant's closest German friend, Joachim Ribbentrop.
A politically and socially ambitious businessman, the forty-one-year-old
Ribbentrop, following a respectable military career in the Great War, had
built a profitable business in wines and spirits. His wife, Anna Elisabeth
(known as 'Annelies'), who nurtured and indulged these ambitions, was
the daughter of Otto Henkell, whose eponymous brand of sparkling wine
earned him the sobriquet of Germany's 'champagne baron'. Their marriage
brought Joachim money, social advancement and career successes that
outpaced his modest talents, surprising both his few friends and many
enemies.

Within two years, Hitler would send the quite unqualified Ribbentrop
as his ambassador to London, before appointing him Germany's foreign
minister. At this point, he held no office in the Nazi hierarchy but had won
favour by lending his villa for secret meetings between Hitler and established politicians at which alliances were made that led to the National
Socialist Party (NSDAP) assuming power. The gauche new chancellor of

Germany was impressed by the wine merchant's cosmopolitan elan and trusted him for ad hoc advice on foreign affairs. That summer, after months of lobbying, Hitler finally appointed Ribbentrop to the grand sounding but inconsequential post of Special Commissioner of the Reich Government for Disarmament Questions.

The Ribbentrops made a handsome couple, photogenic and always immaculately dressed. Joachim favoured Savile Row suits while Annelies patronised the best dressmakers in Paris, Berlin and London. Elegantly furnished with French antiques set on Persian rugs, their villa was designed in the then-fashionable Arts and Crafts style, with a dash of Alpine kitsch. Important artworks hung from its walls, with pieces by Nazi-approved contemporary German painters displayed alongside leading French Modernists so as to raise the tone of their collection above their less sophisticated neighbours. Dahlem was a prosperous suburb favoured by the Berlin bourgeoisie and once home to successful German Jews, with many of whom Tennant's hosts had once happily socialised. Now it was ever more popular with the National Socialist elite, including Himmler, who owned a villa nearby.

Outside, the villa boasted a swimming pool and tennis court set in a well-kept lawn, laid out in the English style Ribbentrop so admired. Scented by lilac flowers, dotted with fir trees and surrounded by rhododendrons, birches, willows and laburnum, it reminded another British visitor of Surrey or Sussex.[1] To the rear, a series of French windows led on to a generous terrace, protected from the sun by a large canvas awning, where on the very warm Saturday evening of the last day of June, Ribbentrop hosted the dinner party.

Tennant had asked for Himmler to be included at the dinner, as he wished to lobby the head of the SS to release certain political prisoners being held without trial in the newly constructed concentration camps. Several hundred of these had sprung up in the previous two years to house illegally held 'political prisoners' under hideous conditions of extreme brutality – in what the Nazis dubbed 'protective custody'.

Short-sighted, weak-chinned and pasty-skinned, the diminutive former chicken farmer was far from the Nordic ideal of National Socialist folklore. Focused on building the police state, Himmler had none of Ribbentrop's cosmopolitan veneer and little to do with Germany's foreign policy. Though he had no obvious interest in meeting the Briton, he did favour friendship with England and admired the British upper classes – particularly for their eating of porridge, which he believed had fuelled their historic success.

Unbeknown to Tennant (and probably Ribbentrop as well), Himmler's mind was on other things that evening. Hitler, Hermann Göring and he were in the final hours of preparation for Operation Hummingbird. Soon dubbed the 'Night of the Long Knives', this orgy of murderous violence had been planned to purge the NSDAP of rivals to Hitler. It would consolidate his hold over the apparatus of state and secure the supremacy of the highly trained SS over its bitter rival, the unwieldy and undisciplined SA, whose thuggish bullying of German citizens and intimidation of foreign visitors damaged the country's reputation at home and abroad. It would also end the life of Ernst Röhm, head of the SA, Himmler's former mentor and Hitler's friend and colleague. Röhm had been lobbying to take charge of national defence by absorbing the small German army, constrained by the Treaty of Versailles, into the SA, now numbering over three million members. This horrified the Prussian officer class and the business and aristocratic supporters on whom Hitler relied to burnish his reputation internationally. Involving over one thousand arrests and around a hundred extrajudicial killings (including that of the former German chancellor Kurt von Schleicher and his wife), the purge confirmed Hitler as the supreme administrator of German justice and cemented Himmler's status at the core of the Nazi high command.

As butlers served French haute cuisine from the well-staffed kitchen and wine from the excellent cellar, Tennant, more brave than subtle, took Himmler 'case by case' through a list of prisoners supplied by his cousin, Margot, Countess of Oxford and Asquith (widow of the Liberal prime minister). Himmler had priorities far more pressing than the humanitarian concerns of a British businessman so was quickly irritated by his persistence. There followed 'quite a scene' as he nearly choked, before shouting at his dinner companion, 'I don't remember that during the South African war the Germans were invited to inspect your concentration camps – I don't remember that when Hitler was in prison any of you English showed any interest in how he was treated – you ought to go down on your knees and thank God we have got those scum under control.'[2]

With dinner unfinished, Himmler left the table and then the villa.
Tennant assumed this was due to their contretemps, but, as later emerged,
it was to take a telephone call from Hitler summoning him to join Hermann
Göring at his country hunting estate to coordinate the next day's purge in
the German capital. There, they directed the arrests, brutal interrogations
and summary executions undertaken by SS and Gestapo officers in an 'evil
atmosphere', as one eyewitness recalled, of 'hate, nervousness, tension,
above all of bloodshed'.[3]

Unaware of events unfolding across Germany that night, Tennant and
Ribbentrop stayed up until three in the morning in the garden, enjoying
Scotland's finest old whisky in their shirtsleeves while talking over how
best they might promote friendship between their two countries. The next
day, the hung-over Briton returned to London by train. Tennant admitted
he 'could not believe his eyes' when he read of the bloody purge executed
overnight from the pages of the scandalised English Sunday papers.[4]

On the face of it, Tennant and Ribbentrop were unlikely friends. In his
exculpatory memoir, published in 1957 (eleven years after his friend was
hanged in Nuremberg for war crimes), Tennant sought to justify their relationship. Admitting he liked him from the outset, he explained Ribbentrop
was not yet the preening and tactless fool he later became as ambassador
in London, nor the evil errand boy for Hitler he became as Reich foreign
minister. The two men shared an enjoyment of shooting, fishing and paintings, and Tennant thought him a 'better than average' violinist.[5]

Poorly educated, having left school at fifteen (a disadvantage that fuelled
his insecurities), Ribbentrop nonetheless spoke excellent French and his
English was so fluent it was said his German had a British accent. His
admiration for England's culture, royal family and capital city, evident in
his library and garden, was deep-seated and sincere but also aspirational
and sometimes dangerously obsessive. In 1909, he had spent a year in
South Kensington learning English. Astonished by the volume of traffic in
Edwardian London and awed by the skill of the white-gloved policemen
directing it, he later told the Führer he wished one day to show him the
view of the City from the Mansion House. In Ribbentrop's study, his admiration for England was obvious, with English books ranging from Lytton
Strachey's *Elizabeth and Essex* to Harold Nicolson's biography of his father,
T. E. Lawrence's *Revolt in the Desert*, George Bernard Shaw's *The Intelligent*

Woman's Guide to Socialism and Capitalism and novels by Dickens, Wells and Forster neatly shelved alongside German and French volumes.

Both men were polyglot, royalist, imperialist patriots with a mounting suspicion of Soviet Russia and Bolshevism. By strengthening business between their two countries, they believed diplomatic relations would improve, and peace be preserved. But despite their burgeoning friendship, Tennant was under no illusions about Ribbentrop's deficiencies. He warned a British politician, though 'extremely likeable', how he was 'very long-winded and rather a bore' and it took undue time for him to 'grasp or to explain things'.[6]

The novelist Muriel Spark described Tennant as 'one of those City business personalities who are usually seen but not heard'.[7] The previous year it was he who had opened London's doors for Ribbentrop and so helped to launch a diplomatic career which would have catastrophic consequences. He had been born into a fantastically wealthy Scottish family which owed its fortune to Charles Tennant, the weaver turned chemist who patented bleaching powder and revolutionised the textile industry at the end of the eighteenth century. This allowed him to set up the St Rollox chemical works in Glasgow, the world's largest, and found a business that enriched his descendants and was merged into ICI in 1926. While his cousin, Christopher, Lord Glenconner, served as chairman, it fell to Ernest to lead the family's successful surviving business, C. Tennant & Son.

Ernest Tennant cultivated his expertise on the new German government and would later be acknowledged by Hitler as a 'determined pioneer of Anglo-German understanding'.[8] One of the first three British soldiers to visit Berlin after the Armistice, he was a surviving member of that much mythologised golden generation of young Edwardians, so hard hit by the war and the subsequent rise of communism that those two traumas defined their worldview thereafter. Tennant's loss of family and schoolfriends in the war was extraordinarily high. At Eton, he had been a member of 'Pop', the elite school prefects. His closest schoolfriend, Julian Martin Smith, who served as best man at his wedding, had been the first British volunteer killed in the opening weeks of the war. Within a year, Tennant's adored younger brother Alan ('Bunny') had died, leaving what Ernest remembered as a 'terrible loss for our very happy and united family'.[9] By 1916, nineteen of his fellow school prefects, seven of his male relations and his brother-in-law had all died. Put another way, two-thirds of his closest male friends and family had been killed, a mortality rate nearly four times greater than typical for army officers in the trenches.[10]

His memoirs reveal how agonised he was to have survived. The army having rejected him due to his poor lungs and injuries sustained in a lion attack in Africa, the Intelligence Corps finally accepted him in 1916 and posted him to France. There he deployed his significant business skills answering questions from the House of Commons about trade, ranging from the cement industry to rubber contraceptives, which the Germans were using to keep hand grenades dry. After the war, the British government sent him to lead a handful of officers into shattered and revolutionary Berlin, which they reached on the first through train from Cologne, bringing their own food and staying at the once luxurious Hotel Adlon. They were to advise the War Cabinet on the food situation, then worsened by the blockade by the British Navy. Published as a white paper, their report linked food shortages, shattered transport links and unemployment with the risk of famine and rising Bolshevism. Warning 'probably both... will ensue before the next harvest', it nonetheless recognised peace terms were not yet agreed so cautioned against lifting the 'menace of starvation' by a 'too sudden and abundant' resupply of food.[11]

The Allies had instigated the blockade at the outbreak of war and maintained it well into peacetime. Estimates of unnecessary post-war civilian deaths ran into the hundreds of thousands and this legacy would trouble Tennant for decades. Writing twenty years later to the prime minister, he explained how seeing children in hospital with 'hunger madness' had driven his determination to rebuild friendship between the two countries.[12] Following the completion of this mission, the Cabinet sent him to Italy, disguised as a railway engineer and with his Italian-speaking wife, to report on the food situation for the Supreme Economic Council recently established at the Paris Peace Conference.

In the following years, Tennant visited Germany often on business and saw the National Socialists rise to power. Only months into the new chancellorship, he published an article on 'Herr Hitler and his Policy' in *The English Review*, a conservative literary periodical. This would open the door of 10 Downing Street to Joachim Ribbentrop and sow the seeds for his becoming ambassador to London. Its immediate result was an invitation for Tennant to give a speech at Ashridge College, the political training school run by the Conservative Party. He pulled no punches in painting the grimmest picture of how Berlin had looked just after the Armistice. No dogs or cats had survived; they had been eaten and their skins used for leather. There was no coffee, soap or textiles; what little the civilians had was ersatz. Men's shirts were made from nettle fibre. Sheets, underclothes and pyjamas were cut from paper while burnt barley and acorns were served as coffee. Half of the women were dying in childbirth from lack of nourishment. Children in hospital were so starved they were but 'little skeletons who would not eat but tried to hide any food they were given under the bedclothes so as to keep it in case they grew still hungrier'.

Tennant was impressed by how Hitler had united the country under one party and planned a national economic revival. Sympathetic to the insult felt by the Germans at press criticism in foreign, especially British, newspapers, he explained how Hitler blamed 'international Jews' and Catholics for these attacks and lambasted his foreign ministry for failing to protect him. His influence over both the diplomatic corps and the military had been restricted by his Faustian pact with the ageing President von Hindenburg. This arrangement suited those aristocratic, conservative German soldiers and diplomats who scorned the low-born Austrian corporal and were unnerved by the thuggish SA. Isolated from the levers of diplomatic influence at home, Hitler urgently wanted friends overseas and despite its hostile press, England remained his first choice. His ideal was an Anglo-Saxon world in which Greater Germany would dominate Continental Europe, leaving Britain free to nurture her far-flung Empire as long as she did not interfere with his adventures on the other side of the Channel.

Unlike others, Tennant recognised the Third Reich as no passing fad; 'nothing except the invasion of Germany or the early death of Hitler can now shake the power of the Nazis.' He had been arguing against their vicious persecution of German Jews since 1932, which had 'grossly insulted' the whole race and shocked the world. But rather than shunning the new regime, he believed the British could best help the Jews and other victims of the regime by making friends with Germany. He acknowledged a 'powerful strain of the bully' in the typical Prussian, and flippantly suggested 'if the Germans could take themselves a little less seriously and we could take them a little more seriously there would be a better chance of mutual understanding.'[13]

Following his speech, a government minister, J. C. C. Davidson, chancellor of the Duchy of Lancaster and a past chairman of the Conservative Party, approached him for a copy of his notes to pass on to his close confidant, Stanley Baldwin, de facto deputy to Ramsay MacDonald, the ailing prime minister. Surprisingly, this was Baldwin's first briefing on Hitler's young government. Eager to fill the gap, Tennant suggested to Davidson that, given MacDonald's frailty, Baldwin should travel to Berlin and be the first Cabinet minister to meet the new chancellor. Davidson agreed to host a private lunch at his home in November 1933 to introduce Ribbentrop and Tennant to his friend, and for them to propose such a visit, bypassing both the German embassy in London and the British Foreign Office.

Davidson had no doubts his lunch guest, despite lacking government or Party credentials, spoke for Hitler. Ribbentrop outlined their ambitions to better Anglo-German relations; his themes would become an all-too-familiar litany. The British press swallowed propaganda from 'internationally-minded persons, mainly Jews' and nobody could understand modern Germany unless they came in person. Bolshevism posed the greatest threat to European civilisation so Germany deserved the means to defend herself and could not remain a 'second-rate power'. Hitler would never rejoin the League of Nations, a 'sounding board for war and completely incompetent as a negotiating body', but was far too busy rebuilding the domestic economy to have 'any leisure for the consideration of a possible war'. Despite old enmity, Ribbentrop assured his lunchmates Germany wanted friendly arrangements with France, but more urgently a naval agreement with Britain. He impressed Davidson with his sincerity and his pride in how the Nazis had outflanked the communists. Reassured by 'vague references' to his territorial ambitions being only eastwards, including Russia, Davidson accepted Hitler's thesis that another war would lead to 'universal Bolshevism through the breakdown of European civilisation'.

All present expressed delight at the lunch. Ribbentrop invited Baldwin to meet the Führer. Ribbentrop briefed Hitler by telephone on the discussions. Davidson wrote a 'most secret' government report that found its way into MI5's files. Baldwin thanked Tennant for arranging it, declaring, 'I like that man, I like his face.'[14] That afternoon, he invited the German to present himself at a 'house in Downing Street' with instructions to ring the bell but not give his name.[15] The prime minister joined the tea; Ribbentrop found both Baldwin and MacDonald congenial and soon whisky replaced tea.

Buoyed by the refreshments, Ribbentrop asked for a follow-up meeting to include Sir John Simon, the foreign secretary, who along with his officials had been unaware of these discussions. Indecisive, over-lawyerly and plagued by self-doubt, Simon, who held the office for nearly four years, was by any measure one of Britain's least successful foreign secretaries. One wit went as far as to label him the 'worst since Ethelred the Unready'. This second meeting, four days later, went less well. Frustrated by being kept in the dark and appalled by this amateur diplomacy, Simon raised myriad objections, insisted such arrangements had to go through the proper diplomatic channels, and an hour-long argument ensued.

The ambitious concept of a summit between Hitler and the genial Baldwin, who feared flying, disliked abroad and was wary of foreigners, soon became a totemic obsession for Ribbentrop, Hitler and Tennant. Its meandering progress offers a useful barometer of Ribbentrop's volatile relationship with Britain. Though never realised, it did frame the context for the series of visits by other senior British politicians who headed over to Germany to take coffee with Hitler, each essentially deputising for the elusive Baldwin.

Although no closer to booking his flight to Berlin, Baldwin did the next day make a 'witty and constructive' speech in the Commons about Anglo-German relations, which, according to *The Times*, impressed the House. Warning against an arms race with Germany and urging her back into the League of Nations, he reminded MPs how Napoleon's France, then 'viewed much like the Germany of today', had after Waterloo gone on to become the 'most pacific nation in Europe'.[16] The price of German bonds rallied in the City.

Only a few weeks later, Tennant returned to Berlin to meet Hitler. The chancellor lamented Allied statesmen were hurrying around Europe 'from Paris to Rome and from Rome to London' discussing him without ever coming to meet him. He proposed a three-day summit with Baldwin suggesting, as he could not leave Germany and assuming the Englishman did not want to come to Berlin, they meet in a frontier town or on a battleship moored off Hamburg. Intrigued, Tennant reminded his host that Baldwin had yet to be appointed prime minister, and so asked why he particularly wanted to meet him. Hitler admitted his admiration stemmed from Baldwin's extraordinary gesture as First Lord of the Treasury when, embarrassed by the war profits of his family firm, he had given half his fortune back to his country to help reduce the national debt and set an example to other citizens.

Tennant promised the Führer he would continue to lobby Baldwin to visit Germany but, despite another amiable meeting in Downing Street, failed against unified Foreign Office opposition. Half-hearted plans were then developed for Davidson and a principal private secretary to go in Baldwin's stead but quickly foundered. Tennant remembered bitterly how this had been the point when the 'professional diplomats and the permanent officials of the Foreign Offices of Britain and Germany linked arms to form a barrier against any amateurs intruding into their orbit and to prevent statesmen going over their heads and having direct negotiations.'[17] Reconciled to the fact the instinctively pro-French and anti-German British diplomats would never help better Anglo-German relations, he now accepted his only option was to cultivate alternative and essentially amateur diplomatic conduits to Berlin and Munich. He would deploy his considerable business skills and persuasive charms to recruit support not just from his fellow businessmen but more widely from high society, military, sporting and other internationalist elites.

The dining room at the refurbished Reich Chancellery in Berlin where Adolf Hitler hosted Ernest Tennant, the Ribbentrops, Lord Rothermere et al. for the celebration of the tenth anniversary of his release from prison, 19 December 1934.

2

ROAST CHICKEN AT THE CHANCELLERY

JUST BEFORE THE 1934 CHRISTMAS HOLIDAYS, SIX MONTHS AFTER his fraught introduction to Himmler, Tennant returned to stay with the Ribbentrops and join a dinner party celebrating both Anglo-German friendship and the ten-year anniversary of Hitler's release from prison following the failed Beer Hall Putsch. That August, President von Hindenburg had died, and Hitler had amalgamated the presidency and the chancellorship into the role of Führer (with the overwhelming support of the German voting public). The two dozen honoured guests included General Göring, then minister president of Prussia, with his fiancée, the actress Emmy Sonnemann; the foreign minister, Konstantin von Neurath and his wife; and Joseph Goebbels, the minister of public enlightenment and propaganda, with his. Tennant could now deepen his connections within the Nazi high command.

Steel-helmeted sentries and SS guards greeted Tennant and the Ribbentrops as they drove through the iron gates of the Reich Chancellery at 77 Wilhelmstrasse. Formerly the home of Chancellor Bismarck, the two-hundred-year-old palace had just been refurbished to the new chancellor's specifications by the architect Gerdy Troost. Hitler had condemned the decorative scheme of his Weimar predecessors as giving the impression of a 'warehouse or municipal fire station' and internally of a 'sanitorium for consumptives'. He damned the chancellor's private office as the 'tasteless room of a sales executive of a mid-sized cigarette and tobacco company'.[1] Tasked with removing vestiges of the municipal, along with any lingering whiffs of tuberculosis and stale tobacco, Troost claimed inspiration from contemporary English design, de-cluttering the overwrought fittings and heavy dark furniture, remodelling the interiors with clean lines and white walls to let in light and air, all to create the best in twentieth-century dictator chic.

Hitler disliked formal entertaining, especially of foreigners, so the ongoing refurbishment had given him the perfect excuse to avoid such receptions. But now a beaming Führer, in evening tails and white tie, welcomed each guest with elaborate courtesy. While the men wore evening dress or party uniform and the women were elegant in long gowns, General Göring cut the most spectacular figure, resplendent in a 'comic opera' uniform, green with white facings, festooned with braid and medals and accessorised by a huge sword. Tennant thought nonetheless he looked unhealthy and 'enormously fat'.

Having women at such events was unusual, but the inclusion of foreigners was unprecedented. The four British guests of honour had already proved themselves friends of the regime so were privileged to be the first non-Germans to dine with the Führer at the refurbished Chancellery. Lord Rothermere, proprietor of the *Daily Mail* newspaper empire, was known for his support of both Hitler's National Socialism in Germany and Sir Oswald Mosley's fascism back home. Driven by a dread of Bolshevism, and having lost two sons in the trenches, he was haunted by the ghosts of the Great War. He was accompanied by his surviving son, Esmond Harmsworth, a former aide-de-camp to the prime minister Lloyd George at the Paris Peace Conference, and his father's successor as chairman of Associated Newspapers. The fourth guest, George Ward Price, served as the *Daily Mail*'s special correspondent in Berlin, and had already secured two exclusive interviews with Hitler in which his unctuous prose about the Führer's love of children and animals had endeared him to his host. He published *I Know These Dictators*, an enthusiastic account of his dealings with the totalitarian states, and had been a founder member of the January Club, set up by Mosley to recruit upper-class supporters for his British Union of Fascists.

Decorated with bowls of fresh flowers – red lilies and white lilacs – the enormous reception room was also covered with a Persian rug so vast, Tennant ventured it must be the world's largest. Hitler admitted with glee it had been destined for the Geneva headquarters of the League of Nations but, following some complication, had been diverted to Berlin. The redesigned dining room with bright ivory-coloured walls led out to the adjoining park through glass doors. The guests sat in comfortable armchairs around a large oval table laid with 'beautiful china, glass and silver – all modern and severe' and decorated with large pots of trailing pink begonias.[2]

Tennant noted that, while the senior Nazis liked and admired Hitler, they were afraid of him, adding drily that the term 'easy-going intimacy' could never be used in the context of their relations with the boss.[3] The *placement* at these dinners remained a source of angst among the Führer's lieutenants and guests which he loved to provoke. Frau von Neurath, wife of the foreign minister, acted as his hostess, while her bitter rival, Annelies Ribbentrop, sat next to the Führer. Tensions simmered between the two women and, indeed, between their husbands. Tennant felt honoured to be seated on Annelies's other side, only one place away from their host and next to the renowned Wagnerian opera singer who would entertain the party after dinner.

Hitler delighted his guests as he reminisced about his time in jail and boasted how he had converted most of his custodians, including the governor, to National Socialism. Ward Price appreciated how, with the 'simplicity of genius', he repositioned his failed putsch and ignominious imprisonment into a 'glorious martyrdom'.[4] Despite the evening's absurdities, Tennant found Hitler an easy host and this evening added to his fascination with the man. But he was never wholly star-struck, admitting how although his followers 'look upon him almost as a God', his own first impressions had been disappointing. Though admiring his 'striking dark blue eyes, kindly, and very intelligent', he found him physically unprepossessing. His harshest criticism was for the 'most unfortunate moustache… a black blob covering the whole of his lip between his nose and his mouth'.[5] He warned a British politician that Hitler could be 'very temperamental' and 'so easily roused to a condition of excitement' that any future negotiations with British ministers would be difficult. Tennant saw Göring as the 'most spectacular' figure in the Nazi firmament, a 'throwback to the Middle Ages', but while intrigued by his overblown schoolboy antics, the massive train set, his tame lion cub and his conjuring butler, he also recognised him as 'efficient, cruel and ruthless'.

Tennant thought the food, served by footmen in mess jackets, well cooked but rather simple. Thick white soup before roast chicken and vegetables were followed by a sorbet and then cheese and biscuits. Hitler ate little and drank only water. The paucity of alcohol was a disappointment.

No cocktails were offered before dinner, and only limited wine during the meal. When the party rose from the dining table, Hitler, who disliked the smell of cigarettes, led the non-smokers into one room, while most of the guests, desperate to smoke, repaired to another. Here, away from the Führer's disapproving gaze, the mood relaxed as 'liqueurs, beer and whisky were flowing freely, and the air was blue with cigar smoke.' Torn between his need for nicotine and the opportunity to ingratiate himself with the Führer, Tennant managed a 'quick puff' before joining Ribbentrop, Rothermere, a few of the ladies and their host in the fresher air.

The singers from the Berlin Opera delighted the Führer, who congratu-lated the performers personally and presented a bouquet of flowers to each woman. Tennant enjoyed sitting beside Frau Goebbels, whom he admired – 'rather a personality, a good-looking blonde with dark eyebrows and well dressed'. He was intrigued by her small, club-footed husband, whom he recognised as the most intelligent of Hitler's inner circle. Like many others, he underestimated Goebbels, confessing after the war he had seen no signs of the 'bursting virility' that made him a 'satyr with women, who found him irresistible'. Nor had he recognised him as 'one of the most evil and dangerous men in Germany'.

Now confirmed as one of only a handful of Britons welcome at the Nazi top table, Tennant offered a conduit between the Party and Britain's government and elites. But despite this success, he returned to London frustrated at how during the two years since Hitler had come into power 'repeated opportunities of better understanding had been missed'.[6] His and Ribbentrop's initial efforts to build credibility in Whitehall through Baldwin, MacDonald and Davidson had fizzled out. With neither the patience nor the contacts to woo politicians and diplomats, he decided to focus his talents on gaining British support from his natural milieu – businessmen, financiers, soldiers and aristocrats. Playing to their respective strengths, he would now rely on his new collaborator, Philip Conwell-Evans, to pick up the pieces of the failed political campaign by orchestrating a series of visits to Nazi Germany by leading British public figures.

From the time of his return to London in 1934, Conwell-Evans dedicated the rest of that turbulent decade to building amity between Britain and Germany, most particularly through his secretaryship of the Anglo-German Fellowship. Then, and ever since, a controversial organisation, it was founded two years after Hitler's appointment as German chancellor to encourage better 'understanding' between the two countries, and thereby 'contribute to the maintenance of peace and the development of prosperity'. In this role, for which he was professionally qualified given his experience with Commons committees and his fluency in German, Conwell-Evans weaved comfortably through the murky corridors of Britain's diplomatic relations with National Socialist Germany, working with a small group of colleagues. Conwell-Evans went on to deploy his special talent for friendship to earn the trust, respect and patronage of leading statesmen and civil servants on both sides of the North Sea. But, as Martin Gilbert (his fellow historian and friend, who now defended Conwell-Evans's reputation) wrote in the 1960s, he had moved from the 'simplicity of walks on the Heath, and talks with poets and essayists, from passivism and socialism and good works' into the 'maelstrom of foreign affairs', and that maelstrom was appeasement.[7]

Conwell-Evans's first political recruit was Philip Kerr, the Liberal politician and writer. He had succeeded his cousin to become the eleventh Marquess of Lothian as well as Earl of Ancram, Earl of Lothian, Viscount of Briene, Lord Ker of Newbattle, Lord Jedburgh and Baron Ker of Kersheugh. In Lothian, Conwell-Evans had found a patron who combined a global reputation for international affairs, a heartfelt desire for peace and impeccable political connections. As Lloyd George's secretary at the Peace Conference at Versailles in 1918 and his *éminence grise* on foreign affairs, he had drafted Article 231, the notorious 'war guilt' clause holding Germany responsible for the outbreak of hostilities. Yet he had never lost his conviction that the French had been needlessly harsh on the vanquished Germans. His ancient titles and four stately homes impressed the Nazis, but he was far from the stereotype of a declining aristocratic reactionary, being firmly on the political left, liberal in both senses, and thus well aligned with his new friend Conwell-Evans. The charming, popular, persuasive and engaging Lothian was never comfortable in ermine. His father, a poorly paid army officer, had brought up his children in a modest dower house. The son preferred to live and dress informally, admiring the more relaxed social mores of the US, and he famously arrived at the coronation of George VI in a battered Austin Seven.

Lothian proved much more interested in Germany than either MacDonald or Baldwin. He and Conwell-Evans corresponded in late 1934 to plan a trip to Germany in the new year. In December, Lothian gave a speech at Chatham House in which he voiced his concerns over whether Germany might start 'playing power politics in Europe, especially Eastern Europe'.[8] Conwell-Evans chided this was not the case and warned that, by stationing the majority of the British fleet in the North Sea, the government risked provoking the Germans. By Christmas Eve, Lothian confirmed he hoped to go to Germany to talk with some 'really representative Nazis about their ideas about the future'.[9]

Despite their starkly different social backgrounds and financial means, Conwell-Evans and Lothian became close colleagues, good friends and frequent correspondents. Conwell-Evans was a welcome guest at Blickling, Lothian's magnificent Jacobean mansion in Norfolk. They shared a passion for internationalism and understanding among nations and worked together at the Rhodes Trust, which funded scholarships at Oxford University for students from Great Britain's colonies and dominions as well as from the US and, somewhat controversially, from Germany. Each contributed to papers and debates at the Royal Institute of International Affairs at Chatham House. Both were lifelong bachelors who shared a tendency towards ill health, especially nervous exhaustion through overwork.

The two Britons were excited about the upcoming trip. Lothian saw his friend's involvement as an 'immense advantage', while Conwell-Evans saw the meeting as a perfect opportunity for Germany to 'make clear to an independent Englishman of very great influence what the aims of the Nazi government are'.[10] They enlisted help from Ribbentrop but, as he had already alienated the German foreign ministry, Conwell-Evans sensibly also sought official blessing from the German embassy in Carlton House Terrace. A lunch was arranged for the two men with Leopold von Hoesch. The popular ambassador to the Court of St James's since 1932, von Hoesch was a cultured bachelor and close to both the Prince of Wales and his mother Queen Mary. The Times admired his 'beautiful English... soft, modulated tones' and doubted 'whether Germany possesses any diplomatist of more exceptional gifts, riper knowledge and experience, or more attractive per-sonality'.[11] Tennant considered him a friend and fed him intelligence on what was happening in Berlin, as Hitler distrusted professional diplomats so much he kept his own ambassador 'completely in the dark'.[12] The distrust was reciprocated and contemporary London saw von Hoesch as no friend of the National Socialists; the foreign secretary recognised him as 'certainly not of the Nazi gang', while the secretary of the Board of Deputies of British Jews agreed he was 'notoriously anti-Nazi in his views'.[13]

Following the lunch, von Hoesch telegraphed to Berlin urging the Führer to honour Lothian with a personal meeting as he would be 'without doubt the most important non-official Englishman who has so far asked to be received by the Chancellor'.[14] He confirmed Sir John Simon, the foreign secretary, had blessed the mission despite his earlier objections to Ribbentrop and Tennant's amateur diplomacy. Simon valued his friend Lothian's advice, allegedly preferring it to that from his own Foreign Office, so asked him to report back promptly on his return before the visit to London by the French premier for discussions on Germany. Neither a blind admirer of nor uncritical apologist for Hitler, Lothian wrote in 1933, 'like most liberals' he 'loathed' the Nazi regime but argued Britain should be 'willing to do justice to Germany'.[15] He insisted every time he saw Ribbentrop, or had contact with Nazi headquarters, he would tell them the main obstacle to better Anglo-German relations was the 'persecution of the Christians, Jews and Liberal Pacifists'.[16]

Notwithstanding this official blessing from both sides, the veneer of amateurism was maintained. Lothian was formally visiting Germany as the director of the Rhodes Trust, an independent charity, and was 'in no sense an emissary' for the British government. But there was no doubting he represented the wider political milieu, however informally, rather than the mercantile interests of earlier visitors as led by Tennant.[17] As such, this set the template for a series of audiences between the German chancellor and well-meaning, distinguished, but still unofficial British political visitors. It also launched Conwell-Evans and Tennant on the path to being recognised as the most effective facilitators for these types of summits.

Von Hoesch was shrewd in his estimation of Lothian, whose influence and political friendships were wide, spanning four British prime ministers. A devoted Liberal and loyal to his old boss Lloyd George (to whom he recommended Conwell-Evans), he had also served in Ramsay MacDonald's Labour Cabinet, and would later lend his Norfolk home to the Conservative prime minister Stanley Baldwin when he suffered a nervous collapse from the pressures of office.

Lothian recommended Conwell-Evans for membership of the Travellers Club. Founded in the aftermath of the Napoleonic Wars by a group of aristocratic politicians and diplomats led by Viscount Castlereagh, the foreign secretary, it welcomed overseas visitors, foreign diplomats and British gentlemen who had 'travelled out of the British Isles to a distance of at least five hundred miles from London in a direct line'. Unlike other St James's clubs that tended towards domestic politics, sports and gambling within tight cliques, this was outward-looking, hospitable and internationalist. Stanley Baldwin had been one of nine prime ministers to join, preferring to eat lunch there alone and undisturbed. A short walk across St James's Park from the 'Office', the foreign secretary was traditionally a member, and the club was so much frequented by his colleagues it became known as the 'Foreign Office canteen'. The Japanese, Bulgarian, Serbian, French and Italian ambassadors were granted honorary membership and, subject to Foreign Office blessing, each German ambassador and his first secretary had been similarly privileged since 1927. When Ribbentrop arrived as ambassador, he much enjoyed the club's facilities and remains (at the date of writing) the only member to have been hanged.

As its official historian noted, the Travellers Club has long been popular with spies as well as diplomats, which, when burnished by its frequent representations in popular fiction from Arthur Conan Doyle to Graham Greene, has given it 'a certain aura'.[18] Prominent British spymasters, including heads of both the Secret Intelligence Service (MI6) and MI5, joined, while other members achieved notoriety as Soviet double agents, including Donald Maclean, John Cairncross and Anthony Blunt. For an impoverished tailor's son in an era and milieu in which social connections were essential, membership of this prestigious and congenial club offered an invaluable leg up the greasy pole. Here, Conwell-Evans would rub shoulders with Cabinet ministers, gossip with rising young diplomats, share scoops with journalists and entertain German embassy staff, spies and fellow promoters of peace. Immediately, it became his London base, both as a champion of Anglo-German friendship and as a clandestine intelligence agent.

And so, in January 1935, Conwell-Evans took Lothian to Berlin. Feted by the Nazi leadership, they met the foreign minister, Konstantin von Neurath, discussed disarmament with Field Marshal von Blomberg, the minister of war, took coffee with Rudolf Hess, the deputy führer, all before a two-hour meeting with Hitler himself. Following his usual monologue on the evils of Russia and communism, the Führer tried ironic humour by asking why France, with a population smaller than her neighbour, was allowed the larger army. By that logic, Germany's should be larger than Russia's, and Luxembourg's the largest in the world. Lothian reiterated he had no 'official position nor diplomatic mission' but did pave the way for a visit by British Cabinet ministers, promising to report favourably to his government. As the meeting ended, his host insisted 'the greatest madness was the war of 1914 between... the English and the Germans' to which Lothian responded by quoting Cecil Rhodes's hope that the US, Britain and Germany would 'together preserve the peace of the world'.[19]

The disarmingly charming Lothian had made such a favourable impression in Berlin that the Führer applauded him as the 'most helpful Englishman' he had met so far.[20] He returned to London convinced of Hitler's sincerity, reporting on his meeting in *The Times*: 'Germany does not want war and is prepared to renounce it absolutely... provided she is given real authority.'[21] He sent copies of Conwell-Evans's transcript of the interview to the prime minister, Simon, Baldwin and Ribbentrop.

Barely a month after their trip, Conwell-Evans returned from a holiday in Switzerland to a summons from Berlin. The Führer wanted to talk about the Anglo-French declaration, to which the Germans had been slow to respond. This joint communiqué (the 'London Declaration') had been issued twelve days earlier, following a meeting between senior British and French ministers. Condemning unilateral rearmament, it proposed a general settlement with Germany on arms and air power limitations. Conwell-Evans, with customary directness, encouraged Hitler to make Ribbentrop his 'ambassador at large', claiming somewhat ambitiously his friend was already 'much beloved in England'.[22] Only hours later, the Germans issued their response, excluding mention of the French and offering discussions with the British. German diplomats had to admit to their furious French counterparts this clumsy ploy to drive a wedge between the two allies had originated from Ribbentrop's office.

A date in early March was set for Sir John Simon, with Anthony Eden as his deputy, to visit Berlin to explore some form of Anglo-German agreement. Anxious to prepare his friend for his first meeting with the German dictator, Lothian explained that Hitler did not like dealing through written documents, preferring personal contacts and discussions, so suggested von Hoesch be encouraged to fly to Berlin to agree the agenda with the Führer ahead of the meeting.[23] Tennant, also just back from Berlin, agreed the Germans wanted a visit by the foreign secretary but insisted they would have a far greater chance of engendering true 'political friendship' if Baldwin and MacDonald went with him. Such a delegation would give the prime minister and his anointed successor a direct relationship with Hitler, who was convinced 'things are never achieved by notes, only by men', rather than having to rely on 'second-hand opinion' as they had done to date.[24] Ten days later, Ribbentrop telephoned Conwell-Evans to suggest Lothian join the trip and to advise Simon not to pressurise the Germans into joining the Eastern Pact, a treaty being championed by the Russians and French, as this would be given a 'most emphatic refusal'.[25] Conwell-Evans countered by urging the Germans to develop a modus vivendi with the Russians but Ribbentrop remained unconvinced they wanted good relations in any circumstances.

Predictably, neither Baldwin nor MacDonald showed any interest in joining Simon's meeting with Hitler. At this point, it was easy to interpret these amateur initiatives as attempts to build a wholly separate and competing diplomatic axis that bypassed and antagonised the formal diplomatic channels. As A. L. Kennedy, *The Times* journalist, remarked in his journal, the 'way things are done now is curious… after the famous Anglo-French communiqué of February 3 Hitler wished to find out what sort of reply would be considered satisfactory in England… he mentioned this to Ribbentrop… Ribbentrop telephoned across the North Sea to Conwell-Evans, C-E asked Lothian, & Lothian asked Simon – & the answer went back through the same chain!'[26] Only later would the British Foreign Office and German foreign ministry see the merits in engaging with Conwell-Evans and his colleagues.

Just days before their scheduled departure, a string of contretemps raised the diplomatic temperature throughout Europe and disrupted the plans. The British government published a white paper criticising the Germans for unilateral rearmament and proposing a fifty percent hike in spending on the cash-strapped RAF over five years in response. As Simon remembered, Hitler took 'umbrage at this plain speaking' and at once succumbed to a 'diplomatic cold' as an excuse to postpone the meeting.[27] Three days later, Göring boastfully unveiled his cherished Luftwaffe, a provocative contravention of Article 198 of the Treaty of Versailles. Within a week, the French government announced the extension of their compulsory national military service from one to two years. This gave Hitler the opportunity to announce the next day Germany's reintroduction of military conscription, again in breach of Versailles, and the creation of a *Wehrmacht* (unified armed forces) with a peace strength of thirty-six divisions, numbering over half a million men.

The first of Hitler's 'Saturday Shockers' had been, as one of his diplomats remembered, 'carefully timed'; knowing the British ruling classes enjoyed a weekend stretching from Friday evening to Monday morning, it had been calculated to wrong-foot London into being slow and disorganised in its response.[28] Paranoid about leaks, Hitler had even kept his own foreign ministry in the dark on the announcement. En route to meet von Hoesch, Conwell-Evans spotted the news in the evening papers so had the unexpected task of briefing the German ambassador. Writing several years later after war had broken out, an embittered Conwell-Evans explained how, by restoring conscription, Hitler had undermined the security provisions of the Treaty of Versailles but even that had failed to 'jolt' hesitant British ministers as they continued to believe his 'lavish professions of peace'.[29] With the benefit of grim hindsight (and acknowledging his own naivety at the time) he pinpointed this as a critical juncture at which Britain played into Hitler's hands through a toxic cocktail of inaction, snobbish underestimation of the Austrian corporal, preference for Empire, ennui about anything across the Channel, and – despite distaste for the well-publicised Nazi cruelties – reluctance to interfere in another sovereign state's internal affairs. This diplomatic neglect, as Tennant explained, fuelled the inferiority complex of the National Socialists, given British ministers were only too happy to travel to the Continent to meet their French and Italian counterparts.

The Cabinet had debated cancelling the already postponed visit but agreed to go ahead, so on Sunday, 24 March 1934, Simon and Eden finally arrived in Berlin for the first meeting between a British Cabinet minister and Hitler, who had now been chancellor of Germany for twenty-six months. The two Englishmen preferred Hitler to Mussolini. Simon saw 'nothing particularly striking about Hitler's appearance, though his eyes are expressive of his determination and he has the hands of a musician', contrasting his 'simple bearing' with Göring's 'bouncing and bemedalled flamboyance'.[30] Hitler's tailoring impressed the famously well-dressed Eden. Simon invited the Germans to send representatives to London for further discussions, especially on relative naval strength. To the surprise of the heads of both the navy and the foreign ministry, Hitler indicated he wanted Ribbentrop to head the delegation despite his lack of experience in either naval or diplomatic matters. Simon returned to London believing, like his friend Lothian, that Hitler was sincere in his professions of peace, but he was under no illusions about the extent of his ambitions; Germany was determined to rearm, Hitler planned to bring all Germans, including Austria, within her borders, and would, before joining any European security measures, insist on the return of those former German colonies (such as German South West Africa, now Namibia) appropriated by the Allies during and after the Great War.

Conwell-Evans met privately in Downing Street on 1 May with Ramsay MacDonald, the day before the prime minister had to give a major speech on Germany in the Commons, a last intervention on foreign affairs before handing over to Baldwin. Conwell-Evans recognised his friend's 'physical and mental powers' were 'rapidly failing' and he had proved ineffectual in promoting Anglo-German diplomacy.[31] Reviewing the effect of the London Declaration, MacDonald admitted to the House that the Allies were finally 'moving from the Versailles regime' to which they had been so wedded since the war. He appealed directly to the Germans to negotiate on arms, his tone both whinging and cajoling. Though chiding Germany for breaching Versailles, he argued this issue remained within the remit of the League of Nations rather than his government. Applauding the Simon visit, he offered to take Germany at its word. All told, he gave Hitler everything he wanted.

Though Tennant and Conwell-Evans had persuaded MacDonald and Baldwin to meet Hitler's special envoy and to make friendly speeches in parliament, they were no closer to sending either to Germany. The fantasy of the new prime minister visiting Berlin rumbled on throughout his premiership but would never gain any real traction. Though firmly embedded as the upstart Ribbentrop's primary British advisers, they were also shrewdly building connections with the other senior Nazis, especially Göring, Hess and, crucially, Hitler himself. They had support from the German embassy in London and, at least, civil tolerance from its British counterpart in Berlin.

The Lothian visit had been considered a success and, through him, they had influence over the less-than-inspiring British foreign secretary.

But they needed a bigger dog to really impress the Führer. A British statesman of global repute, international presence, worldly, charming and intelligent. Encouraged by Ribbentrop and supported by the German embassy, Tennant determined to persuade David Lloyd George to substitute for Baldwin. The former prime minister had recently written an article favourable to Germany in the *Sunday Pictorial*, prompting Tennant to write, with impressive chutzpah, introducing himself as a 'student of German affairs', who had visited Germany more than 130 times since the Armistice.[32] Intrigued, Lloyd George replied within a week.

Perhaps it was a sense of unfinished business. Lloyd George had last been to Germany in 1908 as Chancellor of the Exchequer. Though interested in the country's economic and social reforms, privately his mission had then been to persuade the Germans to de-escalate the arms race, but he had made no progress because neither the Kaiser nor Chancellor Bülow would receive him. Now he welcomed Tennant and Conwell-Evans into his inner circle as trusted guides to modern Germany. Within a month, Tennant wrote urgently from Berlin following dinner chez Ribbentrop insisting disingenuously it was now Lloyd George and not Baldwin whom the Germans wanted to visit Berlin.[33]

But all this amateur diplomacy needed to be paid for. Here, Tennant's strong connections in business and finance put him on firmer ground. While Conwell-Evans focused on the politicians, he would canvass support from the citadels of British capitalism, persuading captains of industry and leading City financiers to help him build Anglo-German friendship and for their firms to finance it. Central to his plan was margarine.

Unilever House, Victoria Embankment, London. The art deco headquarters of Unilever, the Anglo-Dutch multinational food and household products giant which was the Anglo-German Fellowship's main sponsor and host for its board meetings and annual general meetings.

3

MARGARINE, RUBBER AND GOLD

BARELY A MONTH BEFORE THE 1929 STOCK MARKET CRASH, LEVER Brothers, Britain's leading soap maker, merged with the Margarine Union of Holland to create Unilever. Responsible for one third of the world's edible oils and fats, it immediately became Britain's largest company. With 34,000 employees in over one hundred subsidiaries in Germany, it was the largest foreign corporate investor in the country. Despite the challenges of rebuilding her economy after the Great War and the subsequent economic rollercoaster, Germany had the largest population in Europe, was the world's third largest importer, and remained Britain's main European business partner.

Hitler's appointment as chancellor had unsurprisingly alarmed the boardrooms of Unilever and its British peers. Rising nationalisation, trade restrictions and government regulations threatened Unilever's interests, most urgently in margarine. Developed in nineteenth-century France and later marketed by the Dutch, margarine served as a staple of the urban German diet as a cheaper substitute to butter. Unilever supplied over two-thirds of the country's margarine needs, a foreign near monopoly that would worry any government. Dairy farmers, who had voted for Hitler in numbers, saw their butter sales threatened, so legislation had been introduced requiring butter to be added to margarine. The new regime's anti-Semitism presented Unilever's board of directors with further challenges. Required to Aryanise its subsidiary boards by asking Jewish directors to step down, one director ruefully regretted the firm had little choice but to 'swim with the Aryan current'.[1]

German industry in the Weimar era had been broadly expansionist. Its companies had looked to source raw materials from around the world and export well-respected German-made goods in return. But the new National Socialist economic model prioritised self-sufficiency and the development of synthetic raw materials to compensate for a dire shortage of natural resources and the country's loss of colonies. Soon it became economically essential for Unilever and other foreign firms to 'swim' in such currents, rather than a question of political ideology.

Unilever's chairman, Francis D'Arcy Cooper, is acclaimed as a titan of his generation of businessmen. Soon after Hitler came to power, he published an article politely critical of the new German policy, pointing out the production of synthetic raw materials and other moves towards self-sufficiency had unsurprisingly alarmed those countries supplying the raw materials. Flattering the German people who had contributed so much to the 'spiritual treasures and material progress of mankind', he appealed for a restoration of free trade.[2] This, he argued, would benefit all countries.

Ernest Tennant had, since the summer of 1933, been advising D'Arcy Cooper and Unilever's board on Germany and lobbied hard on the company's behalf, opening previously closed doors, introducing the directors to both Adolf Hitler and Wilhelm Keppler, his economics adviser. This had evolved into a British trade mission led by Unilever and including the giant oil joint venture, Shell-Mex & BP and the Dunlop Rubber Company. Travelling with the blessing of Montagu Norman, the Germanophile Governor of the Bank of England and *soi-disant* 'Pope of the City', and with the consent of the Board of Trade, the group was welcomed at the highest levels in Berlin. The delegates, several of whom had left London 'extremely hostile' to Germany, were charmed by Hjalmar Schacht, Norman's Anglophile friend and counterpart at the Reichsbank, who gave them lunch. Following constructive talks at meetings with Ribbentrop, Keppler and Hitler himself, they returned home confident this was an administration with whom they could do business.

Buoyed by this early success in introducing businessmen and politicians to the National Socialist leadership, Tennant and Conwell-Evans determined to create a vehicle for their vision. Given their starkly different backgrounds and expertise, quite how the two men met is uncertain, but Tennant's business connections impressed Conwell-Evans, who told a colleague he was a 'very decent chap, very sincere, and working jolly hard for good relations'.[3] The Anglo-German Fellowship was conceived to serve as a bilateral friendship society to promote good understanding between England and Germany. Recognising, with dry understatement, the German revolution had resulted in a 'good deal of estrangement', the launch brochure hoped the new venture would promote peace and prosperity. As it was emphatically non-political, membership would not 'necessarily imply approval' of National Socialism, but its members were urged to discourage 'misunderstanding'.[4] The Fellowship planned to be unashamedly elitist, drawing members from business, society, the military and all parties in the Houses of Parliament. With its emphasis on peace and prosperity over politics and diplomacy, it drew on a long history of distinguished London-based Anglo-German friendship groups dating back to the nineteenth century. Its immediate predecessor, the Anglo-German Association, had disintegrated following disagreements over how to deal with the new Germany's mistreatment of German Jews.[5]

On 11 March 1935, Tennant brought together a group of British business leaders, several of whom had joined the trade mission the previous autumn, at his City offices. D'Arcy Cooper took the chair and was joined by representatives from the rubber, steel, banking and insurance sectors. Julian Piggott, manager of the British Steel Export Association, represented his industry, which had suffered a severe recession, with European cartels halving production. Charles Proctor served as the UK managing director of Dunlop, the largest rubber goods manufacturer in Britain. A vital strategic raw material, rubber was used in military equipment ranging from tyres to dinghies and infantrymen's boots. Dunlop had been active in Germany since the nineteenth century but the German government had sequestered its local operations in 1914. It had re-invested after the war and now owned the country's second largest tyre factory, but trouble threatened as the new regime forced it to buy local raw materials, join cartels and deny its parent company dividends.

A senior partner from Price Waterhouse had agreed to audit the Fellowship. Appointing the country's leading firm of accountants for the relatively mundane task of reviewing the new organisation's books was evidently intended to establish its fiscal respectability. It also emphasised its independence from the NSDAP, which some critics (including within MI5) suspected of being its covert source of funding. Temporary headquarters were arranged at the Hotel Metropole, close to Trafalgar Square.

Though well past its Edwardian glory days, when the King had entertained his guests in its Royal Suite, this would suffice until funds allowed something smarter.

Tennant and Piggott had briefed Leopold von Hoesch, the German ambassador, who 'thoroughly approved' of the scheme and promised his support. The attendees consented to serve on the new organisation's Council. Eight companies each subscribed fifty pounds to cover launch expenses and agreed to appoint a prominent politician rather than a businessman as chairman. Given the public profile of their recent visit to Berlin, Conwell-Evans was asked to sound out the Marquess of Lothian. Briefing his new friend, he emphasised the new organisation's respectability, promising it would be led by 'very big business people' with real influence and was not a 'hole and corner affair'.[6] The new Council agreed to meet next in the panelled boardroom at Unilever House on Victoria Embankment. Completed two years previously, this huge neoclassical art deco palace still sits proudly overlooking the Thames and Blackfriars Bridge at the point where London's West End meets the City. The Anglo-German Fellowship was moving up in the business world.

The Fellowship boasted of the great and the good it had attracted from the cream of British industry and finance. That such luminaries should sign up to a new and untested body was testament to both the persuasive skills of Tennant, Piggott and D'Arcy Cooper, and the pressing need to address uncertainties around Anglo-German trade and finance. Fifty-nine companies had been enlisted as corporate members with other prominent businessmen joining as individuals. Three of the best-known captains of industry joined: Lord McGowan, Sir Josiah Stamp and Lord Nuffield.

A Glaswegian chemical industrialist, Harry McGowan served for two decades as the autocratic chairman of Imperial Chemical Industries (ICI). Another modern multinational giant, this had combined four leading British chemical companies as a defensive response to the creation of IG Farben, Germany's largest chemicals conglomerate, creating the third largest company in Britain. ICI would turn out to be the Fellowship's most generous donor after Unilever. But *why* is less obvious. While others were threatened with the loss of German subsidiaries and markets, as the major British manufacturer of explosives, ICI was already benefitting from Britain's tentative rearmament and had been unusually intertwined with the British government for many years. McGowan was close to Walter Runciman, president of the Board of Trade, while his finance director was friendly with Sir Horace Wilson, the chief industrial adviser to the government. The company's official historian has explained how the authorities sought its help with what we would now deem industrial espionage, as no other organisation could match ICI's combination of 'scientific talent, industrial technology, and managerial skill'.[7] Encouraged by ministers to investigate IG Farben's innovations, such as its process for producing synthetic petrol, it continued to supply valuable intelligence sourced in Germany, on occasion direct to the foreign secretary.

A polymath who bestrode business, finance, government and academia, Sir Josiah Stamp was known by the newspapers as the 'busiest man in England', serving as chairman of the London, Midland and Scottish Railway, the world's largest transport organisation, a director of the Bank of England, and chairman of the London School of Economics. Lord Nuffield, previously William Morris, had founded Morris Motors, by then Britain's leading car producer with half the domestic market. An early proponent of rearmament, he had expanded into the manufacture of aeroengines in 1929.

Though raised to the peerage, these three barons were self-made men, so far from the stereotype of conservative British landed aristocrats sympathetic to Hitler's ideology as perpetuated in popular fiction. Stamp was the son of a shopkeeper and a milliner; Nuffield's father worked as a draper and McGowan's was a brass fitter. Each had left school and started work before his sixteenth birthday. They were eager to avoid war and to build modern, profitable British industrial companies to lead their sectors internationally.

Beyond these three, industrial support for the Fellowship ranged across major industries, each challenged by the turbulent post-war economy. Sir Leonard Lyle chaired Tate & Lyle, the largest sugar refiner in the UK, supplying three-quarters of the country's needs. Sir Alexander Walker, grandson of the eponymous Johnnie Walker, had merged his whisky company into Distillers to create Britain's sixth largest industrial concern. Walker admired Hitler and was friendly with Ribbentrop, who had distributed Johnnie Walker in Germany. Charles McDougall of McDougalls, pioneers of self-raising flour, represented his family firm and the wider food industry.

Britain's two largest oil companies, Shell Transport and Trading and the Anglo-Iranian Oil Company (later BP), each sent directors. Piggott recruited his colleagues from the recession-hit metals sector, including Firth-Vickers Stainless Steels and United Steel. Having seen their exports halved since the mid-twenties under pressure from import controls and competing man-made fibres, several textile companies also joined the Fellowship. Younger companies in high-technology sectors signed up too, including Imperial Airways, Ever-Ready (the pioneers of electric torches, radios and batteries), Automatic Telephone & Electric Co, and Triplex Safety Glass, who supplied windows for cars and planes.

The Fellowship saw the encouragement of travel and tourism between the two countries as central to its mission. Thomas Cook, Britain's most famous travel agent, sponsored its monthly journal and seconded an employee, Elwyn Wright, to work as administrative secretary. The great transatlantic shipping companies from both countries, devastated in the Great War and now suffering from the worldwide economic recession, were eager to improve Anglo-German links. The German firm Hamburg-Amerika, whose pre-war fleet had been the world's largest, shipping five million emigrants from Europe to the US, joined both the Fellowship and the Deutsch-Englische Gesellschaft (DEG), its German sister society, and sponsored their publications. British rivals were similarly supportive, with the Blue Funnel Liverpool shipping line joining as a corporate member and P&O, now the largest fleet in the world, represented by a director.

Having now rebuilt their international businesses, few industrialists favoured war, but many could profit from the rearming of Britain. Morris, ICI, Dunlop and others were later able to switch their businesses on to a war footing. In stark contrast, the City of London had been doing so much profitable business with Germany, financing its rebuilding and growth, its exposure both to the country and to the wider risk of hostilities could be fatal. The billions lent to the country by British banks and bond investors dwarfed the direct investment in German industry.[8] The last war had resulted in financial chaos and robbed the City of its centuries-long cherished independence from government. After a decade of rebuilding, the stock market crash followed by the European banking crisis had triggered an existential trauma for London's banks. The three directors of the Bank of England, Frank Tiarks, Sir Josiah Stamp and Sir Robert Kindersley, tasked by the British government with managing that crisis, now joined the new Fellowship. Tiarks served on the Council and represented the merchant bank J. Henry Schröder & Co, while Kindersley chaired its successful rival, Lazard Brothers.

Widely considered one of the leading international financiers of his generation, Tiarks was the epitome of a successful Anglo-German. During the Great War he had helped the Bank of England deal with the fallout from severed financial relations with Germany, and then worked for the Admiralty tracking German submarines. In the first few days of the war, he had saved his firm from British government seizure by arranging for Bruno Schröder, and thereby their partnership, to be swiftly naturalised as British. Despite this, Bruno's earlier sponsorship of the Anglo-German Union Club (a precursor to the Fellowship), his charity to prisoners of war on both sides, and his elder son serving in the German Army, led to questions in parliament and angry letters being sent to *The Times*. Asked to explain his divided loyalties, Bruno reflected it felt as if 'his father and mother have quarrelled'.[9] Tiarks agonised similarly. Following the sinking of the *Lusitania* in May 1915, he determined to dissolve the firm, only to be dissuaded by the Governor of the Bank of England, who deemed it contrary to the national interest.

Insurance companies and commercial banks also offered their support. Then as now, London served as the centre of the international insurance market. Its leaders joined the Anglo-German Fellowship as corporate and individual members, led by Sir Percy MacKinnon, the recently retired chairman of Lloyd's of London and including directors from Commercial Union, Guardian Insurance and Norwich Union. Better financed and more domestically focused than their merchant banking colleagues, the high street banks were less exposed to the German market. Nonetheless, their directors also joined in numbers, including Robert Barclay and Sir Donald Horsfall from Barclays, Lord Barnby, Sir Leonard Lyle and Walter Runciman from Lloyds, and Sir Alexander Roger and ICI's Lord McGowan from the Midland.

Potential corporate members of the Fellowship would certainly have been reassured by the German commercial bona fides of its sister society, the DEG, and the reciprocal facilities offered in its comfortable and well-equipped clubhouse in central Berlin. The launch brochure boasted of how this offered an 'open sesame' to Germans in government, business and the professions and so would be much more than just an 'agreeable meeting place'.[10]

Alongside a handful of ardent senior Nazis such as Ribbentrop, the list of fifty-eight DEG founding members includes several who were later identified by Soviet intelligence as being 'big financiers negatively disposed against the new Nazi regime'.[11] Among them were four of the most prominent German industrialists of the twentieth century: Robert Bosch; his nephew Carl Bosch; Hermann Bücher; and Carl Friedrich von Siemens.

Whatever their politics, these German business leaders believed that internationalism should be more profitable than nationalism. Far from being willing dupes of National Socialism, several were politically liberal and, in some cases, vocally critical of the new government. They were clubbable men of business (and they were all men), cut from similar cloth to their Fellowship counterparts, who favoured economic appeasement over protectionism. They had done business with Britain long before Hitler's (and in several cases the Kaiser's) geopolitical adventures had disrupted the centuries-old traditions of trade between the Anglo-Saxon countries. But the path they had to tread through the moral maze was far more difficult than that of their British colleagues. Each of their firms would be later rightly vilified for heinous war crimes, including the use of slave labour and equipping the Nazi war machine with the hideous tools of the Holocaust such as Zyklon B and other extermination equipment.

Robert Bosch had founded the eponymous spark plug pioneer that blossomed into a global electrical engineering giant. His success as an industrialist, social reformer (introducing eight-hour working days) and philanthropist (leaving most of his wealth to charity) brought him fame and respect on a par with Nuffield or Schröder. A lifelong Anglophile, Bosch had worked in England for Siemens Brothers in the 1880s, and fifty years later developed a joint venture with Joseph Lucas of Birmingham. Dismayed by the Great War, he had dedicated himself to the promotion of international understanding. On meeting Hitler in his first year in office, an unimpressed Bosch had provoked the new chancellor's ire by urging him to seek rapprochement with France, suggesting the English model of constitutional monarchy would be best adopted in Germany, all before asking his host: 'You must feel quite odd sitting on Bismarck's chair'.[12]

Returning to Britain in 1936, German intelligence agents trailed Bosch as he visited Gordonstoun, the Scottish boarding school founded by his German Jewish friend, Kurt Hahn, and later favoured by the British royal family. Back in Germany, Bosch actively supported resistance to Hitler and challenged the anti-Jewish policy directly with the ministry of economics. He supported the Berlin chief rabbi, hired Jewish boys as apprentices and funded Jewish charities – for all of which the Yad Vashem Shrine of Remembrance in Israel posthumously awarded him the title 'Righteous Among the Nations'.

Robert was close to his nephew, Carl, the Nobel Prize-winning chemist and chairman of ICI's great rival, IG Farben, the world's largest chemical company with nearly a quarter of a million employees. Just before the Great War, Carl and Jewish-born chemist Fritz Haber had developed the Haber-Bosch process for the synthetic production of ammonia for artificial fertilisers and explosives. Six world-leading German chemical companies had merged to create Frankfurt-based IG Farben and had expanded into pharmaceuticals, inventing two of the world's bestselling drugs, aspirin and (initially for legitimate clinical use) heroin.

While it later capitulated to the regime, financing the NSDAP, facilitating some of the worst horrors of the Nazi era and exploiting wartime slave labour, IG Farben's political leanings until the early thirties had been liberal. Anxious to avoid the extremes of both Nazism and Communism, it had supported moderate and business-friendly politics such as Gustav Stresemann's German People's Party. Carl had refinanced the struggling liberal newspaper *Frankfurter Zeitung*. His company employed many Jewish scientists, and half its supervisory board were Jewish, so his objection to anti-Semitism had been both professional and personal. Invited to meet Hitler even before his illustrious uncle, he had challenged him about the treatment of the Jews. The Führer had lost his temper, ludicrously insisting Germany could survive the next century 'without physics and chemistry', before throwing him out.[13] Bosch never stopped criticising the government, openly challenging its economic policy, and questioning the Führer's infallibility well into 1939.

Carl's friend, Hermann Bücher, served as managing director of Allgemeine Elektricitäts-Gesellschaft (AEG). Founded in the late nineteenth century by the Jewish Rathenau family, it had bought some Edison patents and had an association with Vickers in Britain. As well as inventing the hairdryer and tape recorder, AEG made aircraft, fridges, irons and train locomotives. Like his two Bosch friends, Bücher had little affection for the new regime, calling for international arms controls and challenging National Socialist economics.

AEG and Siemens together controlled Germany's electrical sector. Carl Friedrich von Siemens, son of the founder, had rescued his company after the Great War and built it to be the fourth largest private sector employer in the world. Having pioneered telegraphy and invented the electric dynamo, the company developed the first electric railway, street lights, lifts, streetcars and drills before introducing traffic lights, medical X-rays and television into Germany. Its links with Britain dated back to the establishment of Siemens Brothers in London in 1858. The firm exported a third of its production so was threatened by Germany's increasing enthusiasm for autarky (economic self-sufficiency) and export control. While his company provided funding to the NSDAP once it assumed power, Carl Friedrich expressed his personal disgust with National Socialism from both a commercial and moral perspective and used his group's international network to find work for his Jewish friends, colleagues and assistants overseas. When it became clear he would soon be forced to expel his remaining Jewish employees, von Siemens pensioned them off so they would, at least, have some financial resources.

Support for the Deutsch-Englische Gesellschaft ranged across finance, commerce and industry, just as it did for the Fellowship in London. Leading German banks, including Westfalenbank, Commerz Bank and Deutsche Bank, sent directors. The chairmen of the Hamburg-Amerika Line and of the Norddeutscher Lloyd company of Bremen represented the shipping industry. Other prominent German businessmen who joined included the chief executive of Adler-Werke, the Frankfurt-based manufacturer of cars, bicycles, motorcycles and typewriters, and the managing director of Zeiss-Werke of Jena, the inventor of the first single-lens reflex camera and manufacturer of binoculars, rifle sights and microscopes.

Unsurprisingly, the founders were proud of the economic power wielded on both sides of the North Sea by the sponsors of the Fellowship and the DEG. Just five of their number – D'Arcy Cooper, Stamp, McGowan, Carl Bosch and Siemens – between them employed over a million staff. Eager to cement their status as the foremost champions of friendship between the two countries, they lobbied for official recognition on both sides of the North Sea. Three days after the founding meeting, Piggott visited the Department of Overseas Trade in Whitehall to seek ministerial blessing for the new organisation. He outlined its *raison d'être* to the minister, Colonel Colville, and his four officials (the splendidly named Anstruther-Gray, Picton Bagge, Pickthall and Brinsley-Richards) explaining confidentially they were inviting Lord Lothian to be the chairman.

But, despite this open approach to officialdom, the Whitehall mandarins were at once suspicious. Within ten days, they sent a confidential minute of the meeting, with all the supporting papers, to Frank Newsam, a senior official in the Home Office, copied to the Foreign Office. Newsam, who had previously served as principal private secretary to four Home Secretaries, had been put in charge of a new division set up to monitor pro-German groups such as the British Union of Fascists. The Special Branch of the Metropolitan Police were asked to investigate and produced a report three weeks later. This was sent to Guy Liddell, deputy director of counterespionage at MI5, who opened a file on the Anglo-German Fellowship. Inspector Morse (yes, really) and Superintendent Canning explained it had been intended as the successor to the 'old Anglo-German Club' following the problems it had faced around its Jewish members. They recognised the new organisation had sponsorship from the German authorities and prominent National Socialists but did not allow Germans to join as members.[14] Now the wheels of government were turning quickly, and the MI5 file began to swell. And so developed the early suspicions of the Fellowship's founders and supporters as 'fellow travelling' with the Third Reich, 'supping with the devil', or 'sleeping with the enemy' that would haunt them in the lead-up to the Second World War and have done so ever since.

Joachim Ribbentrop, the German ambassador to London,
shooting at Broadlands, Lord Mount Temple's country estate
near Romsey in Hampshire, 2 December 1936.

4

THE PRINCE AND THE POPPY

Joachim Ribbentrop arrived in London on Sunday, 2 June 1935 for a conference at St James's Palace to advance those discussions about limits on naval rearmament initiated when Sir John Simon, the British foreign secretary, had finally met the German chancellor. Just promoted to 'ambassador extraordinary and plenipotentiary on special mission', this title – though more Gilbert & Sullivan than *corps diplomatique* – gave Ribbentrop the ambassadorial rank he so craved. Presciently, *The Times* worried Hitler might go on to replace experienced government figures such as the state secretary Bernhard von Bülow, or even his chief, the foreign minister Konstantin von Neurath, with this wine-salesman-turned-dilettante-diplomat.[1]

Following a farewell lunch at the British embassy in Berlin, Ribbentrop landed at Croydon aerodrome with a retinue of nearly one hundred advisers, assistants and secretaries. Alongside specialists from the German navy were two foreign ministry officials, Erich Kordt and Paul-Otto Schmidt. Von Bülow had attached the thirty-two-year-old Kordt, a career diplomat, to Ribbentrop's staff officially as an aide, informally as a watchdog to report back on his boss's manoeuvres and excesses. Kordt had been responsible for assigning the thirty-six-year-old Schmidt as Hitler's personal interpreter, a post he held well into the war. An exceptionally gifted linguist with an excellent memory, Schmidt had been senior interpreter during Gustav Stresemann's chancellorship, and at the Simon meeting had impressed the Führer, who spoke only German. Like many senior diplomats and German businessmen financing the DEG, Kordt and Schmidt were wary of the Nazis and sceptical about the competence and motives of their new master. They found a kindred spirit at the German embassy in the form of Wolfgang zu

Putlitz, another young diplomat; each chronicled Ribbentrop's exploits in memoirs published after the war.

Within hours of Ribbentrop's arrival, tensions were brewing between the amateur and professional diplomats. Von Neurath, who disliked Ribbentrop, thinking him both opportunist and amateur, had agreed to his dispatch to London only following assurances from von Hoesch that the British would reject Hitler's terms, leading to a very public failure. The antipathy was mutual; Ribbentrop had never forgiven the suave ambassador for excluding him from Paris embassy receptions in the twenties. Ignoring procedure and smarting from the recent cold shoulder, Ribbentrop succeeded in ensuring the London embassy had no role in the conference. He had, however, accepted an invitation to watch the celebrations of George V's seventieth birthday from the embassy's generous terrace overlooking the Mall, giving the German visitors a privileged view of the procession to and from Horse Guards Parade. This was the English ceremonial and military pageantry Ribbentrop so admired at its absolute best. Pointedly snubbing their embassy colleagues, he instructed his delegation to colonise the right side of the terrace while the von Hoesch camp congregated on the left-hand side by the Duke of York steps. As the King led the mounted procession followed by his four surviving sons back to Buckingham Palace, His Majesty graciously took the salute from the embassy party. Following diplomatic protocol the resident staff bowed and curtsied, while Ribbentrop and his party ostentatiously gave the Hitler salute.

Shrewdly, Hitler had proposed Germany be allowed to ignore the Treaty of Versailles to rebuild her navy to a tonnage equivalent to one third of Britain's. No German had forgotten the British naval blockade maintained after the Armistice, so a strengthened navy would be popular at home. Limiting the German *Kriegsmarine* in this way sounded unthreatening to others, but in reality trebled its strength. *The Times* pointed out that, given the British Navy had to be 'scattered over the seven seas' at all times, the thirty-five percent would give Germany near parity in European waters.[2] Hitler prioritised his land and air forces, and had no intention of honouring the treaty in any event. His timing was lucky too. With MacDonald handing the Downing Street keys to Baldwin and Samuel Hoare replacing Simon at the Foreign Office, the National Government was distracted. Apparently without irony, the ineffective MacDonald regretted to Conwell-Evans that his retirement meant he would be unable to maintain his detailed interest in foreign affairs.[3] His friend, writing several years later, concluded the new leadership had brought neither 'fresh vigour nor clearer thinking' to foreign policy.[4]

The British public's profoundly pacific sentiment had not been lost on a government facing an election within sixteen months. The country had just held its first ever referendum – the Peace Ballot – at which over eleven million, nearly forty percent of the electorate, had voted. Ninety percent favoured Britain remaining a member of the League of Nations and supported disarmament, along with prohibitions on the sale of armaments for profit and the principle that members should rally to defend any attacked nation, ideally by economic and other non-military measures. This fed what Lord Halifax, himself hardly a Cabinet hawk, wryly dubbed a 'high tide of wholly irrational pacifist sentiment' in Britain.[5] Notwithstanding the post-war romanticising of those brave voices challenging appeasement and urging rearmament, theirs was not the will of the people. Their misalignment with the public mood strayed into frustration with democracy itself; Winston Churchill and Harold Nicolson (as Alan Allport recently highlighted) even blamed the sentiment on the enfranchisement of women.[6]

Following several days of encouraging talks, the naval conference adjourned for the Whitsun holiday, so Ribbentrop flew to Hitler's alpine retreat to update his master. Though not yet concluded, the mission signalled heady success for the excited envoy, who was buoyed at being taken seriously in private meetings by both the foreign secretary and the prime minister. Recognition in London society soon followed. The famous hostess Lady Cunard arranged a lunch at which a delighted Ribbentrop was introduced to Edward, the Prince of Wales, whom he quickly identified as the ideal royal patron for his mission to improve relations between the two countries.

Lionised by the press as the world's most famous bachelor, the glamorous prince admired Hitler's social reforms and liked Germany, having enjoyed his holidays there right up to 1913. His mother, Queen Mary, had been born German and spoke English with a German accent. Like Ernest Tennant, he had returned to the country immediately after the Great War and seen it sympathetically at its lowest ebb. Such affinity was reciprocated. As the contemporary journalist and author Philip Gibbs noted, the Germans called him 'the Prince' as if 'he belonged to them'.[7] Despite their mutual antipathy, von Hoesch and Ribbentrop agreed on the merits of bringing Edward into this sphere of Anglo-German relations. Von Hoesch reported the prince worried about the 'too one-sided attitude' of the Foreign Office.[8] Only the previous month, he had hosted him at a dinner at which Edward's cousin, Princess Cecilie of Greece and Denmark, had urged him to make public his support for closer links to Germany.

Ribbentrop realised his best means of channelling the prince's sympathies and stardust to the Reich's advantage was through the Royal British Legion. Established as an amalgam of four veterans' organisations as the Great War ended, the Legion had Field Marshal Haig as its president and the prince as its patron. Though easily bored by royal duties, Edward relaxed in the company of veterans and found his role a happy extension of his morale-boosting wartime visits (often by bicycle) to the troops in the trenches. Earlier that year, Ribbentrop had approached the Legion's foreign affairs expert, Colonel Crosfield, to propose fraternal meetings between British Legionnaires and their German counterparts. Alert to the diplomatic sensitivities, Crosfield had sounded out the Foreign Office's views at a meeting with Anthony Eden, who raised no objection but did warn him the Germans were using their ex-servicemen groups for propaganda.

At the Legion's annual meeting that same month, Edward gave a sensational, controversial and pivotal speech. As he rose to speak he was met by spontaneous singing of 'God Bless the Prince of Wales'.[9] With encouragement from the president and chairman, he proposed a Legion deputation should go to Germany: 'There could be no more suitable body or organisation of men to stretch forth the hand of friendship to the Germans than we ex-servicemen, who fought them in the Great War, and have now forgotten all about that.'[10] Though immediately received by loud cheers from the hall, the subsequent heat and noise it created surprised both the prince and the Legion. Promising a 'hearty welcome to British veterans', *The Times* reported that Ribbentrop, Hess and Göring, who sent congratulatory telegrams to the prince, were delighted by the proposal and that it had prompted Hitler to focus on Anglo-German relations.[11]

The British authorities were less ecstatic but baulked at rebuking the popular heir to the throne. Aneurin Bevan, the firebrand Labour MP, asked in the Commons if the new foreign secretary knew about the mission and if it had been blessed by the government. Hoare parried that it should be for the ex-servicemen's associations to decide but was guardedly supportive. Bevan pointedly encouraged the Legionnaires to visit those German ex-servicemen now incarcerated in concentration camps, before pressing the foreign secretary as to whether he approved of the proposal. Hoare replied primly he could neither approve nor disapprove on the grounds it was not a 'matter within the competence' of his office.[12] But the King had no such qualms; summoning his eldest son for a dressing-down, he asked, 'How often have I told you my dear boy never to mix in politics, especially where foreign affairs are concerned. The views you expressed yesterday, however sensible, are, I happen to know, contrary to those of the Foreign Office.'[13]

Now back in England for the last leg of the conference, Ribbentrop was thrilled to be invited by Lord Lothian to spend a weekend at his North Norfolk home. Conwell-Evans, who accompanied the party, told Lothian he would never forget Ribbentrop's 'awe' as the car turned into the famous central drive leading up to Blickling Hall. Set in five thousand acres and one of England's most important Jacobean mansions, this had been in Lothian's family since the 1840s. Having inherited it from a cousin in 1930, Lothian had restored the house and estate after years of neglect, repainting the main rooms in light colours and replacing heavy Victorian furniture with Chippendale and Hepplewhite. A comfortable retreat for politicians, academics and writers, it was here he also welcomed prime ministers, generals, fellow liberals, internationalists and distinguished overseas visitors, including Jawaharlal Nehru, later India's first prime minister, with his daughter, Indira Gandhi.

Ribbentrop's party toured the grand hall, elegant drawing room and galleried library hung with ancestral portraits and tapestries before enjoying the formal gardens where immaculate lawns, ancient clipped yews and flower beds had been redesigned in the latest English style. This showcased the best of England that Ribbentrop hoped to emulate in miniature in the library and on the lawns of his suburban Berlin villa.

Like those other aristocrats later castigated as appeasers, the Astors at Cliveden, the Londonderrys at Mount Stewart and the Mount Temples at Broadlands, Lothian was hoping to repay the hospitality he and Conwell-Evans had enjoyed in Berlin by cosseting Hitler's inner circle. Whether at tea in the stately homes of England or over coffee and cakes with the Führer at Berlin or Berchtesgaden, they hoped to cultivate personal connections, build trust and engender mutual respect by breaking bread together. Their ambition was to civilise the Nazis.

A refreshed Ribbentrop returned from Norfolk to pull off the first of his unexpected diplomatic triumphs. To Hitler's delight, Britain had signed the Anglo-German Naval Agreement, thereby precipitating the collapse of the only two-month-old Stresa Front. Established between Britain, France and Italy in response to Germany's reintroduction of conscription, the Front was intended to bolster Austria's independence and to restrain Germany from any further breaches of the Treaty of Versailles. Conwell-Evans was excited, promising Lothian the agreement proved Germany wished for 'real and permanent' friendship.[14] Neither the French nor the Italians had been consulted about the naval talks and, to further infuriate the French, it had been signed on the 120th anniversary of the Battle of Waterloo. Hitler called it the 'happiest day of my life'.[15]

Armed with his signed treaty, encouraged by the prince's speech (for which he took credit although von Hoesch had done the groundwork), and emboldened by his social successes, Ribbentrop turned his attention to the ex-servicemen in earnest. An invitation was issued to the Legion and a month later cheering crowds greeted a delegation of six senior officers in Germany, led by the chairman, Major Fetherston-Godley, with a 'most cordial reception' widely reported in the European press.[16] Joining the party was Captain Melville Hawes RN, a former naval attaché in Berlin, soon to be appointed with Ernest Tennant as joint honorary secretary of the new Anglo-German Fellowship, who furnished his previous Foreign Office colleagues with a report on the visit. Soon after arrival, the group were spontaneously received in his Chancellery by the Führer, who quizzed them for nearly two hours about their experiences in the Great War. His translator Schmidt remembered, but for the language barrier, it might have been a 'typical meeting of old comrades'. They met the leaders of the German ex-servicemen associations and were hosted to dinners by Himmler and Ribbentrop. After visiting a settlement for disabled men, they toured the new Dachau concentration camp, presumably prompted by Aneurin Bevan's comments in the Commons before they left for Germany. Now with properly built wooden huts, sleeping bunks and basic washing and toilet facilities, this had evolved from one of the early 'wild' camps. For the benefit of the distinguished visitors, fit and well-fed SS men substituted for the brutalised inmates. While fooled by the substitution and impressed by the food and the surrounding countryside, the solitary confinement facilities had unnerved the Legionnaires, who, Schmidt noted, had become 'daily more critical' as their visit progressed.[17]

The Prince of Wales's clarion call to improve Anglo-German friendship had brought the fourteen-year-old British Legion and the just-launched Anglo-German Fellowship into a fruitful partnership. The Legion lent military respectability to the Fellowship's anti-war agenda and royal gloss to its social aspirations. The Fellowship and its sister organisation in Berlin offered the veterans the comforts of its well-appointed clubhouse in central Berlin and impeccable connections to the National Socialist leadership. The King's first cousin, the Duke of Saxe-Coburg and Gotha, served as president of both the Deutsch-Englische Gesellschaft and the German ex-servicemen's associations now lobbying for affiliation with their former enemies. Soon the two organisations were sharing both members and social events. Four of the Legion's most senior officials joined the Fellowship as members and its chairman, vice chairman and general secretary all enjoyed its hospitality.

The Fellowship's new chairman cemented these links between royalty and the military veterans. Following Lothian's, no doubt polite, refusal to take on the role, probably due to his mounting workload, the Council approached Lord Mount Temple. Given his immaculate royal connections, military record and political pedigree, the sixty-eight-year-old former Conservative government minister had been an astute substitute. Formerly the Rt. Hon. Colonel Wilfrid Ashley MP, he was grandson of the social reforming seventh Earl of Shaftesbury. He had inherited estates in Ireland and England from his great-grandmother, the renowned political hostess, Emily Cowper, sister of one prime minister, Lord Melbourne, and wife to another, Lord Palmerston. Though invalided home from the South African war, Mount Temple returned to active command in the Flanders trenches before serving as a parliamentary private secretary in the War Office. As minister of transport, he had introduced one-way streets, roundabouts and arterial roads – the precursors of motorways. Originally like his family a Liberal, he had crossed to the Conservatives and developed increasing suspicions of anything leftish, becoming chairman of the Anti-Socialist and Anti-Communist Union. Mount Temple moved effortlessly through gilded political, aristocratic and royal circles. As his biographer summarised, 'every social asset was his – good looks, immense charm and real brilliance as a public speaker.'[18] His first wife had been the only child of Sir Ernest Cassel, the fabulously rich and decorated Edwardian philanthropic magnate, friend and financier to King Edward VII after whom their first daughter, Edwina, had been named. The Prince of Wales, the groom's first cousin, served as best man at her wedding to Lord Louis Mountbatten, which Queen Mary and Queen Alexandra also attended. Mountbatten was a great-grandson of Queen Victoria and both his parents were German royals by birth. Both the Cassel and Mountbatten families had, like the Schröders, suffered public opprobrium for their German connections during the Great War.

Back in 1926, Mount Temple had hosted an Anglo-German economic conference at Broadlands, his Hampshire estate, which offered a pre-Nazi model for industrial cooperation driven by business not politics. Held in response to a Continental iron and steel cartel, the attendees were leading businessmen from both countries. The conference had been held secretly, but when inadvertently leaked to the press in Berlin, resulted in protests from both the French and Italian ambassadors; nonetheless it had been deemed a success.

Mount Temple was a vocal friend to the Jewish community. His beloved first wife, Maudie, who had died in her early thirties and to whom he was devoted, had been Jewish. He highlighted the widely publicised and quickly condemned persecutions in Germany only weeks after the National Socialists came to power, presiding at a meeting attended by two thousand people at the Whitechapel Art Gallery. This resulted in the launch of a Jewish Emergency Committee in response to the atrocities, prompting hate mail to him from across the North Sea. Celebrating the disproportionate contribution to German cultural life of the small population of Jews (630,000 out of 64 million), he argued at the meeting it should be impossible for 'Christian men and women to look on in silence' while this minority faced such an existential threat. Stressing the history of British protests against such attacks, he urged the British government to 'open the gates of Palestine as wide as possible.'[19]

Now back in the thick of Anglo-German relations, Mount Temple agreed, as his first act as chairman of the Fellowship, to fly to Germany to join the National Socialist *Parteitag*, the party rally held each year in Nuremberg. Ribbentrop arranged an audience for him to meet the German chancellor, despite his crowded schedule. In order for him to have sufficient time to enjoy this and the other delights of the rally, Tennant had persuaded Mount Temple to give up two days' partridge shooting.

Adolf Hitler on his way to deliver an oration at the 1935 party rally in Nuremberg. Seated behind him is propaganda minister Joseph Goebbels.

5

BEER AND SAUSAGE AT NUREMBERG

EACH SEPTEMBER, THE PROPAGANDA HIGHLIGHT OF THE National Socialist annual calendar was the *Parteitag* held in Nuremberg. Labelled the *Reichsparteitag der Freiheit* (Rally of Freedom) the 1935 gathering celebrated the reintroduction of compulsory military service and the promised liberation of Germany from the shackles of Versailles. A million delegates crowded the narrow streets of this medieval city – one with potent associations with the Holy Roman Empire – which sits at the heart of Germany and close to Munich, the nerve centre of the NSDAP.

Three weeks earlier, Ernest Tennant had arranged for Ribbentrop to invite Group Captain M. G. Christie CMG, DSO, MC to the rally. A former British air attaché in Berlin and Washington, Grahame Christie had set himself up as a self-employed independent intelligence agent based on the Dutch-German border, from where he could closely monitor the rearming of Germany's military and particularly its air force. His education, training and character would make him the perfect candidate to infiltrate Hitler's inner circle. Given his unique skills and exploits as a pilot in the Great War, he had earned degrees of credibility with, and trust from, his former enemies which it is hard to exaggerate. The most significant relationship he developed was with Hermann Göring, whom he had first met in early 1931 when Göring served as a representative from Bavaria in the Reichstag, a year from being appointed its president. From then on, they corresponded often and met on several occasions for long talks about aviation and Anglo-German relations over glasses of whisky. These meetings gave Christie a unique and invaluable insight into the build-up of the Luftwaffe which he conscientiously reported back to London.

This was the first rally to welcome foreigners in any number. Ribbentrop had taken the lead in issuing invitations to his new British friends, attracting a mix of the admiring, curious, prurient and plain suspicious. Following his recent diplomatic triumph with the naval treaty, this was his first chance to shine within the Nazi firmament at home. Having been only a minor figure, he was, as his biographer noted, now a 'celebrity everyone wanted to meet'.[1] Many British visitors travelled under the aegis of the new Anglo-German Fellowship. Alongside Tennant, several have left their impressions of this extraordinary occasion, including Henry Williamson, author of *Tarka the Otter* and a supporter of Oswald Mosley, and Micky Burn, a junior reporter in the Rothermere press. Williamson noted the 'thousands of foreign guests; lines and lines of Mitropa coaches filled with military attachés, secretaries, embassy underlings, Oxford Groupists, Boy Scout bosses, journalists, social lecturers [and] industrial millionaires'.[2] Burn was a friend of Unity Mitford who, with her sister Diana Guinness (by then enjoying an adulterous affair with Mosley) and their brother Tom, were among the Führer's guests of honour.

The mistreatment of German Jews quickly surfaced as an issue. Following rumours published in the *Jewish Chronicle*, the London papers reported on plans to introduce anti-Jewish legislation at the rally. Tennant had already warned Christie he had been alarmed by the 'disgusting' campaign of that 'horrible man' Julius Streicher, the *gauleiter* of Franconia and publisher of the viciously anti-Semitic Nazi newspaper *Der Stürmer*.[3] Frustrated by how even internationally-minded Germans failed to see how this threatened their efforts, he insisted that if he and Mount Temple were drawn into any anti-Jewish demonstrations, it could be fatal for the nascent Fellowship. Streicher, he was convinced, was 'the world's public enemy No. 1 and far and away the main obstacle to better Anglo-German relations'.[4] An alarmed Ribbentrop telephoned at once to promise there would be no trouble.

Tennant nonetheless was unconvinced by Ribbentrop's reassurances that the Jewish question would not be an issue and so, anxious not to embarrass the chairman, postponed Mount Temple's visit until October at the earliest. But he was sufficiently mollified by Ribbentrop to make the journey to Nuremberg himself that weekend and to bring his wife

Eleonora, while Conwell-Evans and Christie travelled separately. From the outset, the Tennants' trip was still fraught. Though married to Ernest since 1912, Eleonora was ill-suited to life among the British bourgeoisie. She was fiercely independent, having stood unsuccessfully as a Conservative parliamentary candidate in the staunchly Labour-voting London docklands at the recent general election. On their early morning flight to Berlin from Croydon aerodrome, Eleonora felt 'righteously indignant' when she read about Hitler's speech to several thousand German girls and young women. Promising his audience the reintroduction of conscription would deliver them 'braver and better husbands', he insisted that bearing babies would be their 'great triumph' whereas women entering politics 'degraded themselves [and] degraded parliament'. As her husband wryly noted, 'had it been possible to step out of the aeroplane while still over England, she would have gone home'.

Arriving in Nuremberg, the fractious couple battled through ranks of Brownshirts and civilians lining the streets to the Grand Hotel, Hitler's favourite, where Ribbentrop's office had arranged them a comfortable room. A frantic schedule of social events had been laid on for the British visitors. But neither tea with the Duchess of Brunswick, the Kaiser's daughter, nor a vast banquet hosted by Himmler at the headquarters of the SS improved Eleonora's mood, so she returned home the next morning by train.

Accommodated in new grandstands and terraces designed by Albert Speer, the visitors watched a quarter of a million uniformed men and boys in serried ranks goose-stepping with flaming torches under skies lit up by searchlights. For the first time, the rally featured Göring's cherished Luftwaffe, with displays of brand-new fighters and bombers flying over the crowds in a swastika formation. The British delegates felt welcome and admired the efficiency, lack of litter and *esprit de corps*. But, within a day, the now wifeless Tennant admitted to fatigue: 'the vastness, sameness and duration of the spectacles made them somewhat difficult for the British to digest'. Similarly, Williamson felt a 'bit weary of the incessant march-past' while Burn complained 'everything went on far too long.'[5]

Conwell-Evans was having a better weekend than Tennant. He had dined with the Duke and Duchess of Brunswick, which he'd found 'thrilling', and had seen 'everybody'. The two Britons were honoured to be driven alongside Ribbentrop to lunch at the castle right behind the open-topped

Mercedes-Benz carrying the Führer through the city's narrow streets, bedecked with swastikas and 'enveloped in a continuous roar of cheering from hundreds of thousands of people who packed the pavements and filled every balcony, dormer window and battlement'. Tennant marvelled at how Hitler stood to attention beside the driver without complaint. Conwell-Evans felt 'fearfully bucked' when picked out by Hitler from the other English guests at the reception for a conversation.[6]

A special meeting of the Reichstag to pass new legislation had been hurriedly convened for that evening in response to rumours circulating in the London press and an incident in New York where Jewish dock workers had pulled down the swastika from a visiting German boat. The parliamentarians sat on red velvet chairs listening to Hermann Göring, the Reichstag president, spitting anti-Semitic venom as he commended the new laws which he required them to pass. The Flag Law adopted the Nazi swastika as the German national flag. The Law for the Protection of German Blood and German Honour forbade marriage and sexual relations between Aryans and Jews. The Reich Citizenship Law deprived German Jews of their citizenship and therefore their political rights, making them subjects rather than citizens of the German state. As inspiration for these soon-to-be-notorious Nuremberg Laws, the National Socialist legal experts had studied the US 'Jim Crow' racial segregation laws, then vigorously enforced in the southern states of America. The purpose of both sets of legislation was to create a caste system which marginalised despised minorities, depriving them of basic human rights and unifying the white Aryan majorities in doing so.[7]

Tennant thought the pretence of parliamentary process farcical, noting that any Reichstag member questioning the proposed legislation would have resulted in scenes reminiscent of an H. M. Bateman cartoon. But soon his attention wandered from this democratic charade, as his nose was 'tickled with a delicate aroma of beer and sausage' emanating from the adjoining restaurant. As they returned to the Grand Hotel a torrential thunderstorm caught his party, so he attended that evening's banquet in wet clothes. But the rain failed to dampen his admiration for the athleticism of the young Duchess of Brunswick who, he mused, 'must have been an antelope in a previous existence' given how fast she ran through the crowd. They were joined at dinner by a motley group including the Maharaja of Kapurthala, two British MPs, Lord Rennell, former ambassador to Rome, two of Mosley's

Blackshirts in uniform, the Duke of Coburg, and the 'young and beautiful' Unity Mitford, who Tennant noted really believed Hitler to be 'divine in the Biblical sense'.[8] Ribbentrop presided, 'tired but happy', over this assortment of guests, nicknamed 'Ribbentrop's kindergarten'. The Führer had just agreed to stand as godfather to his new son, Adolf, and his English friends had presented him with a silver christening cup. By the end of dinner, a Pooterish Tennant could report his clothes had 'dried up very nicely… except for the trouser legs'.

While continuing to enjoy their hosts' hospitality, Tennant and Conwell-Evans could not ignore the brutal new anti-Jewish legislation. At a lunch hosted by Hitler, Tennant was seated next to Alfred Rosenberg, leader of the NSDAP's foreign policy office and the only senior Nazi other than Ribbentrop to have visited London in an official capacity. Tennant, who thought Rosenberg a 'most unpleasant… little man of undistinguished appearance', explained the Germans were alienating world opinion through their 'insults' to the Jews.[9] Having signally failed to persuade Rosenberg at the lunch, he and Conwell-Evans demanded to see Ribbentrop that Monday morning. Conwell-Evans lectured their German friend till he went 'black in the face', but with similarly negligible effect.[10]

Tennant's analysis in his contemporary report of Ribbentrop's justification for the persecution makes uncomfortable reading to the post-Holocaust historian. Though reiterating his condemnation of Streicher's 'cruel and vulgar anti-Jewish campaign', he accepted the Germans might want to 'curtail the influence on German life and culture acquired by certain sections of the Jewish community'. He did nonetheless hope his mission would do nothing to 'worsen the position of the Jews in Germany and some day… may be able to help them'.[11] Conwell-Evans had been navigating a similarly rocky moral path in his assessment of the Third Reich. At a talk in late 1933 on 'Impressions of Germany' given at Lord Noel-Buxton's London home (the text of which he sent to MacDonald and Lothian) he had reminded his audience the purpose of the 1919 blockade had been to impose the 'unjust' Treaty of Versailles on Germany. This had directly resulted in the deaths of 'at least 750,000 men, women and children'.[12] While calling for the abolition of concentration camps and the restoration of the Reichstag, he did defend the new regime, suggesting English newspapers were 'exaggerating atrocities' committed by only a 'very small minority of roughs'. Given the extent of well-documented National Socialist brutality in its first year of power, this now seems astonishingly misguided.

Conwell-Evans had argued to German ministers the 'rehabilitation' of the Jews as a race should be essential if Germany wanted friendship with England. Otherwise, the harassment of Jews would be compared to the Revocation of the Edict of Nantes. He had prominent Jewish friends in both Germany and Britain and, in one case at least, arranged the emigration of a family to England. His history professor in Königsberg, Hans Rothfels, had been born into a wealthy Jewish family. Even though he had converted to Lutheranism before the First World War and was a well-regarded nationalist historian (who later wrote one of the first histories of the German resistance), the Nazi authorities could not ignore his Jewish ancestry. The British consul in Berlin had been unhelpful, so Conwell-Evans arranged with the Home Secretary to secure entry permits for the family and then found Rothfels a two-year teaching post at St John's College, Oxford. He cultivated friendships with other Jewish or part-Jewish intellectuals including Professor Arnold Bergstraesser, the respected political scientist forced to leave Germany, and Alfred Zimmern, one of the founders of Chatham House and later the first secretary-general of UNESCO, whom he recommended to Ramsay MacDonald for a peerage. A. L. Kennedy, leader writer at *The Times*, appreciated such efforts and proposed him as the paper's next Berlin correspondent, noting Conwell-Evans 'hates the Jew-baiting and the persecution of the Church'.[13]

But it is his correspondence with Rose Rosenberg which gives us the most pertinent insight into Conwell-Evans's attitudes to the 'Jewish question' in National Socialist Germany. One of the most successful Jewish women in British public life, Rosenberg had been born in East London in 1892, and was like her friend the child of a tailor, in her case a Jewish migrant from Russia. Known as 'Miss Rose of No. 10', she served as Ramsay MacDonald's personal secretary for thirteen years and was the first woman allowed in the Strangers' Dining Room in the House of Commons. As a breathless American journalist wrote at the time, 'she knows more of the inside dope on home politics and world politics than anyone in the kingdom outside of MacDonald and King George'.[14] It is clear from their correspondence that Conwell-Evans had developed an (almost certainly platonic) *tendresse* for Rose. Anxious to impress on her his sincerity, he had written as early as

October 1933 offering 'some hopeful things to say' to the prime minister about the 'possibility of Hitler changing his attitude towards the Jews'.[15] Later, he personalised the issue, asking 'can I do anything for the cause which doubtless you personally have at heart? I need hardly tell you that I have been doing my utmost for the Germans of Jewish extraction.' He insisted: 'I have <u>passionately</u> pleaded in Berlin with important Nazis – again and again for the German Jews... I shall go on doing so.'[16] There is no hint of Rosenberg, an evidently shrewd judge of character, doubting his sincerity and she replied, 'You cannot imagine how deeply I feel on the whole subject. I do appreciate all you are doing, nevertheless, and urge you to continue your good efforts.'[17]

Conwell-Evans and Tennant journeyed home from Nuremberg rebuffed and demoralised. Fierce gales had twice forced their flight across the North Sea to make emergency landings back in Belgium; switching to a boat, they finally reached home and 'very rough it was'. Though relieved he had left behind the chairman Lord Mount Temple (to whom he described the event as 'complete pandemonium'), Tennant thought the trip still worthwhile, as he had to keep 'up to date' with the Nazis or their actions became 'completely incomprehensible'.[18]

Grahame Christie, Tennant's second invitee to the *Parteitag*, had meanwhile been observing the Germans through a sharper lens. Though soon to become Conwell-Evans's closest co-conspirator, his first allegiance was to Sir Robert Vansittart, the permanent undersecretary at the Foreign Office. A published poet, playwright and later movie scriptwriter, Vansittart served three prime ministers and five foreign secretaries and was the antithesis of the stereotypical British civil servant. Immaculately dressed, generous, witty and artistic, his second marriage to an enormously wealthy heiress supported a lifestyle unusual for a government employee, complete with a grand mansion in Park Street, Mayfair and an exquisite William and Mary manor house in Denham in Buckinghamshire. Dubbed by Conwell-Evans as the 'stormy petrel in the doldrums of appeasement', alongside his friend Winston Churchill and Duff Cooper, 'Van', as he was known to all, would be the most determined critic of the British government's policy of appeasement.

In his voluminous correspondence with Vansittart, Christie predicted the regime's direction of travel with eerie accuracy, recognising the threat of Hitler's foreign policy and seeing through the layers of obfuscation, misinformation and misunderstanding. Confident in his judgement of the German psyche, he noted that for them war was a 'highly moral institution', and so young Germans were being trained to die for the Reich. The League of Nations was being ignored internationally and the advance of air power would be the decisive factor in future conflicts. Christie emphasised that the recovery of German-speaking territories was their foremost priority, with 'diversions' planned to bring tensions to a head approximately three years later, in 1938, in the disputed Memel Territory, Austria and then Czechoslovakia. The Germans, he warned, were confident neither the French nor the British were willing to risk war to protect any of these faraway countries.[19]

*Hermann Göring and his wife Emmy attending the opera
ball at the Staatsoper, Unter den Linden in Berlin.*

6

WHISKY WITH GÖRING

ENGINEER, PRIVATE PILOT, AIR FORCE OFFICER, INTELLIGENCE agent and latterly art collector, Grahame Christie was the epitome of the gentleman amateur, a character from fiction in the mould of John Buchan's Richard Hannay or Ian Fleming's James Bond. Among his many remarkable achievements, he earned the respect, trust and friendship of Hermann Göring.

Apart from a short obituary written by his nephew for *The Times* and sporadic mentions by specialist historians, his story is still largely untold. Admired by his friends for physical and intellectual courage alike, he had once flown his out-of-control plane into the side of a hangar to avoid injuring the ground staff, 'escaping death only by a miracle'.[1] He had been born in 1881 in Edgbaston, the affluent Birmingham suburb, to John and Annabella Christie. His father had prospered by arranging the series of amalgamations that created the London City and Midland Bank (now part of HSBC Group). His mother had died before his second birthday so he and his older brother 'suffered rather at the hands of governesses'.[2] The third of these became the second Mrs Christie and left the boys traumatised by the very notion of stepmothers. Following school at Malvern College, which he disliked and where he admitted to being lazy, Christie moved to Germany where he became fluent in the language and qualified as an engineer. Awarded the degree of *Doktoringenieur* with first class honours in chemistry by the University of Aachen, he ran the English subsidiary of the Otto Coke Oven Company, a German business owned by family friends, for which he invented techniques for recovering by-products from coke production. Beyond his engineering and language skills, Christie was an intrepid outdoor sportsman. An avid mountaineer and natural skier, according to his family he taught Captain Scott to ski before his famous expedition to Antarctica.

In 1913 Christie commissioned an early monoplane from the Yorkshire designer Robert Blackburn. Weighing less than one thousand pounds (about that of an average horse), this motorised carpentry was powered by an eighty-horsepower engine to speeds of up to seventy miles per hour. Still a novice, Christie employed a professional pilot and together they toured the north of England, giving displays above enthralled crowds, most of whom had never seen powered flight. That October, the plane's manufacturers challenged their Lancashire rival, A. V. Roe, with its Avro 504 biplane, to a hundred-mile race ending in Moortown in Leeds, with checkpoints in York, Doncaster, Sheffield and Barnsley. The *Yorkshire Evening News* sponsored a silver trophy and a crowd of twenty thousand assembled to watch what was unsurprisingly dubbed the War of the Roses. After various dramas, including the Avro missing a checkpoint and a terrier getting caught in the Blackburn's wheels, victory was declared for Yorkshire. Widely covered by local newspapers, the race was captured in photographs and a series of postcards showing the victorious Christie and his pilot in their plane.

When war was declared the next summer this early flying experience proved invaluable. Christie donated both his private planes to the army and enlisted as a military pilot with the rank of second lieutenant in the two-year-old Royal Flying Corps. The new corps was small and ill-equipped, with only two thousand personnel spread over five squadrons, four flying rudimentary aeroplanes and one operating observation balloons. Pilots paid for their flying lessons, so a private income was an advantage.

Aged thirty-three, Christie was old for a pilot, with most of his colleagues a decade younger and with only a few hours of flight training. A photograph survives of him standing in front of the biplane in which he earned his Royal Aero Club aviators' certificate. With flight overalls worn over a thick cream sweater, the still boyish-looking second lieutenant Christie leans his right arm on the propeller with his left hand resting confidently on his hip, a leather helmet framing precise, delicate features set in a moon-shaped face. Four years later, he ended the war a wing commander and lieutenant colonel with the Military Cross and a Distinguished Service Order. The frontispiece of his squadron's official history, dated 1919, shows him immaculate in service dress with wings and medal ribbons proud above his left breast pocket. The same youthful, delicate features and kindly eyes look out but with none of the swagger of the earlier portraits.

Christie avoided the limelight so effectively and was so modest about his achievements that details of his war service are sketchy. He climbed the military ladder quickly, staying at the centre of the action and the forefront of aeronautical innovation. He made his first notable contribution at the Battle of Loos in September 1915, the largest Allied offensive since the start of the war, where fierce fighting resulted in fifty thousand Allied casualties. Flying a miscellany of primitive planes, the Royal Flying Corps lost many pilots and machines to both fire from the ground and harassment by German *Fokkers* equipped with machine guns. Christie demonstrated for the first time the efficacy of tactical bombing (the dropping of bombs from aircraft onto targets of immediate military value), now a mainstay of modern combat aviation. His squadron had been ordered to attack the train junctions and locomotive sheds behind enemy lines at Valenciennes, an especially challenging task as their planes were equipped neither to carry nor drop bombs. Undaunted, on the afternoon of the second day of battle, Christie, supported by a second pilot and plane, braved appalling weather to get airborne. Maintaining a height of nearly five thousand feet (and so a mile high) out of range of small arms fire from the ground, he dropped a 112 lb bomb onto twenty train trucks, each unexpectedly loaded with live artillery shells. The detonation, as one historian drily recorded, resulted in a 'temporary cessation of all traffic at this great junction at a vital time'.[3]

As the largest air battle fought to date, Loos represented a turning point for both Christie, now promoted to captain, and the young Royal Flying Corps, which had matured from bit part player on the Western Front to take a vital role within the British Expeditionary Force. The following spring, Christie returned to England to assume command of No. 50 Squadron, newly formed to defend the south coast against German Zeppelins, the first military threat to British homes since the Napoleonic Wars. Christie's technique involved positioning his enemy with the moon on the far side, so what little light it emitted would silhouette these huge airships.

Within nine months, the now Major Christie returned to France to set up No. 100 Squadron, the first bombing unit to fly at night. Described by Brigadier-General Trenchard as one of his 'best weapons', its first mission was to attack the aerodrome at Douai, where the legendary Red Baron, Manfred von Richthofen, ran what one of Christie's officers (in a splendidly mixed metaphor) dubbed a 'veritable nest of… the flower of the German

Flying Corps'. All eighteen of Christie's planes took to the air at night and succeeded in wrecking the Red Baron's aerodrome's hangars, grounding his famous 'Flying Circus' for several days and disturbing his sleep.[4]

Christie's squadron fought through the major battles of 1917 from Vimy Ridge to Passchendaele. In retaliation for German bombing raids on civilians in England, they were tasked with strategic night bombing deep into the German industrial heartlands, targeting major cities, especially railway stations, junctions, goods sidings, steelworks and even moving trains. As one of his pilots gleefully remembered, this had 'many of the characteristics of big game hunting'.[5] Though now promoted to wing commander and lieutenant colonel, Christie continued to fly combat sorties, irking both his commanders, unhappy with a senior officer taking such personal risks, and his juniors, resentful of his scrutiny.

The Royal Flying Corps merged with its naval counterpart to become the Royal Air Force in April 1918. Five squadrons with a few dozen planes and 2,000 staff had mushroomed to 150 squadrons, over 3,000 aircraft and over 100,000 personnel. Christie ended the war with a permanent commission and was sent by the new RAF to South America to advise various countries on their nascent air forces. Soon after the Armistice, he was decorated for the third time, created (like Fleming's Bond) a Companion of the Order of St Michael and St George. A small brass plaque commemorates him in the order's chapel in St Paul's Cathedral in London.

Christie's 'good' war had sharpened his essential traits: bravery, overwork, dogged determination, secrecy and an aversion to war. But despite his affection for Germany's culture and people, he obsessed about the threat of her nationalism and militarism and developed a profound distrust of her political and military leaders. The war had also taken its toll on his health; he never fully recovered and so went on half-pay from the RAF. He had recovered sufficiently by 1922 to accept a posting to Washington as the air attaché to the British embassy. Here, his combined charm, diplomacy and military intelligence well suited the role, and within a year he was promoted to group captain. As a colleague remembered, the 'cleverest aeronautical engineers' saw him as their equal while as a decorated combat pilot the 'keenest of the American aviators' respected his judgement. Blithely exploiting these connections, he soon gathered so much technical intelligence on the emerging US air services that his Whitehall masters, sensitive to any risk of Anglo-American diplomatic embarrassment, worried he was straying into espionage.[6]

Christie's workload had been prodigious, with him spending, according to a contemporary, weeks sleeping in trains and working at a rate which would have 'killed most men'. Not yet fully recovered, he ended his posting ill again, returning to England for an extended rest cure before being appointed air attaché at the embassy in Berlin. Now the Foreign Office, alarmed by German rearmament, better valued his accomplished intelligence gathering. As in the States, his engineering degree earned him admiration from the aeronautical scientists while his flying record brought him respect from the military. Now, he explained poetically, his job would be to 'wander aimlessly amongst the Boche herds with our ears laid back, eyes front, but our mental antennae extended in the endeavour to select and sift from the bewildering multiplicity of wavelengths a few significant signals'.[7] By all accounts, he was a highly effective attaché.

As Conwell-Evans remembered, Christie had warned, well before Hitler came to power, that Germany would soon become a 'menace to Great Britain and Europe' for the second time that century. When Ramsay MacDonald's government proposed withdrawing British troops from the Allied-occupied Rhineland six years ahead of schedule, Christie feared Germany would take 'considerable liberties' with the treaties and agreements designed to restrain her. Reaching for Biblical precedent, he suggested 'having shorn Samson's locks we should keep his scalp closely cropped until he shows the definite tendency to handle the ass's jawbone in a more delicate manner'.[8]

But, with his health still variable, he fully retired from the now much-diminished peacetime RAF. At his valediction, his friends hoped he would rest and recover sufficiently to help the development of aviation with 'his experience and his brilliant intellect'. He did indeed soon return to deploy both. Despite sixteen years in a poorly paid military career and the financial crises of the late twenties, Christie was still very rich. As a committed bachelor with no family to support or limit his movements, he set himself up as an independent intelligence agent. Firmly in the Richard Hannay mould, he used his wealth, expertise and contacts to launch a mission to 'gather and compare information bearing on German designs from as many authoritative sources as possible'.[9] With no formal employer and unpaid, he acted like Hannay as a gentleman amateur, something unusual outside of fiction.

Now Christie would spend eight months of each year at Huis Wylerberg, the home of Marie Schuster-Hiby, his German 'godmother', which sits in hills overlooking the Rhine valley and was then just into German territory on the Dutch-German border near Nijmegen. (Annexed by the Dutch in 1949, it is now in Holland and remains the only territory not returned to Germany post war.) Huis Wylerberg was designed by Otto Bartning, a pioneering Bauhaus architect, and is one of the most innovative German expressionist buildings, with a star-shaped plan and asymmetrical facades. Old friends of the Christie family, the Schuster-Hibys owned the Otto Coke Oven Company where Grahame worked before the war. As a teenager Marie had been au pair to the Christie boys soon after their mother had died. A maternal bond developed between them; a framed photograph of him remains on her desk to this day.

Though committed opponents of National Socialism, Marie and her daughter Alice were distantly related by marriage to Hermann Göring. At Wylerberg they developed an artistic and musical salon, hosting concerts, including new works composed and performed by Jewish musicians. For seven years, they used the house and a hotel in the village to facilitate the escape of German Jews into Holland. Quite how many succeeded is unclear, but as they could shepherd up to fifty across the border in a single night this could have run to many hundreds or even thousands. Tragically, the Dutch authorities quickly captured many and returned them to Germany.

The Schusters had attracted the suspicions of the German authorities, which Marie and Alice parried bravely. They would welcome enquiring SS and Gestapo officers into the house and leave them to wait in the comfortable music room while tea or coffee was prepared. Given time to admire the silver-framed photograph of General Göring prominent among the family pictures on the piano, the suitably refreshed young officers quickly lost their curiosity and remembered they had other citizens to harass.

From Wylerberg, Christie covered Germany, Austria, Czechoslovakia and other European countries, while the Travellers Club served as his London headquarters. The quality of his connections in Germany was quite exceptional, ranging from loyal but boastful Nazis inadvertently sharing military intelligence to opponents of the regime deliberately passing state secrets.

Christie had first met Hitler in 1932 with Rudolf Hess at the Kaiserhof Hotel in Berlin. He had left the meeting 'quite unimpressed' with the NSDAP leader, whom he assessed as a 'rather vain and vacillating demagogue' able to 'sway the masses' but with no sense of humour and an inferiority complex. Like Tennant and Simon, he had been struck by Hitler's 'expressive' eyes but deplored the 'grotesque Charlie Chaplin' moustache and 'small mouth with tight thin lips which express petulance, meanness and cruelty'.[10] Christie's wide group of friends within German aviation and industrial circles dated back over twenty years and included vocal critics of National Socialism such as Robert Bosch. He found it easy to make friends in the fraternity of airmen, for whom an impressive flying record seemed far more relevant than nationality or political allegiance. Men like Erhard Milch, the state secretary of the Reich Aviation Ministry, Göring's loyal deputy in the Luftwaffe and a founding DEG member, provided him with first-hand intelligence on the build-up of the German air force. While air attaché in Berlin, Christie had befriended Hugo Junkers, the founder of the renowned Junkers Aircraft and Motor Works, who later refused to cooperate with the new government and was arrested for high treason. Christie's most productive source of detailed secret intelligence was a military adviser to Junkers, Captain Hans 'Johnnie' Ritter, a South German who had also served as assistant to the military and air attachés at the German embassy in Paris.

But for where the Nazi regime was heading and what its leaders were planning, Christie could rely on his ebullient, effusive, indiscreet friend and *Gesprächspartner* (talking partner) – Hermann Göring. The British security sources had failed in their attempts to cultivate reliable sources close to the head of the Luftwaffe, so this promised intelligence gold. The primary recipient of Christie's reportage was Robert ('Van') Vansittart, whom he had befriended in twenties America. This became the foundation of Van's famous 'private detective agency', of which Conwell-Evans soon became another highly effective agent. In Vansittart, as Conwell-Evans remembered, Christie had found a 'friend upon whose discreet silence he could entirely rely, and one whose brilliant and unconventional mind was quickly responsive and sympathetic to his voluntary efforts to help'. As permanent undersecretary at the Foreign Office, Van stood at the centre of the intersection of Great Britain's formidable diplomatic machine and, given his oversight of the security services, served as a vital link between the intelligence gatherers and the decision makers in Whitehall. Christie became for him quite simply 'Britain's best source on the inner workings of the Nazi state'.[11]

*The German national football team give the Nazi salute at
White Hart Lane, Tottenham, London, before playing England
(who would go on to win 3–0), 4 December 1935.*

7

SWASTIKAS OVER
WHITE HART LANE

By OCTOBER 1935, THE NEWLY ESTABLISHED ANGLO-GERMAN Fellowship was ready to be unveiled. It had secured sufficient capital from its business backers to incorporate in London as a company limited by guarantee, with sixty-five distinguished founder members. Lord Mount Temple was confirmed as chairman, a council of nineteen luminaries was appointed and the travel agency Thomas Cook seconded Elwyn Wright to run the office. Soon it was flourishing, with a busy programme of members' events. Nearly 350 members were recruited within a year and 600 within two. The inaugural social event, a banquet to welcome the organisers of the Berlin Olympics, established the template for the Fellowship's larger social gatherings. It invited distinguished speakers and guests of honour from both sides of the North Sea and *The Times* and other newspapers would report on the evening's theme and speeches. In Germany its sister society, the Deutsch-Englische Gesellschaft, was being relaunched under the leadership of the cream of Anglo-German royalty.

While Wright oversaw the coordination for the banquet in London, Tennant's lobbying of Lloyd George to consider a visit to Germany was bearing fruit. The former prime minister invited Tennant to lunch at his estate in the village of Churt on the Surrey-Hampshire border, where he kept pigs and bees and grew fruit, sold in a picturesque farm shop opposite the village pub. They were joined by his two secretaries, Frances Stevenson, then also his mistress, and the long-suffering A. J. Sylvester. Previously private secretary to two other prime ministers, Bonar Law and Baldwin, Sylvester had worked for Lloyd George for twelve years and would do so until his master's death. A skilful secretary, diarist, speed typist, shorthand note-taker and amateur filmmaker, he served as aman-uensis, secretary and valet – a hybrid of Boswell, Miss Moneypenny and Jeeves. Admitting he had chosen Tennant because businessmen were better informed than diplomats, Lloyd George bombarded him with questions, especially around Churchill's recent claims the Germans were spending vast sums on rearmament.

Buoyed by the prospect of a visit by such a senior British statesman to Germany, Tennant returned with Conwell-Evans to stay chez Ribbentrop in Berlin. On the day of their departure, Churchill gave a characteristically robust speech in a Commons debate on foreign affairs just before parlia-ment was dissolved ahead of the general election. Germany, he warned the House, had been rearming at an alarming rate and would this year spend the 'incredible figure' of more than £800 million. Echoing Christie's secret report to Vansittart from the month before (to which he likely had access from Vansittart and other Foreign Office allies), he explained:

> The whole of Germany is an armed camp… A mighty army is coming into
> being. Many submarines are already exercising in the Baltics. Great cannon,
> tanks, machine guns and poison gas are fast accumulating… The German
> air force is developing at a great speed, and in spite of ruthless loss of life. We
> have no speedy prospect of equalling the German air force or of overtaking
> Germany in the air, whatever we do in the near future.

Switching gear, he flattered the Germans with compliments that he might have borrowed from the Fellowship's publicity material. Bearing no grudge against the country and no prejudice against its people, he promised he had 'many German friends, and… a lively admiration for their splendid qualities of intellect and valour, and for their achievements in science and art'. Echoing the sentiments of the Prince of Wales, he promised, 'The re-entry into the European circle of a Germany at peace within itself, with a heart devoid of hate, would be the most precious benefit… which alone would liberate Europe from its peril and its fear, and… the ex-Service men, would go a long way in extending the hand of friendship to realise such a hope.' But changing tack again, he explained, 'We cannot afford to see Nazidom in its present phase of cruelty and intolerance, with all its hatreds and all its gleaming weapons, paramount in Europe at the present time.'[1]

The next day, while Tennant and Conwell-Evans were with the Ribbentrops, a copy of Churchill's speech was handed to their host, who, 'very white and angry', insisted in a clumsy but chilling attempt at humour: 'Mr Churchill is quite wrong in his figures… we are not spending a paltry 800 millions on rearming. We are spending £10,000 millions a month. We are turning out 25,000 aeroplanes a day and 1,000 big guns a minute.' Rising to his theme, Ribbentrop joked of how 'Herr Hitler is just about to pass a law making any woman liable to concentration camp who fails to have twins in 1936, triplets in 1937 and quadruplets there after and the ratio must be at least three boys to one girl… we aim at a population the size of India,' before asking 'my God what can you do with men who make wild statements like that?' Returning to London, Tennant briefed Lloyd George (who was much amused by the reaction to Churchill's speech) and extended his open invitation to Germany, explaining the Führer was an admirer and so he would be very well received.[2]

Meanwhile, the Fellowship team were arranging an upcoming dinner with Hans von Tschammer und Osten, the Reich Sports Leader, as its guest of honour. The XI Olympiad, scheduled for the summer of 1936, offered the new Fellowship an ideal launch pad for their message of Anglo-Saxon amity. More controversially, it also offered a propaganda platform for Hitler to show the supposedly civilised side of National Socialism. Just a week before the Olympic banquet, the Council had arranged a private dinner in honour of the ambassador, Leopold von Hoesch, at the Dorchester Hotel, the newly built modernist temple to luxury on Park Lane.

The evening provoked a fracas that nearly strangled the Fellowship at birth. Lord Eltisley, a former MP and a Council member, challenged the German government's treatment of Jews in his speech which Elwyn Wright, the ardently pro-Nazi secretary, deplored as a 'violent attack'.[3] The ambassador reported to Berlin in more measured tones how 'several of the English guests had voiced their disapproval of Nazi internal policy and had expressed misgivings about its long-term effect upon Anglo-German relations.'[4] Either way, Hitler was furious and demanded the recall of those Germans just arriving in London for the banquet. Only the rapid intervention of Ribbentrop, playing down the accuracy of von Hoesch's report, averted a disaster.

Having aborted his visit to Nuremberg because of the anti-Jewish legislation, Mount Temple's first public outing as chairman was the Olympic banquet, with this second controversy still warm to the touch. But tempers were quickly cooled and von Hoesch returned to break bread with the Fellowship, supported by his chargé d'affaires, the charmingly mannered but ardent Nazi, Prince Otto von Bismarck (grandson of the Iron Chancellor), and Karlfried Graf von Dürckheim-Montmartin, the energetically Anglophile head of the English section of Ribbentrop's private office. The president of the Deutsch-Englische Gesellschaft, the Duke of Saxe-Coburg and Gotha, brought a contingent from Germany including von Tschammer und Osten, Theodor Lewald, president of the Olympic organising committee, and Carl Diem, its secretary-general.

The previous day a football game had been played between England and Germany at White Hart Lane in north London. The first friendly international between the two countries in five years, this had political, diplomatic and sporting significance, triggering widespread controversy. Not least because the swastika, recently adopted as the German national flag, flew above the home ground of Tottenham Hotspur, a team – then as now – proud of its support from London's Jewish community. The English Football Association had invited ten thousand German supporters, their travel sponsored by the German *Kraft durch Freude* (Strength through Joy) state leisure organisation. Jewish groups and the Trades Union Congress had lobbied the British government to ban the game. The authorities had argued to keep sports and politics separate, and that a ban would hand Joseph Goebbels a propaganda triumph. The German fans were carefully shepherded throughout their trip and behaved well while eight hundred police kept order between anti-fascist protesters and pro-Nazi supporters. Fritz Szepan, the German captain (nicknamed 'Greta' for his blond hair), remained determinedly apolitical: 'We have nothing to do with governments. Herr Hitler has sent us no message. We are here as sportsmen to play football against the best in the world. The game's the thing, is it not?'[5]

One England fan took matters into his own hands. Ernie Wooley, a tool maker from Shoreditch, scrambled onto the roof of the West Stand and cut the lanyard on the flagpole, causing the offending swastika to fall to the ground. He was arrested at once and charged at Tottenham Police Court with criminal damage valued at 3s 6d, but the chairman dismissed the case. As to the game itself, the *Manchester Guardian* concluded that while the 'experts must decide whether it was good football, it was certainly good fun'. Unlike in the preceding game against Italy, the Germans were so well behaved that the play had been 'amazingly clean' and the 'amount of handshaking was almost comical'.[6] Unusually, given later form, England won three goals to nil.

Mount Temple, while proposing the health of the DEG, applauded the good nature shown by both players and spectators. In his response, the Duke of Coburg reported 'widespread sympathy in Germany for the English people, the depth of which was not yet fully understood in Britain'.[7] Von Tschammer und Osten claimed the 'language of sport was international' and should be an 'educative and cultural force of the first order'. Dr Lewald briefed his fellow diners on plans to welcome the forty-nine countries competing in the Olympics. Commenting on the football match, he argued, to cheers, that it showed the German sportsman was a 'good fighter and a good loser too'.

Only two months old and with no official role in international sport, the Fellowship had done well to attract members of both Houses of Parliament, two of Britain's three International Olympic Committee members and other celebrated gentleman amateurs to the dinner. The Fourth Estate was well represented, including Guy Butler, the athletics correspondent for the *Morning Post*, who as a sprinter had won four Olympic medals including a gold. He was joined by fellow journalists including Ralph Deakin, the foreign news editor for *The Times*, and Sir Roger Chance MC, who would later serve as press attaché at the British embassy in Berlin.

Not to be outdone, the relaunched Deutsch-Englische Gesellschaft held its augural event in Berlin a month later, inviting a gaggle of senior National Socialists, Anglo-German royalty, British diplomats and friends of Germany. The opening ceremony for the newly furbished clubhouse at 30 Bendlerstrasse in the heart of Berlin's diplomatic district was followed by dinner at the prestigious German Aero Club. The Duke of Coburg presided, supported by the Duke of Brunswick, the deputy president, with Mount Temple leading a party of Fellowship visitors from England. The senior Nazis arrived in force. Rudolf Hess as Hitler's deputy was the highest-ranking, supported by von Tschammer und Osten and General Franz Ritter von Epp, Reich governor of Bavaria, alongside the ever-present Ribbentrop. Sir Eric Phipps, the British ambassador, led an embassy contingent including his minister, military attaché and air attaché. The attendance of such senior diplomats was a vote of confidence in the fledgling sister societies, especially given the equivocal attitudes of their masters back in Whitehall.

Coburg spoke warmly of the 'depth of feeling in Germany in favour of understanding between the two countries', comparing the pride of the subjects of the British Empire with that of the followers of the Third Reich.[8] After dinner, the entire party was invited to join General Göring and over two thousand guests, including Berlin's *corps diplomatique*, German royalty and nobility at a ball so lavish it astonished the international press, who struggled to pick out any aspects of socialism in this display of National Socialism. Celebrating the general's forty-second birthday, the State Opera House had been redecorated with cream satin hung from the walls and staircases and fountains installed just for the night. Ribbentrop and Göring also hosted the English contingent for private lunches over the rest of their stay in Berlin.

Conwell-Evans deployed his charm to secure the support of the British embassy and its consulates under three successive ambassadors. He had built a rapport with Phipps and his predecessor, Sir Horace Rumbold, and would do so with his successor, Sir Nevile Henderson, too, despite their three quite different personalities. Rumbold had charted the rise of National Socialism in a series of drily witty memoranda sent back to Whitehall, only to be relieved of his post by a nervous foreign secretary. He had challenged Hitler about his persecution of Jews, prompting a 'hysterical bawling with his hair falling over his eyebrows' in response, behaviour Conwell-Evans thought unlikely to impress the ambassador, who always insisted on 'preserving the decencies and conventions of social life'.[9]

But the Berlin embassy offered a poisoned chalice for any diplomat, made worse by Britain's disjointed foreign policy. Transferred from Vienna to replace Rumbold, Phipps also struggled to cultivate friends within the German hierarchy. But while Vansittart, his brother-in-law, remained frustrated by the amateur diplomacy of the Fellowship and its ilk (with the exception of Christie, whom he always deemed a professional), Phipps was more sanguine, thinking it best to 'avoid giving the Germans reasons to suppose, by adopting a sulky attitude, that the Embassy disapproves of any efforts, however unauthorised on our side, to promote Anglo-German agreement and understanding'. Though he declined an honorary chairmanship of the Fellowship, Phipps did agree to attend the ceremony and to entertain 'ambulant amateurs' when they came to Berlin, as 'a friendly meal' might prevent the 'complete nobbling of the missionary by the ineffable Ribbentrop', who believed most British diplomats to be 'rabidly Germanophobic'.[10] He did, however, warn the ailing King George V, three days after attending the launch, that these enthusiastic initiatives might raise 'false German hopes as regards British friendship and cause a negative reaction in England, where public opinion was very naturally hostile to the Nazi regime and its methods'.[11]

Notwithstanding the ambassador's concerns, these tentative attempts to civilise the Nazis were well received in Germany. In a year-end round-up on the country headlined 'Friendship with Britain', the Berlin correspondent of the *Observer* reported on how the efforts to 'increase political friendship' were appreciated. The naval pact had been welcomed with 'terrific jubilation' and Sir John Simon's visit, the British Legion delegation, the football match in London and the foundation of the Anglo-German Fellowship had all 'played their part in the persistent wooing of Britain'.[12]

Meanwhile, fresh from celebrating the relaunch of the Deutsch-Englische Gesellschaft in Berlin, the Duke of Coburg returned to London on a mission blessed by Hitler, who hoped to manipulate the royal cousinhood for his own purposes. Briefing the waiting newspapermen at Croydon aerodrome, the duke explained his purpose was to strengthen the Anglo-German Fellowship. With him came a party of German veterans for a return visit following the British Legion trip to Berlin the previous July. Having placed a swastika-emblazoned wreath at the Cenotaph and given the Nazi salute, they motored down to Richmond to visit the poppy factory before a tea party at the Legion's headquarters, joined by the German ambassador and the Schröder family.

The Legion hosted a welcoming dinner at the Army and Navy Club with guests including Vansittart and Duff Cooper. Its president had been about to propose the loyal toast when he was handed a telegram warning 'the King's life is moving peacefully towards its close'. Toasts to the dying monarch were drunk and both the German and British guests were 'deeply moved'.[13] A lunch hosted by the Fellowship the next day was hurriedly postponed, the expedition curtailed, and so the delegates returned home early. That night, eased on by a generous dose of cocaine and morphine administered by his doctor, the seventy-year-old King George V succumbed to bronchitis.

At the funeral held a week later, Coburg, his first cousin, slow-marched behind the gun carriage carrying the late king's body from Westminster Hall via Paddington Station to its final resting place at Windsor. Born a British royal prince in 1884 in Esher in Surrey, Charles Edward was also born the second Duke of Albany, as his father, Queen Victoria's youngest son, had died of haemophilia before his only son's birth. Educated in England, the fifteen-year-old prince had been removed from Eton, which he enjoyed, and sent to Germany. There, his formidable grandmama required the reluctant teenager, who spoke little German, to assume the throne of her late husband's principality, the tiny duchy of Saxe-Coburg and Gotha with a population of less than a quarter of a million souls. Thus Charles Edward, a fatherless British schoolboy, became Carl Eduard and the head of the minor Teutonic family whose name, through astute dynastic manoeuvrings, now graced the royal families of Belgium, Portugal, Bulgaria and the United Kingdom of Great Britain and Ireland and the Empire of India. His other first cousins sat on the thrones of Germany, Russia, Spain, Sweden, Norway, Romania, Greece and the Netherlands. By then styled the Duke of Saxe-Coburg and Gotha, he visited England often and remained close to his British cousins. His uncle, King Edward VII, made him a Knight of the Garter and stood as godfather to his eldest son, while his devoted sister, Princess Alice, married Prince Alexander of Teck (the Earl of Athlone), brother to Queen Mary, now the grieving royal widow.

The funeral showcased the best of British royal ceremonial: a solemn and dignified celebration of the late King-Emperor. The slight, lonely figure of the new king, Edward VIII, led the funeral procession, supported by his three brothers and followed by five European kings, the French president, heads of state and crown princes from around the world. Dressed in great-coats and capes worn over the finest creations of Europe's royal tailors, they marched ahead of a flotilla of carriages carrying the widowed Queen and the other veiled royal ladies swathed in mourning black. The black and white film footage of the funeral cortège does little justice to the colourful array of dress uniforms on display. The military escort, festooned with medals, included the Brigade of Guards in scarlet and black, the Royal Marines in blue tunics set off by impeccably white Sam Browne belts, while shining silver breastplates elevated the red and blue of the Household Cavalry. Alongside the coffin marched the Gentlemen at Arms in skirted red coats trimmed with blue velvet cuffs and facings, embroidered with the Tudor royal badge, accessorised with gold aiguillettes, ceremonial sticks of office and cavalry swords. Beside them, carrying pikes, came the Yeomen of the Guard in royal red tunics with purple facings, gold lace ornaments, red knee-breeches and red stockings. The King's coachmen and footmen escorted the royal carriages, immaculate in flame-red capes and gold frogging.

Especially striking was the assortment of headgear worn by the male mourners. The King and one brother wore admirals' bicorne hats, the other brothers, plumed busbies. The Gentlemen at Arms escorted them in helmets with tall swan feather plumes, the Yeomen in flat pork pie hats, trimmed with red, white and blue rosettes, the guardsmen in black bearskins, the Royal Marines in white pith helmets, and the Household Cavalry in pale blue plumed silver helmets. Not to be outdone, the foreign dignitaries, representing the late King's dominions and beyond, sported all manner of gilt-badged peaked caps, busbies, fezzes, kepi, turbans and top hats.

Marching alongside this enfilade of millinery, the stooped Coburg, with his short back bent by rheumatism, strikes an incongruous, even absurd figure. Formerly an enemy combatant and now a general, dedicated Nazi, and SA *Obergruppenführer*, he wore the distinctive German coal scuttle steel helmet (*stahlhelm*) over a plain grey greatcoat with a black armband and Sam Browne belt. Dressed as if for battle, without medals, epaulettes, gold frogging or ceremonial sword, he looks far older than his fifty-one years, dragging his left foot, the result of a tobogganing injury.

Two decades before, the outbreak of the Great War had shattered the duke's comfortable existence as a prominent Anglo-German royal. Though in Britain visiting relations at the time, he had chosen to serve with the German military. The British authorities had deemed him a traitor and stripped him of his English titles. Forced to abdicate his throne following the abolition of the German monarchy, further ostracism followed when George V forbade the Prince of Wales from attending the wedding of Carl Eduard's daughter to a Swedish prince. Convinced the war fought between his cousins had been a never-to-be-repeated mistake and Bolshevism presented the greatest threat to Europe, Coburg had embraced the full spectrum of anti-democratic and far-right movements that had mushroomed in the political chaos during the Weimar Republic.

But though underdressed and denied the royal decorations bedecking his fellow mourners, this was now a heady return to British royal favour for Coburg and his duchess. While he marched only a few rows behind the British princes, she rode beside the crown princesses of Denmark and Sweden in a state landau drawn by a pair of Cleveland Bay horses. At the dinner that night, he was seated at the new king's table in the white and gold dining room, where the fifty most honoured guests ate off the state service of gold plate.

A better king than his father, George V's popularity had built steadily between the Great War, much of which he had spent visiting hospitals, and the celebration of his Silver Jubilee the year before. But he was a narrow-minded conservative Victorian patriarch who, as his eldest son wrote, disapproved of 'Soviet Russia, painted fingernails, women who smoked in public, cocktails, frivolous hats, American jazz, and the growing habit of going away for week-ends'.[14] In sharp contrast, his forty-one-year-old heir seemed cosmopolitan, well travelled, socially enlightened, a better speaker, charming, quicker-witted, internationally popular and highly photogenic. With Edward's accession to the throne, the prospects for Anglo-German friendship had never seemed better. Now Hitler had a direct channel through his devoted acolyte Coburg to a British throne on which sat a monarch far more sympathetic to the German cause than his father. Highlighting his respect and admiration for the British monarchy, Hitler attended a memorial service for the late king at the Anglican church of St George in Berlin. Von Hoesch reported to the foreign ministry that the new king felt a 'warm sympathy for Germany' which might influence British foreign policy.[15]

All this was a boon for Coburg. Staying with his sister Princess Alice at her apartment in Kensington Palace, he entertained to dinner both appeasers, including Neville Chamberlain and J. J. Astor, proprietor of *The Times*, and two anti-appeasers, Anthony Eden and Duff Cooper. He also joined a state dinner at Buckingham Palace, took tea with the widowed queen and had several private conversations with the new king.

Reporting to Hitler in a misleading and self-aggrandising memorandum, Coburg claimed Edward wanted an alliance between the two countries, thought the League of Nations a 'farce', disliked the Russians, and wanted to meet Hitler in person. Keen to ingratiate himself with the Führer, he stressed the King's frustrations with constitutional monarchy and representative democracy, declaring he planned to 'concentrate the business of government on himself'. Hoping to serve as the main conduit between the two heads of state, he claimed his cousin had asked him to visit often to discuss 'confidential matters' between the two countries.[16] All this fuelled Ribbentrop and Hitler's continuing misinterpretation of constitutional monarchy, their overestimation of the executive authority of a British monarch, and their belief Edward had real ambitions to be 'England's Führer'. Meanwhile, as Stanley Baldwin, Anthony Eden and Joachim Ribbentrop quickly learned, the new king's only genuine interest in foreign affairs related to Mrs Ernest Simpson, a twice married American socialite with whom he was besotted.

German troops in the Kaiser Strasse in Freiburg, 9 March 1936.

8

VISTAS OF UNLIMITED AGGRESSION

JUST BEFORE ONE O'CLOCK IN THE MORNING ON SATURDAY, 7 March 1936, a telephone call from the Continent interrupted Vansittart's weekend at his grand Mayfair town house. His friend and most dependable informant, Grahame Christie, was calling to alert the British government about secret German orders to re-militarise the Rhineland the next day. This was the first of Hitler's military adventures since coming to power and his third weekend surprise sprung on his European neighbours. Ribbentrop had shrewdly recommended scheduling it over a weekend when, as the British ambassador later ruefully admitted to the foreign secretary (despite the old king's disapproval of the custom), 'members of the Cabinet would be "dispersed" to their weekend retreats and therefore no immediate counter-move could be decided on.'[1]

The strategically sensitive Rhineland roughly defines Germany's western border and is bisected by the country's longest river as it flows from a glacier high up in the Swiss Alps through Germany, Belgium and Holland before emptying into the North Sea. Having traced the German-Swiss border, the Rhine passes through Cologne, the former headquarters of the occupying British army following the Great War, where the German military fortifications were demilitarised into large public parks. Further north, the river reaches Strasbourg, the totemic Franco-German border city; originally French, this had been ceded to Germany for half a century and restored to France only in 1918. For Germans, *der Rhein* embodied their natural protection from any military incursion from the west. Associated with national pride and Franco-German enmity long before the Great War, it had been fought over for centuries. Germanic peoples living along its banks had suffered attacks by French neighbours from the Thirty Years' War in the seventeenth century to the Napoleonic Wars in the nineteenth.

Ever since the Middle Ages the French had yearned to hold sway over the land on the river's left bank and ideally the river itself, so losing Alsace-Lorraine in the Franco-Prussian War had been a national trauma. By the twentieth century, the river was totemic even for the British, who needed France as a buffer against any aggression by Germany. As Baldwin had warned two years previously, the advent of bombers meant the English Channel no longer offered the protection it had since the days of the Spanish armadas. Now the 'old frontiers' had gone and so 'when you think of the defences of England, you no longer think of the chalk cliffs of Dover; you think of the Rhine.'[2] In similar vein, the river's strategic importance had been highlighted to Conwell-Evans by no less an authority than Marshal Foch, whom he had met on a train in the 1920s. Pointing to the Rhine, the former supreme allied commander had said, 'you see that… there will be another war because you [i.e. the British] didn't give us that part of the world.'[3]

Germany had reconfirmed the terms agreed at Versailles in the Locarno Pact in 1925, accepting Allied occupation of the Rhineland for a decade with permanent demilitarisation thereafter. Precluded from having troops, fortifications or military equipment on the left bank and within fifty kilometres of the right, this offered some safety margin between France and Germany, the two historic enemies. But the Germans resented being unable to control or defend their borders, so the river remained a touchstone of nationalistic feeling. The song 'Die Wacht am Rhein', with its catchy refrain, 'the Rhine, the Rhine, our German Rhine, who will defend our stream, divine?', had almost been adopted as the German national anthem between the wars.

Rumours of an incursion into the demilitarised zone had been circulating for months. Christie had warned of the German plans as early as the previous summer while Conwell-Evans had advised Lothian that the 'most dangerous aspect for the future is the demilitarised zone.'[4] In February, he and Tennant had warned leading British statesmen that the planned Franco-Russian alliance would lead to Germany feeling 'her encirclement has been completed' and she would take 'drastic steps to meet the situation.'[5]

The German press had initiated a campaign against the restrictions while, back in London, the foreign secretary had asked his staff what concessions could be extracted from Hitler in return for allowing German troops back into the zone.

The preparations for remilitarisation, of which Christie had exact details, were made in conditions of such rigorous secrecy that the action, when it came, would be sudden and unexpected. Most observers assumed Hitler would wait at least until after the Summer Olympics in Berlin, which he was carefully staging to shine the best light on his regime, and indeed he had originally planned to make the move in 1937. To maintain the element of surprise, he only briefed his Cabinet ministers at the last moment and the staff of the propaganda ministry were kept in their offices overnight. Christie's briefing by telephone included the precise timing, locations and scale of the reoccupying military force. He also explained how Hitler hoped to mollify international outrage with a seven-point plan of palliative diplomatic sops he would lay out in a memorandum issued simultaneously with the coup. Germany would offer to rejoin the League of Nations, sign non-aggression pacts with neighbours, offer guarantees to Belgium and Holland and give a twenty-five-year moratorium on any claims for the return of former German colonies.

Twelve hours later, at eleven o'clock in the morning, German troops approached the Hohenzollern Bridge in Cologne. Opened in 1911 by Kaiser Wilhelm II, this magnificent structure forms the city's main crossing, carrying four train lines and one road over the Rhine. Newsreels and press photographs of the day evoke memories of the Great War. Small boys run ahead of smiling infantrymen marching to the beat of traditional military bands towards the towers of Cologne's cathedral on the western side. Still Germany's most visited tourist attraction, this Gothic masterpiece built over six centuries was another powerful emblem of German *Kultur*. Mounted cavalrymen follow light horse-drawn field guns and carts laden with supplies as delighted crowds waving handkerchiefs welcome the soldiers. Women press flowers into their buttonholes as priests bless the progress of the reoccupying force. While many spontaneously offer the Hitler salute, the atmosphere is relaxed, festive and civilian, in contrast with the staged, martial triumphalism of the Nuremberg rallies. As his troops were crossing the bridge, Hitler had been some five hundred kilometres east at the Kroll

Opera House in Berlin. Facing the burned Reichstag across the Königsplatz, this served as the home of the German parliament and a special meeting had been called for that Saturday afternoon. Six hundred bemused deputies attended in full uniform, along with journalists and international diplomats. The Führer triumphantly announced that after three years the 'struggle for German equal rights can be regarded as closed'.[6] William Shirer, the American journalist, recorded the rapture as 'little men with big bodies and bulging necks and cropped hair and pouched bellies and brown uniforms and heavy boots' heard these words, leaping to their feet 'like automatons, their right arms upstretched in the Nazi salute'.[7]

The success of the initiative was far from guaranteed. Hitler's agitated military and diplomatic advisers urged caution. The army's commander-in-chief, Werner von Fritsch, was certain the French would mobilise their troops for a counter-incursion into the demilitarised zone. Far from being a force of overwhelming size and strength as feared by the French, only about thirty thousand troops were involved. Of these, only a few advanced anywhere close to the border as their nervous commanders had strict instructions to withdraw at any sign of the expected French military response which they had little confidence they could resist. As Christie learned two months later, the troops had been issued only with blank ammunition and Hitler boasted he had given the adventure no more than a five percent chance of success. Conwell-Evans wrote that the German leader had 'ventured upon his greatest gamble with the dice at that time heavily loaded against him', while his biographer concluded, 'one French division would have sufficed to terminate Hitler's adventure'.[8]

The Führer's timing had been impeccable. While the British and French governments had had months to plan their response, he had still caught them by surprise. Choosing that weekend allowed time for national celebration in Germany, while slowing the reaction of those, especially the British, who might have protested but were (with Vansittart the exception) away from London. The dilatory international response to this diplomatic and military outrage would prove critical to the trajectory of Hitler's regime. In London, the anaemic press reaction in the Sunday papers shocked Ivan Maisky, the Russian ambassador. Unable to gauge the reactions of the usual 'influential people' enjoying their weekends, he sensed in such complacency a 'new and dangerous turn towards Germanophilia in British policy'. He worried Hitler's seven points would give his English supporters, such as Lords Londonderry and Rothermere, ammunition to 'sow terrible confusion in the minds of lily-livered pacifists and spineless Labourites' so they would believe Hitler's professions of peace would solve the German problem.[9]

The Fellowship's Council felt similarly unnerved, sending a letter of protest to the Führer begging him to 'undo what he had done'.[10] The German ambassador shared his Russian colleague's alarm but for different reasons. On the Tuesday, von Hoesch sent a memorandum to his masters accepting the British public did not 'give a damn if the Germans occupy their own territory', but warned the British government had been disturbed by the betrayal of Locarno and the Houses of Parliament were 'charged with disquiet, anxiety and, indeed, perplexity'.[11] Bravely speaking truth to power, he compared this with the fevered weeks before the declaration of war in July 1914 and assessed the risk of war as evens. This was not what Hitler wanted to hear.

The next day von Hoesch met with Lord Lothian, who agreed that, while the British public were mostly indifferent and often sympathetic to the reoccupation, the incident might provoke a military alliance between Britain, Belgium and France. This would bring Britain into the sphere of the Franco-Russian pact encircling Germany with the 'grand alliance' that Churchill so favoured, but which Lothian feared would aggravate rather than contain Hitler. Germany should instead keep her troops back from the French frontier and 'rest content with this symbolic act'.

Now back from their weekends, Anthony Eden, the newly appointed foreign secretary, and his deputy, Lord Halifax, hurried to France for talks with the French ministers, agreeing to convene a meeting of the Council of the League of Nations in London to discuss the crisis. They invited Germany to send a delegate to argue their case, and after some prevarication, Hitler dispatched a reluctant Ribbentrop. After three weeks shuttling between London and Germany on his special plane and with political distractions in France, Italy and Spain set against a background of near universal pacifism among the British and French public, the League only issued a condemnation of the German action. Hitler had got away with it.

The collective inaction of the allies had 'stupefied' Grahame Christie, who had seen a real chance of Russian support to build a unified front against Germany. Instead, as he told Vansittart, Britain was 'committing suicide' as the Continental balance of power would now shift from France and her allies to Germany and hers. Hitler's hugely popular success in the Rhineland had opened 'vistas of unlimited aggression', with ninety-eight percent of German voters supporting it in a plebiscite. Göring and Ribbentrop had triumphed over those moderates, especially in the army, who had counselled caution. Hitler had reconfirmed his view that the democracies were supine and gutless and would never march to support Austria or Czechoslovakia. Three months later, Christie reported to Vansittart that the Nazi leaders were already discussing the 'annihilation of France by a swift use of tanks, armoured cars and air attack'. The Führer now saw himself as a new Caesar, a successor to Charlemagne.[12]

Though lacking Göring's bombast and bravura, Ribbentrop was riding high. Hitler honoured him with a celebratory boat ride down the Rhine, where 'cheering crowds converged on the banks' to greet their victorious leaders.[13] Tennant realised Ribbentrop would now be even harder to constrain and their relations cooled from that point forward. And yet it was essential he and Conwell-Evans should sustain their friendships with Ribbentrop and Christie with Göring to preserve peace between their two countries. Alarmingly and disastrously, two of the most convinced Anglophiles in Hitler's inner circle, for whom an invitation to take tea with the King or shoot pheasants at Chatsworth had the most appeal, were now emerging as the Führer's most hawkish councillors.

Just a month after the remilitarisation of the Rhineland, the fifty-four-year-old Leopold von Hoesch died suddenly in his bedroom in Carlton House Terrace. This robbed the diplomatic corps of a skilled champion of Anglo-German amity and left this vital diplomatic post unfilled for many critical months. His *New York Times* obituarist acclaimed the German ambassador as a 'gentleman trained in the best traditions of the old diplomacy', who had been 'immune to the contagion of violent, swashbuckling nationalism' and dedicated to 'easing the relations between his country and its Western neighbors'.[14] The King telephoned the embassy to offer his condolences. His government arranged for his swastika-draped coffin to be carried with full honours by six bear-skinned guardsmen, followed by Cabinet ministers and other dignitaries down the Mall past Buckingham Palace to Victoria Station. From there, his cortège was escorted to Dover, where a nineteen-gun salute was fired and a lament played by a lone piper as he was transferred to a British destroyer for his final journey back to Germany. He left behind his much doted-on dog, Giro. Buried at the top of the Duke of York steps on Carlton House Terrace, his is still the only Nazi-era German memorial in London.

Though ascribed to a heart attack, von Hoesch's death has never been satisfactorily explained. It triggered rumours the Gestapo had poisoned him (via his toothpaste) or he had taken his own life out of despair with the direction taken by the National Socialist government he so distrusted. The death of his counterpart in Paris, another old school diplomat sceptical of the Nazis, a few weeks earlier in similarly suspicious circumstances only served to fuel such conspiracy theories further.

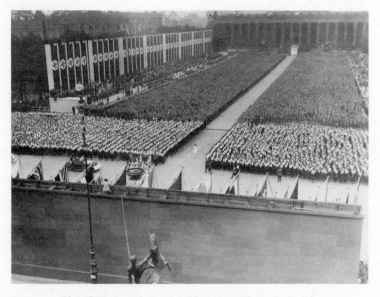

The Olympic torch is carried into the stadium during the opening ceremonies of the XI Olympic Games at the Olympic Stadium in Berlin, Germany, on 1 August 1936.

9

MAYFAIR RUSHING
HITLERWARDS

THE DIPLOMATIC DUST KICKED UP BY THE RHINELAND CRISIS settled quickly, much to Hitler and Ribbentrop's delight. That summer of 1936 went on to reach a zenith of Anglo-German amity with two propaganda triumphs for the Nazis – the Summer Olympic Games held in Berlin followed by the arrival of David Lloyd George. Having hosted its first banquet to promote the Olympics the previous December and lobbied the former prime minister to take coffee with Hitler, the Anglo-German Fellowship would continue to play its part in both landmark events.

Before leaving for the Games, the Fellowship hosted its second banquet on 14 July at the Dorchester Hotel. Held in honour of their royal highnesses the Duke and Duchess of Brunswick, this was to be far grander than the Olympic dinner and cemented the Fellowship's evolution from an earnest lobbying body funded by businessmen into an elite organisation attracting royalty, aristocrats, military men, leading politicians from across the political spectrum, and a sprinkling of spies.

The Brunswicks were an intriguing double act with an impeccable royal pedigree. Born a prince of the United Kingdom and directly descended from George III, Ernst August headed the royal House of Hanover and was another cousin to George V. Princess Viktoria Luise of Prussia was the former Kaiser's only daughter and a great-granddaughter of Queen Victoria. Their wedding in 1913 had reunited the estranged royal houses of Hohenzollern and Hanover. It was the last great family gathering of the European sovereign cousins, including Tsar Nicholas II of Russia and King George V, barely a year before the Great War set the families on opposing sides in history's bloodiest conflict. The young couple's privileged position in both British and German royal families was shattered when, like his Coburg cousin, the duke was stripped of his British titles and forced to abdicate his German dukedom and disestablish his duchy.

Ribbentrop was friendly with the Brunswicks, floating plans with Hitler to restore a puppet German monarchy to cover National Socialist constitutional outrages with a fig leaf of royal respectability. He had even suggested their schoolgirl daughter, Frederika (later Queen of Greece), be married off to her second cousin, the much older Prince of Wales. (The poor girl's mother had herself been offered up to the same prince as a potential future queen a quarter of a century before.) The Brunswicks were a photogenic couple: diarist and former spy Robert Bruce Lockhart, a guest at the dinner, shared Tennant's enthusiasm for the duchess's physique, noting she looked 'browned and athletic'.[1] Though politically ineffectual, they cooperated wholeheartedly as pliant Nazi propaganda tools, especially in England.

Ernest Tennant had befriended the Brunswicks chez Ribbentrop and cultivated them as a socially impeccable bridge between the sister organisations. He saw them often at the villa in Dahlem and, rather than flowers or chocolates, would bring the duchess a Finnan haddock or kippers. Both Brunswicks remained close to their British royal cousins and at ease in English society, with a son at Oxford and Frederika at a traditional English girls' boarding school. Having deposited the princess there, they paid visits to the King and Queen and the Duke and Duchess of York, the first visit to Buckingham Palace by one of the Kaiser's children since the war. As such it was a tentative step on the path of reconciliation between the two countries, with the vestigial German royal families offering a tantalising alternative to National Socialism.[2] Lloyd George had explained to one German royal that, had his family retained its throne, the 'headaches' surrounding Hitler might have been avoided while Churchill had conceded that the loss of the monarchy had left a 'yawning gap' into which Hitler had stepped.[3]

The Brunswicks were very hospitable to English visitors from the Fellowship and the Royal British Legion. They entertained the Tennants to tea during that ill-fated Nuremberg trip and hosted Conwell-Evans at their castle at Blankenberg. Ever the alert historian, he was struck by the similarity between the family's flag and the Royal Standard at St James's Palace. He found them 'overwhelming in their kindness' and was especially touched when the duke drove him personally to the railway station.[4] Heady stuff for a tailor's son from Carmarthen.

The Fellowship was determined to reciprocate; one member welcomed them for the weekend near Ascot after which they stayed with another on the Isle of Wight. Alongside Lord Lothian, who gave the main address, no fewer than five marquesses graced the banquet, including Lords Carisbrooke, Londonderry, Zetland, and Douglas & Clydesdale. Prince Alexander Mountbatten, the Marquess of Carisbrooke, had joined the Fellowship and he and his wife were the first resident British royals to attend one of its events. The epitome of an aristocratic Conservative politician and the Fellowship's noblest recruit, Charles Vane-Tempest-Stewart, the seventh Marquess of Londonderry, was a cousin and protégé of Winston Churchill. He was thought so well connected that 'even the King calls him Charley'. His huge wealth funded a London house staffed by forty-four servants and country estates in Durham and Northern Ireland, which he and his ambitious wife deployed to advance his never-more-than-second-division parliamentary career. As minister for air and an aviation enthusiast, he had rearmed the depleted RAF by introducing the Hurricane and Spitfire fighters and pioneering the first use of radar. He had introduced Ribbentrop to another flying peer, Douglas Douglas-Hamilton, the glamorous thirty-three-year-old marquess famed in both Britain and Germany as the first pilot to fly over Everest. As his son explained, 'aviators in those days were regarded in much the same way as the early astronauts, and aviation was looked upon as a top priority by the leaders of the Third Reich'.[5]

A phalanx of lesser members of the Houses of Lords and Commons, both Liberals and Conservatives, joined the dinner. Several of the Fellowship's original business backers attended, alongside an impressive representation from the armed services, many of whom served their king in the Royal Household and so moved easily in Court circles. The Royal British Legion was particularly proud of its royal patronage and in his speech Major General Sir Frederick Maurice, its president, awarded the royal couple honorary membership of the Legion. Other senior Legionnaires joined him, including Colonel Ashwanden, vice chairman and an aide-de-camp to the King. As at the Olympic dinner, several of the military guests were ageing veterans of veldt, trench and sea, but this time the guest list included younger serving officers who would go on to fight the Germans with distinction in the next war, such as the Douglas-Hamilton brothers, Lieutenant Colonel the Hon. Everard Wyndham, colonel of the Life Guards, Captain Thomas Troubridge, formerly naval attaché in Berlin, and Wing Commander Sir Louis Greig, who had mentored the young Duke of York and shepherded his betrothal to Elizabeth Bowes-Lyon.

Prince Otto von Bismarck, as acting chargé d'affaires at the embassy, represented the German government at the top table and proposed the chairman's health. The tone changed when Lord Lothian used his speech to warn about German misbehaviour, although he made no direct mention of the persecution of the Jews and other minorities. Circumstances, he said, were at a critical stage both 'full of hope and full of menace'. He accepted the Treaty of Versailles (which he had helped draft) was now irrelevant and Germany had the right to rearm. But choosing his words carefully, he warned Hitler that the 'internal policy' of his regime offered a 'serious obstacle' to the establishment of good relations between the two countries before concluding, 'everyone knows what they are.'[6]

Conwell-Evans was delighted by the evening and effusive about Lothian's speech. The dinner had cemented the Fellowship's respectability both in London and abroad. Increasingly confident in its prospects, the Council signed a lease on an office at 223 Cranmer Court, a newly built block of serviced flats on Sloane Avenue in Chelsea. With six rooms, including one for visitors, this proved an ideal base for the growing administration. By October, the Fellowship was comfortably installed and had raised two thousand pounds in subscriptions and donations. While Tennant focused on charming the corporate backers, Conwell-Evans served as the political secretary, and Elwyn Wright, the salaried secretary, oversaw the administration, chased membership fees, managed the events and handled the company secretarial duties, ably supported by the redoubtable Betty Pomeroy and two stenographers.

The Council agreed to embrace the dark art of public relations, and so tasked a new department with producing marketing materials, including a membership brochure, an annual report and a monthly review. Seeking youth and intelligence, the first recruit was a recent graduate of Trinity College, Cambridge who wrote well, was socially connected and spoke German. He joined the Fellowship both as an employee and a member and a photograph of him enjoying the Brunswick dinner appeared in *The Tatler*, the society magazine.[7] This talented and charming young man was the son of St John Philby, the famous author, Arabist and explorer. Christened Harold Adrian Russell, he is better known by his childhood nickname – taken from Rudyard Kipling's eponymous novel about a boy spy – Kim.

Ribbentrop had been issuing invitations to his new English friends, including from the Fellowship and the Legion, to join the summer Olympiad in Berlin that August. The high point of British social engagement with the National Socialist regime, the British ambassador dubbed it 'Mayfair rushing Hitlerwards'.[8] Though the Games have been widely studied by historians, limited analysis has been undertaken on the British contingent of over one hundred peers, peeresses, MPs and their wives who came to Berlin that summer. While Ribbentrop took the lead, the top Nazis including Hitler, Göring and Goebbels also saw the opportunity offered by the Olympics to woo the British elite and so joined in welcoming them to Berlin. The Fellowship's members had access to the DEG's comfortable clubhouse in Berlin, which issued tickets to over fifty English visitors daily.

Into this bacchanalia of Anglo-German affability swept Sir Robert Vansittart. Already devouring Christie's secret intelligence, the flamboyant head of the Foreign Office had decided to use the Olympics to see the Third Reich in person. Lady Vansittart had agreed to substitute as embassy hostess for her indisposed sister, the ambassador's wife, so Sir Robert claimed to be coming along in a personal capacity. But *The Times* reported diligently on every step of this glamorous couple in Germany and, sensitive to the absurdity of this charade, he titled his lengthy secret report 'A Busman's Holiday'. He had arranged private meetings with most of the Nazi leadership, including Hitler, Ribbentrop, Göring, Goebbels, Hess and von Neurath (no less than six times), as well as with bankers and industrialists. Discreetly, he also met individuals linked to the nascent German resistance to Hitler, including the three 'most intelligent' journalists, Karl Silex, editor of the *Deutsche Allgemeine Zeitung*, Paul Scheffer, editor of the liberal *Berliner Tageblatt*, and Rudolf Kircher, Berlin correspondent for the *Frankfurter Zeitung*.

Hitler was wrong-footed by his well-dressed guest who was fluent in German and stood over six foot tall in his immaculately stockinged feet, as he had been expecting instead a 'small man of Jewish appearance'.[9] The British visitors were treated to a fortnight of receptions hosted by the Party leaders, each anxious to outdo his rivals with ever more opulent and civilised hospitality. The first extravaganza was a gala dinner held by the Ribbentrops to celebrate his much-heralded appointment as ambassador to London to replace von Hoesch, whose death in April had left the post open for five months. With the president of the Olympic committee as guest of honour, six hundred guests enjoyed vintage Pommery champagne, crowded into a vast marquee pitched on the lawn where Tennant had previously infuriated Himmler.

Ribbentrop's triumph was soon eclipsed by Göring's party, which left the eight hundred guests 'gaping at the display and the splendour', reminding the MP and diarist Chips Channon of the 'fêtes of Claudius, but with the cruelty left out'. Von Neurath hosted six hundred, including the Olympic committee and leading statesmen, at his castle in Charlottenburg. Goebbels then arranged for two thousand guests to be ferried by liveried crew in motorboats to his party on Peacock Island on the Havel River. In comparison, the British embassy party thrown for Empire Olympians had been, sniped Channon, 'boring, crowded and inelegant'.[10] (This echoed their country's anaemic medal count, in which they ranked only tenth, below countries as small as Hungary, Finland and Sweden.) Finally, the Führer threw a spontaneous and sumptuous dinner in honour of the Vansittarts in the Reich Chancellery dining room, for which they extended their 'holiday'. Sir Robert noticed how the 'Olympic truce' had improved the Führer's mood.[11]

Prominent among the British contingent were the Douglas-Hamilton family led by the glamorous Marquess of Clydesdale, who with his two brothers and a sister were each provided with a chauffeured car by the German government. He was keen to investigate the rearming of the German air force, and during the trip he befriended the Haushofer family, themselves close friends of Rudolf Hess. Karl Haushofer, Hess's mentor and former professor at the German Academy, is credited with developing the intellectual framework of *lebensraum*, as explored in Hitler's *Mein Kampf*. The Anglophile Karl was a DEG founding board member and had been awarded honorary life membership of the Royal British Legion. His son Albrecht shared his affection for England and served as Hess's personal guide and a special adviser to both Hitler and Ribbentrop. MI5 later assessed him as the 'greatest authority in Germany on the British Empire'. It was he who introduced Clydesdale to Göring, who, unable to resist showing off to such a famous aviator, arranged for a tour of the Luftwaffe, allowing the marquess to size up Germany's air power. These links between the Douglas-Hamilton family and Nazi Germany would come under the closest scrutiny when, in May 1941, Rudolf Hess parachuted onto their ancestral Scottish estate seeking peace with Britain.

Fellowship and other British visitors returned home with varying perspectives. Lord Rennell wrote to *The Times* with glowing appreciation for the 'remarkable man of vision who directs the destinies of Germany'.[12] Lord Decies criticised the Germans for bending the principles of amateurism and warned of a 'new race of energetic, virile young people... ready to go anywhere under the orders of the Führer... fully armed, equipped with the best of war materiel, and an air force second to none'.[13] Vansittart worried about the 'over specialisation of athletics' and predicted, thinking well beyond sport, these 'intense people are going to make us look a C3 nation.'[14] But it had been an immediate triumph for both Anglo-German amity and National Socialist propaganda. As one analysis concluded, 'if lavish hospitality alone could have forged a link between Germany and Britain, the Olympic fortnight would have done the trick, for the entertainments were on a prodigious scale, and carried out with a degree of taste which agreeably surprised even the most critical of visitors.'[15] Ribbentrop had been thrilled by the Vansittarts coming to Berlin and hoped it might change his attitude towards Germany. All of this created ideal conditions for Germany to welcome the most celebrated British statesman to visit the country for many years.

David Lloyd George, the former British prime minister, meeting Adolf Hitler at the Berghof near Berchtesgaden in September 1936. Behind them are Ribbentrop and Paul-Otto Schmidt, the official interpreter.

10

COFFEE WITH HITLER

At ten in the morning on Wednesday, 2 September 1936, Ernest Tennant stood on the railway platform at London's Liverpool Street Station. He waved goodbye as his colleague Philip Conwell-Evans led an excited David Lloyd George, who disliked flying, on board a train bound for Munich. Stanley Baldwin came only in spirit, as Anthony Eden, the foreign secretary, still vetoed him visiting Germany in person. Two of the prime minister's inner circle, Tom Jones, his close confidant and a former deputy secretary to the Cabinet, and Lord Dawson, his doctor, were joining the expedition, tasked with reporting back on the new Germany. Mrs Baldwin had also asked them to bring back some blue gentian flowers as a reminder of her honeymoon in Bavaria.

Tennant felt delighted; after years of painstaking lobbying, they had finally persuaded a venerated British statesman to travel to Germany to meet Hitler. Lloyd George was coming in the benevolent wake of the Berlin Olympics and the surprisingly cultivated festivities during which the Third Reich had succeeded in presenting its civilised side far more effectively than any of its earlier conventional diplomacy. The former British prime minister had the intelligence, the charm and the wiles to build on this wave of goodwill to further civilise the Nazis.

The night before, the mostly Welsh-speaking party had celebrated in a light-hearted mood their departure for the three-week tour with a dinner at the Savoy. Part motoring holiday, part diplomatic mission, and part economic fact-finding tour, Lloyd George's entourage led by Conwell-Evans included two of his offspring: his son Gwilym and, less eagerly, his daughter Megan. Each, like their father, a serving Liberal MP, they were supported by his private secretary, A. J. Sylvester, and two young Welsh civil servants,

Emrys Pride and Ben Bowen Thomas, who had been sent ahead by plane as scouts and aides-de-camp.

This would prove to be the high-water mark of the Anglo-German Fellowship's successful summer of diplomatic marriage brokering. Contrary to Lloyd George's mischievous suggestion to journalists, this trip had been no last-minute whim, dreamt up over a recent lunch enjoyed with Ribbentrop. Rather it was the fruit of sixteen months' patient lobbying and planning by Jones, Tennant and Conwell-Evans. Though out of government for fourteen years, the 'Welsh Wizard' remained a political giant among pygmies, popular both at home and abroad. Hitler's admiration for the Great War premier strayed into hero worship, while Ribbentrop boasted that 'the Germans have in Hitler their Lloyd George.'[1]

For Ribbentrop, this was correspondingly the zenith of his Anglophile charm offensive, following his recent appointment as ambassador to the Court of St James's and the accession to the throne of his new friend, Edward VIII. Though he had failed to deliver Baldwin to meet his Führer, Lloyd George offered a respectable proxy and was the biggest fish yet caught. That August's Berlin Olympics had been a global propaganda triumph, exceeding the organisers' best hopes, while the next month's Nuremberg rally would be the most welcoming to fashionable Londoners fascinated to see the National Socialist regime in its full glory.

The meetings between Lloyd George and Hitler were subject to intense scrutiny by the British press at the time, and they still polarise opinion. Conwell-Evans was the sole member of the British party allowed to join the private audience with Hitler, and his original typed transcript of that meeting has only recently been rediscovered. Most of his fellow guests also left personal accounts of the trip, including Jones, Dawson, Sylvester and Pride, while Paul-Otto Schmidt, Hitler's interpreter, included an account from the hosts' perspective in his memoirs. Lloyd George's own reflections appeared in an ill-judged *Daily Express* article and in an interview in the *News Chronicle*.[2] Remarkably, nearly an hour's colour footage of the adventure survives in two films taken separately by Sylvester and Lloyd George's chauffeur.

Detailed planning had started at once following the recent lunch with Ribbentrop. Lord Lothian had recommended Conwell-Evans to Lloyd George as an 'admirable liaison officer… acceptable to both parties.'[3] Sylvester duly telegraphed his old colleague, who immediately accepted the role on the basis his fellow Welshman would need someone who 'knows the situation and the good and the great and who can speak the language and take independent notes'.[4] Conwell-Evans flew back from Germany to Lloyd George's Surrey home, where the older man took 'an instant liking' to him. This affection was reciprocated. Conwell-Evans had admired the former prime minister since before the war when Lloyd George had come as a guest of honour to a dinner at Jesus College, Oxford (famous for its Welsh connections), and the students had shown their admiration by banging the tables with their spoons. Now he flattered him as the 'only man who understood Hitler and Hitler understood'.[5]

After his disappointing election campaign and exclusion from the new Cabinet, the opportunity to step back onto the international stage appealed to both Lloyd George's vanity and his political ambitions. Anxious to re-engage with foreign affairs, he had already offered himself to Baldwin as foreign secretary, suggesting he might help deal with Germany. Insisting, disingenuously, that he was unconcerned by the country's rapid rearmament, he claimed an interest in the German roads programme, a need to review the condition of the nonconformist churches and a hope to discuss his war memoirs with General Ludendorff, victor of the Battle of Tannenberg. Though well disposed towards the defeated Germans since the 1919 Peace Conference, when he had argued for them to be treated generously, he did not know the country well and there seems a sense of unfinished business. His last visit had been as Chancellor of the Exchequer, three decades before, officially to study its economic and social reforms but with a hidden agenda to de-escalate the mounting arms race. Both the Kaiser and the chancellor had refused to meet him, so he had achieved little. Just as pensions reform had provided his cover story back in 1908, now the study of the German economic miracle provided the backdrop. But it was the impending threat of war that really overshadowed both expeditions.

Before catching his train, Lloyd George lunched with his friend Ivan Maisky, the amiable but not always dependable and often mischievous Russian ambassador and diarist, with whom he had explored an Anglo-Soviet axis to restrain Germany. Maisky considered his lunch companion the 'outstanding' British statesman of his era but was perturbed by his new-found enthusiasm for the German Führer. Urging caution, he précised those sections of *Mein Kampf* covering Hitler's plans for Russia excluded from the English translation. Meanwhile, Conwell-Evans flew back from Germany and dined with Sylvester at the National Liberal Club. He confirmed that Ribbentrop was overseeing the logistics and the German government would book and pay for their hotel accommodation.

A calm crossing from Harwich brought the party to Flushing in Holland by late afternoon. Two German chaperones – a senior shipping executive and Baron Geyr, the military attaché at the embassy in London – were on hand to escort them south to the Bavarian Alps. The previous night's cheerful atmosphere continued when they stopped in Cologne at midnight; Sylvester, Gwilym, Conwell-Evans and Geyr, careful not to wake the sleeping Lloyd George, explored the city's centre, admired the cathedral and visited a pub before rejoining the train in the early hours.

The party reached Munich less than twenty hours after leaving London to be met by Lord Dawson and Tom Jones. After lunch they motored in three cars on to the picturesque town of Berchtesgaden. One hundred and fifty kilometres south-east of Munich, the town and its environs were a popular tourist destination close to the Austrian border but now also served as the geographic hub for the National Socialist machine in south-eastern Germany, and so much more than just their summer retreat. The Führer engineered a psychological advantage over visiting foreign statesmen by receiving them here rather than in the capital, Berlin. Even by plane this would be an arduous journey, equivalent to the British prime minister inviting foreign statesmen to meet him at a fishing lodge at Loch Lomond in Scotland rather than in Downing Street.

Having themselves arrived by plane, the Ribbentrops treated the visitors to dinner at the Grand Hotel. Frau Ribbentrop charmed Tom Jones, recognising him as the prime minister's intimate and so most worthy of her cultivation. But her husband irritated them all by 'harping on Russia and the spread of Communism in Spain, France and China and the menace to India'. Tired, but relishing debate, Lloyd George countered that Russia's nationalism, imperialism and militarism were greater threats than her Bolshevism and anyway, the 'French peasant will never go communist'. Mischievously prodding Ribbentrop about Winston Churchill, he explained that while his old friend was currently 'terribly pro-French', the Germans should try to bring him into their 'church'. The challenge with Winston, he went on, was how he fought 'everybody in turn… one day, it is Russia, now it is Germany'.[6]

Six months prior to their visit, *Country Life*, the leading British magazine specialising in country pursuits, had helpfully provided the visitors with a guide to the Führer's Bavarian home in a gushing profile entitled 'Hitler as Countryman'.[7] He had originally rented this 'cosy but modest' eight-roomed wooden chalet known as Haus Wachenfeld in the late 1920s and bought it when he became chancellor of Germany. Perched two thousand feet above Berchtesgaden, it overlooked the five-mile-long Königsee lake, on which he would row his favoured guests in a small wooden boat. By 1936, *Mein Kampf*, Hitler's hugely successful autobiographical manifesto, had sold three million copies. This generated royalties which the author claimed unconvincingly were sufficient to fund an ambitious refurbishment. The 'peasants' cottage' blossomed into a huge villa complex renamed the Berghof, or Mountain Court. Forty rooms were added, including a great hall measuring ninety by forty feet, a cinema and a bowling alley, swallowing up the original wooden building. The mountain complex would serve as the Führer's political and personal headquarters for much of the year.

The day after their arrival in Bavaria, Lloyd George enjoyed a leisurely lunch with the Ribbentrops on the terrace of their hotel, sheltered from the blazing sunshine by the establishment's entire supply of large umbrellas. Sylvester's Cine-Kodak film shows the two men contentedly puffing on cigars ahead of Hitler's own car arriving to collect them. Conwell-Evans accompanied them for the ten-minute drive to the Berghof, leaving the rest of the party at the hotel feeling excluded and disgruntled. As the open-topped car drew up to where the long flight of stone steps from the house met the alpine road, their smiling host was already coming down to greet his guest. Dawson recognised this stratagem as pure theatre, enabling the Führer to position himself above his guests and then 'descend to meet them in proportion to the occasion'.[8] Lloyd George had been honoured by an almost full descent and now, as his biographer noted, 'face-to-face were the statesman who had dominated the First World War, leonine with flowing white hair, a still bewitching figure, and the restless, magnetic personality of Hitler'.[9]

Karl Huhle's famous photograph of the two leaders meeting with a warm handshake illuminates the generation gap. Hitler, twenty-seven years younger, sports a contemporary-cut suit of light brown cloth. His trousers have turn-ups while his shirt is soft-collared and finished by a brightly patterned silk tie – very much the Continental dictator at home. Lightly holding a felt hat in his left hand, Lloyd George is the epitome of an Edwardian parliamentarian, with a dark three-piece suit, a formal stick-up collar and plain tie held in place by a gold pin. On a ribbon around his neck hangs a pince-nez. This outdated eyewear was a studied prop, like Churchill's cigar, Chamberlain's umbrella and Thatcher's handbag, each so beloved by cartoonists.

From here, Conwell-Evans's typed notes take up the story. With a bearing seemingly 'very modest and simple', Hitler so venerated his visitor he could 'hardly keep his eyes away from him'. He led them through the broad entrance hall painted light green and furnished with cactus plants – perhaps more alpine sanatorium than dictator's mountain-top headquarters – to his private sitting room. Along the way, Lloyd George correctly identified a portrait of a small boy as the young Frederick the Great, astutely suggesting he had 'suffered from the stern rule of his parents', to which the delighted Führer laughed with 'eyes beaming with benevolence and admiration' and replied proudly it had been the only surviving portrait of the king taken from life.

While orderlies poured coffee and served pastries and fruit, Lloyd George, perched uncomfortably on a backless bench, opened with a remark about the wonderful weather before questioning his host in a 'quiet persuasive way' through the two interpreters, Conwell-Evans and Schmidt. Soon they found common ground on how the 'tragic upset' of the Great War necessitated understanding between Germany and Britain. Lloyd George insisted it would be essential not just for the sakes of the two countries but to 'preserve Western civilisation itself'. Hitler convinced his listeners his 'fervent wish' for friendship with Great Britain had been his 'dream' since his youth. He offered his guest his well-worn Faustian pact: in return for his recognising the 'vital interests' of the British Empire, England should accept German hegemony on the Continent, which was necessary for her to maintain a 'proper standard of life' for her people. As with earlier British visitors, Hitler fixated on the 'disintegrating force' of Bolshevist ideology which threatened the 'existence of the nation states of Europe', comparable to the 'Mohammedan invasion'.[10] As Lloyd George later told Maisky, every time Russia had been mentioned, Hitler's 'lips began to twitch convulsively' and soon he would be 'shouting again, all but foaming at the mouth'.[11] The visitors complimented Schmidt on his rapid and fluent interpretation of his master's voice. He drily explained he had covered this subject many times before.

Anxious to shift his host from such ideological *idée fixe* and on to diplomatic solutions, Lloyd George suggested the upcoming Locarno conference might result in a strengthened treaty between England, France, Germany, Italy and Belgium. Pressed to agree, Hitler insisted Germany should be treated as an equal and worried about Moscow's influence. Lloyd George admitted the recent Franco-Russian treaty presented a serious difficulty. But could Hitler agree to an air pact between the three main Western European powers? Yes, subject to a common defensive position and their building on Ribbentrop's naval treaty as the first step. When Germany's rearmament programme had been discussed, Hitler explained without apparent irony that this had not helped his popularity at home and was unpleasant to him personally, as he much preferred civil infrastructure such as his beloved *autobahnen*, which generated better economic and social returns.

Unlike most British guests, Lloyd George did get a word in edgeways, moving the German dictator away from his customary ranting monologues on to meaningful diplomatic dialogue on sensitive topics. Bringing Conwell-Evans as his own interpreter and adviser had been shrewd, compensating for his lack of German and neutralising the agenda control his host achieved through Schmidt and his own monolingualism. Though impressed by Hitler, Lloyd George had not lost his critical faculties, as Churchill and others later suggested. Picking up on his challenge to Ribbentrop the night before, and mindful of his lunch with Maisky, he warned Hitler his focus on Bolshevism 'might be regarded… as an obsession' and predicted Germany's 'unhealthy relations' with Russia would be a problem. He also challenged Hitler on his support for the Nationalists, a 'purely reactionary and military party', in the seven-week-old Spanish Civil War. Both sides were 'extremists' and 'savages'. General Franco was 'no statesman' and had 'little or no experience of war', in contrast to Hitler, whom he flattered for spending fourteen years creating a 'new spirit' in the German people.[12] Highlighting atrocities such as the massacre of over one thousand prisoners by Nationalists at Badajoz two weeks previously, he suggested a strengthened Locarno alliance could accelerate the end of that brutal conflict.

Conversation lightened and widened to mutual interests, from the Great War to the regeneration of the German economy. Hitler excitedly shared his new four-year economic plan, on which Göring had briefed the cabinet that same day, and which would be unveiled at Nuremberg ten days later with ambitious plans for greater autarky. With the development of ersatz raw materials such as rubber, petrol and cotton, it would preserve precious foreign currency for the 'necessities of life' – eggs, butter, cheese, meat and fats. Lloyd George shared Hitler's child-like pride in his road programme, having seen the new autobahn himself. Hitler explained how the new road design reduced casualties by two-thirds; in the first week motorists typically drove at 120 kph but soon settled down to a more sedate 80 kph and still 'reached their destination in record time'. Lloyd George had been impressed by the Führer's grasp of economics, later telling Tom Jones he wished Neville Chamberlain, then Chancellor of the Exchequer, could be 'closeted with him for an hour'.[13]

The two statesmen left the three-hour meeting mutually enthralled. Lloyd George returned to his hotel, as Sylvester remembered, 'in great form, very delighted with his talk and obviously very much struck with Hitler'.[14] Megan flippantly greeted her father with the Hitler salute. Returning it without irony, he insisted he was 'really a great man'.[15] Later, Lloyd George told Maisky he found Hitler to be 'unpretentious, modest and quite well-educated'.[16]

The distinguished doctor prescribed a whisky and soda followed by a lie down for his over-excited patient. Conwell-Evans met with Jones and Schmidt to draft a press communiqué, reporting how discussions had centred on the European political situation, with the visitor also interested in the new roads and the German economy.[17] Separately, Jones persuaded Conwell-Evans to dictate his extempore recollections to him, as Ribbentrop had petulantly objected to his taking notes. Schmidt recorded it had been 'one of Hitler's best days... refreshed by his stay in the mountains, slightly bronzed by the sun, [and] obviously delighted by the recognition implied in the visit from the world-famous statesman'.[18]

Following the triumph of this first encounter, the Führer invited Lloyd George's whole party back to the Berghof the next day. Arriving in a convoy of Mercedes, the tourists admired the breathtaking views of the Alps as

Hitler greeted each of them personally at the top of the steps. Sylvester's film shows Hitler as the perfect host. Animated, charming and welcoming as white-gloved SS officers serve his guests tea, coffee, slices of cold ham and hard-boiled eggs cut in halves, he munches on a personal supply of Zwiebacks and *petit beurre* biscuits. Joachim and Annelies Ribbentrop joined as hosts alongside Otto Meissner, the state secretary responsible for welcoming foreign dignitaries, 'fat and jolly in a grey knickerbocker suit'.[19]

Hitler presented Lloyd George with a signed photograph in a silver frame, applauding how he had 'galvanised the people into a will to victory'. Having thanked him warmly, Lloyd George teasingly asked if it could sit alongside Foch, Clemenceau and other Great War leaders. His new friend did not object but admitted he would struggle if it were put next to Erzberger and Bauer, the German Socialist political leaders whom he blamed for the 'stab in the back' at the Armistice.

As the Führer then went on to sign photographs for the others, they all grasped the historical importance of the 'great War Leader of the British Empire' meeting the 'great Leader who had restored Germany to her present position'. Conwell-Evans concluded they were witnessing a 'symbolic act of reconciliation between the two peoples'. Dawson and Jones begged Hitler to excuse the prime minister's absence on health grounds and, weeks later at Nuremberg, with the glow from this visit fading, Jones reported Hitler had wept at the vanishing prospects of ever meeting Baldwin.[20]

As they prepared to say their farewells, the host and chief guest were admiring the tapestries when Lloyd George asked Conwell-Evans to invite the Führer to visit England. He promised he would be 'acclaimed by the British people', echoing Baldwin and MacDonald, who had proposed the same through Ribbentrop, Tennant and the German ambassador back in 1933. In response, Hitler threw up his hands in a gesture Conwell-Evans interpreted as his wishing it 'might be true'.[21] Though non-committal, he reiterated he felt 'passionately interested in the furtherance of Anglo-German understanding'. As proof of this, he was sending Ribbentrop, his 'best man', to London as ambassador.[22] How wrong this would prove to be.

After the excitements of the trips up the hill to the Berghof, that evening the Lloyd George entourage repaired to a beer garden. There they 'made whoopee' under the trees, listening to the band and watching the local youth as they danced and flirted. In the days following, they made good use of their extended stay in Germany. Rudolf Hess treated them to tea in what the Germans considered a 'castle' but Sylvester thought closer to a 'London suburban villa of moderate size'. They visited neat workers' cottages with tidy vegetable gardens, model farms with immaculate white chickens and land reclamation projects being cleared by bare-chested Aryan youth. Having been mobbed by enthusiastic youngsters at a girls' camp, Lloyd George toured Hitler's new Munich headquarters and later gave the Nazi salute as he inspected ranks of SS and SA rehearsing for the Nuremberg rally.

Throughout the trip, Conwell-Evans was never far from Lloyd George's side, lively and smiling, energetically translating, explaining and liaising. The films and his commentary show how well received Lloyd George had been in Germany, especially by the young. In Berchtesgaden, locals in traditional costume photographed him as he admired the sights. Young Germans crowd the gleaming Mercedes cars and spontaneously salute the former British prime minister; there is no concealing the old man's delight at this recognition and warmth of reception. In several respects, Lloyd George was paving the way for the next prime minister, Neville Chamberlain, who two years later would be hailed in Germany for bringing peace to the Anglo-Saxon world.

A few days later, the party travelled to Augsburg to a celebration lunch held at the grandest hotel in town. Favoured by Hitler and famed for its cuisine, the locals joked that to 'dine well in Munich, you must go to the *Drei Mohren* in Augsburg'. The landlord flew the Union flag alongside the swastika to welcome his British guests. It had been in this very room, Ribbentrop announced, where Hitler had decided to reoc- cupy the Rhineland. A commemorative menu signed by the guests sur- vives in Conwell-Evans's papers. Danish fish with salt potatoes followed Londonderry bouillon, then young partridges in a champagne and herb sauce served with more potatoes (this time mashed), finished off with a raspberry omelette, cheese and fruit. Jones noted it had been all 'perfectly cooked and was voted the best so far'.[23]

Despite the holiday atmosphere and Berchtesgaden's touristic delights, the menace of National Socialism had never been far below the surface. Pride reported he and the other youngsters were 'sharply disturbed' by the number of uniformed SS and other men who 'far outnumbered the citizens on holiday in shorts'.[24] Even *Country Life* noticed the Berghof had been surrounded by barbed wire and armed guards, but blithely trusted its purpose was just to keep out 'well-meaning admirers and excursion visitors'.

Looking for some degree of balance, Lloyd George did meet with some opponents of the National Socialist regime, including leading German Baptists and several of Conwell-Evans's German friends who shared that antipathy. In his *Daily Express* article, Lloyd George acknowledged that the 'restraint on liberty', especially the censorship of the press, had been 'repellent'. Along with 'every well-wisher of Germany', he prayed 'Goebbels's ranting speeches will not provoke another anti-Jewish manifestation' and in his interview with the *News Chronicle* emphasised he 'deplored Hitler's political and religious repression, a terrible thing to an old Liberal' like himself (notwithstanding he raised none of these concerns at his tea parties with the Führer). He assured his readers he did not advocate the 'immuring of political opponents in concentration camps' and thought the persecution of the Jews was a 'grave and deplorable thing'.[25]

So, while a public relations coup for Ribbentrop, Lloyd George's visit had not been an unmitigated propaganda success for the National Socialists. Nor was the stage management wholly under Party control. On the German side, Geyr and Schmidt were both old-school foreign ministry, later entwined with the conservative resistance to Hitler. Ribbentrop had been unexpectedly passive during the trip; when challenged on Russia, according to Schmidt, he had been a 'shadow', and 'scarcely uttered a word' during the main talk.[26] The picture of the meeting shows him holding back, six steps down from his master, nervous and unsure, while it is Schmidt who supervises the introductions.

The morning following the tea party, Jones urged Lloyd George to brief the prime minister and the foreign secretary before speaking to the press. Dawson pressed him to share his impressions of the Führer in the upmarket *Daily Telegraph* rather than Lord Beaverbrook's populist *Daily Express*. Foolishly ignoring this counsel, Lloyd George published his hastily drafted and sensationalist article under the heading 'I talked to HITLER', just a week after his return. Hyperbolic in its enthusiasms and careless in its implications, the article compared Hitler to George Washington, calling him a 'born leader of men' and admiring his 'magnetic, dynamic personality with a single-minded purpose, a resolute will and a dauntless heart'. Ever the egalitarian, Lloyd George praised the new social structures in Germany which meant 'provincial and class origins no longer divide the nation.' The shadow of the Great War – especially the 700,000 who had 'died of sheer hunger in those dark years' – is mixed in with a strong dose of mea culpa. Accepting Germany had breached the Treaty of Versailles, he suggested she had been no worse than the other European countries. Urging realism, he warned Germany's rearmament had left the country 'impenetrable to attack except at a sacrifice of life which would be more appalling than that inflicted in the great war'[27] – words written in the hope of charming the Führer and civilising his administration which have dogged Lloyd George's legacy ever since.

These ventures into print met with immediate criticism in other newspapers and from politicians. But Tennant and Conwell-Evans were nonetheless delighted, celebrating over lunch at the Travellers Club. An 'overjoyed' Tennant wrote congratulating Lloyd George on the article. Having been treated with 'great suspicion' by his friends for defending Hitler, he now felt 'immensely encouraged' to find support from someone as famous as the former prime minister.[28] Hitler and Ribbentrop had assured him at Nuremberg they had been much encouraged by his visit. Lloyd George had been grateful for Conwell-Evans's support, sending a 'token of appreciation', presumably the signed photograph that became a treasured keepsake. Conwell-Evans reported to Sylvester on the 'tremendous' benefit of the visit in Germany; Lloyd George's 'sense of fair play' had been the 'talk of the country' and the youth admired 'his energy, youthfulness and great broadness of mind'. Hitler had Lloyd George's photograph on his mantelpiece and now understood the meaning of the English phrase 'grand old man'.[29]

Ribbentrop's biographer concluded that the meeting had 'filled Hitler with a renewed burst of anglophile enthusiasm', while Lloyd George's saw it as the 'rhetorical climax of inter-war appeasement'.[30] Writing both with the benefit of hindsight and with his own legacy in mind far more than his friend's, Winston Churchill opined 'no one was more completely misled than Mr Lloyd George, whose rapturous accounts of his conversations make odd reading to-day.' He concluded that Hitler had a 'power of fascinating men, and the sense of force and authority is apt to assert itself unduly upon the tourist'.[31]

Several historians have challenged the Churchillian orthodoxy, offering more nuanced interpretations of Lloyd George's Anglo-German game plan.

Commenting on the notorious newspaper article, the distinguished Welsh historian Kenneth Morgan wrote that it would be 'wrong to see him as just an uncritical advocate of appeasement'; Lloyd George had urged greater rearmament, especially of the air force, so Britain could 'confront the dictators from a position of strength'.[32] Another historian reminds us that he 'seldom limited his political manoeuvres to one line', while a third asked, 'who fooled whom in this Alpine encounter?'[33] In 1942, Hitler himself suggested that had Lloyd George been in power there might have been an Anglo-German understanding in 1936 – albeit with Britain as a junior partner in his adventures.

There are many reasons why a liberal British statesman might choose to flatter Hitler. Lloyd George was naturally promiscuous in his praise of dictators. Hoping to protect his friend Ivan Maisky from the brutal and unpredictable Soviet purges, he had sent a 'warm message of admiration' to Stalin, lauding him as the 'greatest statesman alive!'[34] Even Churchill appealed to Hitler's vanity when it suited his rhetoric, as late as November 1938 issuing a statement to the press (itself easily quoted out of context) explaining that he had 'always said that if Great Britain were defeated in war, I hope we should find a Hitler to lead us back to our rightful position among the nations'.[35] Whatever else, it seems unfair to paint one of Britain's greatest twentieth-century statesmen as the Führer's dupe. Guided by his friends in the Anglo-German Fellowship, he had, at least, made every effort to civilise the Third Reich.

PART TWO

October 1936–November 1938

Adolf Hitler with the British ambassador, Sir Nevile Henderson, in the Hotel Deutscher Hof during a tea party for the foreign guests at the NSDAP Reichsparteitag in Nuremberg, 12 September 1937.

11

PREACHING BROTHERLY LOVE
TO A ROGUE ELEPHANT

While Lloyd George toured Germany, his friend and protégé, the new king, Edward VIII, had been cruising the Eastern Mediterranean in a steam yacht accompanied by a handful of close friends and courtiers. Among them had been the still married Wallis Simpson. That autumn of 1936, soon after both expeditions had returned to Britain, photographs of the couple appeared in the foreign press and gossip spread among *haute société* about the King's affair. But the British newspapers, stifled by the press baron Lord Beaverbrook, kept a dignified silence. Most of Edward's subjects remained unaware of the romance that would provoke the country's biggest constitutional crisis for decades.

While the British monarch focused on matters romantic, his ministers and subjects were absorbed in domestic issues. The Jarrow March was highlighting the unemployment and poverty caused by the closure of the town's shipbuilding works. The Battle of Cable Street in East London pitched marchers from the British Union of Fascists and a police escort against upwards of 100,000 anti-fascist demonstrators. Two days later, the BUF's leader, Oswald Mosley, married his mistress Diana Mitford in a private ceremony with Adolf Hitler as their witness.

That autumn, Germany and Italy signed a protocol setting up a diplomatic axis between Rome and Berlin. Both governments were covertly supporting General Franco's Nationalists in the by now raging Spanish Civil War. An international conference for non-intervention in that conflict was held in London with widespread support for neutrality, driven by the fear any intervention could spark a larger European war. The British prime

127

minister embargoed sales of munitions to Spain. In Soviet Russia, Joseph Stalin initiated his campaign of domestic terror, the Great Purge, with his first Moscow trial of former party leaders. In the US, President Roosevelt delivered his infamous speech to the Chautauqua Institution in which he insisted, 'we shun political commitments, which might entangle us in foreign wars; we avoid connection with the political activities of the League of Nations', before giving his personal perspective on war.

> I have seen war. I have seen war on land and sea. I have seen blood running from the wounded. I have seen men coughing out their gassed lungs. I have seen the dead in the mud. I have seen cities destroyed. I have seen 200 limping, exhausted men come out of line — the survivors of a regiment of 1,000 that went forward 48 hours before. I have seen children starving. I have seen the agony of mothers and wives. I hate war.[1]

This was the complex and fraught diplomatic atmosphere into which the accident-prone and intellectually deficient Joachim Ribbentrop finally headed to take up the ambassadorship to the Court of St James's. Here he had the opportunity to build on the excellent work of his much admired predecessor, placing himself at the forefront of London's *corps diplomatique*, as master of a senior embassy, living in an Eaton Square house (rented to him by Neville Chamberlain), with invitations from London's society hostesses dropping on his doormat, and a son heading for Eton College. Having assured Lloyd George he was sending his best man to London, Hitler's parting words to Ribbentrop were: 'Bring me the English alliance.'[2]

What could possibly go wrong?

Sir Eric and Lady Phipps hosted a farewell dinner at the Berlin embassy for the Ribbentrops and included Conwell-Evans, in the wake of his success in shepherding Lloyd George around Germany. Phipps felt pessimistic about the mission. Placing the 'lightweight' Ribbentrop 'near the bottom of the handicap', he found him 'irritating, ignorant and boundlessly conceited'.[3] Any failure to fill the elegant shoes of the emollient Leopold von Hoesch would worsen Anglo-German relations while any success would fuel his ambitions which so outstripped his talents. Sir Eric warned the Foreign Office that Hitler had hinted success in London could be rewarded with the real prize – the foreign ministry – despite his envoy's ignorance of both government and diplomacy. Vansittart shared his brother-in-law's pessimism, warning of how the new ambassador would bypass diplomatic processes to report directly to Hitler. Even Ribbentrop, having lobbied so hard for the London posting, now felt, as Van noted, 'markedly unenthusiastic' about leaving for London.[4] He delayed taking up this sensitive post, empty for nearly six months, in favour of wooing the Japanese and politicking in Berlin, much to the irritation of the British Foreign Office. His enemies in the Party, especially von Neurath, Goebbels and Göring, expected him to fail and expose his shortcomings. And he knew it. Only Hitler sounded optimistic.

The Ribbentrops headed to London in special train carriages attached to the *Nord Express* with an entourage of forty-four retainers, including two Gestapo men tasked with spying on his unfortunate underlings. His two key lieutenants were Ernst Woermann and Erich Kordt. Phipps rated both diplomats as excellent, explaining to London that they were both looking forward 'with much misgiving to their task of keeping their master straight'.[5] The first would replace as counsellor the urbane and properly aristocratic Prince Otto von Bismarck, who had been acting chargé d'affaires and risked, with his beautiful Swedish wife, outshining the socially anxious Ribbentrops in London's diplomatic jungle. The thirty-three-year-old Kordt, who had gone with Ribbentrop to the naval conference the previous year, now returned to London as first secretary. He had promised to report back to von Neurath, his true *patron* in Berlin, on his boss's manoeuvrings.

From the moment they stepped onto the Victoria Station platform on 26 October 1936, a cocktail of social ineptitude, personal insensitivity and unlucky timing blighted the Ribbentrops' time in London. Ignoring the convention that an ambassador makes no public comment *en poste* before presenting his credentials to the head of state, he proffered the Hitler salute for half a minute before giving an unscheduled press conference to the assembled journalists and photographers. True to form, his message was that Anglo-German friendship should serve as a bulwark against Russian communism, 'that most terrible disease', rather than on its own merits. The next day's newspapers were as unimpressed by the speech as by the violation of protocol. Even his own press officer had been appalled by his lack of tact.

The first social rebuff to embarrass the family was their failure to secure a place at their school of choice for Rudolf, their eldest son. Ribbentrop, a keen student of British elites, had set his sights on the most famous. Founded by King Henry VI in 1440, Eton College had already educated fifteen of Britain's prime ministers, including Walpole, Pitt, Wellington and Gladstone. Eton's dominance of the Foreign Office was notorious, and half a dozen of the Cabinet had attended the school, including Eden, Londonderry and Halifax. Ribbentrop had asked Vansittart over lunch in Berlin to use his influence to secure Rudolf a place, convinced the school would show him 'how English boys live, and he will be able to teach the Hitler Youth'.[6] But the fifteen-year-old had been too old for the usual entry, had not been 'put down' for a place at birth, and had not been to a suitable preparatory school, so his would have to be a special case. Van approached the headmaster, Claude Elliott, who on the grounds of the boy's age refused and recommended Stowe instead. In the end, a place had been found (following pressure from the British government) for Rudolf as a day boy at Westminster School, close to the embassy. There, the unfortunate Rudolf failed to impress his schoolmates, especially the young Peter Ustinov, who remembered him being daily deposited by a 'huge white Mercedes' driven by an embassy chauffeur with whom he exchanged 'Heil Hitler's before hurrying into morning prayers.[7] His sister, Bettina, fared no better at Heathfield girls' boarding school near Ascot where, according to Vansittart's daughter Cynthia, the other girls were 'awful to her'.[8]

None of this should have mattered had Hitler not so fixated on Eton and had Ribbentrop not been so anxious to impress his master by succeeding in London. The Führer believed the school had helped Britain win the Great War on the basis its Officers' Training Corps served as a paramilitary organisation with 'military instruction as [its] first duty'. This he had explained to an amused Anthony Eden at their first meeting, arguing, as his guest had been appointed an officer in the Great War straight from school, that he must have received his military training as a pupil. The future foreign secretary had pointed out that the training had been negligible and the field days little more than opportunities for illicit smoking. His 'completely unconvinced' host had shaken his head, disregarding his clarification as 'patriotic deception'.[9] Two years later, despite his mounting hostility to England, Hitler sent a Hitler Youth leader to visit the school for inspiration for the elite *Adolf-Hitler-Schulen* he was launching that year. A delegation from Eton had been invited to visit these newly established training grounds for future SS officers and other elite Nazis. (By 1940, secret German planning documents designated Eton for immediate takeover for the education of the sons of top-ranking Nazi officers as part of Operation Sealion, the invasion of Great Britain.)

So just as they admired but misunderstood Britain's constitutional monarchy, so Hitler and Ribbentrop idealised but misread the 'Old School Tie' tradition. Nor were they alone in struggling to decode Britain's social customs. As the American journalist Virginia Cowles patiently explained to her US readers:

> This tradition is not, as many Americans imagine, preserved by a snobbish group which takes delight in singing sentimental songs about their lost youth and sworn to 'stick together' at any cost. Eton, for example, which supplies England with seventy-five percent of its ruling class, offers no tangible evidence of a 'fraternity'. It is a curious but important paradox that Old Etonians seldom wear Old Etonian ties, never have re-union dinners, and rarely refer to their school except in anecdotes directed either at the sanitary arrangements or the stupidity of their masters.[10]

Ribbentrop's social stumbling had been worsened by his unhappy timing. The day before he arrived, Mr Justice Hawke, the judge at the Ipswich Assizes, granted Mrs Simpson her decree nisi. Within weeks, Britain was consumed with the national crisis surrounding the King's determination to pass the throne to his younger brother in order to marry an American double divorcée deemed unsuitable as Queen. The abdication delivered a cruel setback for both Ribbentrop's diplomatic mission and the Fellowship's monarchist aspirations. It robbed both of their royal friend and de facto patron – albeit each had been more imagined than real – and Hitler considered it a disaster. Notwithstanding his interest in modern Germany, Edward had been distracted from foreign affairs throughout his short reign. Similarly, the prime minister, who had cautiously welcomed Tennant's earlier overtures and had blessed Lloyd George's mission, now had little time for

Anglo-German subtleties as the crisis unfolded. As Eden later remembered, Baldwin had begged not to be troubled 'too much with foreign affairs'.[11] Buoyed by his success in navigating the choppiest of waters in switching kings, he was anyway steaming towards his longed-for retirement.

Amid these excitements, only days after Edward signed the instrument of abdication handing the throne to his younger brother and left the country for Austria, the Fellowship hosted its third grand banquet on 15 December 1936, this time at Grosvenor House on London's Park Lane. Held to welcome the ambassador, this provided the forum for Ribbentrop's first formal speech after the false start at Victoria Station. In doing so, the Fellowship aped the dinners held by the Pilgrims' Society, the oldest and most prestigious Anglo-American bilateral friendship society, with whom it shared several members. With royal patronage and membership drawn from political, diplomatic and military elites, the Pilgrims by tradition (which continues) hosts the first speech on British soil by an American ambassador, while the first given by his British counterpart is always to its sister organisation, the Pilgrims of the United States.

Two moments of farce punctuated the evening. The first arose during the preparations of the hotel's ballroom when simmering tensions between the organising secretary, Elwyn Wright, and the honorary secretary, Conwell-Evans, bubbled to the surface. Without approval, Wright had borrowed a flag from the German embassy which he had hung behind the top table alongside a Union flag. Convinced this would lead to the Fellowship being 'branded as Nazis', Conwell-Evans had demanded its removal, but Wright had flatly refused. And so, the seventh Marquess of Londonderry, until recently His Majesty's secretary of state for air, duly toasted the German ambassador in one of London's grandest hotels with a 'great blatant swastika' as his backdrop.[12] His audience included a dozen fellow members of the House of Lords, another dozen knights of the realm, the high commissioner of South Africa, and most of the Fellowship's Council, accompanied by their wives. Praising his hosts as a 'great factor for good', Londonderry deplored the arms race and insisted it was time to 'close rapidly the vista of war and open up the glorious one of peace'.

In his reply, which must have run to half an hour, Ribbentrop eulogised the Anglo-German Fellowship as having started life as a 'delicate young sapling' which had now grown into a 'firm young tree' which he was sure would not easily be 'uprooted by antagonistic winds or even a storm'. Having announced scholarships for British students at the universities of Hamburg and Berlin, he moved on to international politics. Acknowledging 'misunderstandings and misinterpretations' leading to 'missed opportunities' over four years, he returned to familiar tropes. The world's nations were divided into the 'haves' and the 'have nots'. Germany, stripped of her colonies, was firmly among the latter. Her four-year economic plan focusing on self-sufficiency should not cause alarm to her British friends. Bolshevism was the common enemy. Mirroring Londonderry, he concluded that 'another conflict between their two great nations, another universal world war, would mean the unavoidable victory of world revolution, bolshevism, and destruction of everything dear to them from generations.'[13]

The speeches provoked such mixed reactions that a fracas broke out between two tables. On one, which included the Fellowship's solicitor, Gerald le Blount Kidd, there were objections to Ribbentrop's words. A guest on a neighbouring table, George Pitt-Rivers, leapt to the ambassador's defence and damned the 'platitudinous discourses' of the other speakers. Voices were raised. Tempers flared. Matters reached a head, with Le Blount Kidd pointing firmly at Pitt-Rivers and loudly announcing, 'If that man applies for membership of the Fellowship, I will see that he is not admitted.'[14] Pitt-Rivers was attending as a guest of his secretary and lover Catherine Sharpe, an attractive twenty-three-year-old member who had been introduced to Hitler by her cousin, Unity Mitford. Twice married and twice her age, Pitt-Rivers was the spectacularly wealthy landowning grandson of the founder of Oxford's eponymous museum of anthropology. Having inherited huge estates and an interest in anthropology from his grandfather, he had developed his own less innocent enthusiasms – for eugenics, anti-Semitism and anti-Bolshevism. Le Blount Kidd was good to his word and lobbied the Council to refuse him membership of the Fellowship on the grounds of his extremism. The chairman, Lord Mount Temple, agreed, informing the meeting that Pitt-Rivers was 'mad... all his family are mad', and that his famous grandfather had been 'notoriously mad'. Another attendee reported that the Athenaeum Club had deeply regretted admitting the grandson as a member while a third reminisced that he had 'once shot a man in a hotel in Johannesburg'.[15]

Barely six weeks later, Ribbentrop returned to Berlin to witness Hitler give a major speech to the German Reichstag promising peace, which was widely reported internationally. The Führer called for international cooperation, better trade, the return of German colonies, restrictions on armaments (especially for the air force) and reiterated his desire for an agreement with England. *The Times* approved, and in the House of Lords Mount Temple reassured his fellow peers that the Germans 'bear us no ill will for the War, and all they want is to resume the old relationship which existed between our two countries before the War in 1914'.[16] Criticising the Franco-Soviet Pact and Foreign Office hostility to Germany, he asked, 'Why should we always do what the French ask us to do and never do anything to placate and to help the Germans?' Ribbentrop sent a letter of thanks.

In January, the Fellowship held its first annual general meeting at Unilever House and issued its annual report to a membership now close to five hundred. Reviewing its first year with satisfaction, it noted the three successful banquets, the warm welcomes extended to parties of ex-servicemen, Hitler Youth leaders, miners and singers from Germany, and the delegations sent to the Olympic Games and opening of the DEG clubhouse in Berlin. The Council regretted the 'sad passing' of the previous ambassador, von Hoesch, who had been the Fellowship's first guest and so supportive, but barely drew breath before trumpeting its 'special pleasure' in welcoming his successor, who ranked 'foremost among German public men in promoting Anglo-German friendship'.[17] Looking forward to a second year of progress, plans were announced to grow the membership throughout the country and establish a Ladies Committee, presumably to broaden the focus away from the middle-aged London businessmen who had started it. The Fellowship's published accounts, audited by Price Waterhouse, underpinned its financial transparency and solvency to challenge any suggestion it was being under-written by the German government or the Nazi party.

As well as the new German ambassador in Carlton House Terrace, the new year brought a new king, George VI, and within months a new prime minister and a new ambassador to Berlin. But all was not well in the Fellowship's comfortable new offices in Chelsea. In February, Tennant had proposed to Mount Temple that Conwell-Evans should replace the increasingly erratic Elwyn Wright as full-time paid secretary. Wright took his proposed removal badly and found an unexpected source of support from the group of troublemakers protesting about George Pitt-Rivers's rejected membership.

Ribbentrop had cemented his reputation for diplomatic clumsiness by startling the King with a Hitler salute rather than the customary bow from the neck as he presented his credentials. This earned him the nickname 'Brickendrop' from David Low, the *Evening Standard*'s celebrated cartoonist. Meanwhile, at the Foreign Office, plans were afoot to replace his opposite number in Berlin. Having determined his brother-in-law, Eric Phipps, had been temperamentally unsuited to representing his country in National Socialist Berlin, Vansittart arranged his transfer to the far more congenial embassy in Paris. 'Too soon,' thought Conwell-Evans, given how well Phipps had ensured his government understood 'Hitler's intentions'.[18]

Phipps's replacement would be the inexperienced and maverick Sir Nevile Henderson. Then ambassador to Buenos Aires, he was a likea-ble Old Etonian whose Savile Row suits and red buttonhole earned him the reputation as the best-dressed man in the Foreign Office. Naturally Germanophile and suspicious of the French, like Lloyd George, Lothian and Tennant, he had been in Paris for the 1919 peace talks and shared their view that the Germans had been unfairly treated. Vansittart had returned from Berlin convinced that the embassy needed to build better rapport with the Nazis. He had assessed Henderson as 'good with dictators' given his close friendship with King Alexander of Yugoslavia, who shared his passion for shooting game. Invitations to shoot with Old Etonians were already helping to civilise senior Nazis; Lords Londonderry and Mount Temple had hosted Ribbentrop to ordinary shooting weekends at their estates. Henderson's prowess at field sports quickly endeared him to Göring but cut less ice with the vegetarian and animal-loving Führer, who dismissed him as the 'man with the carnation'.

The new ambassador had been well disposed to the Fellowship from the outset, and initially that admiration was reciprocated. He had befriended Mount Temple on the SS *Cap Arcona* in March that year as they both sailed back to Europe from the US. Conwell-Evans praised him to the chairman as 'so different from his predecessor' and the Council gave a private dinner in London to wish him bon voyage.[19] Before leaving for Berlin, Henderson met privately with Chamberlain, who would replace Baldwin as prime minister that May. No written record survives of their meeting, but Henderson claimed that Chamberlain had outlined his attitude towards Germany and asked him to take a more sympathetic line with the Nazis than his predecessors. Rightly or wrongly, Henderson took this as a personal mandate to placate Hitler at all costs, often in conflict with the Foreign Office. He knew from the outset his mission was controversial, admitting to Eden that he would be accused of being 'pro-Nazi'.[20]

Within a month, the Deutsch-Englische Gesellschaft hosted a welcome dinner at its Berlin clubhouse for His Majesty's ambassador, further embedding the twin societies within the Anglo-German diplomatic circuit. The Duke of Coburg played host to his Eton schoolmates, Henderson and Tennant, with Mount Temple representing the Fellowship. Following the Pilgrims model, Henderson gave his maiden speech, flattering his hosts who had contributed 'so much to a better understanding between nations'. Taking 'advantage of the licence granted [him] by Mr. Chamberlain', he quoted a Great War poem that included the emotive line, 'who dares put a rifle to his shoulder to kill another mother's darling boy?' An appalled Grahame Christie reported to Vansittart that declaiming this 'American pacifist doggerel' to an audience of 'tough militant German leaders' was as worthwhile as preaching 'brotherly love to a rogue elephant'.[21] Having praised Hitler's regime, Henderson then urged its critics in England to 'lay less stress on Nazi dictatorship and much more emphasis on the great social experiment which is being tried out in this country'.[22] This he later admitted had caused the most offence back home, with critics in the House of Commons giving him the sobriquet of 'our Nazi British Ambassador'.[23] The speech sent shock waves well beyond Berlin and London. Ivan Maisky, the Russian ambassador, warned his friend Vansittart it had caused 'amazement in Moscow, not to mention more definite emotions'.[24]

In reply, Coburg expressed his delight that the 'highest representative of Great Britain in our Fatherland has the fullest sympathy for our work' and was thus in lock step with Ribbentrop, who gave 'his warmest interest and fullest support in the pursuance of its aims to our sister society'.[25] But in London, less flattering parallels between the two new ambassadors were being made. Oliver Harvey, the foreign secretary's private secretary, hoped nervously in his diary that they had not sent 'another Ribbentrop

Left: Ernest W. D. Tennant, founder of the Anglo-German Fellowship, with his butterflies in a portrait by Edward Halliday, 1937.

Right: Joachim Ribbentrop (left), Reich disarmament representative, dressed as an English gentleman, in London with Erich Kordt (right), legation secretary, May 1934.

Leopold von Hoesch, the German ambassador to London and an early sponsor of the Anglo-German Fellowship, with his beloved dogs on the terrace of the German embassy at Carlton House Terrace.

Malcolm Grahame Christie in his Blackburn Type 1 two-seat monoplane in 1914. The pilot, Harold Blackburn, sits at the rear with Christie as passenger in the front.

Blickling Hall, near Aylsham in Norfolk, home of Philip Kerr, the 11th Marquess of Lothian.

Huis Wylerberg near Nijmegen on the German-Dutch border, home of Grahame Christie's godmother, Marie Schuster-Hiby, which served as the base for his Continental adventures and through which the Schuster-Hiby family helped many Jews to escape from Germany.

Marie Schuster-Hiby and her daughter, Alice, before the Second World War.

Alice Schuster and Grahame Christie in the 1960s.

The funeral procession of Leopold von Hoesch, the German ambassador to London, passing Buckingham Palace, 15 April 1936. Von Hoesch's sudden death robbed Anglo-German relations of a talented champion and opened the way for his disastrous successor, Joachim Ribbentrop.

The Duke of Saxe-Coburg and Gotha gives the Nazi salute having laid a wreath in homage to Great Britain's war dead on the Cenotaph in Whitehall, London. The duke was leading a delegation of German ex-servicemen on a three-day visit that coincided with the return of Neville Chamberlain, the British prime minister, from his second meeting with Adolf Hitler in Germany. Police officers afterwards formed a guard to prevent the removal of the wreath while people filed past, 24 September 1938.

Top left: Douglas Douglas-Hamilton, the Marquess of Clydesdale (later 14th Duke of Hamilton and 11th Duke of Brandon), carrying his gear to the plane prior to take-off from Heston Aerodrome for the first ever flight over the summit of Everest, 16 February 1933.

Top right: H. A. R. ('Kim') Philby, The Times journalist, member of MI6, Soviet intelligence agent and traitor, who set up the publicity department for the Anglo-German Fellowship, c. 1940.

Gertrud Scholtz-Klink (left), Germany's 'women's leader', and Lady David Douglas-Hamilton, head of the British Women's League of Health and Beauty, watch a group of young women train in London, 8 March 1939.

David Freeman-Mitford, Lord Redesdale (left) with his wife, Sydney, and their daughter Unity Mitford at a concert during an Anglo-German Fellowship meeting at Victoria Hall, Bloomsbury, London. With them is Dr Sigismund-Sizzo Fitz Randolph, the German press attaché (far right), 15 December 1938.

Banquet given in honour of TRH the Duke and Duchess of Brunswick by the Anglo-German Fellowship at the Dorchester Hotel in London. The duke was the first cousin of the late King George V, and the duchess was the daughter of former Kaiser Wilhelm II. The tables are decorated with Union flags and swastikas, 14 July 1936.

Edward Wood, the Viscount Halifax, lord president of the Council, attends a dinner of the Anglo-German Fellowship at the Grosvenor House Hotel, London. From left to right are Halifax, the Duke of Saxe-Coburg and Gotha, president of the Deutsch-Englische Gesellschaft, and Joachim Ribbentrop, the German ambassador to London, 2 December 1937.

David Lloyd George, the former British prime minister (second right), with Joachim Ribbentrop, placing a wreath on a German war memorial in Munich. Behind Lloyd George are (left to right) Philip Conwell-Evans, Lord Dawson of Penn, Tom Jones and Major Gwilym Lloyd George, 7 September 1936.

An SS orderly serves tea and coffee to David Lloyd George and his party at the Berghof, Hitler's Bavarian mountain retreat. Ribbentrop sits between Hitler and Lloyd George, 7 September 1936.

Philip Conwell-Evans looking at the cine camera with which A. J. Sylvester films the tea party hosted by Hitler for Lloyd George and his party. Behind Conwell-Evans, (from left to right) Lord Dawson, Paul Schmidt, Megan Lloyd George and Tom Jones listen attentively to the Führer, 7 September 1936.

to Berlin.[26] He was right to worry and shrewd in making the comparison as both men (between whom little love was lost) were vain, foolish and proud. Each would circumvent diplomatic process to feed the deluded vanities of their mercurial heads of government rather than their foreign ministries.

While in Berlin, Mount Temple used the opportunity to meet Hitler for the first time and to see von Neurath. Conwell-Evans had arranged the appointments through Ribbentrop, bypassing both the embassy in Berlin and the Foreign Office in London, who had tried to nix the meetings. This provoked a furious outburst from Vansittart who, following a request from the chairman to debrief the prime minister in person, fired off an irate memorandum insisting 'the P.M. should certainly not see Lord Mount Temple – nor should the Secretary of State'. Rising to his theme, he insisted it was time to 'put a stop to this eternal butting in of amateurs – and Lord Mount Temple is a particularly silly one' before reminding his readers that 'Sir E. Phipps rightly complained of these ambulant amateurs'.[27]

Hitler's professions of peace would soon, as Ian Kershaw put it, 'prove even more cynical than it appeared at the time'.[28] Mount Temple's vocal support seems correspondingly naïve. That same month, Christie confirmed just how naïve. Claiming to be worried about 'deteriorating' Anglo-German relations, Göring had invited him for a 'heart-to-heart' talk. They had avoided politics over lunch before retiring to his private office for a two-and-a-half-hour discussion.

The general expressed his frustration at Great Britain obstructing both the return of Germany's colonies and her expansion on the Continent, especially regarding Austria, suggesting both the Nazi Party and the German public were now seeing the British as their 'chief enemy'. Christie insisted his country would resist any aggressive acts to force *Anschluss* but might accept a 'mutual friendly agreement with Austria whereby the latter would not yield her entire independence to the Reich but got fair play'. To this, a smiling Göring replied that the 'measure of independence is purely an internal German affair' and then asked why Britain cared about Czechoslovakia's fate. Christie explained that whatever he had heard from his ambassador in London or from the newspapers, Great Britain would honour her duties to the League of Nations and stand behind France's obligations to defend Czechoslovakia from any 'unprovoked attack'. Conversation then ranged across international relations, from the attitudes of the Italians to the prospects for the Low Countries and the situation in Asia, before returning to Central Europe, on which Christie pressed his host for clarity.

'What is Germany's aim in Europe today?' he asked.

'We want a free hand in Eastern Europe. We want to establish the unity of the German peoples (*Grossdeutsche Volksgemeinschaft*),' the general replied.

'You mean to get Austria?' asked his lunch guest.

'Yes'.

'You mean to get Czechoslovakia?'

'Yes'.

'You mean to get Rumania?' he continued, and here Göring hesitated before replying.

'No, but when Austria and Czechoslovakia belong to Grossdeutschland, then of course Rumania and Hungary would come into the bloc as partners. Yugoslavia is our friend, anyhow.'

Christie then pushed for greater clarity on the fate of the Czechs. To this, Göring replied, smiling cynically:

'Probably about half of them would die on the battlefield, and the other half would join their friends in Russia...'

The general then raised the threat of a frustrated Germany forming alliances with other countries. Would a pact with Russia threaten British interests in Persia and Afghanistan? Christie agreed it might limit the spread of communism but still an Anglo-German alliance would be preferable. Göring then boasted with obvious menace about the 'close friendship' developing between Germany, Italy and Japan.

Taking back the initiative, Christie challenged Germany's Five-Year Plan and its combination of autarky and barter. Arguing that it would require 'high tariffs, subsidies, contingencies, clearings, export and import licences', he predicted it would isolate Germany from Great Britain, France and the US, who were together advancing the benefits of free trade. Here, he thought he may have struck home.

Now looking uneasy and 'very grim', Göring could not feign his usual breezy insouciance. Turning the conversation to the Great War, he admitted Germany had been slow to learn how her 'most dangerous and tenacious enemy' had been Great Britain. But in summing up, Göring still dangled the prospect of a deal: 'above all things we want cooperation with Great

Britain... there are people in the Nazi party who do not wish this, but the leader and myself are longing for it... the door is not yet shut.'

Christie had been gathering evidence from both Hitler's resolute followers and his harshest critics to warn the Foreign Office about Nazi aggression for years. Armament production in Germany was now 'proceeding at an astounding rate and the supply of raw materials could barely keep abreast of the demand'. Speculating armed conflict would be the likely outcome, he ventured (with impressive foresight) that the end of 1939 would be the 'probable date when the Nazis would launch the war'. They had four immediate aims: to separate France from Russia; to separate Great Britain from France; to 'pave the way for the early conquest of Austria and Czechoslovakia'; and to rearm aggressively, especially the Luftwaffe. Summing up his report to Vansittart, he wrote, 'Only by a firm front and an increased display of defence force can we prevent Hitler and the party yielding to the temptation of war if they stolidly adhere to their present policy. We must see that an attack on London appears to them to be a very, very costly adventure.'[29]

*Reception held at the German embassy to celebrate the coronation
of King George VI with Field Marshal Werner von Blomberg
representing the German government. Left to right: the Princess of
Hessen (second figure), the Duchess of Kent and Ribbentrop listening
to Frida Leider, the singer from the Berlin Opera. 13 May 1937.*

12

THE BRICKENDROP CIRCUS

MAY 1937 BROUGHT THE CORONATION OF KING GEORGE VI AND Queen Elizabeth, held on the day that would have seen his elder brother crowned. It was a glorious national and international occasion as delegates from the Empire and around the world descended on London to join the celebrations. As such, it offered Ribbentrop and his allies a springboard for greater Anglo-German collaboration, possibly even a formal alliance, just as the Olympics had the summer before. The Fellowship's commentary on the celebrations in its *Monthly Journal* nicely illustrates both its ardent royalism and its wider preoccupations that spring. Underscoring its loyalty to the British Crown, it celebrated the 'peoples of his Majesty [being] at peace with their neighbours in all the five continents' and insisted, a touch defensively, there would be nothing disloyal in 'promoting relations of friendship with the most powerful nation on the Continent of Europe'.[1]

The Germans entered the celebrations with outward enthusiasm, but their engagement seemed somewhat muted compared to what might have been the case if it had been the openly Germanophile Edward VIII being crowned at Westminster Abbey. The question as to who should represent the Führer was an added source of tension from the outset. Both Göring and von Neurath had volunteered, each eager to join the quest for an English alliance. Göring sent his chief of personal staff, Colonel Karl Bodenschatz, on a reconnaissance mission during which he visited Oxford and took tea at the Plough Inn near High Wycombe. But news of his coming had leaked to the British press and provoked vocal objections from the Labour Party and Jewish groups, which infuriated Göring.

Von Neurath wanted to continue his discussions with Vansittart from the previous summer and assess the damage done by his ambassador in

London. But Ribbentrop, threatened by Göring's charismatic flamboyance and von Neurath's polished professionalism, vetoed both. Hitler instead sent Field Marshal Werner von Blomberg, the German minister of war and commander-in-chief of the Wehrmacht. The fifty-eight-year-old aristocrat and army officer had endeared himself to the Führer during both the Night of the Long Knives and the remilitarisation of the Rhineland. Though a convinced National Socialist and an advocate of aggressive rearmament, he had been steadfast in preserving the army's independence from the Party and had outmanoeuvred Röhm, Himmler and Göring in their attempts to encroach on the army's authority to benefit the SA, SS and Luftwaffe, respectively.

Von Blomberg went down well in London. Conwell-Evans felt honoured to be appointed his 'English ADC' and arranged an excursion outside London. Capitalising on the arrival of such a civilised German minister to a landmark royal event, the Fellowship hosted a reception at the May Fair Hotel, with members paying six shillings each to join him for tea. Chamberlain thought him a 'very pleasant agreeable man of the world who talks extremely good English'.[2] Conwell-Evans found him 'extraordinarily kind and friendly'. Meanwhile, keen to take advantage of the celebratory mood to burnish their social credentials in London, the Ribbentrops had decided to throw a sumptuous house-warming reception at the just refurbished German embassy on the day after the coronation.

Only a month before the excitements of the coronation, Conwell-Evans had escorted the German ambassador for a 'pure holiday' to Cornwall, accompanied by an entourage including Reinhard Spitzy, his twenty-five-year-old private secretary (who left an entertaining account of the trip), senior aides, servants and a nurse, but neither Frau Ribbentrop nor their children. The county was charged with significance for Ribbentrop and the trip marks the last flush of his heartfelt affection for England. As Tennant later confirmed to Neville Chamberlain, this was the point when his 'state of mind of seeking friendship with this country' had ended.[3]

Having spent a happy year learning English in London aged sixteen, Ribbentrop's next sight of the British Isles had been in August 1914, following the outbreak of war in Europe. Returning from New York to enlist in the German army, his ship had been passing within sight of the Isles of Scilly when a British destroyer intercepted her, and sailors had boarded with fixed bayonets. All but two of the German passengers were arrested and interned in Falmouth. Ribbentrop was excused arrest by a British intelligence officer, one Captain Wally, with whom he had found Canadian friends in common and who accepted his claim to be medically unfit for military service. Now, twenty-three years later, having returned in triumph to England as his government's most senior envoy, he had vowed to revisit the royal duchy during peacetime. Over tea with a correspondent from the *Western Morning News and Daily Gazette*, he enthused how he had never forgotten the 'beautiful sight of those tall cliffs, many-hued in the glow of a setting sun, and the wonderful green of the turf at their summit'.[4]

Moments of farce punctuated the journey west. To Spitzy's horror, the reserved compartments provided at no extra cost by the railway company included three private Pullman carriages with a restaurant car and library. Ribbentrop had hoped to travel incognito as 'Mr Williams', because the London newspapers were chiding him and his wife for their extravagances. Now he was furious to find photographers waiting at the station following a tip-off, albeit his mood later improved as he settled into the luxurious train. At Exeter, their carriages were decoupled onto a private express train taking them to St Ives, the picturesque former fishing port, where they were greeted by the mayor. The best rooms with sea views had been reserved at the newly refurbished Tregenna Castle Hotel, where further comedy ensued when it emerged the ambassador from Japan was coincidentally also a guest. Appalled in case their meeting was construed as a secret conspiracy against the host nation, the Japanese diplomat made his excuses and returned to London the next morning.

The Ribbentrop party soon relaxed, playing golf on the hotel's nine-hole course, tennis on its grass courts and riding horses over the rugged local countryside. Colonel Edward Bolitho, lord lieutenant and local master of foxhounds, lent them sure-footed hunters and entertained them at his house near Penzance. The British intelligence services had asked Bolitho to report any indiscretions once tongues had been loosened by his wine cellar. Although later subject to muttered criticisms for hosting the Nazi leader in the county, there is no evidence Bolitho, a veteran of the trenches (he tactfully took down his souvenir bullet-riddled German helmet), had any sympathies for the regime. His daughter, Agnes, impressed the smitten Spitzy as the model of Aryan womanhood, a 'true representative of the contemporary Nordic ideal, though rendered more human through humour and youthful exuberance.[5] Away from his controlling wife and the chaos of his embassy, Ribbentrop seemed to really enjoy the holiday and his affection for the region was evidently sincere. The hotel went to great lengths to make him feel at home, even arranging a cake decorated with a swastika at a tea party to meet the local press.

On a reconnaissance trip to London the previous autumn, Annelies Ribbentrop had decided the von Hoesch embassy had neither the grandeur nor sufficient National Socialist chic for her husband's mission. Three adjoining houses on Carlton House Terrace had been knocked together to create grander public spaces, their fine Regency interiors stripped out and refurbished in the monolithic neoclassicism deployed at the Chancellery in Berlin. Eighty-two cream-coloured telephones were installed for the Ribbentrops' personal use, including one by his bath, from where he directed his embarrassed staff. The building had been secretly fitted with hidden listening devices ('Dictaphones') so his Gestapo henchmen could listen in on the far-from-loyal staff of the ever-more-paranoid ambassador. The largest drawing room (of five) had been extended to one hundred feet, modern furniture and rugs imported from Germany and German paintings commandeered from reluctant museums to be hung on the walls. Chips Channon thought the result 'impressive by sheer size but... far from beautiful'.[6]

The *News Chronicle* billed the reception, with around 1,300 guests, as 'one of the biggest... held in London for many years'. Ribbentrop dropped his first brick with the invitation. At his insistence, this had been drafted in German rather than English, as the language of his host country, or French, the lingua franca of diplomacy. (Mischievously, Peter Rodd, son of Lord Rennell and husband to Nancy Mitford, replied in Yiddish.) The guests of honour were the Duke and Duchess of Kent, brother and sister-in-law of the King. Widely admired for their film-star looks, the newspapers reported how the duke's 'scarlet tunic uniform and the dark blue ribbon of the Garter' perfectly complemented the duchess, beautiful in 'white satin with a necklace of sapphires and diamonds and a tall tiara to match'.[7] Despite a competing reception at the Austrian Legation that night, London society came to see just how civilised the Nazis could be. The weight of traffic approaching the embassy was so great that many guests had to finish the journey through the gridlocked streets on foot.

The guest list ranged far wider than the usual Anglo-German enthusi-asts. In its *Monthly Journal*, the Fellowship boasted how it is 'seldom that a gathering so representative of the British Empire has assembled at a foreign embassy'. Neville Chamberlain (only a fortnight away from moving next door to 10 Downing Street), Anthony Eden, Lord Halifax and Sir Thomas Inskip, minister for coordination of defence, all came with their wives, as did von Blomberg's opposite number, Duff Cooper, secretary of state for war and leading critic of appeasement. The senior ranks of the British armed forces came to see their counterparts face to face, including the air chief marshal and the Admiral of the Fleet. The Royal British Legion was represented by its president and chairman. The dominion prime ministers and the high commissioners of Australia, Canada, Southern Rhodesia and South Africa represented the Empire. Foreign royals joining the melee included the crown princes of Belgium, Greece, Japan and Saudi Arabia. Other notables with no obvious interest in international diplomacy ranged from the Bishop of London and the Lord Mayor to the headmasters of Eton, Harrow and Winchester. The newspaper barons Lords Rothermere and Kemsley led the press contingent, supported by Geoffrey Dawson, the appeasing editor of *The Times*, and Hitler's favourite British pressman, George Ward Price from the *Daily Mail*. The Fellowship proudly reported that its council had fielded eighteen, led by Mount Temple, Tennant, Conwell-Evans and D'Arcy Cooper. Well over a hundred Fellowship regulars were listed among the guests, including three of its marquesses and four of its peers. As well as Duff Cooper, other convinced anti-appeasers who came to see the Germans up close included the Churchills and the Vansittarts.

The principal singers from the Berlin Opera and two dance bands had been brought over to entertain the guests. Horcher, Berlin's most famous restaurant, supplied the food, flown in on specially chartered planes. One embassy official remembered 'unlimited supplies of lobster, caviar and champagne', noting the 'comparatively modest catering at Buckingham Palace could not hold a candle to the lavishness of Ribbentrop's hospitality.'[8] But, despite this civilised indulgence, the abiding memory for most of those present had been the congestion. Chamberlain called it a 'terrific crush' and, even with the enlarged reception rooms and marquees installed over the terrace, the Court and Social correspondent of the *Sunday Times* waspishly headlined his report 'Crowded German Embassy'. General Gamelin, the chief of the French General Staff, lost a military decoration in the confusion, while the wheelchair of an elderly Fellowship member got stuck in a doorway. Such was the crowd, most of the foreign guests had escaped by midnight, leaving their hosts to finish off the food and drink, much of it still untouched. General Milch, head of the Luftwaffe, was spotted snoring contentedly on a sofa with his feet on a silk-embroidered armchair, his hairy chest exposed through an open shirt, while a colleague, Captain Jäger, vomited on the carpet. The SS orderlies tasked with clearing up the mess grumbled for days.

Ribbentrop insisted his party had been a 'complete success' *because* of the crowds. But Annelies would have been sensitive to the teasing of the English newspapers and socialites. While the *Sunday Times* gossip columnist had gushed about her frock of 'softly falling chiffon of a light blue which might be termed duck's egg or light periwinkle', he could not resist adding in parentheses it had been a colour 'also worn by Mrs Eden on this night'.[9]

Ribbentrop similarly claimed to have enjoyed the coronation, even though it was for George not Edward. But even in the hallowed abbey the Ribbentrops were unable to avoid the childish schoolboy teasing that delights the English but so puzzles foreigners. The congregation, many clad in heavy ermine robes or Court dress and well refreshed beforehand, had to be seated hours in advance, so they risked (as Channon remembered delicately) 'possible bladder complications', given the scarcity of lavatories in the building.[10] Arrangements had been made for the scholars of Westminster School to usher any caught-short guest to the limited facilities in response to a raised arm. Alert to the ambassador's reputation for gaffes and irritated by his son's hectoring advocacy of the Nazi cause, they chose to interpret any arm raised by a Ribbentrop as a National Socialist salute…

Von Blomberg used his visit to charm London's great and good and Ribbentrop hosted two lunches in his honour at the embassy. The first centred on the retiring Baldwin and his court, including the Edens, Londonderrys, Vansittarts, Kemsleys, Rothermere, Lothian and the Archbishop of Canterbury. The second was for the newer brooms, led by the Chamberlains and joined by the Coopers, Hoares, Halifaxes and Churchills. Von Blomberg called on Eden at the Foreign Office, where the foreign secretary thanked him for representing the Führer and for the German press's enthusiastic coverage of the coronation. Although the field marshal passed on Hitler's worries about tensions over Spain, Italy, Russia, the League of Nations and the return of colonies, Eden still thought it an 'exceptionally cordial' interview and hoped the 'impression which the ceremonies in this country since his arrival have made upon him' as well as the 'kindness of the reception accorded to him both officially and by the populace' may have encouraged his 'desire to attempt to make use of his visit to better Anglo-German relations'.[11] On the Sunday, Conwell-Evans and von Blomberg motored down to Sandwich in Kent to visit Waldorf and Nancy Astor at their sixteen-bedroomed Arts and Crafts 'seaside cottage' beside the town's famous golf courses. Stopping en route in Canterbury, the archbishop, fresh from crowning the new king, showed them the cathedral. Conwell-Evans reported to Mount Temple that his charge had been delighted with his reception everywhere, and 'charmed' with the Anglo-German Fellowship.[12] He gave the German a copy of Trevelyan's history of England as a souvenir of his visit.

Return visits by 'influential Englishmen' to Berlin remained Ribbentrop's obsession. He still had Baldwin's name atop a list of those whom he claimed improbably had agreed to come to Germany to meet the Führer that summer. Also included were Inskip, Lord Derby (a former secretary of state for war, ambassador to Paris and racehorse owner), Ribbentrop's whisky supplier Sir Alexander Walker, and (astonishingly) Winston Churchill, whom he still hoped to transform into a 'friend of Germany'.[13] Lord Halifax should be encouraged to visit but only after the others had sweetened the atmosphere by paving the way.

As it turned out, Halifax was the only politician from the list to travel to Germany later that year and he circumvented the German ambassador to do so. Lord Lothian and Conwell-Evans, both anxiously seeing signs of deteriorating Anglo-German relations, went first for further meetings with the Nazi leaders. Before seeing Hitler, they had a 'long and stormy' meeting with Göring on the morning of 4 May. He had declined a translator, so Conwell-Evans had to interpret. Echoing Christie's meeting a few weeks before, he complained at such length about the Spanish Civil War, colonies, communists and the British resistance to any German expansionism that he was late for his lunch with Hitler. Clearly shaken, the duo then met with

Hitler for a similarly long and fraught audience, despite being joined by the affable Schmidt.

This time there would be no coffee. Hitler, in 'one of his less amiable moods' berated them on similar themes to Göring but did still argue for 'better understanding between these two great peoples of similar race, whose cooperation would render the maintenance of security in Europe so much less onerous, and so much less expensive'. As they left, Conwell-Evans remarked upon how Hitler now seemed very embittered against England and Lothian agreed that the situation had become 'both more dangerous and more soluble'. In a report sent to the British prime minister, the dominion prime ministers and the Foreign Office, Lothian argued for concessions to prevent Germany resorting to force with 'terrifying strength, decision and violence'.[14]

Lothian had been quicker to shift his views on Hitler than is generally acknowledged. Maisky recognised this period as a crossroads for the British ambulant amateurs and their National Socialist friends. Having noted Lothian's Germanophilia had faded in late 1936, by the following April he reported how he was now actively suspicious of Germany.[15] Clearly regretting his earlier placatory comments about Hitler, Lothian sent his report to his friend Norman Davis, the president of the US Council on Foreign Relations, asking him to share it confidentially with President Roosevelt. With the conviction of a convert, Lothian now started on his path towards the British embassy in Washington, from where he would influence the US president and his advisers to garner American support for Great Britain's war against Hitler's Germany. Building on his understanding as a prominent appeaser, gained under the auspices of the Fellowship and the guidance of his friend Conwell-Evans, this gave him credible intelligence and, counter-intuitively, unusual authority when briefing the president on the Nazi threat.

The rising distrust in Anglo-German circles caused fracture lines that were hard to ignore. A week after the coronation, Ribbentrop received a letter from Berlin accusing the Fellowship of hostility to National Socialism and 'Jewish sympathies'. Objection had been taken to Conwell-Evans demanding the swastika be taken down at the Ribbentrop dinner and to his recent visit with Lothian to Berlin. He and Tennant hurried round to the embassy to discuss the letter, but the ambassador suggested they 'take no more notice of the affair'.[16] Despite this sangfroid, those close to him agreed this had been when Ribbentrop fell out of love with England and the English, triggered by disappointment with his and his wife's social advancement in London and the realisation his diplomatic mission had failed. Conwell-Evans diagnosed an inferiority complex caused by him being 'treated like a commercial traveller by the British aristocracy' who saw him as a figure of fun.[17] The thin-skinned Joachim and even thinner-skinned Annelies had tired of David Low's cartoons, the public-school pranks, the teasing of their children at school and the snide remarks from society hostesses and gossip columnists. As Ribbentrop's biographer concluded, the 'former Anglophile, the man on whom Hitler had counted to bring home *rapprochement*, suddenly emerged as a violent antagonist of Great Britain'. From now on, he would represent Britain to Hitler as Germany's 'most dangerous enemy' and therefore the 'main obstacle to her ambitions'.[18]

Social niceties apart, the abdication threw Ribbentrop's flawed judgement on Great Britain into sharp relief. Thoroughly misunderstanding the limits put on the monarch by the unwritten constitution, he had been sure the King would never abdicate, and now blamed the turn of events on a Jewish plot. His fantasy of Edward as an English Hitler undermined his credibility as an arbiter of Anglo-German diplomacy. But the new king was quickly followed by a new prime minister in Neville Chamberlain, the arch advocate of his own very particular flavour of appeasement. So ironically, at the point when Ribbentrop finally abandoned his hopes for an English alliance, as the historian Gerhard Weinberg concluded, the constitutional crisis 'helped open rather than close the way to a British approach to Berlin.'[19]

The man who might mitigate the damage done by Ribbentrop was his immediate boss, Konstantin von Neurath. Though denied his trip for the coronation, he was determined to visit London that summer. The British government, now firm in its belief that face-to-face meetings could bridge the choppy waters of international diplomacy, wanted the German foreign minister to propose what concessions Germany needed to guarantee peace in Europe. Von Neurath accepted, only to cancel shortly after, blaming the alleged attack on the German warship *Leipzig* by communist Spanish submarines. Henderson supposed Ribbentrop had forced the cancellation, just as he had blocked von Neurath and Göring joining the coronation. The Chamberlains had been planning a 'cocked hat lunch... with enormous zeal' and Neville regretted the cancellation in speeches at the Albert Hall and in the House of Commons. *The Times* shared the PM's disappointment, noting that it meant the loss of a 'promising opportunity for fruitful discussions of just those Spanish problems and incidents' used as excuses for the cancellation, before reminding its readers that the Simon-Eden visit had gone ahead despite Hitler reintroducing conscription.[20]

Conwell-Evans and Christie were furious. Christie berated Göring that 'much good work had been undone' and von Neurath coming to London might have led to a 'most helpful discussion of all kinds of existing questions and obstacles'.[21] Meanwhile, Conwell-Evans met with Ribbentrop in London, just before he returned to Germany for summer holidays, to insist that the government would be open to proposals, but Ribbentrop petulantly insisted there was no point as the British would just refuse them. An 'evidently somewhat shaken' Conwell-Evans hurried across St James's Park to the Foreign Office to update Vansittart, who at once prepared a memorandum for the prime minister, foreign secretary and Halifax. So now Vansittart – who only two months before had been so damning of the 'ambulant amateurs' – and the Foreign Office were welcoming Conwell-Evans and listening to his intelligence on Germany. Recognising him as 'one of the leading influences' on the Fellowship, Van explained that he was also Ribbentrop's 'principal guide and adviser in this country' and his wise advice to the ever more erratic German ambassador had been both 'sound and persuasive'.[22]

*Sir Robert Vansittart, permanent undersecretary of state for
foreign affairs. As well as oversight of the British Secret Services,
Vansittart had established his own intelligence gathering
service known as 'Van's private detective agency'.*

13

SHARKS, STALIN AND INSPECTOR MORSE

BY THE SUMMER OF 1937, WITH A NEW KING CROWNED, THE trauma of the abdication could finally subside. Neville Chamberlain, the new prime minister, felt supremely confident in his policy of appeasing Germany, backed by an ideologically sympathetic ambassador in Berlin and a compliant Cabinet in Downing Street. Now joining his friend Christie as one of Sir Robert Vansittart's most trusted intelligence assets, Philip Conwell-Evans was equally welcome in both the neoclassical splendour of the British Foreign Office and the austere modernism of its German counterpart. With the membership of the Anglo-German Fellowship (of which he had been full-time secretary since February) rising from 450 to 700 over the year, he was building very satisfactorily diplomatic bridges between the two countries. The Fellowship reported proudly how, during that summer, members of its Council welcomed approximately a thousand German tourists arriving each week by boat at Greenwich Harbour. Meanwhile, hundreds of thousands of British tourists visited Germany, and as one contemporary commentator noted, 'almost without exception they came back with favourable impressions.'[1] The facilities of the DEG clubhouse in Berlin were soon overstretched as it hosted thirteen thousand visitors during the year.

But all was not well at the Chelsea offices. Despite income from subscriptions doubling and ticket sales for events rising by a quarter, the Fellowship was living beyond its means, so its cash reserves halved over the year. Unilever continued to contribute generously but Ernest Tennant's initial success in raising commercial sponsorship had not been sustained and other corporate donations were dwindling. More sinisterly, the Fellowship had attracted unwanted attention from external groups, dragging it into the murky worlds of far-right extremism and state-sponsored espionage.

The first viper in the nest was Elwyn Wright, Conwell-Evans's predecessor as secretary. Even though he had only served in the role for eighteen months, his tenure would taint the organisation's reputation and fuel accusations that it was institutionally pro-Nazi ever after. Wright had taken his redundancy badly, insisting his replacement by Conwell-Evans had been unconstitutional and a false economy. With close links to Germany, including a brother-in-law in the SS, his anti-Semitism was never far below the surface. Claiming that there was a 'grave state of unrest' among the membership, he was frustrated by the Fellowship's equivocal attitude towards the Nazi experiment and urged the 'supine' Council to support the regime against attacks from the British Press.[2] Matters escalated when he sent a letter to Le Blount Kidd, the Fellowship's solicitor, asking if he had any 'Jewish blood'.[3] When challenged on such anti-Semitism by Conwell-Evans, he defended the Nuremberg Laws as a 'stern necessity' in the German government's handling of its Jewish minority.[4]

Cut adrift from the organisation, Wright dropped any pretence at moderation and launched a vendetta against the Council. He had found a deep-pocketed patron in George Pitt-Rivers, who shared his views, and together they assembled a clique of pro-Nazi and anti-Semitic members to escalate their hurt at being marginalised into a battle to wrest control of the organisation from the moderates on the Council. Richard Griffiths, who has chronicled British 'Fellow Travellers of the Right' in a groundbreaking trilogy, identified those 'sharks lurking in the shallows' (many of whom were interned for their views during the Second World War) whose activities have given the Fellowship its 'rather ambiguous status' ever since.[5]

But careful analysis of the organisation's membership and guest lists has found that only about five percent are known to have shared Wright's extreme views. (By comparison, a greater percentage were Old Etonians – albeit with some overlap…) That small but vocal minority of initially enthusiastic members did include some of the nastiest sharks. Captain Billy Luttman-Johnson had founded the January Club to attract middle-class supporters to Mosley's British Union of Fascists. Major General J. F. C. Fuller, the famous military strategist, another friend of Mosley, later controversially attended Hitler's fiftieth birthday celebrations. Major Francis Yeats-Brown, a former British Indian army officer and yoga enthusiast (whose bestselling 1930 memoir, *The Bengal Lancer*, was made into a hugely popular film starring Gary Cooper), was Hitler's favourite British author and returned that admiration with gusto. Vice-Admiral Sir Barry Domvile, the former director of naval intelligence, believed a Jewish-Masonic alliance was overtaking the world and so founded The Link, a populist pro-Nazi group. C. E. Carroll served as the virulently anti-Semitic editor of the *Anglo-German Review*. The most prominent of the female Hitlerites was Margaret Bothamley, secretary of The Link's central London branch, a founder of the Imperial Fascist League and a member of an array of other far-right societies, including the Nordic League, the British People's Party and the Right Club.

This motley crew rallied support for Pitt-Rivers and Wright's campaign to oust Mount Temple, Tennant and Conwell-Evans from their senior positions. They claimed that 'Zionist forces' now controlled the Fellowship while the Council aimed to 'corrupt or crush' National Socialism, had ignored the membership, represented Jewish business interests and exploited undue influence over Ribbentrop as ambassador.[6] Mount Temple tried to calm the situation by inviting Pitt-Rivers for lunch at Broadlands, while maintaining a civil correspondence with Wright well after Conwell-Evans and Tennant had lost patience. His efforts failed and in June the rebels tried to corral the ten percent of the membership needed to call an extraordinary general meeting to change the leadership. Working together, Pitt-Rivers and Wright sent a package of inflammatory correspondence to Ribbentrop outlining their allegations, a fourteen-page diatribe to a DEG official in Germany and – most damagingly – a sycophantic letter in schoolboy German to Joseph Goebbels, the minister of propaganda. But while this campaign damaged the Fellowship's relations with the Germans, and has sullied its historical reputation, the agitators failed to unseat the Council and gradually migrated away to deploy their pro-Nazi and anti-Semitic energies with other organisations that more closely shared their beliefs.

While the Fellowship was being confronted by its far-right membership, it came under more subtle attack. Despite having only a small office and a handful of staff, it had been secretly infiltrated by undercover agents working for the Russians, the British and even the Board of Deputies of British Jews. The Russians got in first. Joseph Stalin, the general secretary of the Communist Party of the USSR, did not share Pitt-Rivers and Wright's conviction the Fellowship was hostile towards National Socialism. He particularly wished to monitor any signs of improving relations between London and Berlin, which in his worst fears, and Hitler's best hopes, might lead to an anti-Communist alliance against Russia. Stalin's secret police, the NKVD, had instigated a programme to recruit young British idealists loyal to the Communist cause and infiltrate them as long-term agents into key institutions within the Establishment. Arnold Deutsch (codenamed OTTO), probably the most successful spy recruiter of the century, led the initiative. His first success had been Kim Philby, whom he recruited on a bench in Regent's Park in 1934. Philby had married a Jewish Austrian communist and, following a stint as a courier for the communists in Vienna, had returned to London looking for a job. As his left-wing politics in Cambridge and Vienna were no secret, his handler had encouraged him to pivot from these youthful enthusiasms to a new persona sympathetic to Nazi Germany. As he recollected, within a few weeks he had 'dropped' his political friends, begun attending functions at the German embassy and joined the Fellowship.[7]

At about the same time, the Fellowship's executive committee had agreed to set up a publicity department staffed by bright young Cambridge graduates. Clever, well connected and socially adept, Philby spoke German and wrote well, so seemed well suited for the job. He had most likely been introduced to the Fellowship by Sir Roger Chance, a journalist friend of his father's, who had found him a previous job as a sub-editor on a magazine and was an enthusiastic member. Employed in the new department in late 1935, Philby had also joined as a member within a few months and attended the Brunswick dinner. His friend and fellow Soviet agent, Guy Burgess, also undertook some paid work for the Fellowship although never joined as a member.

It has been widely assumed in the extensive literature on the Cambridge Spies that for these two Cambridge graduates and novice Soviet agents, joining a supposedly pro-Nazi organisation had been, as one recent study put it, a neat 'somersault in their politics' undertaken in order to bury their communist pasts.[8] While helpful to some extent, this was not their primary motivation – especially if we accept a more nuanced interpretation of the Anglo-German Fellowship as being more Germanophile than pro-Nazi. Their Soviet masters wanted them to penetrate the British Establishment, not dabble with an extremist or eccentric organisation with allegiances to a foreign state and recent enemy. Rather it had been the Fellowship's respectability, its political and diplomatic access and its elitist credentials that attracted these social-climbing intelligence agents and their employers. Philby insisted that joining served as more than just a smokescreen, explaining that any 'overt and covert links' between Britain and Germany would seriously concern the Russian government; so this had marked the beginning of his 'actual work' for the Soviet Union.[9] These were certainly important early steps in the career of what MI5's official historian has called the first of 'the ablest group of British agents ever recruited by a foreign intelligence service'.[10]

By the summer of 1936, Kim Philby had been spending about a week each month in Germany on behalf of the Fellowship. He became absorbed in setting up a new *Anglo-German Trade Gazette*, which never made its first issue after the German authorities switched their funding to the more resolutely pro-Nazi *Anglo-German Review*. Tennant and Mount Temple were nonetheless pleased with his work, and it seems he helped edit the *Monthly Review*. For a young man of twenty-four, he was given significant responsibility and access to the German leadership, including Ribbentrop and Goebbels. Despite later claiming to have found his fellow members 'profoundly repulsive', he enjoyed the Fellowship's social activities, dating and possibly seducing Lady Margaret Vane-Tempest-Stewart, Lord Londonderry's second daughter, whom he met at the Brunswick dinner.[11]

Philby's work for the Fellowship gave him the springboard for his much better remembered later career moves. When his handlers proposed he go to Spain as an aspiring journalist investigating General Franco's Nationalists, the German embassy in London supplied him with credentials, and he was also accredited to *Zeitschrift für Geopolitik*, the journal run by Karl Haushofer, Hess's mentor and a DEG founder. Soon after, *The Times* took him on as a correspondent covering the war.

MI5 had opened its file on the Fellowship several months before Philby joined and kept a close eye on its endeavours right up to the outbreak of war. Inspector Morse, a leading Nazi hunter tasked with monitoring espionage risk among pro-Germans in England, and Superintendent Canning of the Metropolitan Police's Special Branch, were asked to investigate. Their report, dated April 1935 and sent to Guy Liddell, MI5's deputy director of counterespionage, noted that, though sponsored by them, the Fellowship was neither controlled by the National Socialists nor admitted German members. But not until the summer of 1937 did Maxwell Knight, head of MI5's section responsible for monitoring fascists and communists, dispatch agents to visit the Fellowship's Chelsea headquarters. Their quarry was fellow travellers of the right rather than Soviet agents and, crucially, they were late, so missed the opportunity to expose certainly one (and possibly two) of the most dangerous Soviet spies of the twentieth century.

The MI5 agents were impressed by the building, a block of 'modern high-class flats', and estimated the rent at not less than £350 per annum. Having gained access to the office, they noted its six rooms, including a well-furnished visitors' reception room. With a perhaps surprising interest in interior decoration, they admired the 'expensive modern style fittings'.[12] While finding no evidence of illegal behaviour, they grumbled that the Fellowship's activities were 'wholly directed towards making English people friendly towards Germany and not towards making Germans friendly towards England'.[13] This is patently unfair, given its extensive social activities with its German counterparts and the many thousands of German tourists it had welcomed to Britain.

That autumn, Knight arranged for his close friend and trusted agent, Jimmy Dickson (codenamed M/3), to apply for membership and supplied him with the one guinea subscription fee.[14] Dickson promised his spymaster he would actively engage with the Fellowship's activities.[15] As he had not been introduced by an existing member, an interview was arranged at Cranmer Court, where Conwell-Evans explained that there had been earlier attempts by undesirable elements to join with the 'intention of causing friction'. While he passed the interview, Dickson seems an odd choice for the job; a chain-smoking civil servant at the Ministry of Labour, he was a former RAF pilot and sometime fascist with a weak heart who wrote lowbrow thrillers in his spare time.

There is no evidence in the MI5 files of Dickson generating any valuable intelligence and about six months later, Knight infiltrated a more glamorous second agent into the Fellowship. A twenty-six-year-old Austrian divorcée, Friedl Gaertner urgently needed a work permit and a job in London. Her sister, Liesl, a former exotic dancer, had recently married the brother of Stewart Menzies, the deputy head of MI6, who had recommended Friedl to MI5. At their hour-long first meeting the initially sceptical Knight had assessed Friedl, herself a sometime model and cabaret singer, as an 'extremely level-headed and intelligent person' before noting her 'very considerable personal attractiveness'.[16] She would be willing to work for the British security services in England and, with German as her mother tongue, he suggested she join the Nazi party and mix with the German colony in London to monitor its activities. As she objected to his suggestion that her working cover should be as a 'mannequin' (a fashion model), he found her a day job as secretary to his friend Dennis Wheatley, the hugely success-ful thriller writer. Her lascivious male colleagues gave her the codename GELATINE – because they thought her a 'jolly-little-thing'.

Gaertner took to her new career with alacrity. Having befriended Betty Pomeroy, the office secretary at Cranmer Court, she was able to supply Knight with perceptive and balanced first-hand accounts of the Fellowship's inner workings. Frictions were building within the organisation as it faced up to Neville Chamberlain's ultimately calamitous interpretation of appease-ment, apparently unaware it was being watched by intelligence agents and monitored for trustworthiness by its supposed German friends. Infiltrating the Fellowship had been her first undercover assignment for MI5 and proved her mettle as an agent, just as it had for Kim Philby working for the Russian intelligence services.

Lord Halifax, British Cabinet minister, meeting Adolf Hitler at the Berghof near Berchtesgaden following his private visit to the Berlin Hunting Exhibition, 20 November 1937. German foreign minister Konstantin von Neurath can be seen to the right of Hitler.

14

SENDING A CURATE
TO VISIT A TIGER

ARRIVING IN BERLIN IN MAY 1937 TO TAKE UP HIS POST AS Britain's new ambassador, Nevile Henderson had learned of plans to hold an international hunting exhibition in the city later that year. Under sponsorship from Hermann Göring, who had added *Reichsjägermeister* (Game Warden of the Reich) to his many roles in the National Socialist state, other European countries were being encouraged to put together exhibits. The new ambassador, also a field sports enthusiast, had been shocked no plans had been made for his country to be represented given how many Germans and Britons shared that passion.

That September, Henderson controversially attended the annual National Socialist *Parteitag* (the 'Rally of Labour') at Nuremberg. He did so without the blessing of London, breaking the precedent set by his predecessor and embarrassing his French and US counterparts, who had planned to boycott what promised to be an ever-more extravagant showcase of Nazi propaganda. The experience enthralled him; he reported rapturously to the Foreign Office that the 'effect, both solemn and beautiful, was something like being inside a cathedral of ice' and that the serried ranks of marching standard bearers and SA men had looked 'incredibly beautiful'.[1] Though delighted by his gift of a bowl of customised SS china filled with sweets, he had been disappointed not to meet the Mitford sisters. He did meet Göring, who repeated his worry, earlier shared with Christie, about how the Germans increasingly perceived Britain as an enemy. Together, they concocted a plan for Lord Halifax to come over for the International Hunting Exhibition.

At six foot five, Halifax, the former viceroy to India, now lord president of the Council and leader of the House of Lords, was tall enough, senior enough and aristocratic enough to impress the Nazis as the epitome of the Anglo-Saxon sangfroid they so admired. Intelligent and unflappable, Chamberlain trusted him, and he was respected by his fellow Cabinet members. Thought to have done a good job in the negotiations following the Rhineland crisis, it was suggested his success at dealing with Mahatma Gandhi had equipped him to handle another troublesome vegetarian in the shape of Adolf Hitler. Most importantly, he was an excellent huntsman and a fearless master of the Middleton Foxhounds in his beloved North Yorkshire, despite having only one functioning arm.

To give it the least degree of British governmental blessing, the Foreign Office insisted the visit be classed as entirely private and unofficial, a pretext Lloyd George called 'innocent, though amusing and rather ridiculous'.[2] Diplomatic sensitivities were heightened because the Duke and Duchess of Windsor had the month before undertaken their ersatz state visit to Germany. Prince Loewenstein, president of the German Hunting Association, duly extended the invitation through the good offices of *The Field*, then, as now, a periodical favoured by the hunting and shooting set rather than an obvious conduit for diplomatic summits. A meeting between the master of foxhounds and the animal-loving Führer had been admitted as a possibility, but only if both men's busy schedules allowed.

Something similarly vague had been floated to the press when Lloyd George made his pilgrimage to Berchtesgaden, but this time the absurd cover story crumbled almost at once. Contrary to post-war mythologising, as Halifax's most recent biographer has shown, Eden and his Foreign Office, though uncomfortable, were privy to the decision for him to go. But while Ribbentrop and the Fellowship had helped to organise the earlier British visits, this time von Neurath and Henderson took charge and, at the Foreign Office's specific request, kept Ribbentrop in the dark.

Eden gave Halifax firm guidance that he should insist on Germany respecting Austria and Czechoslovakia's democratic independence, just as Christie had back in May. Of course, neither men nor their advisers knew of how, only a fortnight before, Hitler had unveiled his strategy to a tight group of senior colleagues at the secret and pivotal 5 November Hossbach Conference. This meeting had included von Neurath, the war minister von

Blomberg, Göring as head of the Luftwaffe, and his counterparts from the army and the navy. At the meeting, Hitler promised to subjugate Austria and Czechoslovakia in short order, with force if necessary. He ordered his military commanders (who had arrived thinking the meeting had been called to discuss steel allocations) to prepare for a general war against Germany's 'hate-inspired antagonists', France and England, within five years. For this, they were neither prepared nor confident of success.

On the evening of Thursday, 18 November 1937, the British having failed to move the meeting to Berlin, Halifax and Ivone Kirkpatrick, the first secretary at the embassy, accompanied by von Neurath and Paul-Otto Schmidt, the foreign ministry interpreter, travelled overnight to Bavaria on Hitler's special train. They were comfortably accommodated in two private coaches, each including a sitting room, sleeping compartments and a bathroom. Overly attentive staff plied their guests with whisky and soda every half-hour. As they arrived at the snow-covered Berghof, Hitler waited at the top of the flight of steps to receive Halifax (now wearing two sweaters, to the amusement of Eva Braun and her friends). This first encounter between the two statesmen had been ill-fated from the outset, when Halifax, by his own admission, mistook the brown-coated, black-trousered, silk-stockinged Hitler for a footman. He had been about to hand his hat and coat to the diminutive dictator until hastily corrected by von Neurath hissing '*Der Führer, Der Führer*' into his ear.

The contrast with Lloyd George's arrival is stark; then, a beaming Führer had bounded down the steps to greet his revered guest. But in the fourteen months separating the two visits, political and diplomatic sands had shifted and the persona of the two British politicians could hardly have been more different. The three-hour meeting with the patrician Halifax would be tense and awkward. Their host, according to Kirkpatrick, was in such a 'peevish' mood that the conversation was 'distinctly sticky'. Halifax opened their private talk by touching on the taboos Lloyd George had avoided – the mistreatment by the Nazis of the Church, the Jews and the trade unions. In response, Hitler grumbled about his difficulties with the democracies who had rebuffed his offers of disarmament and attacks on him by English newspapers and MPs. His mood worsened when Halifax pointed out his repeatedly ignoring treaty obligations meant Great Britain and France were unsurprisingly wary of his overtures. Halifax then veered off Eden's brief by suggesting Austria and Czechoslovakia might come under German influence so long as the process were peaceful. He also hinted that colonies might be restored if his host could only play the good European. Unlike with Lloyd George, Hitler showed no interest in disarmament and seemed cynical and non-committal when Halifax ended the talk by hoping for direct Anglo-German negotiations.

Von Neurath and Kirkpatrick (whose memoirs provide a wry account of the trip) then rejoined them in the 'hideous' dining room for a 'rather indifferent meat lunch' albeit washed down with plenty of wine. The conversation opened with an irritable exchange about weather forecasts and the discomforts of flying, following which the hunting exhibition in Berlin was mentioned. This prompted Hitler to assert there was no point in shooting game: 'You go out armed with a highly perfected modern weapon and without risk to yourself to kill a defenceless animal.' The party having repaired to the huge sitting room for coffee, two SS men demonstrated the famous giant window, but conversation proved no easier. When India came up, Hitler suggested to its former viceroy that Britain's challenges on the subcontinent could be quickly remedied by first shooting Gandhi and then continuing to execute senior members of the Congress Party until they fell into line. At this, Halifax gazed at his host with a 'mixture of astonishment, repugnance and compassion'. Following a stiff and awkward pause for formal photographs by Heinrich Hoffmann, Hitler's court photographer, the visitors returned to the special train where, over a restorative cup of tea, an embarrassed von Neurath excused his master on the grounds he had been 'tired and out of sorts' but promised the meeting had still been useful. Tellingly, he emphasised how 'excellent' it had been to bring Hitler in 'contact with the outside world'.[3]

Having stopped the train to dine in Munich, they travelled overnight to reach Berlin in time for breakfast. Halifax then enjoyed a far more congenial lunch with General Göring at his Prussian estate, served by footmen dressed in eighteenth-century liveries. The host went out of his way to charm his guest and the still firmly bowler-hatted Halifax, like other British visitors before him, had been mostly amused by the absurd Göring, whom he characterised as a 'modern Robin Hood… a composite impression of film-star, gangster, great landowner interested in property, prime minister, party-manager, [and] head keeper at Chatsworth'.[4]

That evening at a dinner hosted at the British embassy, this better atmosphere prevailed as Halifax was courted by the more moderate and more civilised Nazi leaders, including von Blomberg, who had charmed London at the coronation, and Hjalmar Schacht, the Anglophile Reichsbank president, who pressed the case for returning German colonies. A similarly congenial tea party at the embassy followed with Joseph Goebbels whom, as had Vansittart, Halifax admitted to liking. When the minister for propaganda complained about the Berlin correspondents of British newspapers goading Hitler and his administration, Halifax pointed out they had been stationed in Berlin for many years without prior complaint. With a 'shameless and charming smile', Goebbels explained: 'We did not complain in the past because Germany was not rearmed… we complain now because we are strong enough to do so.'[5] Reminding his tea companion that Britain maintained a free press, Halifax nonetheless promised to have a quiet word.

Halifax wrote up his notes on the train back to London and briefed the Cabinet the next day, concluding that Hitler was focused on the return of colonies and did not want war. With the benefit of hindsight (especially about the Hossbach Conference) and given his intelligence and experience, this seems astonishingly naïve. Conwell-Evans thought both sides had misread each other, with Hitler interpreting friendliness as an 'expression of British timidity'.[6] Kirkpatrick admitted it failed to alter events but argued the embassy had benefitted from the relatively rare opportunity to meet Hitler and his senior paladins.[7] Given the ease and frequency with which Conwell-Evans, Tennant and Christie had accessed the National Socialist inner sanctum, this admission is startling.

The meeting had achieved little as an exercise in diplomacy but did give the future foreign secretary a direct view into the belly of the beast. This had been 'ambulant amateurism' at its most amateur – neither an official visit properly organised through the foreign offices and embassies, nor an unofficial, plausibly deniable meeting arranged through the ostensibly neutral offices of the Anglo-German Fellowship. Sympathetic biographers have characterised it as the 'high-water mark' of Halifax's appeasement, a time when he had been 'badly taken in' by the senior Nazis, but explained, 'Nothing in Edward's upbringing had equipped him with the instinct to fathom the true wickedness of these men.'[8] Churchill later struggled to imagine 'two personalities less able to comprehend one another' than the 'High Church Yorkshire aristocrat and ardent peace-lover... and the... demon-genius sprung from the abyss of poverty, inflamed by defeat, devoured by hatred and revenge, and convulsed by his design to make the German race masters of Europe or maybe the world'.[9] Lloyd George felt similarly sceptical, comparing the enterprise to 'sending a curate to visit a tiger'.[10] Schmidt noted that Hitler also favoured a clerical allusion, dubbing his visitor the 'English parson'.[11]

Halifax turned hawkish over Germany faster than often credited and soon his views diverged from Chamberlain's line of unquestioning appeasement.[12] Philip Conwell-Evans and Grahame Christie were guiding Halifax on this change of tack to an extent that is often underappreciated by commentators. Beyond the black comedy and chilling insights into Hitler's mindset, the contrast between his encounter with the 'Holy Fox' in November 1937 and that with the 'Old Goat' the previous autumn serves at least three purposes. It maps the evolution of Hitler's disillusion with Britain; it illuminates the personality types needed to charm and decipher Germany's dictator face to face; and it convinced Halifax of the need for his government to find better counsel, beyond its embassy and Foreign Office, on how to handle this monstrous regime. Might the ambulant amateurs be useful after all?

The prime minister, whose ability to misconstrue Hitler would define the next eighteen months, had nonetheless been pleased with the visit. He told his sister it had gone well, particularly as Halifax had been able to invite von Neurath to revive his aborted visit to London. The Fellowship, despite having had no role in its clumsy choreography, publicly shared this enthusiasm. The *Monthly Journal* reported that its members had welcomed the visit and that the German public had seen it as a 'promising first contact' between the two governments.[13] The optimism of the country sports set was even less guarded; in a Christmas message to readers, *Country Life* credited the editor of its rival *The Field* for contributing to the 'now historic rapprochement' between England and Germany through the visit, which should therefore 'enable thorny problems to be approached in a hopeful atmosphere'.[14] Sadly, their confidence that Europe had become a safer place was misguided. Great Britain had missed its chance to civilise Hitler; he had left the diplomatic room, fed up with not being taken seriously by London, and Neville Chamberlain had disastrously failed to spot his leaving.

Less than two weeks later, the Anglo-German Fellowship welcomed nearly five hundred guests, with Lord Halifax as the keynote speaker, to the Grosvenor House hotel for its second annual Christmas dinner. As this was his first engagement with the organisation and he was the most senior government figure to attend a dinner, this represented a coup for the Fellowship. His speech was especially newsworthy as he had been Chamberlain's emissary to Germany and would replace Eden as foreign secretary within two months. The chief German guest was the Duke of Coburg, and he was joined by Ribbentrop, only two months from promotion to foreign minister, and Vansittart, in his last month as permanent undersecretary, who brought his wife. Mount Temple praised the duke's work with war veterans before reporting that the membership had reached seven hundred, including citizens from 'all parts of the British Isles', an emphasis presumably designed to mitigate any suggestion it operated as a metropolitan elite.[15] Both the *Manchester Guardian* and *The Times* reported the knowing laughter when Halifax wryly reminded his audience that his Germany trip had been to visit the hunting exhibition. He warmly praised the work of his hosts in promoting 'understanding between nations';[16] photographs of the evening show him relaxed and smiling, in contrast to his awkward hauteur in Germany.

Ribbentrop claimed credit for the visit on behalf of the sister societies, on the grounds they had created a better atmosphere in Anglo-German relations, despite he and they having been excluded from the arrangements. The German embassy in London reported to Berlin that the dinner had been a success and that the press had covered it satisfactorily. Halifax's enthusiasm for the Fellowship's mission survived the dinner; he wrote with evident sincerity to Conwell-Evans that it would have a 'good effect' and he had been glad to contribute.[17] Now the Fellowship had the ear of the new British foreign secretary, and the increasingly professional amateurs could come to the aid of the struggling amateur professionals. The Fellowship was ready to fill the vacuum in Anglo-German diplomatic relations that dated back to the early part of the decade. The chairman and Council proudly reported to the membership that nearly seventy members of both Houses of Parliament had now joined, before sending traditional festive greetings and hoping 1938 would be witness to 'great progress along the road to a permanent friendship between Great Britain and Germany'.[18]

*Enthusiastic crowds greet Adolf Hitler as he arrives
in Praterstrasse in Vienna, March 1938.*

15

CLEARING THE DECKS

On New Year's Day 1938, Sir Robert Vansittart relin-
quished his post as permanent undersecretary after eight years as head
of the Foreign Office. Having refused to vacate his well-appointed office
next to the foreign secretary, he had been given the newly created and
grand-sounding title of 'chief diplomatic adviser to the government' and
created a Knight Grand Cross of the Order of the Bath (GCB) but stripped
of executive authority. This would be the first step of the process which
Conwell-Evans ominously labelled 'clearing the decks', whereby Neville
Chamberlain rearranged his team of close advisers to marginalise and
isolate those opponents to appeasement within his government and civil
service.[1] Winston Churchill was particularly exercised about Van being
'kicked upstairs', telling Sir Eric Phipps, now the ambassador in Paris, that
it would antagonise the French and be 'represented as a victory for the
pro-Germans in England'.[2] Van's replacement was to be Alec Cadogan,
who had just returned as the well-respected ambassador from China to
be a calming and efficient successor to the volatile, emotional and often
provocative Vansittart. An effortlessly patrician Old Etonian, he had, like
Van and Tennant, excelled at school and Oxford, served at the Paris peace
talks and later worked well with Eden as foreign secretary, urging him and
Vansittart to revise the Treaty of Versailles.

The British prime minister increasingly relied on Sir Horace Wilson, his
closest adviser and 'only real friend', for foreign policy advice.[3] The epitome
of a career civil servant, Wilson had held the vague and misleading title
of 'chief industrial adviser' throughout the thirties. He had been seconded
to the Treasury for service with the prime minister in 1935 and would
be promoted to permanent secretary of the Treasury, and so head of the

entire British civil service, four years later. Cut from quite different cloth to the patrician Vansittart and Cadogan, Wilson was the gifted son of a furniture dealer and a boarding house landlady. He had attended neither public school nor Oxbridge but worked his way up from boy clerk, taking a night school degree at the London School of Economics. Serious, intelligent and diligent, he had wide experience of government, finance, industry and economics but, disastrously, had no knowledge of diplomacy, international relations or Germany.

Both knighted for their services, Wilson and Vansittart had reached the pinnacle of Britain's internationally respected civil service and jealously guarded their offices, located right beside their masters'. But there the similarities end. Vansittart was a multilingual playwright and poet, charming, highly strung and very rich. He despised Wilson, who was modest, controlled, reserved and quiet. While Van had been the arch anti-appeaser for years, Wilson would be the architect of Chamberlain's particular and disastrous recipe for appeasement. The former's star waned as the latter's rose; recognising his unique hold over the prime minister, Conwell-Evans, Christie and Tennant determined to develop some influence over Wilson to buttress their close links with Vansittart and Halifax.

Thus, the see-saw of diplomacy tipped as the intelligent British critics of Germany lost influence to the doves while in Berlin, in horrible symmetry, the hawks were tightening control and fuelling Adolf Hitler's distrust for Great Britain, which would soon harden into loathing. The Führer had been getting his own ship combat-ready by removing any 'obstacles to war' within his diplomatic and military leadership.[4] Ribbentrop, still bitter at being excluded from the Halifax summit, had sent a painstakingly crafted, disingenuous and absurdly misleading memorandum to Hitler, signalling the changing fortunes of Anglo-German relations. This served as both his letter of resignation as ambassador, the role he now loathed, and job application for the appointment he most craved – foreign minister of the Third Reich. He now claimed Britain and France would never allow German expansion in Eastern and Central Europe and would fight unless outgunned by Germany and her allies. Chamberlain's appeasement symbolised the perfidious British playing for time while Halifax's visit had been an intelligence gathering exercise. Skilfully, he used Edward VIII's truncated reign both as justification for his earlier misguided confidence that he could secure an alliance and to excuse his abject failure to do so following the abdication. The King, he insisted, had been forced to abdicate because he had refused to co-operate in an anti-German policy, while Vansittart, Germany's 'toughest opponent', had in fact been promoted such that England should now be considered Germany's 'most dangerous enemy'.[5]

The full absurdity of this interpretation is clear from the deliberations of the British Cabinet Foreign Policy Committee, which had been set up following the Rhineland crisis. Now convened to debrief on Halifax's fraught encounter with Hitler, this was chaired by the prime minister, with senior Cabinet ministers joined by Vansittart, Wilson, Cadogan and (most unusually) the ambassador to Berlin. Far from preparing for war, it was exploring restoring German former colonies in return for her rejoining the League of Nations and agreeing to abolish bombing aeroplanes. In a refrain soon to become the leitmotif of his ambassadorship, Henderson begged his colleagues not to provoke Hitler and to put any suggestions only in the most tentative way. Meanwhile, Christie reported to Vansittart that the German foreign ministry had lost its last shreds of independence. A foreign policy split was widening among the Nazi leaders, with the moderates – von Neurath, von Blomberg and Göring – still favouring an understanding with Britain, while the radicals – Himmler, Goebbels, Rosenberg and Ribbentrop – wanted to 'go the whole hog' with Italy and Japan.[6] The Führer leaned towards the latter camp.

Three of the seven attendees at the Hossbach Conference had expressed doubts about the wisdom of Hitler's ambitions for hegemony in Continental Europe back in November 1937. Von Neurath, the foreign minister, had finally persuaded Hitler to accept his resignation and Ribbentrop had been appointed to succeed him in early February. Christie reported that this had been met with widespread surprise, even to Ribbentrop himself, who had been out of favour with his beloved Führer since the awkward Halifax meeting. The second sceptic, General Werner von Blomberg, who had so charmed his London hosts at the coronation, was seen internationally as a calming presence among the Nazis. His removal had been engineered around a scandal. Hitler and Göring had served as witnesses at his wedding to a woman twenty-five years his junior whose humble origins had already raised eyebrows among his class-conscious fellow officers. When the Berlin police unearthed the bride's police record for prostitution and theft in a massage parlour, the unlucky field marshal was forced to resign after forty years' loyal service to the German army. General Werner von Fritsch, the third of the Hossbach sceptics, had opposed military aggression against Austria and Czechoslovakia and struggled to protect the army from Nazi interference. As commander-in-chief of the army since 1933, he was an obvious candidate to succeed von Blomberg but had himself been forced to resign on trumped-up homosexuality charges. Hitler then made himself both war minister and supreme commander of the armed forces, promoted Göring to general field marshal in the army as a sop for being denied the war ministry, and appointed committed Nazis to other senior military posts. Now with direct control of the key offices of state, Hitler held his last ever cabinet meeting in early February. He had tightened his grip over the soldiers and the diplomats who had sneered at the low-born Austrian corporal and jealously defended their independence from the Nazi Party. His dictatorship was nearly complete.

But all was not quite lost for the forces of moderation within the foreign ministry. Despite initial fears he would order a purge of the conservatives and replace them with his motley band of acolytes, Ribbentrop was persuaded to retain many of the veteran civil servants who had served the Weimar Republic. Crucially, Ribbentrop appointed Conwell-Evans's friend Erich Kordt, on whom he depended to polish his diplomatic communiqués, as his *chef de bureau*. This kept Kordt at the heart of German foreign policy-making, with impeccable access to both foreign minister and chancellor. Anxious to keep a trusted ally in Carlton House Terrace, Erich arranged for his brother Theodor to replace him as counsellor in London. This secured the family's direct, secure and covert channel of communication with the British government through Conwell-Evans and Vansittart. Though now based in Berlin, Erich's status as a founder of the DEG offered plausible cover to continue his regular meetings with the Fellowship's secretary. The brothers enlisted their cousin Susanne Simonis, a reporter for *Deutsche Allgemeine Zeitung*, to shuttle between Berlin and London with key messages, using her journalistic credentials as cover.

With his private network of family and friends secure in Berlin and London, Erich set about bolstering the moderates in the now Nazi-dominated foreign ministry with three critical appointments. He encouraged the nomination of Ernst Freiherr von Weizsäcker as state secretary – so

Alec Cadogan's opposite number. A protégé of von Neurath, von Weizsäcker was another old school diplomat and not yet a Party member. Paul-Otto Schmidt, who had translated during Lloyd George and Halifax's visits and also sympathised with the opposition to Hitler, was assigned as the Führer's personal interpreter, while Herbert von Dirksen was appointed to succeed Ribbentrop as ambassador to London.

Notwithstanding this new cast list in the Wilhelmstrasse, the Fellowship leaders continued to cultivate their unique (albeit by now strained) friendship with the promoted Ribbentrop, while strengthening their bonds with his far-from-loyal senior staff. Critically, Christie still nurtured his decades-long rapport with Hermann Göring who, though denied the war ministry and ceding influence to the despised new foreign minister, stubbornly kept a hand in German foreign policy. The British security services particularly valued Christie's intelligence as they lacked any direct access to Göring, who was now reported as better inclined towards Great Britain and urging Ribbentrop to be more 'forthcoming'.[7] Having failed to bring him over for the coronation, a plan had been developed for Lord Derby, the renowned horse owner, former war minister and ambassador to Paris, to invite Göring to the Grand National at Aintree in March. Perennially popular in Germany, the famous horse race offered sporting cover for a private visit akin to Halifax's to Berlin for the hunting exhibition. In parallel, the Jockey Club planned to charter a ship to bring parties of German racing fans to Liverpool. Such an excursion to England, led by the new field marshal, might break the diplomatic ice and neutralise Ribbentrop's toxic influence.

The London diplomatic staff was further revised later that month when an emotional Anthony Eden, frustrated at being sidelined by the prime minister and opposed to craven pandering of the dictators, resigned as foreign secretary. His replacement was his deputy, the unflappable Lord Halifax, who (for the moment) remained dependably loyal to the prime minister and his flavour of appeasement. Alec Cadogan would support him as permanent secretary and Oliver Harvey as principal private secretary. Cadogan shared many of Van's suspicions of the rising threat from Germany but interpreted his role on lines more pragmatic and realpolitik, all of which he recorded in his unauthorised diary. Harvey had served devotedly as Eden's private secretary and did so for his successor also, albeit without the same rapport. Penned by a convinced anti-appeaser, Harvey's diaries complement Cadogan's in offering piercing insight into the conflicts prevailing between the Foreign Office and Downing Street. The personalities of the suave, upper-class, internationalist Old Etonians at the Foreign Office – Halifax, Vansittart and Cadogan – were in stark contrast with the doggedly two-man clique in Downing Street – Chamberlain and Wilson, business-like, financially literate, expert managers, but also provincial and narrow-minded. Here we can see the crux of the tensions between the two power bases struggling for control over Britain's foreign policy.

Christie exposed the German government's true intentions when he reported on a secret lecture given by Göring on 8 February to a group of senior Luftwaffe, army and war ministry officials. In chilling detail, he laid out the Third Reich's international ambitions and the ruthless tactics needed to implement them. Hitler now had the incorporation of his mother country into a greater Germany – *Anschluss* – on the top of his wish list. A month earlier, Christie had reported rumours of a forthcoming putsch, which would be positioned as the spontaneous wish of the local populace.[8] It had been hoped this would mollify their nervous Italian neighbours for whom an independent Austria had served as a buffer against an expansionist Germany. As the German army was not yet ready to attack Britain or France, the *Anschluss* would be followed by the *Eroberung* (conquest) of Czechoslovakia with an early blitzkrieg (lightning war), following which Hungary and the Balkan states would naturally come under Germany's economic control. Göring remained convinced that by deploying overwhelming air power, it would be possible to 'bring Czechoslovakia completely to its knees' before the 'slow-moving western democracies' had a chance to mobilise their forces. German mechanised land forces would then advance across the Austro-Czech frontier and reach Prague, followed by the infantry in large numbers.

Christie noted how the airmen and the economists had applauded this grim plan while the soldiers, who knew how ill-prepared Germany was for a protracted war, had been less enthusiastic. Her economy was so fragile that unless industrial resources and raw materials could be commandeered by geographical expansion, Göring's four-year plan seemed unlikely to work. The enormous appetites of rearmament had led to critical shortages of iron, steel, rubber, aviation fuel and tungsten and the previous autumn's poor harvest meant food was in short supply. Tennant had come to the same conclusion, reporting to Mount Temple that an increase of just five percent in demand for butter, meat, eggs, bread and milk would trigger national shortages. Consequently, Christie urged the British government to engage with the reasonable elements in the country to support those army leaders trying to prevent Germany heading into a disastrous war.[9]

In early March 1938, Joachim and Annelies Ribbentrop returned grudgingly on the Nord Express for a three-day visit to bid their formal goodbyes in London. What should have been a last hurrah quickly turned to debacle. Tensions had been building between Germany and Austria following a fraught meeting at Berchtesgaden between Hitler and Kurt Schuschnigg, the Austrian chancellor. Hitler had bullied his fellow dictator to promote Austrian Nazis to critical cabinet posts. This was especially difficult med-icine for Schuschnigg to swallow given that it was Austrian Nazis who had murdered the previous chancellor, Engelbert Dollfuss, only two years before. Desperate to preserve his country's independence and with Nazis fomenting trouble on the streets of Vienna, Schuschnigg had called a snap referendum on the question of independence to be held that Sunday. Fearing a popular vote in favour of independence would thwart his dream of a Greater Germany, Hitler was now incensed.

Apparently unaware of the drama unfolding back home, the Ribbentrops pulled into Victoria Station to be greeted by a large contingent of Metropolitan Police, as protestors had gathered in central London to demand the release from prison of prominent critics of the Nazi regime. Mounted police were stationed outside the German embassy, while officers patrolled the nearby Duke of York steps, the Mall and Piccadilly. Arriving to meet Halifax and Cadogan at the Foreign Office, Ribbentrop was initially flattered to see a crowd gathered outside. Assuming them friendly, he raised his arm in salute only to be heckled with shouts of 'Ribbentrop get out' and 'Release Niemöller'.[10]

That night, the departing ambassador and his wife hosted a huge recep-tion at the embassy to say farewell to the British government, London's *corps diplomatique* and their other friends in the country. Despite the evident failings of his ambassadorship, most of those who had attended his house-warming party only ten months before now returned to enjoy more excellent champagne at Carlton House Terrace. Presumably now more out of duty rather than affection for their hosts, this included the Chamberlains, many of the Cabinet, the British Legion leadership and an extensive contingent from the Anglo-German Fellowship.

The next day the prime minister and his wife treated the Ribbentrops to a farewell lunch at 10 Downing Street. They had gathered prominent politicians and their wives, including the Halifaxes, Hoares, Simons, Inskips, Londonderrys, Churchills and Cadogans, to join the celebration. The already awkward lunch descended into near farce over the coffee. Chamberlain and Halifax had spent twenty minutes urging their guest to promote better mutual understanding and therefore peace, when a Foreign Office messenger arrived with telegrams for Cadogan. Hitler had issued an ultimatum demanding Schuschnigg's resignation and the cancellation of the plebiscite, while German troop movements had been reported on the Austrian border. As the party broke up in disarray, Winston Churchill took his leave of Frau Ribbentrop with an amiable wish for friendship between England and Germany, to which she acidly replied, 'Be careful you don't spoil it.'[11]

Having sent her back to the embassy, Ribbentrop was taken down to be berated in the prime minister's study. But as neither he nor his ministry had been briefed on the enterprise, he was as bewildered as his hosts and intensely embarrassed. Halifax visited Ribbentrop for tea that afternoon and found him 'frankly mystified' by the reports from the Continent and unable to accept Hitler might have acted without consulting his foreign ministry. Halifax reiterated that Germany should avoid any 'exhibition of naked force' and not try to replicate the circumstances with Czechoslovakia.[12] But such warnings had no effect; Chamberlain later concluded that Ribbentrop remained 'so stupid, so shallow, so self centred and self satisfied, so totally devoid of intellectual capacity that he never seems to take in what is said to him'.[13]

Just before dawn the next morning, another Saturday, German troops rumbled into Austria in a blatant breach of the Treaty of Versailles, their tanks decorated with greenery and decked with German and Austrian flags. The border posts were open and they faced no resistance, but progress fell short of Teutonic efficiency. Fuel shortages, worsened by icy conditions, resulted in most of the tanks breaking down and blocking the narrow roads, while a scarcity of maps meant the commanders had to rely on Baedeker tourist guides to find their way to Vienna. After delays, Hitler set off on Saturday afternoon in a six-wheeled, open-topped Mercedes-Benz followed by senior Nazis in a fleet of staff cars for the journey from Munich to Vienna, his first visit in twenty-four years to the country of his birth. Along the way, a visibly emotional Führer stopped at his birthplace, revisited his childhood home and laid a wreath on his parents' graves. In scenes reminiscent of the Rhineland two years before, delighted and often hysterical crowds of proudly bemedalled Great War veterans, women bearing flowers and small children waving flags greeted the invading Germans as they progressed slowly past houses draped with swastikas to the sounds of pealing church bells and village bands. The journalist George Ward Price joined Hitler's entourage and secured an interview with the triumphant Führer. When the party stopped overnight in Linz, having been welcomed by a crowd of 100,000, he was given first use of the establishment's only telephone so that *Daily Mail* readers could read the story first-hand. Back in London, the startled Cabinet met in emergency session and the prime minister was furious that his escape to Chequers for the weekend had been delayed.

The Führer's caravan, escorted by thirteen police cars, finally arrived in Vienna as hundreds of Luftwaffe fighter planes droned overhead, to be welcomed by vast crowds chanting *Sieg Heil*, cheering and screaming with delight. The next day, half a million people listened to their new leader's address from the balcony of the Imperial Palace in the heart of Vienna. So rapturous had been the welcome for the Germans, Hitler decided to incorporate Austria immediately as a province of the Third Reich rather than establishing it as a protectorate as planned. Now 75 million German-speaking people were united in one nation.

While, to Chamberlain's relief, not a shot had been fired to effect the long-awaited *Anschluss*, its ugly side quickly emerged. Heinrich Himmler orchestrated a hideous campaign of persecution by German storm troopers and local Nazis against Austrian Jews. Jewish shops were looted. Young and old were brutally humiliated, with men stripped naked and forced to clean the streets with acid while elderly Jewish ladies were made to climb into trees and impersonate birds. One hundred thousand Jews fled Vienna by any means available. Many were pulled off the few packed trains leaving the stations before they reached the Czech border while others attempting to escape in vehicles or on foot blocked the roads to

Prague. Passports were destroyed and assets confiscated. Many Viennese Jews resorted to suicide.

Yet again Hitler's shrewd – or maybe just lucky – timing mitigated the expected diplomatic protests. Racked by industrial disputes and domestic political instability, France had no sitting prime minister as the government had collapsed two days before. In the House of Lords, the Archbishop of Canterbury had risen to thank Hitler for 'preserving Austria from a civil war'.[14] The US authorities were content.

Ernest Tennant remained sympathetic to the cause of a Greater Germany, but the Fellowship's Council felt alarmed enough to write to Ribbentrop criticising the German government's action. Christie was less convinced, predicting that the invasion of Austria would be only 'one small step toward other and bigger events'.[15] All in all, despite mild diplomatic protests and some alarmed press reports, as Conwell-Evans later glumly concluded, 'Britain, France and Italy remained passive. Austria ceased to exist.'[16]

Ribbentrop was unhappy. Hitler had ordered him to remain at the embassy in London, where he had to rely on the BBC to keep him abreast of events, stoking his paranoia about Hitler excluding him from Germany's greatest foreign adventure to date, and of losing out to Party rivals, especially Göring. Adding further insult, Hitler had recalled von Neurath from retirement to provide a calming influence on his fellow diplomats, making Ribbentrop look ever more ridiculous and feeding what the contemporary journalist Leonard Mosley called his 'jumbled mass of tortured frustrations, of imagined snubs and rebuffs, all of them floating like sores in his brain and turning him into perhaps the most dangerous man in Europe today'.[17]

The impact of *Anschluss* had been barely absorbed when, in May 1938, rumours reached Prague, Paris and London of German troops massing on the border of Czechoslovakia. Created twenty years earlier from fragments of the Austro-Hungarian Empire, Chamberlain's 'far away country' was a multi-ethnic state with a land mass slightly larger than England. Germany bordered it to the west and north, Austria to its south and Poland, Hungary and Romania to its east. Though small, as the only surviving democracy in Central Europe, backed by much cherished guarantees from France and Russia, its very existence infuriated Hitler, whose visceral loathing of the Czechs dated back to childhood. As the industrial workshop of the old empire, noted for its manufacture of cars, trams, aircraft, ships and weapons (particularly the famous Skoda works, whose armaments production in 1938 exceeded all of Britain's), it was enticing both to Hitler in his search for *lebensraum* and to Göring hunting industrial assets. The absorption of Austria into the Third Reich had alarmed the majority of Czechs and inspired their German-speaking minority. With their frontier with Greater Germany lengthened, now they were vulnerable on three sides and their fortifications facing Germany largely redundant.

Three million *Sudetendeutsche*, about a fifth of the country's population, formed the majority in the region bordered by Germany and Austria known as the Sudetenland. Friction between the two communities had been long-standing as the Czechs had suffered domination from Vienna under the Habsburg yoke for three hundred years, while the aspirational German speakers denigrated their Slav neighbours. Many Czechs had deserted to fight alongside the victorious Allies in the Great War while their German-speaking neighbours joined the vanquished. Systematically excluded by the Czech majority from government and commercial opportunities, the Sudetens had also suffered disproportionately from unemployment, so many British were sympathetic to their cause, including the government, Churchill and Christie.

On 13 May 1938, Christie brought Konrad Henlein – the half-German, half-Czech leader of the Sudeten German Party in Czechoslovakia (SdP) – to London, where the British government and press warmly welcomed him. It had been widely hoped this charming, mild-mannered former gymnastics teacher might offer a civilising influence on Hitler's ambitions. Christie took him to lunch with Winston Churchill at his Victoria flat, where they were joined by Archibald Sinclair, the Liberal leader, and Professor Lindemann, Churchill's scientific adviser. Writing afterwards to thank him for lunch, Christie flattered their host, stating that Henlein thought he represented 'the *real* strength of the British' in stark contrast to 'those wretched defeatists whose gutless attitude encourages both ends of the Axis to rev up their demands relentlessly.'[18] Christie also arranged for Henlein to give a talk at Chatham House (where he, Conwell-Evans and Lothian were active members) at which the Sudeten claimed the Prague government's links with Moscow meant Czechoslovakia would be 'Russia's aircraft carrier'.[19] Through Vansittart, he arranged for Harold Nicolson to host a tea party to introduce him to other young Labour and Conservative MPs similarly suspicious of Germany. Fortified by sandwiches, scones and a Dundee cake, the party seemed convinced of the Sudeten leader's reasonableness but warned him an aggressive absorption of the Sudetenland into the Reich would force a war.

Barely a week after Henlein's charm offensive in London, on the evening of Friday, 20 May, reports reached the British Foreign Office of mechanised German troops moving towards the Czech frontier and of local disturbances ahead of municipal elections due on the Sunday. Fearing a carbon copy of the *Anschluss*, the Czechs called up their reservists and overnight mobilised nearly 200,000 well-trained and well-equipped troops to man the country's border defences. The British and French ambassadors demanded explanations from von Weizsäcker at the foreign ministry, who insisted (quite possibly correctly) there was no truth to the reports. Henderson ruefully reminded him he had received similar reassurances only hours before the German army marched into Austria. He was sent to meet a 'pugnacious and truculent' Ribbentrop, who threatened that Germany would indeed invade if there were any bloodshed and the Czechs would be 'exterminated... women and children and all'.[20] The French, backed by the Russians, confirmed they would honour their treaty obligations to defend Czechoslovakia. In London, Halifax was recalled from a visit to Eton College, where he was a fellow, and Chamberlain truncated his weekend's fishing in Hampshire so the Cabinet could meet on both Saturday and Sunday. Meanwhile, under instruction from their ambassador, worried British embassy staff chartered a special train carriage to evacuate their families from Berlin. Hitler had ruined another weekend.

Halifax sent a private message via Henderson to Ribbentrop urging moderation and patience and called in the German ambassador, who denied any unusual troop movements. To this day, it is unclear as to whether he and his colleagues were telling the truth. Despite driving for over a thousand miles that weekend, the British military attaché and his deputy found no evidence of any such activity. Knowing Czechoslovakia to be next on his shopping list in any event, Christie and Conwell-Evans believed Hitler had backed down under coordinated Allied pressure. The foreign democratic press agreed, with even the French newspapers proclaiming it a victory for England. Though the original reports had been exaggerated and possibly fabricated, the May Crisis had humiliated both Hitler and Ribbentrop.

Amid these crises, social niceties were maintained, with little outward acknowledgement of the worsening situation. On the Wednesday before that traumatic weekend, the Anglo-German Fellowship held an afternoon reception for Herbert von Dirksen, the new ambassador, a polished and experienced diplomat who disliked his predecessor as much as his British colleagues did, so despite the rising tensions they found him a much easier customer. One hundred and fifty guests welcomed the new envoy – who had previously served as ambassador in Tokyo and Moscow – including the Foreign Office's top brass, R. A. Butler, undersecretary of state for foreign affairs, Alec Cadogan, the new permanent secretary and Vansittart, the chief diplomatic adviser.

The May Crisis, this most perilous of non-events, had immediate and profound consequences. Within a fortnight, an infuriated Hitler had crystallised his plans, codenamed 'Case Green', to 'wipe Czechoslovakia off the map' that autumn. One of Christie's informants (named by the historian Patricia Meehan as Captain Wiedemann, Hitler's adjutant) had sent him a letter, forwarded by Vansittart to Halifax and by Harvey to the prime minister, confirming that the crisis had resulted in a 'complete muddle and lack of direction'. This had so seriously damaged Hitler's personal authority, he was now 'moved by a wild desire for revenge', and prone to such 'brutal outbursts' and 'Sphinx-like silences' that his underlings feared for their lives should they dare contradict him.[21] The historian David Faber has captured the dark irony: 'Hitler was all the more enraged that he had been prematurely accused of being on the point of committing a crime that he did indeed intend to commit, but had not yet had the opportunity to carry out.'[22]

Interpretations of this rare diplomatic outmanoeuvring of the German regime varied. Vansittart, Conwell-Evans and Christie thought the coordinated, robust protests by the democracies, alongside the swift mobilisation of the Czech military, proved standing up to Hitler had been both essential and effective. In stark contrast, Nevile Henderson had only agreed to such a firm stance on condition it should never be repeated for risk of further provoking the Führer's ire.

As spring slipped into summer, this sense of chaos within Anglo-German relations continued. Despite Ribbentrop's new loathing of Britain, his mood swings and his undiplomatic outbursts, both Tennant and Conwell-Evans tried their best to support cordial relations and some shreds of affection for him well into 1939. Their assessments of his mercurial temper were discussed at the highest levels. At a Cabinet meeting on 22 June, the foreign secretary reported that Conwell-Evans had challenged Ribbentrop, who had accused Great Britain of 'whipping up the war mind in Europe', to support talks between the Czechoslovakian government and Henlein.[23]

That same month, while in Berlin on business, Ernest Tennant had been invited by Ribbentrop, whom he had not seen for a year, to tea at his 'immense Schloss' in the hills at Sonnenburg, some fifty miles east of Berlin. Having sent him a car, the foreign minister was waiting dressed in white cotton plus fours and flanked by a Scottish golf professional and two caddies on the imposing front steps of his recently acquired eighteenth-century house. Ribbentrop challenged his alarmed friend to a round on his private nine-hole course. Though naturally *sportif*, Tennant had not picked up a golf club for thirty years, as a lion had badly mauled his arm before the Great War. But he overcame his disability and lack of practice to win each of the first five holes. Ribbentrop then behaved in a way Tennant later realised had been 'rather revealing', losing his temper, hitting all his balls into a distant wood and stalking home in a rage.[24] The Scottish golf professional, foolish enough to celebrate the British victory, was sacked shortly afterwards.

Cornwall Gardens, Kensington, London, location of Conwell-Evans's flat where the key secret meetings with representatives of the German resistance to Hitler were held with British civil servants.

16

THE OSTER CONSPIRACY

NUMBER 31 CORNWALL GARDENS SITS IN THE SHADE OF MAG-
nificent plane trees on the north side of a quiet square close to Kensington
Gardens. For Philip Conwell-Evans, recently moved from a bedsit in
Bayswater, this offered a respectable address convenient for the Travellers
Club and the Palace of Westminster, and only a brisk walk from Vansittart's
Mayfair mansion across the park. Laid out during London's expansion westwards in the second half of the nineteenth century, these proud Italianate
terraces were built for prosperous Victorian middle-class families with
phalanxes of servants, but now, with their facades darkened by a half century's soot from chimneys, nearby trains and the thickening traffic of the
Cromwell Road, the area had lost the confidence of its Edwardian heyday
and the houses had been sub-divided into flats let to writers, artists, office
workers or as pieds-à-terre. Conwell-Evans's modest bachelor flat on the
ground floor of number 31 would become the unlikely forum for a series
of clandestine visits by envoys from the budding German resistance, now
plotting a coup against Hitler, to meet Whitehall's two most senior mandarins, Sir Horace Wilson and Sir Robert Vansittart.

Erich Kordt was the first to arrive, sent back to London by Colonel-
General Ludwig Beck, chief of the German General Staff, whom Conwell-
Evans assessed as 'perhaps the ablest, certainly the most respected of the
old school' of German military leaders. Beck was working with four other
German generals and an admiral on a plan to unseat Adolf Hitler, led by
Major General Hans Oster, deputy head of the *Abwehr*, the German military
intelligence service.[1] The plan for the coup was straightforward and robust.
Should Hitler order the invasion of Czechoslovakia, General Erwin von
Witzleben, whose command included the critical Berlin Defence District,

would lead a Panzer division into Berlin with the cooperation of sympathetic colleagues heading the Berlin police force. Erich Kordt would open the doors to welcome the plotters into the Reich Chancellery. Hitler would be arrested and tried, or maybe just shot. Though concentrated on Berlin in the first instance, it seemed reasonable to assume, having removed Hitler from power, that the rest of the country would be keen to avoid another European war and fall into line behind the replacement government. Working together, these men arguably had a greater chance of success than any earlier – or, as it would turn out, any later – plot against the Führer. Rightly or wrongly, they saw Conwell-Evans and his colleagues within the Fellowship as the best means of liaising with the British government to ensure its support for a post-Hitler regime.

But rather than support any diplomatic, military or domestic challenge to Hitler's aggression that summer, Neville Chamberlain's determined master plan was to continue appeasing the German dictator. He had decided to send a mediator to Prague to oversee the fraught negotiations between the Czech government and the Sudeten German Party. His chosen candidate, recommended by the ever-present Horace Wilson, was the sixty-seven-year-old Viscount (Walter) Runciman, a Liberal peer and former president of the Board of Trade, whose party spent seven weeks in Czechoslovakia in August and September. Though nominally independent of government, the reluctant Runciman had been directed to apply pressure on the unfortunate Czechs to make concessions to the Sudetens, unaware Hitler had instructed their leaders to frustrate any settlement – however generous. Christie had met Henlein secretly in Zurich in early August 1938 and confirmed this cynical plan to the Foreign Office. He had warned Henlein that should Germany launch a military assault on Czechoslovakia, she would not get away with a brief blitzkrieg but rather would face a long and 'grim' European war.

At some point after Conwell-Evans had moved into Cornwall Gardens, he received a summons from Robert Vansittart to the Foreign Office, where Grahame Christie joined them. An agitated Van complained, 'we are not rearming… there is great danger', before asking them to 'write all you know about the Nazis to stir up the government… they must be made aware of the dangers'.[2]

Vansittart then collated Christie's latest intelligence into a memorandum evidencing the planned attack. Hitler, he summarised, had always been 'half balmy' [*sic*] and now sided with the extremists, but was still 'not too balmy to be scared back over the fence if we have the nerve to do it'. Christie acknowledged this to be at odds with the advice coming from the ambassador in Berlin, but argued that the embassy was now too close to the regime to 'pick up the informed murmurings of the malcontents'. Both the Secret Service and Christie's network of reliable informants corroborated Vansittart's analysis. These included a senior army officer, a well-informed Sudeten (who confirmed Henlein's duplicity), a highly placed Reich official, an industrialist, a serving diplomat, a distinguished economist and other dependable friends. Between them, they confirmed: the German leaders were confident they could prevail with a short military confrontation; all former soldiers aged under sixty-five had been ordered to report for duty; agents provocateurs were being sent from Vienna into the Sudeten districts to foment unrest; and Göring had been fast losing influence over the Führer, so only Himmler could advise him now.

But crucially, the citizenry remained opposed to any European war. A frustrated Goebbels had berated journalists for not creating a warlike mentality among the German public. The economist (probably Hjalmar Schacht, now working with Oster) confirmed that Runciman's mission had been doomed to fail, unless Great Britain and France broadcast a convincing warning over the radio in German. He corroborated the soldier's evidence of civilian pacifism, especially among young people, which was shared by many generals. Hitler, who now saw himself as a 'god', was actually 'mad' and the criticism from England and elsewhere of his treatment of the Jews was driving him towards war.

Erich Kordt returned to London in early August, ostensibly for a holiday with his brother, but also met Conwell-Evans for lunch at the Travellers Club. Here, he challenged his friend's belief the Runciman mission might succeed given what they both now knew of Hitler's real thinking. Conwell-Evans later acknowledged Kordt had been quite right; Chamberlain should instead have called an emergency meeting (to include Russia) of the Council of the League of Nations, which would have put Hitler in a quandary and bolstered his moderate generals.

The two friends met again a fortnight later at the Kaiserhof Hotel in Berlin. The occasion was a lunch hosted by Erich's chief, the foreign minister, which would prove no less disturbing than Tennant's encounter on the golf course. It confirmed Conwell-Evans's realisation that the newly promoted Ribbentrop, his sometime friend, holiday companion and enthusiast for England, could no longer be civilised and would provoke Hitler into war with Great Britain. Recently discovered handwritten notes, prepared in collaboration with his friend the historian Martin Gilbert, and some loose pages of draft typescript for a possible book, allow us to reconstruct the discussions at that traumatic lunch. Still smarting from the embarrassments of the May Crisis and ranting against the Czechs for mobilising, Ribbentrop had been adamant the Allied protest had been unjustified, since no German troops had been moved. Believing this to be an outright lie, Conwell-Evans said nothing but gave him a hard stare. Undeterred, an increasingly agitated Ribbentrop shouted, 'If they continue to behave in that way... we would wipe them out... we will massacre the whole lot, seven million of them.'

At this violent outburst, Conwell-Evans, the lifelong pacifist, pointed out sarcastically, 'Such an operation would be difficult as in four years of war the combined artillery of the French, British and Americans succeeded in destroying only two million Germans... Germany has come to a parting of the ways... if you attack the Czechs, we and the French will fight, and your Reich will be destroyed.'

Ribbentrop disagreed. 'Czechoslovakia is not a British vital interest,' he said, before insisting, 'the Empire's resources would not be wasted on such a cause.'

'On the contrary,' replied his lunch guest, 'as the integrity of Czechoslovakia is vital to France, it is equally vital to ourselves... as foreign minister you have a grand chance now of winning the confidence of the Eastern European States; by respecting their integrity you could build up a system of relationships with the Eastern European States analogous to those governing the British Commonwealth of Nations... but if you seek to conquer you will lead to the destruction of Germany.'

'*Quatsch!*' (twaddle) Ribbentrop retorted. 'Words, words, that mean nothing, that is what you always offer.'

'Oh come, come,' Conwell-Evans replied, 'what would satisfy you as far as the Czechs are concerned? [...] Would you be content with autonomy for the Sudetens, or would you prefer a plebiscite letting them choose their fate?'

'I cannot answer these questions; you should not put them to me,' Ribbentrop replied.

'You evidently mean to make war on the Czechs then?'

'Nonsense,' Ribbentrop almost shouted, 'you are drawing wrong conclusions... I never said so.'

Now realising the futility of logical argument and close to leaving in disgust, Conwell-Evans led his old friend to the window and asked whether he had no thought for the lives of ordinary Germans walking in the street. 'Do you want to see those young men – just mutilated bodies – die?'

By now uncharacteristically incensed, Conwell-Evans stormed out of the hotel onto the Unter den Linden, Berlin's famous boulevard lined with lime trees. As he stepped out into the street, Kordt caught up with him, having been sent by Ribbentrop to determine the strength of British opposition to Hitler's plans. Bluntly, he told his friend the position was hopeless and to go back and tell the foreign minister, 'In three weeks we shall be at war.' Returning home, Conwell-Evans admitted to himself Ribbentrop was too craven to Hitler to give cogent let alone wise counsel and compared him unfavourably with Göring, who would have advised the Führer better.[3] Now abandoning all hope of civilising his Nazi friends, he opted to support those in Germany who offered an alternative to Hitler's regime.

Also back in London, Christie visited Lord Halifax to discuss the Central European situation and urge the mobilisation of the navy and air force. An old friend, the head of a major German industrial concern, had telephoned him from Belgium to warn him that the National Socialists were 'in full war cry', but still faced opposition from most of the population, including many in the army, who feared a catastrophe.[4] Military mobilisation would start during the next week and Czechoslovakia would be invaded in September. Christie admitted to Vansittart that both he and the industrialist had previously believed in the 'sincerity and applicability' of National Socialism but had now, like Conwell-Evans, lost faith in any chance of civilising them.

His friend's advice on what Britain should do next had been precise and clear: 'Give the Sudetens a fair deal... no mere verbal protest will help. Hitler won't believe you. Unless our people call a halt to our army mobilisation, answer by mobilising your fleet and air force.' He predicted this would be the only way to break Hitler's 'run of luck and successes', otherwise the result would be 'campaigns of brutality and violence in which rich decadent England will be one of the most enticing objects of attention.'[5]

So, Christie and Conwell-Evans had now supplied the British government with sound, cross-checked intelligence from credible sources that Hitler was insanely bent on conquering Czechoslovakia within weeks, against the advice of most of his generals and with minimal appetite for war among the German population. There was an emerging military and civilian resistance willing to risk their own lives to depose Hitler should he attack. Any hope of moderating this plan through Ribbentrop had to be abandoned given his new loathing of the British and mushrooming sycophancy to Hitler. Though sceptical, Göring could no longer manage the Führer and his instinct for self-preservation meant he played both sides of the coin. The crisis was real and the danger of war in Europe imminent. How and when to respond to this threat would be the British government's greatest preoccupation and would remain so for the next dozen weeks.

Conwell-Evans and Christie were not alone in their volte-face on the Germans that summer. Halifax had secretly offered Lord Lothian, whom Conwell-Evans had twice escorted to Berlin for audiences with the Führer, the ambassadorship to Washington, and he had accepted. Before leaving for a long trip to Australia, Lothian telephoned his friend Jan Masaryk, the Czech minister in London, to confirm he was no longer a Germanophile, having been finally persuaded he had been on the 'wrong road' by the events in Austria and the 'whole cynical cruelty of the regime'.[6] Thus he had evolved from ardent appeaser of Germany into primary cheerleader for Anglo-American friendship; his once close association with the Nazi regime gave him the authority of a convert. His ambassadorship now opened a channel of influence between the Anglo-German Fellowship and the US government, up to and including President Roosevelt, and offered a platform from which to secure American support for Great Britain in any armed conflict against the Germans.

But whatever else might challenge the British government that August, nothing should be allowed to disrupt the English summer holidays. Chamberlain told his sister, while 'the reports from Czecho are by no means encouraging', he still hoped not to truncate his holiday.[7] And so, as soon as he had dispatched Runciman to Prague, and despite a bout of sinusitis, he headed north to Scotland for an extended fishing expedition on aristocratic estates and then a sojourn with the royal family at Balmoral. Alec Cadogan, the permanent undersecretary at the Foreign Office, took his car and his wife to Le Touquet to play golf and the gaming tables for over a month. Oliver Harvey also took a month's leave in France, returning to London only in early September. They had left Halifax dealing with a 'pretty gloomy situation' throughout August.[8]

Into this vacuum stepped Conwell-Evans and Christie. Both keen mountaineers, even they managed a few days' holiday together in the Swiss mountains. In the middle of August, Christie wrote to Vansittart confirming Japan had joined the German-Italian military alliance, with Ribbentrop and the Japanese ambassador both signing the document. Conwell-Evans returned on 23 August to host a discreet meeting at his flat between Theo Kordt and Sir Horace Wilson. Theo, who was deputising for the vacationing ambassador, so temporarily Germany's most senior diplomat in London, now admitted to the prime minister's chief adviser that he was working with the opposition, before detailing Hitler's war plans and urging for a consistent and publicly articulated policy from the British government.[9]

Conwell-Evans rushed back to Berlin the next day, planning to stay for two weeks to attend the *Parteitag*, but returned after only five days to update Wilson in Downing Street and Vansittart in the Foreign Office. Otto Abetz, Ribbentrop's adviser on France, had confirmed to Christie that the planned Czech invasion between 12 and 15 September would be preceded by a disturbance fomented as an excuse for a blitzkrieg. This would be immediately followed by a flood of propaganda offering 'grandiose propositions for world peace' to mitigate the inevitable howls of international protest.

By the next day, Chamberlain felt sufficiently alarmed to recall his Cabinet colleagues from their holidays for what turned into a long and disquieting secret meeting. Eighteen ministers attended and were joined in the Cabinet room by Sir Nevile Henderson, who had been brought back from Berlin. Halifax spoke for an hour, reporting that Germany was partially mobilising and Hitler had determined to fight. The ambassador followed, just as he had in May, to argue emphatically against doing or saying anything which might antagonise Hitler. The meeting concluded with a consensus that conflict was best avoided if the Czechs could be pressed to concede the Sudetenland to Hitler, thus robbing him of any *casus belli*.

Evidently frustrated by such a timorous approach, Vansittart precised Conwell-Evans's intelligence in a memorandum for the foreign secretary, insisting the Germans would absorb, by whatever means, all of

Czechoslovakia rather than just the Sudetenland. Hitler dismissed any counsel of moderation, convinced France and Great Britain would remain neutral. At this point, Vansittart felt the need to explain why the Cabinet should trust Conwell-Evans. Though once Ribbentrop's 'bosom friend' and the 'most ardent Germanophil [sic] in this country', now the 'scales have dropped from his eyes'.[10] The next day, Conwell-Evans was granted an audience with Halifax to recommend (as had Christie) mobilising the British fleet. He then met Kordt and Vansittart again at his flat, following which he penned another letter to the foreign secretary urging him not to try to bluff Hitler, who had a 'strange, uncanny and prophetic instinct of distinguishing bluff and realities'. Before heading back to Nuremburg, he asked for his name to be redacted from any correspondence to protect his German informants, now at risk of arrest and execution, and promised to devote his life to Anglo-German relations.[11]

Winston Churchill had meanwhile been lobbying Halifax on similar lines, suggesting a joint note be drafted from Britain, France and Russia, and blessed by President Roosevelt, calling for a peaceable solution to the crisis and reiterating the support of all three countries for Czechoslovakia. At the same time, he recommended putting the fleet to sea as a visible reminder of British naval strength. Halifax remained unconvinced by the grand alliance plan but did want to make a speech making those explicit warnings to Germany which the Foreign Office had been urging him to give ever since March. Horace Wilson's uppermost priority was still to avoid any initiative that might antagonise Hitler, so he warned Chamberlain against involving the Russians and persuaded Halifax to remove some offending paragraphs in his draft speech.

Finally, on Friday, 2 September, Cadogan returned from his holidays wondering in his diary whether he should 'ever see Le Touquet again'. Having spent the weekend in the office catching up on the volumes of unread paperwork (including the Christie and Conwell-Evans intelligence), he admitted to his diary that there had been 'certainly enough in the Secret Reports to make one's hair stand on end'. That weekend, the German resistance made another approach to the British government when Beck, Franz Halder (Chief of the General Staff of the Army High Command) and Oster sent a retired army friend, Lieutenant Colonel Hans-Werner Boehm-Tettelbach, to warn the English against making any concessions to Hitler. Fluent in English, the colonel came to meet Julian Piggott, one of the Fellowship's founding Council members. The two men had got to know each other soon after the Great War, when the Englishman had served in Cologne as British high commissioner of the Inter-Allied Rhineland High Commission. Piggott now introduced him to an unnamed major in the Intelligence Service and arranged further meetings with other senior British figures, but with little if any effect.

With the crisis deepening, that September saw the lead actors in our story – Conwell-Evans, Tennant, the Kordts, Henderson, Christie, Wilson and most infamously the prime minister Neville Chamberlain – shuttling back and forth by plane between the London aerodromes and Berlin in the urgent search for peace.[12] Despite the well-established formula for British politicians visiting Germany (mostly sponsored by the Fellowship) and the thinner trail of German politicians leaving the Fatherland to visit England, the suggestion Chamberlain might ease tensions by flying to meet the Führer in person – 'Plan Z'– seems to have originated from the prime minister alone.

Chamberlain excitedly told his sister that this idea had been 'so unconventional and daring' it 'rather took Halifax's breath away'.[13] The winded foreign secretary quickly insisted Vansittart should join the meeting, at which point the appalled chief diplomatic adviser fought it 'tooth and nail'. He loudly proclaimed that the British prime minister flying uninvited and cap in hand to the German dictator would be akin to the humiliation suffered by the Holy Roman Emperor, Henry IV, kneeling in the snow in supplication before the Pope at Canossa nearly a thousand years before.[14] Unpersuaded by Van's broad historical perspective, the undaunted Chamberlain presented his cunning plan as a fait accompli to his Cabinet less than a week later and, despite some misgivings, the proposal gained momentum and, quickly, approval.

Publicity poster for the 1938 NSDAP Parteitag *at Nuremberg.*

17

TEA AT NUREMBERG

HELD IN THE SECOND WEEK OF SEPTEMBER 1938, THE TENTH
annual National Socialist Congress had been billed as the *Reichsparteitag
Grossdeutschland* (Party Day of Greater Germany) to celebrate the *Anschluss*.
With tensions mounting throughout Europe, the rally attracted even more
interest than in previous years. Among the journalists from London were
Hitler's favourite Fleet Street hack, the *Daily Mail*'s G. Ward Price; Leonard
Mosley, later the war correspondent for the *Sunday Times*; and Vansittart's
friend, the irrepressible Virginia Cowles. In *Looking for Trouble* (published
in 1941), she captured the now finely tuned, pseudo-mediaeval pageantry
deployed by the Nazis: a 'million red, white, and black swastikas fluttered
from the window-ledges, and the town, swollen to three times its normal
size, resounded to the ring of leather boots and blazed with a bewildering array of uniforms'. Highlighting the particularly fevered atmosphere
that week, she remembered how the hotel lobbies were filled with 'Italian
diplomats in earnest conversation with delegates from Nationalist Spain;
German party leaders smiling at the Japanese, worried French statesmen
cornered with the British.'[1]

As in previous years, Philip Conwell-Evans and Ernest Tennant led the
British contingent of Anglo-German Fellowship grandees, including no
fewer than five members of the House of Lords. Three were senior British
businessmen, while the other two fell more easily into the stereotype of
bumbling aristocratic amateur admirers of Hitler. Lord McGowan chaired
ICI and served as a director of Dunlop, each early backers of the Fellowship.
Lord Stamp, chairman of LMS Railway and the London School of Economics
and a director of the Bank of England, had advised Chamberlain and previous Chancellors of the Exchequer on taxation since the Great War. Lord

Hollenden, a Council member, was president of the Wholesale Textile Association. All three had significant business links with Germany and the Fellowship had previously arranged for both McGowan and Stamp to meet the Führer privately.

But less likely to further the cause of international business or diplomacy were the Fellowship's other two peers, Lords Redesdale and Brocket, who had arrived under their own steam. Accompanied by his wife, son Tom, and fourth daughter, Unity, Redesdale is now best remembered as the inspiration for Uncle Matthew in the novels of his eldest daughter, Nancy Mitford. Famous in fiction for believing 'Frogs are slightly better than Huns or Wops, but abroad is unutterably bloody and foreigners are fiends', the real Redesdale was also a xenophobe and anti-Semite.[2] Tom was friendly with Virginia Cowles, who described his tall, moustachioed father as wandering around Nuremberg with a 'bewildered air as though he were at a rather awkward house-party where (curiously enough) no one could speak any English'.[3]

In a pointed slight to the democratic nations, their ambassadors were accommodated not in the town's comfortable hotels as in previous years, but alongside the foreign journalists in a special train parked in a siding a good twenty minutes from the centre of town. The British ambassador arrived for his second rally intending to stay for just thirty-six hours. But with the frenzy of diplomatic anxiety, he had to stay on for a full five days of celebrations during which the Führer refused to see him. Back in Berlin, his equally stressed first secretary, Ivone Kirkpatrick, took up full-time residence in the embassy to deal with the ceaseless flow of messages and did not leave the building for three weeks.

Untersturmführer Baumann, an attentive and perceptive young SS officer, met Henderson at the station and arranged transport, accommodation and meetings with Party leaders while discreetly charting his guest's ineptitude in a sixteen-page memorandum prepared for the German foreign ministry.[4] The fastidious Henderson, now seriously ill with throat cancer, struggled without his creature comforts, finding the wagon-lits cramped and sleep almost impossible. To add to his woes, he had no easy means of communicating with either his embassy in Berlin or with his masters in London. For security reasons, he had not brought a cypher and – by his own admission, idiotically – he had forgotten to bring any writing paper.

As secretary of the Anglo-German Fellowship, Conwell-Evans had been luckier in his accommodation, Erich Kordt having secured him a room at the Grand Hotel, an honour usually reserved for the Führer's personal friends. But rather than relishing his welcome into the Nazi fold, Conwell-Evans used his privileged status to harvest intelligence on the escalating crisis from his foreign ministry friends. They warned him that Henderson was 'too easily fooled' by Hitler's protestations of peace and not speaking 'plainly' to Ribbentrop, so begged him to intercede personally with the ambassador.[5]

And so, for two hours early on that sunny Thursday morning, secretary and ambassador walked between the railway tracks arguing passionately. Conwell-Evans explained that he and Christie had compelling intelligence Hitler was determined to invade Czechoslovakia within a couple of weeks, so Britain must take the strongest of lines to prevent war. Doggedly convinced any strong statement would provoke Hitler's ire, Henderson urged Conwell-Evans to tone down his warnings but did finally authorise him to return at once to London to brief the foreign secretary. The two men agreed on one thing; Hitler was now almost certainly mad, but they were diametrically opposed as to how to deal with him. Henderson warned Halifax the Führer may have 'crossed the border-line of insanity' so should be handled with kid gloves to avoid provocation, while Conwell-Evans's diagnosis was that, because he was so mad, it would be disastrous to think him open to rational negotiations.[6] Following the heated tête-à-tête between the two Britons, the ever-helpful Baumann arranged a car to take Conwell-Evans back into the centre of Nuremberg en route for London. Knowing him to be a leading light in the Fellowship, he reported to his masters that, as they had made their farewells, Conwell-Evans had evidently been 'striving to conceal a great shock'.[7]

Meanwhile, back in London, the German resistance made its boldest and riskiest approach to date, arranging for their new ally in the embassy, Theo Kordt, to meet secretly with Cadogan, Halifax and Wilson in 10 Downing Street. The journalist Susanne Simonis, the Kordts' cousin, had just arrived in London with a memorised message for Theo from his brother Erich. Now crossing the line from diplomacy to espionage and therefore treason, Theo acknowledged that he represented 'political and military circles in Berlin who wanted *to prevent war by all means*'.[8]

Hitler, he explained, planned to invade Czechoslovakia on the nineteenth or twentieth of that month, so he implored the British government to issue an 'unequivocal statement' over the radio, avoiding the 'niceties of diplomatic language', in terms to impress even a 'semi-educated dictator who thought in terms only of force'.[9] A foreign policy defeat could well, he suggested, unseat the Nazi regime. As Cadogan recorded in his diary that night, Kordt had risked his life by putting 'conscience before loyalty' to betray Hitler's true intentions. Impressed by his visitor's bravery and sincerity, Halifax promised to discuss it with the prime minister and Cabinet colleagues at once. The German walked back to his embassy via the garden gate feeling optimistic.

That evening, Wilson walked round to the Foreign Office to brief Cadogan, who agreed the intelligence was credible enough and the situation serious enough to recall the PM at once from his Scottish holiday and cancel the foreign secretary's trip to the League of Nations in Geneva that week. But, although Kordt and Halifax met again the next day, no ultimatum was issued; Cadogan thought it would be 'fatal', while Wilson believed it would provoke Hitler.[10] As one historian concluded, this had not been 'some little-known emissary' but rather the 'officially accredited second-in-command at the German embassy', so it seems 'extraordinary in hindsight that, because his suggested course of action was so out of step with British policy at the time, no further action was taken or advice sought'.[11] Only weeks later, an embarrassed Halifax admitted to Theo that he had been unable to be 'frank' because, against the Foreign Office's better instincts, they had been developing the plan for Neville Chamberlain to short-circuit diplomatic channels by flying to Germany in person.[12]

The foreign secretary did send an unambiguous message to Nevile Henderson to be delivered to Ribbentrop. This explained that His Majesty's Government felt 'so greatly distressed' by the toxic atmosphere of the Prague negotiations that, if France went to war with Germany to defend Czechoslovakia, the resulting conflict would be one from which Great Britain 'could not stand aside'.[13] Telegraphed to Kirkpatrick at the embassy, who then dispatched it by night train to Nuremberg, somehow it had been leaked to the *Daily Mail*, whose Saturday edition the next morning trumpeted:

BRITAIN WARNS GERMANY TODAY
WILL NOT STAND ASIDE IF CZECHS ARE ATTACKED
INSTRUCTIONS SENT TO AMBASSADOR[14]

Meanwhile Wilson had sent a message from the prime minister to Henderson asking if it were time for the button to be pushed on Plan Z. Chamberlain was eager to go to Germany but wanted his ambassador's guidance as to how (or even if) he might be received. Shrouded in secrecy, this was carried by one of the King's Messengers (known as the 'Silver Greyhounds') rather than risk another leaked telegram. With astonishing disobedience, Henderson refused to deliver the foreign secretary's message. Instead, he explained by telephone, the courier would return with his reply to both communications, written – as he had no writing paper – on blank pages torn from the detective novel he was reading. Leaving Nuremberg early that morning, the exhausted Silver Greyhound flew to Cologne only to miss the London flight, so Cadogan sent a plane to collect him.

Defending his point-blank refusal to pass on the message, Henderson insisted it would have been 'ill-timed and disastrous', promising he had already made the British position as 'clear as daylight to people who count'.[15] Warning that the 'tale of a London aeroplane with a message' had already revived painful memories of the May Crisis for the Germans, he insisted a repeat of that episode must be avoided, otherwise Hitler would be driven 'straight off at the deep end'.[16] Despite the barrage of advice to the contrary, the Inner Cabinet surrounding Chamberlain, including Halifax, Cadogan, Hoare and Simon (both themselves former foreign secretaries), agreed to accept the ambassador's placatory position. Chamberlain had to send urgent telegrams to Paris, Prague and Berlin to deny the *Daily Mail* report, even though at the time of publication it had been true. Vansittart was furious.

That same night, Hitler had gathered his leading generals for a conference that ran into the early hours of Saturday morning. Fired by the febrile atmosphere of the rally and fuelled by the adulation of his massed supporters, he reconfirmed his plans for Case Green – the conquest of Czechoslovakia. By four o'clock that Saturday afternoon, Conwell-Evans had returned to rain-sodden Nuremberg for the annual tea party hosted by the 'smiling and obsequious' Ribbentrop at the Hotel Deutscher Hof. With Hitler as his guest of honour, the other guests included diplomats, other foreign dignitaries and a handful of favoured journalists. Lords Stamp, McGowan and Brocket were honoured to be placed at Hitler's table along-side Ward Price, the Sudeten leader Henlein and the ubiquitous Schmidt to translate. On each table sat a card stating, 'Please Don't Smoke in The Presence of The Führer.'[17]

Less eccentric than Redesdale but more dangerous, the thirty-four-year-old Lord Brocket was an enthusiast for the Third Reich, a wealthy landowner, former Conservative MP and a regular at the Fellowship's dinners. He had entertained leading Germans, including Ribbentrop and district leaders of the Hitler Youth, at his two stately homes. Unhelpfully for the cause of Anglo-German relations, Brocket had developed a rapport with the prime minister who, to Conwell-Evans's frustration, would listen to his young friend's advice on Germany well into 1939. Brocket had been flattered to be seated next to the 'extremely nice and very cheerful' German leader, who during their animated conversation, as Cowles noted from another table, 'several times threw back his head and laughed loudly.'[18] When Hitler confessed to finding the weather and foreign affairs 'rather depressing', Brocket hoped both would soon improve before suggesting the Führer would be bound to like Chamberlain personally if only he could meet him, and the two leaders would get a 'great deal settled'. To this, a pleased Hitler responded, 'It is rather difficult… I cannot leave my country, and meet him in a foreign country, he cannot leave his country and come here, we cannot meet in aeroplanes in the air, and I am always very seasick on the sea!'[19]

While Brocket exchanged facile pleasantries with Europe's pre-eminent dictator, Conwell-Evans managed a hurried talk with von Weizsäcker. With Rudolf Hess and Gestapo officers hovering nearby this was especially risky. The state secretary and Erich Kordt urged him to persuade Chamberlain to write to Hitler proposing a plebiscite in Czechoslovakia, confident this would secure popular German support and prevent disaster. That same weekend Ribbentrop's ambassadors in London, Paris, Washington and Rome were each advising that military action would lead to a general war, but the foreign minister, now thirsting for battle, silenced them by sending all four on compulsory leave for the rest of the month. Before leaving again for London, Conwell-Evans warned Stamp and Tennant of the imminent danger. Tennant remained for the last day and, while discussing the situation with other British visitors, including Ward Price, was interrupted by some uniformed Nazis who, bowing politely, asked, 'May we venture to enquire what you are all talking about so seriously?'

Turning round slowly and adjusting his eyeglass, the famous journalist replied, 'We are just discussing what we are going to do with you Germans after we have defeated you in the next war.'[20]

Back in London, Conwell-Evans saw Halifax for their second meeting in a fortnight to urge him to ignore Henderson's advice, be firm with the Germans and mobilise the British fleet.[21] Anxious to ensure his message was heard, he followed up with a letter that evening and a memorandum (copied to Chamberlain and Vansittart) two days later, underlining the unique circumstances:

> Never in history has a situation existed in which the highest members of the Foreign Office of a great power, and other leading personalities of the state have made appeals through trusted intermediaries to a foreign government to save them from war. Yet that is the position today in respect of Germany and Great Britain: the highest people in the German Foreign Office risking instant execution have placed me in full possession of the aims and plans of Chancellor Hitler, and have described to me his state of mind, bordering literally on the insane, and have almost on their knees begged me to explain to the British government the steps which would enable them to defeat the plans of their insane Chancellor.[22]

These brave individuals were sure the British ambassador was wrongly convincing the Cabinet Hitler wanted peace when, in truth, he planned to attack Czechoslovakia towards the end of the month, confident Britain and France would not intervene. Hitler had promised, 'even babes suckling at their mothers' breasts must not be spared', while complaining that the current peace had made the Germans soft, his old Party comrades had become 'corpulent', his generals were 'too bourgeois to be able to take heroic decisions', and so anyone opposing him would be shot. Only Ribbentrop and Himmler fully supported Hitler's extreme position, while the other German leaders were 'aghast'. Even Hermann Göring, as always playing a double game, quietly opposed Hitler's plans. The German people were 'disturbed and uneasy' and would support a peaceful settlement in Czechoslovakia. It was imperative for Nevile Henderson to be replaced by a 'British special envoy of 1st class ability, of high rank and 1st class renown, with great experience and knowledge of the situation in Germany'.

But Conwell-Evans promised all had not yet been lost; prompt action could 'save Europe from war, and central Europe from collapse and Bolshevism, and restore and preserve that fine German civilisation'. Christie had also hurried back to London that weekend to brief Vansittart on intelligence supplied by Captain Fritz Wiedemann (Hitler's adjutant and commanding officer in the Great War), who confirmed that the Führer had outlined his wider ambitions: 'We must over-run Czechoslovakia as soon as possible… next year is France's turn… the year after [1940] we have to settle Britain and then my world Empire will be completed.'[23]

That same Sunday, Lord Brocket painted a quite different picture to Horace Wilson in Downing Street to be shared with the prime minister, whom he had encouraged the Führer to meet. He explained that his tea-party companion had been in good health and spirits and had promised he had 'no intention whatever of attacking England at any time, or of going to the West or attacking France', joking he would be as likely to want to conquer China.

Notwithstanding Brocket's interference, there is no doubt both the Foreign Office and Downing Street were taking Conwell-Evans and Christie's intelligence seriously. Oliver Harvey, Halifax's secretary, noted in his diary that Conwell-Evans had brought home 'passionate pleas from moderate German leaders begging H.M.G. to take some step to stop their mad Chancellor!'[24] At the Cabinet meeting on Monday, ahead of Hitler's crucial speech closing the *Parteitag*, Halifax told his colleagues that, based on good intelligence, he now believed Hitler was 'possibly or even probably mad' and may already have decided to attack Czechoslovakia '*coûte que coûte*' (no matter the cost). Sceptical as to whether a direct ultimatum would suffice, he cited 'Professor [*sic*] Conwell-Evans' as the source of a report that Hitler had been advised by his ambassador in Paris that France, the United Kingdom and the United States would indeed fight if he attacked Czechoslovakia. After some debate, the Cabinet agreed he *was* mad, and it would not do to try to bluff him, but they should wait to see what he said in his speech that evening before framing a response. Writing to his sister Ida, Chamberlain complained of a 'pretty awful week – enough to send most people off their heads, if their heads were not as firmly screwed on as mine'.[25]

Intriguingly, against this background, even anti-appeasers saw Hermann Göring as a possibly civilising influence on German foreign policy and English traditional field sports as the means to civilise him. At the height of the crisis, Duff Cooper, the First Lord of the Admiralty, wrote to Halifax emphasising Göring's passion for hunting and shooting, suggesting a 'big shoot at Chatsworth [the Duke of Devonshire's estate in Derbyshire], for instance, or at Belvoir, [the Duke of Rutland's estate in Leicestershire] might produce a wonderful effect'.[26]

An adoring, noisy crowd of thirty thousand received Hitler's speech with delight that night as he furiously demanded self-determination for the *Sudetendeutsch* and called President Beneš a liar, but did stop short of threatening war. Still feverishly seeing the glass half full, Henderson reported that despite 'certain violence and ill mannerisms', the German leader had made a good speech, with 'no signs of mania with which he is credited in some quarters'.[27] In London, a crowd of ten thousand gathered outside Downing Street; the *Evening Standard* printed 150,000 copies of the speech; and the BBC interrupted its programmes to broadcast it live. In New York, Wall Street came to a standstill and over one hundred American radio stations relayed it around the country. In Paris, army reservists were called up to man the Maginot Line. On Tuesday, 13 September, Chamberlain's Inner Cabinet convened and, without the full Cabinet being consulted, a cypher telegram stamped MOST IMMEDIATE had been sent to Henderson in Berlin instructing him to deliver the following personal message to Hitler from the prime minister:

IN VIEW OF INCREASINGLY CRITICAL SITUATION I PROPOSE TO COME OVER AT ONCE TO SEE YOU WITH A VIEW TO TRYING TO FIND PEACEFUL SOLUTION. I PROPOSE TO COME ACROSS BY AIR AND AM READY TO START TOMORROW. PLEASE INDICATE EARLIEST TIME AT WHICH YOU CAN SEE ME AND SUGGEST PLACE OF MEETING. SHOULD BE GRATEFUL FOR VERY EARLY REPLY. NEVILLE CHAMBERLAIN[28]

The aeroplane carrying British prime minister, Neville Chamberlain, leaving Heston airport for Germany for his meeting with Adolf Hitler, September 1938.

18

PLAN Z

TWO DAYS LATER, ARMED WITH HIS TIGHTLY FURLED UMBRELLA, the British prime minister left Heston aerodrome just before nine in the morning to make his maiden overseas flight, waved off by Lord and Lady Halifax, Alec Cadogan, Theodor Kordt and two Fellowship stalwarts, Lords Brocket and Londonderry. This was the first of three tortuous, traumatic and then – only fleetingly – triumphant meetings with the German dictator. Hitler had been 'thunderstruck' to receive Chamberlain's request for a face-to-face meeting but had little choice but to accept. Travelling in an eight-seated, twin-engined Lockheed 14 Super Electra, the prime ministerial party included Sir Horace Wilson and William Strang (head of the Foreign Office's Central Department), but no official interpreter. Sustained through the bumpy flight by ham sandwiches and whisky, they touched down at Munich's Oberwiesenfeld airfield four and a half hours later. There, Ribbentrop, von Weizsäcker and the two ambassadors, Henderson from Berlin and von Dirksen from London, were waiting to greet the peace-seeking British prime minister in front of a crowd of several thousand well-wishers. Much to Ribbentrop's irritation, more cheering crowds lined the streets as a fleet of Mercedes cars delivered them to Munich's central station, where the Führer's personal train waited for the three-hour onward journey to his Bavarian retreat.

Doubts about the wisdom of Plan Z extended beyond the Foreign Office. Many miles away in Australia, an alarmed Lord Lothian, hearing of this excursion, told a friend he thought Chamberlain 'heroic and courageous', but feared a diplomatic disaster.[1] Ivan Maisky, the Russian ambassador in London, had been appalled at the sight of the 'leader of the British Empire' going 'cap in hand' to the German Führer.[2] His friend, Winston Churchill, thought it the 'stupidest thing that has ever been done'.[3] But as he shuttled between the two countries with the cheers of both German and English crowds ringing in his ears, Chamberlain was confident he could reach a lasting settlement with Adolf Hitler.

Arriving at the Berghof in the late afternoon in heavy rain, Chamberlain had been impressed by its setting and the views over Berchtesgaden, but underwhelmed by meeting the Führer in the flesh: 'his expression [is] rather disagreeable, specially in repose and altogether he looks entirely undistinguished... you would never notice him in a crowd and would take him for the house painter he once was.' Following tea and cake in the Great Hall, the two leaders repaired to Hitler's private office, accompanied only by Paul-Otto Schmidt, who interpreted. To his dismay, Ribbentrop had not been allowed to join the meeting and vented his pique by later refusing to share Schmidt's notes of the discussions with the British.

The two leaders found little common ground. While Chamberlain's theme was the preservation of peace, Hitler focused on the Sudeten question, claiming fallaciously that three hundred Sudetens had been recently killed by their Czech countrymen and were threatening to invade unless the Sudetenland were seceded to Germany. To his credit, Chamberlain maintained his characteristic sangfroid, even inviting Hitler to visit England, a concept provoking the 'shadow of a smile' in response. He later told his Cabinet he had seen no 'trace of insanity' during their 'frank and friendly' conversation but did note his host's agitation each time Czechoslovakia was mentioned.

After just one session, they agreed to reconvene in a week. The visitors returned to London, this time fortified by chicken sandwiches and claret, to be greeted by Halifax, Kordt and ever larger crowds. Welcomed back to Downing Street by his wife and three thousand excited spectators, Chamberlain boasted to his colleagues that he had now established a 'certain confidence' with Herr Hitler whom, despite his 'hardness and ruthlessness', could be 'relied upon when he had given his word'.[4]

The next day, the French prime minister and foreign minister arrived in London for discussions, during which Chamberlain reassured them Hitler would arrange an 'orderly' handover of the Sudetenland to Germany. During a week of extensive negotiations, the two governments developed the 'Anglo-French plan', which pressurised the unhappy Czechs into allowing their country to be split in two. On 22 September, the prime minister left for his second audience with the German leader, again waved off by Kordt and Halifax. Arriving in beautiful sunshine at Cologne airport to the sound of a band playing 'God Save the King', further crowds welcomed him at nearby Bad Godesberg with flowers and presents. This time, Ivone Kirkpatrick from the Berlin embassy accompanied Chamberlain to serve as his interpreter. With French support and the reluctant agreement of the Czechs, Chamberlain had been confident he had brought everything Hitler had asked for at their first meeting. So he was dumbfounded when, over the next few days, the German leader dismissed the Anglo-French plan as insufficient and presented in its place his 'Godesberg memorandum'. This required the immediate military occupation of Czechoslovakia by the German army, the transfer of materially more territory than suggested at the first meeting, followed by the comprehensive dismemberment of the country. During those already tense negotiations, the million-strong Czech army had been mobilised, at which point Hitler threatened war.

An exhausted and demoralised Chamberlain returned to London but, with his customary mix of vanity, obduracy and naivety, still reassured his Cabinet he had 'influence over Herr Hitler', who now trusted him and would not 'deliberately deceive a man whom he respected'.[5] But the Foreign Office remained unconvinced. On Saturday evening, the normally emollient Alec Cadogan, who had seen all of Christie and Conwell-Evans's reports, decided to challenge his master's support for the prime minister's policy. The next morning, Halifax berated his permanent undersecretary: 'Alec, I'm very angry with you. You gave me a sleepless night… I woke at one and never got to sleep again', before conceding Cadogan had indeed been right. At the Cabinet meeting, when asked to lead the discussion, Halifax mounted an apologetic ('I feel a brute') but firm rebellion against his prime minister and friend, insisting he should refuse Hitler's terms.[6] The worm had turned. The Cabinet was persuaded to overrule Chamberlain and take, as Conwell-Evans and Christie had been urging for weeks, a stronger diplomatic line with Germany and to mobilise the British fleet that same day.[7] As Oliver Harvey noted in his diary, Halifax had 'lost all his delusions about Hitler and now regards him as a criminal lunatic'.[8]

On Monday, the British government confirmed it would, with France and Russia, support Czechoslovakia if Germany attacked. On Tuesday,

Conwell-Evans reported how widespread German public support for the prime minister's mission had infuriated Hitler. As he stood on the balcony of the Reich Chancellery watching a parade of aircraft and heavy artillery passing beneath him, 'crowds of spectators looked on in frigid silence at the troops going by, and neither cheered the Führer nor raised their arms in salute.'[9]

On the same day, Chamberlain made a radio broadcast firstly giving thanks for all the letters of support from the public in Britain, France, Belgium, Italy and even Germany, before confessing he found the responsibility 'almost overwhelming... how horrible, fantastic, incredible it is that we should be digging trenches and trying on gas masks here because of a quarrel in a far away country between people of whom we know nothing.'[10]

On Thursday, Theo Kordt and Cadogan drove Halifax down to Heston to join the rest of the Cabinet in waving off the prime minister for his third pilgrimage to Germany in a fortnight. This time, Édouard Daladier and Benito Mussolini joined him for a 'Four Powers' meeting, but both the Czechs and the Russians were excluded. The French premier and the Italian dictator were each accompanied by their foreign ministers, while Chamberlain had brought Horace Wilson, rather than Halifax or Cadogan, who were left fulminating in London. Quickly the four leaders signed an agreement confirming the evacuation of the Sudetenland within the first ten days of October – essentially everything the German leader had demanded in his Godesberg memorandum.

Having been mobbed by ecstatic Germans as he left Munich, Chamberlain returned to Heston with the celebrated paper promising peace between the two countries, which he had cajoled Hitler to sign. Ernest Tennant had been summoned to join the PM's welcome party. Before leaving for the aerodrome, he sent a friend a vivid report of the national panic during that week when he and his family had had no idea whether it was to be 'peace or war'. His wife, already an air raid warden, and their nineteen-year-old daughter, Vanessa, had been charged with assembling and distributing over thirty thousand gas masks in their neighbourhood. His son Julian had been evacuated from Eton, while Ernest himself had been busy arranging to move his City firm to the supposedly safer Cardiff. The male household servants were deployed to dig a trench while an anti-aircraft searchlight was set up in the grounds of their house. The ever-resourceful Vanessa took charge of a team of Girl Guides to find billets and dig latrines for three thousand recently arrived East End children. By Thursday night, all military personnel had been ordered to return to barracks and anti-aircraft guns were manned. 'The sky was full of search lights and planes were zooming overhead... we thought that the Conference had failed, and that war might break out overnight.'[11]

Huge crowds greeted the prime minister at Heston aerodrome. Chamberlain drove with Halifax straight to Buckingham Palace to be received by Their Majesties and thanked by a relieved and grateful nation. During the journey, Halifax advised the PM not to call a snap general election and urged him to bring Labour politicians into the Cabinet. At the palace, several thousands had been waiting in heavy rain for over two hours to see the first commoner privileged to take the adoring cheers from the famous balcony. Tens of thousands of letters and presents flooded in from relieved admirers around the world; churches held thanksgiving services across Britain; streets in France were renamed in Chamberlain's honour and a newspaper opened a subscription to buy him a house beside a river; and a grateful Dutch nation sent a floral tribute by plane, having stood down their army. Witnessing the jubilation, an unimpressed Orme Sargent, assistant undersecretary at the Foreign Office, concluded, 'You might think that we'd won a major victory, instead of just betraying a minor country.'[12]

Soon, both the royal family and the prime minister returned to Scotland to resume their holidays. Chamberlain, admitting to being 'nearer to a nervous breakdown' than ever before, spent ten days fishing for salmon and sea trout on the Tweed, shooting partridges and reading Disraeli's letters.[13] By signing the Munich Agreement, he had (by his own estimation) preserved peace in Europe, trounced Churchill in the Commons, and with Wilson's help wrested control over foreign policy from the emasculated Foreign Office and obstructive Halifax. In truth, he had alienated Soviet Russia, Czechoslovakia's previous guarantor, and as one recent historian pithily summarised, his 'mad dash to avoid war led him to bargain away a modern Czech army of thirty-seven divisions and to hand over to the German armed forces 1.5 million rifles, 750 aircraft, 600 tanks and 2,000 artillery guns'.[14] Another almost immediate casualty would be war-shattered Spain, where the signing of the agreement ended any hope of an anti-fascist alliance in

Europe, robbing the embattled Republicans of any remaining morale and leading to Franco's total victory and his subsequent dictatorship lasting till his death in 1975.

When Conwell-Evans returned to Germany in the middle of October, Eduard Brücklmeier, one of his foreign ministry friends who had been based at Berchtesgaden during the crisis, told him Hitler had admitted to putting forward his most 'brutal demands', and had been surprised and scornful when they were accepted by Chamberlain. Others in the ministry conceded that the threat of the Royal Navy had deterred Hitler from attacking the Czechs. But, as Conwell-Evans later concluded, 'for the Nazis, Munich had in fact opened up new vistas of unending conquests, bloodless and otherwise, in the west as well as in the east.'[15]

Whatever else Neville Chamberlain signed at Munich, it had been a death warrant for the Oster conspiracy, whose leaders had been only days from arresting and incarcerating Adolf Hitler. Chamberlain's Plan Z had ignored carefully crafted advice and undermined the trust built with the German resistance. And while Britain and France's concessions may have temporarily frustrated Hitler's visceral urge to make war on the Czechs, they had robbed the conspirators of their *casus belli* as the immediate threat of a European war receded. Erich Kordt complained that Munich 'prevented the *coup d'etat* in Berlin', while even the depressed and exhausted Henderson saw the irony of how, 'by keeping the peace, we have saved Hitler and his regime.'[16] Historians agree that the 'ground was cut from under the feet of the most promising attempt to overthrow Hitler', and that this had been the 'last chance for Europeans to stop Hitler from taking the path that would lead to the loss of fifty million lives'.[17] Unusually, Joachim Ribbentrop had been proved right in his advice to Hitler that Britain would, in the end, not fight to protect Czechoslovakia. In this way, the Munich Agreement undermined those potentially moderating influences on the Führer, such as the senior generals and even the mercurial Hermann Göring, because their advice had proved overly cautious.

While Vansittart and the Fellowship's leaders shared the wave of relief at the preservation of peace felt around Great Britain, they had consistently urged a stronger line with Hitler. Under no illusions he would be content with the Sudetenland, their intelligence had mostly been impeccable (with the notable exception being their assessment of Henlein's bona fides). As one leading historian of British intelligence concluded, 'the Munich crisis marked the peak of Vansittart's success as intelligence analyst… his facts were accurate, his reading excellent and his policy Britain's only option other than surrender.'[18] He, and his two most effective 'private detectives', Christie and Conwell-Evans, had been on the right side of history.

Though the Führer had been robbed of his war, Conwell-Evans reported that most Germans realised he had 'clearly been master of the situation throughout' and they admired 'his bellicose tactics and his successful cunning'.[19] Christie reported to Halifax and Vansittart, barely a week after the PM's return, Ribbentrop's gleeful remark that Chamberlain had signed the 'death warrant' of the British Empire. The Germans would now inherit the Empire 'as easily as one inherits the estate of an old aunt during her lifetime, piece by piece, merely by coaxing with persuasive words'.[20] As Conwell-Evans concluded, 'Chamberlain had brought to his country neither peace nor honour, and the tragedy lay in his unawareness of the fact.'[21] But when he bumped into Horace Wilson at the Travellers Club, the prime minister's chief adviser admonished him to 'get on with your Anglo-German Fellowship… don't carry on so with Vansittart.'[22] Meanwhile, MI5 intercepted telegrams showing the disdain Hitler felt for Chamberlain; on his copy of the report, Halifax (who saw Munich as a humiliation albeit better than a war) underlined three times the term the German leader used to describe the British prime minister – 'arsehole'.[23]

Cheering crowds greet the prime minister, Neville Chamberlain, on the balcony of Buckingham Palace with King George VI and Queen Elizabeth following his return from signing the Munich Agreement, 2 October 1938.

19

THE NIGHT OF BROKEN GLASS

THE MUNICH CRISIS AND THE DISMEMBERMENT OF CZECHO-slovakia had absorbed international attention and distracted the world's press from the intensifying persecution of Jews within Germany. They were now being diminished and excluded from German society under measures far harsher than required under the Nuremberg Laws. On 18 October 1938, Berta Grynszpan and her parents were among the twelve thousand Polish-born Jews ordered to leave Germany despite being legally resident for many years. Allowed only one suitcase each, their other possessions were confiscated by the authorities or looted by neighbours. Herded by the Gestapo onto crowded trains bound for Poland, only about one-third made it safely across the border. Upwards of eight thousand were left in limbo on the German side without food, lodging or income. The Grynszpans sent an anguished postcard to Berta's brother in Paris asking for help.

At the dinner hosted the next evening by the Anglo-German Fellowship to honour Ambassador von Dirksen, there was no mention of the abuse of Jews in Germany. Held at Claridge's, this was its first grand gathering since the prime minister's triumphal return from Munich and, whatever the private misgivings of Christie, Lothian and Conwell-Evans, a post-Munich glow bathed the dinner. Three hundred guests attended, half of whom were British, including – just back from Nuremberg – Lords Redesdale and Brocket. Friedl Gaertner had been sent by MI5 to monitor the event and her report adds valuable colour to the coverage in *The Times*.

Opening what was clearly a long night of speechifying, Mount Temple shared his view that, despite the two countries having come 'within an ace of war', never before had they met 'under fairer circumstances'. The ambassador agreed that the 'recent time of great strain and crisis' had brought the 'two peoples nearer together' and created a 'better understanding'.[1] Lord Brocket, before introducing the guest speaker, General Hermann Tholens (deputy chief of the German public service camps), looked forward to a 'time when our national life could be organised on similar common-sense lines to those pertaining in Germany'. Having jeered at the anti-appeasers in the Commons as being 'impotent', he attacked the *Evening Standard* both for publishing extracts from *Mein Kampf* and for the facetious disrespect of its celebrated cartoonist, David Low. The general's keynote speech lasted for over an hour, and was, according to Gaertner, 'so boring that even the most enthusiastic member of the AGF ceased to listen'. She was amazed this 'collection of British people of the middle and upper classes could display the pathetic ignorance of foreign affairs, and German affairs in particular'.

With two hundred new joiners that year, the membership was now close to nine hundred and embraced luminaries from each of the British Establishment elites – royal, political, diplomatic, aristocratic, business, financial, military, sporting and intelligence. In three years, the Fellowship had evolved from an amateur business-backed pressure group irritating professional diplomats and politicians into the most respected forum for the promotion of Anglo-German relations. From being a marginal 'ginger group' of ideologues struggling to influence events, it now had direct and quick access to the British government, including the prime minister, his special adviser, the foreign secretary, his parliamentary undersecretary, the chief diplomatic adviser and the ambassador in Berlin, offering influence over foreign policy beyond envy to modern political lobbyists. In Germany, the Fellowship's leadership had similar access to Hitler and both his champions and his critics. The intelligence garnered by Christie and Conwell-Evans from ostensibly loyal commanders such as Göring and Milch, his deputy in the Luftwaffe, had been balanced by that from those military leaders and civil servants now energetically conspiring against Hitler.

Toasts were drunk to the King and the Führer after a dinner of smoked salmon, honeydew melon, chicken consommé, lobster Newburg and partridge, followed by ice cream and cherries. But soon the Munich glow faded. Only weeks after the dinner, at a Fellowship cocktail party, Friedl Gaertner had been pleased to be introduced to the guest speaker, Dr Karl Silex, Anglophile editor of the *Deutsche Allgemeine Zeitung* newspaper, one of the three 'great dailies' in Germany, whom Vansittart had met in

Berlin during the Olympics. This time, she thought the guests of a 'far more intelligent type' and, unlike General Tholens, Silex made an 'absolutely first-class speech… significantly free from bombast' and therefore 'more likely to make a good impression on the British'. Surprised to find nearly two million people unemployed in Britain and preparations for war such as trenches being dug in Hyde Park, Silex argued that the English should not feel humiliated by Munich nor believe Chamberlain had been forced to sign the agreement because his country had not been ready for war. Suggesting with a 'slight smirk' that perhaps the prime minister 'has another piece of paper… in his pocket', he diagnosed a cultural misunderstanding whereby 'England thinks, quite wrongly, that Germany threatens', while the Germans 'feel that whatever they do England is always against them'. Gaertner feared his 'considerable personal charm' and 'very convincing way of speaking' made him an 'extremely dangerous individual'.[2]

In Paris, seventeen-year-old Herschel Grynszpan received his sister's postcard with the news of their chaotic expulsion to the Polish border. Distraught, he bought a pistol and walked into the German embassy in Paris where, having failed to find the ambassador, he shot five bullets at the twenty-nine-year-old third secretary, Ernst vom Rath, before giving himself up to the French police. The German newspapers quickly blamed the 'Jewish people' for the shooting rather than this disturbed teenager. Within days, all Jewish newspapers and magazines were banned, Jewish children were expelled from Aryan schools, and Jews forbidden to own guns. On 8 November, the fifteenth anniversary of the Beer Hall Putsch, the unfortunate diplomat died from his injuries.

Two days after the shooting, in a night of unparalleled brutality, members of the SA led German civilians (including schoolchildren urged on by their teachers) in vicious attacks on Jews, their homes, schools and sacred buildings. Joseph Goebbels ordered that these should be presented as spontaneous demonstrations. During an orgy of violence extending through Germany and Austria to almost every city, town and village, Jewish-owned shops and businesses were ransacked and looted. A thousand synagogues, many dating back to the eighteenth century, were set alight and their sacred texts desecrated; storm troopers forced Viennese Jews to tear down their own synagogue. More than thirty thousand Jewish men were arrested and sent to concentration camps, where a thousand would later die. In twenty-four hours of carefully planned and ruthlessly executed violence, an estimated ninety-one Jews were killed by fellow Germans and many more took their own lives. Sir George Ogilvie-Forbes, the most senior British diplomat then in Berlin (Henderson being on sick leave), reported to London that there were 'no police… in evidence, and the Fire Brigades were turned out only to prevent the flames from burning synagogues and other buildings from damaging Aryan property'.

There had been nothing spontaneous or chaotic about the violence; soon known as the 'night of broken glass', or Kristallnacht, after the shards of shattered glass littered across the pavements, the violence had been methodical, exhaustive, shocking and impossible to ignore – both at home and abroad. Ogilvie-Forbes explained that there could be:

> no doubt that the deplorable excesses… were instigated and organised by the government. The attacking parties commenced operations at a given hour and singled out with uncanny precision Jewish shops, buildings, and places of business, and it seems that few mistakes were made. In the same way as they had begun, the attackers ceased operations on the word being given by Dr Goebbels, who, in his public utterances, condoned what had been done.[3]

No amount of propaganda by Goebbels could hide Kristallnacht from the world's media. As Conwell-Evans's friend and fellow historian, Martin Gilbert, explained in his compelling chronicle of the pogrom, with several hundred foreign journalists in Germany from all of the main international news agencies and national papers, 'no event in the history of the fate of the German Jews between 1933 and 1945 was so widely covered by the newspapers while it was taking place.'[4] On the twentieth anniversary of the end of the Great War (in which so many German Jews had served their country), the world's newspapers pulled no punches in reporting the events to their readers. The *Manchester Guardian* quickly upgraded its early reports from 'disturbances' to 'outrages' and 'barbarism'. The *Times* reported 'THOUSANDS OF JEWS ARRESTED' in a 'A BLACK DAY FOR GERMANY', while the *Daily Telegraph* told of 'GERMAN MOBS' VENGEANCE ON JEWS' resulting in 'JEWS SHOT DEAD'. The *Washington Post* saw 'JEWS VICTIM OF DAY OF VENGEANCE' while the *News Chronicle* focused on 'EXPLOSIONS, FIRES, PANICS' and the *Daily Herald* called it 'LIKE AIR RAID' with 'BOMBS USED TO SET SYNAGOGUES AFIRE'.

But despite civilian involvement, Conwell-Evans reported that the pogroms had caused 'as great a revulsion of feeling among the German people as they have done in England, and Hitler and the regime have suffered a further loss of prestige'.[5] Ogilvie-Forbes agreed, telling Halifax he had 'not met a single German of whatever class who in varying measures does not, to say the least, disapprove of what has occurred'.[6] As one leading German historian emphasised, Kristallnacht had been 'specifically intended to stifle the euphoria in Germany created by Munich'.[7] Arriving back in Berlin the day after the violence, Conwell-Evans's foreign ministry friends explained that the attacks had been 'deliberately undertaken in order to harden and brutalise the German people, so as to make them less unwilling to go to war'.[8]

Two days after Kristallnacht, Göring chaired a meeting at which it was agreed that German Jews would be forbidden from working in most professions or running businesses and banned from theatres, concerts, cinemas and exhibitions. German Jewry would be fined an 'atonement tax' of one billion marks (equivalent to an astonishing £84 million at the time) as punishment for the murder of the diplomat, and with the twisted logic of the Nazi mind, was held financially responsible for all damage to Jewish property resulting from the pogrom. Ogilvie-Forbes admitted he could 'find no words strong enough in condemnation of the disgusting treatment of so many innocent people and the… appalling sight of 500,000 people about to rot away in starvation'.[9] Halifax was similarly appalled by Kristallnacht and clashed with Chamberlain, who, though 'horrified', refused to provoke Hitler by taking definitive action against Germany or changing strategy.[10]

Even Hitler's most enthusiastic British supporters could not ignore Kristallnacht. The tensions fermenting since its foundation ignited an existential crisis for the Fellowship which brought its leadership's long-standing concerns about German anti-Semitism into the public domain for the first time. The Council met to discuss the crisis and the NSDAP sent Gert Schlottmann, chairman of the Berlin branch of the DEG, to investigate the British reaction. Conwell-Evans gave him a 'long tale of woe', explaining that the persecutions were having a 'disastrous effect on the Fellowship and its work'. Schlottmann initially thought this exaggerated, quoting 'various opinions to the contrary', presumably from the Pitt-Rivers claque. But he was quickly convinced, returning to Berlin 'extremely depressed and very shocked' at both the 'narrow-minded views of the British public' and 'the repercussions which the persecutions have had on the Fellowship itself'.[11]

Lord Mount Temple resigned as chairman (but remained a member) in protest at the treatment of the Jews by the Germans, telling the *Daily Telegraph* he thought that 'all activities should wait for a better time'.[12] The Council published a formal notice, signed by Conwell-Evans, in *The Times* and other newspapers and wrote separately to each member, deeply regretting the events, which 'set back the development of better understanding between the two nations'. Nonetheless, it promised to maintain its support for the appeasing prime minister, suggesting (with little evident conviction) that this would be the 'most useful way of encouraging those friendly relations upon which peace depends'.[13]

There is no reason to doubt Mount Temple's sincerity in resigning. As the former spy and now journalist Bruce Lockhart noted spikily in his diary, he was 'father of two half-Jewesses in Lady Louis Mountbatten and Mrs Cunningham-Reid'.[14] Were he a German subject, the *Evening Standard* pointed out, his 'non-Aryan connection would be enough to make him ineligible for chairmanship of the Deutsch-Englische Gesellschaft'.[15] The Jewish community, previously understandably suspicious of the Fellowship, welcomed this new vocalism; the *American Jewish Yearbook* saw it as evidence that 'even the most ardent advocates of Anglo-German friendship had finally become convinced the persecution of the Jews was more than an internal German problem and much more than a sentimental obstacle in the way of cooperation with the Nazi state'.[16] A grateful private Jewish correspondent begged Mount Temple to use his 'good offices' against the spread of 'Jew-baiting' in Britain.[17] Another Council member, David Mason, a former Liberal MP and ardent Germanophile, who had met Hitler and Goebbels two years before, wrote to *The Times* attacking Goebbels and appealing to 'our common humanity... because the refugee question very directly concerns us as a nation and as individuals'.[18] But not all admired these principled stands; C. E. Carroll, the pro-Nazi founder of the *Anglo-German Review*, wrote gleefully to his fellow enthusiast, George Pitt-Rivers, declaring that Mount Temple's resignation would be a 'big blow' for the Fellowship before asking, 'What will their tea parties be without him now?'[19]

Friedl Gaertner reported that the Fellowship had lost nearly half its membership, that subscriptions had fallen to a 'deplorably low level', and many of the 'influential hosts and hostesses' now refused to support functions attended by Nazi Party members.[20] Betty Pomeroy, the office secretary (whom she thought a 'very intelligent and sincere woman'), was 'genuinely horrified at the recent turn of events' and had characterised the lingering members as 'only a lot of useless fanatics'.[21] Three months later, MI5 noted how disappointed the Nazis now were with the Fellowship: 'Berlin have been counting very considerably on the influence which the AGF might exert during a crisis and it is considered that they completely failed in this in September.'[22] Nor were the German diplomats in London any happier with the damage done. Just a week after Kristallnacht, von Dirksen sent an agitated report to Berlin bemoaning the 'anti-Semitic wave' in Germany which had triggered a 'fresh wave of anti-German feeling' in England, undermining the morale of supportive Britons. All this, he added, had been 'grist to the mill' to the anti-German lobby, who had used it to attack Chamberlain and his policies.[23]

While the weary and disillusioned Tennant wanted to keep the Fellowship going and its mission alive, he was now under no illusion about the Third Reich and the terror of Kristallnacht, which he now knew had been crueller even than reported in the British media:

It is unimaginable. Jews of the best families, diplomats, bankers, ex officers, etc. are going to be forced without money to settle in ghettos being formed in the Grenadierstrasse and surrounding districts, that is in the worst slum quarter of Berlin. From the number of damaged buildings I saw during my short stay in Berlin, the recent destruction of Jewish property must have exceeded any descriptions I have read about. How the Jews are to earn any money on which to exist until they can leave the country remains a mystery. Even leaving the country presents them with insoluble problems. To get a visa from the various consulates requires personal visits to be made to these offices, most of which are situated in streets which Jews are forbidden to enter. The same applies to the shipping company offices. Further, the fares usually have to be paid in foreign exchange which is not available. As far as I can make out the majority of the German people are becoming shocked and disgusted.[24]

Hitler now dropped all earlier pretensions to being a man of peace, recognising it had encouraged pacifism at home and hobbled his negotiations with Neville Chamberlain. He instructed Göring to host a conference to find an urgent solution to the 'Jewish question' and, just a week before Christmas, ordered the Wehrmacht to develop a plan for the liquidation of the rump Czech state. That same week, the British prime minister was still giving speeches appeasing rather than standing up to the dictators, much to his foreign secretary's frustration. Such rhetoric stoked Hitler's conviction that Britain and France would still not go to war for any 'far off' country.

PART THREE

December 1938–May 1941

*Pedestrians glance at the broken windows of a Jewish-owned shop
in Berlin after the attacks of Kristallnacht, November 1938.*

20

THE TWO ENGLISHMEN WHO KNOW GERMANY BEST

THE TURBULENCE OF ANGLO-GERMAN RELATIONS IN THE LAST weeks of 1938 begged obvious questions for Ernest Tennant, Philip Conwell-Evans, Grahame Christie and Philip Lothian as to whether to battle on with the Anglo-German Fellowship and, if so, what its battle might be. Hobbled by the loss of its chairman, members and sponsorship, it was also assailed by bad publicity and hostile questions in the House of Commons. Historians have generally assumed the Fellowship shamefacedly abandoned its activities in the months immediately following Mount Temple's resignation when, in reality, despite growing British public animosity towards Germany, it struggled on for the months leading up to the outbreak of war.[1] But now its only valid purpose was as a conduit through which its champions could dig for intelligence on Hitler's real intentions and develop various last-ditch quests to save the peace.

In December, Tennant and Conwell-Evans returned separately to Berlin while their friend and patron Lord Lothian embarked on a seven-week tour of the United States. The purpose and tone of these three journeys had changed profoundly. As he remembered in his memoir, Conwell-Evans now used the Fellowship as an umbrella under which to 'collect anti-Nazis' in Germany, even deploying transport kindly supplied by the Gestapo to meet his contacts.[2] One such valued informant was Eugen Diesel, a well-connected writer on technology and son of Rudolf Diesel, inventor of the eponymous internal combustion engine. Hostile to National Socialism and linked to the resistance, Eugen warned Conwell-Evans that the Nazis had added Denmark to the list of countries they planned to conquer. He also briefed him about the development of rockets (presumably the precursors of the V-2) designed to be launched from the Dutch and Flemish coasts against London.[3]

The first social event hosted by the Fellowship since the dramas triggered by Kristallnacht was a reception in Mayfair to hear a talk by Colonel P. T. Etherton, a well-known explorer and aviator. Just back from a tour of Germany and the Sudetenland, he had inspected a labour camp, visited the industrial areas and lunched with General Göring at his country house. This was the third Fellowship gathering Friedl Gaertner had infiltrated on behalf of MI5, and she found the tone quite different to its predecessors – not least because the persecution of Germany's Jewish population was raised explicitly as a subject for discussion. Etherton recounted to his audience of 150 guests how he had berated Göring about Goebbels's propaganda attacks on Great Britain and debated the relative competence of the two countries' air forces. Though disturbed by the very visible public notices attacking the Jews, he stressed the 'evident goodness and kindness' of most Germans, counselling against judging a nation by its leaders. Gaertner thought this explicit criticism of the regime gave the evening an 'utterly different' flavour and surprised the audience. She quizzed the membership secretary Betty Pomeroy as to whether Berlin had sent instructions to tone down the blatant German propaganda. Pomeroy admitted the Fellowship now faced a stark choice between adopting an 'entirely new line' or risking extinction.[4]

Lord Lothian had left for the US determined to highlight the threat of Hitler's Germany and to lobby for American help in controlling the seas. Visiting as a private individual rather than as British ambassador designate, he insisted his appointment should remain secret, even to the president himself, so he could speak openly on the German situation. He and Roosevelt met on the second day of the new year; initially booked in as a fifteen-minute courtesy call, it ran to an hour and quickly escalated into a heated debate. The two men had been introduced twenty years before at the Paris Peace Conference, when the young Roosevelt had been assistant secretary of the US Navy and Lothian private secretary to the prime minister. They had most recently met three years before, when Lothian had been a vocal advocate of appeasement. Now he launched into his campaign to persuade the sceptical president that Britain had the mettle to resist Hitler, and therefore needed and deserved American support. FDR ascribed British naivety about the Nazi threat to an over-preoccupation with communism, telling him that the 'wealthy class in England is so afraid of communism, which has constituted no threat at all to England, that they have thrown themselves into the arms of Nazism, and now they don't know which way to turn'.[5] Roosevelt had amiably teased his guest about his previous foolish confidence in the Third Reich, to which Lothian responded robustly by insisting the German threat was now very real and appeasement in England now very dead. FDR then berated Lothian and his country's poor morale: 'I got mad clear through and told him that just so long as he or Britishers like him took the attitude of complete despair, the British would not be worth saving anyway'.[6]

When the president asked whether Hitler was a 'gentleman with whom you can negotiate', Lothian had thrown up his hands and admitted to having been terribly wrong.[7] Ever more impassioned, he was adamant that Britain had 'defended civilisation for one thousand years' but now the 'spear is falling from her hand' and so it was up to the United States to 'take it and carry on'. Though FDR later admitted he had taken all this with a grain of salt, and had asked for more proof, the process of persuading the US into supporting the British in any future European war was now well under way.[8]

While its London sister society struggled to redefine its purpose in the escalating diplomatic crisis, the Deutsch-Englische Gesellschaft expanded ever faster, opening new branches across the country, from Bremen and Hamburg in the north to Munich and Vienna in the south, and from Essen and Cologne in the west to Dresden in the east. Each branch clamoured for support, in the form of visiting lecturers, contacts and hospitality in England from the now painfully under-resourced Anglo-German Fellowship in London. Tennant mused that this late-in-the-day enthusiasm had been a response by the 'best elements' among the German people to the atrocities against the Jews and other 'unpleasant features of the present regime', prompting them to 'stretch out their hands towards Great Britain'. But money remained a problem. Despite securing some funding for the Fellowship from the British Council, with membership fees, corporate donations and income from events all diminishing, its financial state was now parlous. Lobbying the British government for more support, Tennant argued to a Cabinet minister that a 'few thousand pounds' for the Fellowship to support the DEG's efforts inside Germany would be 'immensely valuable', equivalent to equipping several army divisions or to building several naval cruisers.[9] Halifax agreed with the principle, estimating to the Cabinet that the Germans were spending five million pounds a year on sophisticated propaganda which should be countermanded by a campaign involving the BBC, personal business contacts, a British Library of Information in Berlin, pamphlets from the British Council and lecture tours to the DEG and German universities.[10]

The intelligence garnered by Conwell-Evans and Christie now reached the apex of British government. Vansittart commissioned them to collate their thoughts into a joint report which he needed to counteract the advice fed by the ambassador to the prime minister and his chief adviser, as all three clung like drowning men to the flotsam that was their waterlogged dogma of appeasement. While Van's earlier memoranda were criticised for their circumlocutory literary style and often ignored, this one could not have been clearer. Running to eighteen pages, professionally printed and individually numbered, each copy had been stamped THE PROPERTY OF HIS BRITANNIC MAJESTY'S GOVERNMENT, presumably to make it harder to ignore, and labelled MOST SECRET... TO BE KEPT UNDER LOCK AND KEY, doubtless to ensure that anyone who saw it read it. Sending it to the foreign secretary early in the new year, Vansittart shrewdly explained that it had been written by the 'two Englishmen who know Germany best... strong and pronounced Germanophils [sic]' whose earlier enthusiasm for the regime should add credibility and balance to those voices, such as his own, critical of the Nazis since the outset.[11] This crucial document crystallises in print their volte-face on appeasement, gestating for at least eighteen months. Christie admitted he had initially believed in the 'sincerity and applicability' of National Socialism, while Conwell-Evans had welcomed it as a 'healthy force to combat communism'.[12] Both now unequivocally condemned the 'aggressive and fanatical nationalism, racial intolerance and arrogance' of the Third Reich and deplored its 'idolatry of man... worship of physical might [and] contempt for everything humane'.[13]

The document mapped out the path of Hitler's regime over the next few years and hindsight shows it to have been chillingly prescient. Halifax circulated it to the Cabinet Foreign Policy Committee, which included all the most senior Cabinet ministers, ahead of their January meeting. This committee now served as the main forum for discussions around 'Possible German Intentions' and would meet thirty times between that point and the invasion of Poland. Reminding his colleagues that Van's secret sources had shown themselves over the previous year to be 'on the whole, accurate and correct', he insisted on the strictest secrecy as they risked 'liquidation' if anything leaked.[14]

Conwell-Evans opened his section bluntly warning that 'our country and empire are faced by a greater peril than has yet threatened them in their history'. Hitler, he explained, had been 'bewildered' by events, felt 'thwarted' by the Munich Agreement, and had been 'incensed' by Chamberlain scuppering his plans to conquer Czechoslovakia. Now 'little better than a monster in his ruthlessness and cruelty', the German leader was driven by his 'hatred and envy of England', whom he swore would now 'have to dance to our tune'. Were he to update *Mein Kampf*, his only revision would be to withdraw the proffered friendship with an England whom he now saw as Germany's *Todfeind* (deadly enemy).

Like Colonel Etherton, Conwell-Evans urged his readers to differentiate the regime from its subjects. Following the atrocities of Kristallnacht, Hitler now suffered mounting domestic criticism, especially from German women whose 'humane sentiments' were not yet crushed. To do so, they needed to be subjected to continuous propaganda about the 'essential criminality of Jews, the worthlessness of democracy and the ideas of a decadent and weak England'. Ribbentrop and Goebbels were now Hitler's main advisers and allies, with the foreign minister stamping on any 'considerations of prudence' and accusing his more experienced colleagues of 'defeatism'. While Göring may still feel 'grave misgiving' about the path to war, he was no less corrupt than the other German leaders, cheerfully diverting 'vast sums of public money' for their private use.

Liberating the Sudetens, he explained, had merely been Hitler's pretext to induce the Germans to make war. The year 1939 would be the 'most menacing', as they rapidly pushed eastwards in force. Within six to twelve months, they would turn to the west and 'reduce England to the position of a second-rate power'. The conquest of Eastern Europe would advance rapidly, culminating with an alliance between Russia and Germany, possibly within the year.

Bluntly, Conwell-Evans urged his fellow Britons to 'pull ourselves together and take the most drastic measures' or accept that 1940 may 'witness the collapse of the British Empire'. A coordinated programme of propaganda and rearmament would be essential. His German contacts advised him that the regime could be ended within six to twelve months by skilful propaganda offering to cooperate with the German people. Rearmament should be accelerated, with intimidating statistics and lavish illustrations of Britain's fearsome military hardware splashed around in the newspapers to impress the Germans.

Christie, who had been monitoring Germany's military build-up since the 1920s, detailed how the German economy was being primed for war. Jewish property was being confiscated, private enterprise attacked, sourcing of essential materials prioritised, and state-controlled barter introduced. The opposition to Hitler had weakened but might win some popular support if he attacked France or Great Britain. The German army would be broadly loyal to the Führer, as he offered better career prospects to its officers than the alternatives. Great Britain's salvation depended upon the 'adroitness of our statesmen', particularly in separating Mussolini from Hitler. Russia, he predicted, would be pivotal in any future war and may well resist a German invasion successfully if the 'bulk of the Red Army remained intact, adopted the tactics of retreat and refused to desert Stalin or form a Germanophil [*sic*] government'. At that point, Great Britain and France could intervene to bring down the Nazi government and replace it with 'saner men of reason'.

This intelligence harvested by Christie from his well-embedded network in Germany was finally being listened to. How much difference it made is inevitably hard to qualify. But in a short entry in the *Oxford Dictionary of National Biography*, the distinguished historian Donald Cameron Watt has made the strongest case that it did; he concluded that, after the Munich Agreement, Christie's briefings to the British government were 'at least in part responsible for the war scare of the third week in January 1939'. This, he continues, led to the 'adoption for the first time by a British cabinet in peacetime of a commitment of the British Army to a continental war, to the subsequent doubling of the Territorial Army, and then in April 1939 to conscription'.[15]

Alec Cadogan was reassured that the Foreign Policy Committee did not 'pooh-pooh' all this intelligence and recognised that another serious outrage by Hitler, such as an attack on Holland, would bring Britain into a war and so it was time to take the US into their confidence. He therefore drafted a telegram to Washington picking up the key themes of the new year memorandum, all of which echoed Lothian's briefing to the president earlier that month. Promising that 'His Majesty's Government have no wish to be alarmist', but nonetheless signed by the foreign secretary, approved by the prime minister, and sourced from 'highly placed Germans of undoubted sincerity', the cable advised the Americans that Hitler was 'bitterly resentful' about Munich, humiliated by Britain, and planning a 'further adventure' for spring of 1939, possibly including an attack on Holland. Delicately avoiding asking for explicit US support, it did admit it would be a 'great help' if the president had 'any further suggestions to make'. Arriving at the US embassy, Cadogan handed the telegram to the first secretary. Having read it, the shocked American diplomat admitted it made him feel 'quite sick'.[16]

Luftwaffe aircraft perform a fly-by in honour of Adolf Hitler's birthday in Charlottenburg, Berlin, 20 April 1939.

21

NO HAPPY RETURNS
FOR THE FÜHRER

While Lord Lothian completed his US tour, in February 1939 Philip Conwell-Evans returned to Berlin for an eight-day visit to attend a dinner hosted by the Deutsch-Englische Gesellschaft, to lunch with Ribbentrop, and to meet his other foreign ministry friends. It would prove to be his last pre-war visit to the country; soon after, Robert Vansittart warned he could no longer guarantee his personal safety, as the German authorities were watching him. Having enjoyed such rare access to the National Socialists' topmost tables and most powerful corridors for four years, the Nazis now doubted his 'political reliability', suspicious of his links to those sceptical or even actively resistant to the regime.[1] But though isolated from his German informants, Conwell-Evans's personal stock had risen in the eyes of British government decision makers. Paradoxically, at the same time, through a series of missteps, misjudgements and misunderstandings, the reputation of his cherished Anglo-German Fellowship was collapsing almost entirely.

The German guests at the DEG dinner included the state secretary, von Weizsäcker, and other NSDAP leaders, government officials and military representatives, while Sir Nevile Henderson and Lord Brocket gave speeches on behalf of the British guests. The ambassador, just back from six months' sick leave in Britain for cancer surgery, used the event, as he had two years before, to promote Chamberlain's appeasement rather than advance the Foreign Office's more robust line.[2] Calling for a 'firm friendship' based on protecting the 'vital interests of Germany as a continental and Great Britain as an oversea power', he offered Hitler the catnip of a free hand in

Europe in return for the Empire remaining unmolested. Even *The Times*, infamous for its dogged endorsement of appeasement and supportive of this ambassador, had been surprised.[3] As Henderson sat down, the head of the foreign ministry press bureau arrived with a telegram reporting that the House of Commons had voted for a further £150 million for rearmament. When pressed to justify this, the ambassador scrawled, 'peace can only be ensured when Britain is in a position to defend herself' across the offending telegram and signed it.[4] A furious Vansittart advised the foreign secretary that this had created the impression the British were inclined to be 'duped'.[5] A shocked Conwell-Evans reported that the moderate industrialists at the dinner were so alarmed by the ambassador's naivety and indiscretion, they thought it dangerous to even talk with him.[6]

In reply, the Duke of Coburg celebrated the ambassador's acceptance of honorary membership of the DEG (a distinction he shared with Joseph Goebbels), then parroted Hitler's latest mollifying appeals for cooperation before applauding the recently signed Anglo-German Coal Agreement and proposing further trade talks. Henderson proudly reported that the duke's speech had been drafted under Hitler's direction, so exciting the prime minister that he sent a precis to his sister, assuring her it pointed towards peace and that finally the British had 'got on top of the dictators'.[7] At a speech in Blackburn soon after, approvingly covered by the German press, he made conciliatory noises to Hitler. In a report, the US ambassador Joe Kennedy laid out for Washington the tensions now prevailing between Downing Street and the Foreign Office. While the latter believed 'Hitler is not to be trusted at all and… will do something that will provoke trouble any day', Chamberlain's plan would be to 'go along, preparing and arming all the time, but assuming that he can do business with Hitler'.[8]

The lunch hosted by Ribbentrop would turn out to be Conwell-Evans's last ever meeting with his erstwhile friend and so marked the end of an era. The other guests included his bête noire, Lord Brocket, and Walther Hewel, a DEG Council member and Ribbentrop's liaison with Hitler. Ribbentrop, whom Conwell-Evans complained he had 'never found so difficult', was now 'rapidly succumbing to a type of megalomania'. Now not even pretending tolerance, Ribbentrop shocked his guest by insisting 'every Jew must leave Germany'. Launching a tirade of abuse at President Roosevelt, he labelled him the 'mouthpiece of Judah and the instrument of the Comintern', accusing him of hoping to 'bring about the Chancellor's defeat', but did admit he was the only statesman who 'sees through' Hitler.[9]

Conwell-Evans also used his last visit to Berlin to meet his other foreign ministry friends discreetly in a suburb. They confirmed that Hitler had made the decision to 'finish off Czechoslovakia' and the gulf between Ribbentrop and Göring had been widened by their 'personal jealousy and bitter rivalry'.[10] Having moved so comfortably in senior National Socialist circles, Conwell-Evans felt deeply alarmed by the 'atmosphere of terror' and the rising profile of Himmler's SS officers at the German foreign ministry.[11]

Meanwhile, following a tête-à-tête with Hermann Göring, Nevile Henderson sent a telegram to Halifax painting the Berlin atmosphere in a far kinder light. The field marshal was run down, having lost forty pounds on an extreme diet, and planned a rest cure in Italy. Despite himself having been away from Berlin for months, Henderson felt qualified to reassure Göring he expected no 'serious international trouble' and saw no appetite in Britain for a preventative war, except within a 'section of the intelligentsia and of London opinion'. Even Göring, the arch dissembler, admitted he wished he could share Henderson's confidence, especially given the risk of Churchill or Eden replacing Chamberlain as prime minister.[12] Desperate to foster calm and contradicting Halifax's cable to Washington, the ambassador reassured London that the Führer planned no more 'adventures' and insisted 'all stories and rumours to the contrary are completely without real foundation'. Czechoslovakia might be 'squeezed', but Hitler would not 'force the pace unless his own hand is forced', as he would rather 'return to the fold of comparative respectability'. Incandescent, Vansittart insisted to the foreign secretary that 'squeezed' was entirely the wrong word and damned the ambassador as a 'national danger'.

Vansittart forwarded Conwell-Evans's report from his final Berlin trip to the foreign secretary, with a four-page cover note calling it 'one of the most illuminating papers' he had ever read. Knowing Ribbentrop as he did, 'at least ten times' better than did Henderson, Conwell-Evans's intelligence was far more credible than the ambassador's 'dangerous rubbish' and blew his 'fallacious cobweb into the limbo where it belongs'.[13] The report reiterated Hitler and Ribbentrop's hostility to Britain and their low opinion of the strength of the Anglo-French alliance. It also highlighted how the economic challenges facing Germany had driven the vice president of the

Reichsbank, Rudolf Brinckmann, to a very public nervous breakdown. Wages were inflating and the national railway system was breaking down. Hitler's frequent changes of foreign policy were frustrating the General Staff; he had dropped plans to invade the Ukraine and Holland in favour of the incorporation of Bohemia and part of Moravia so that Czechoslovakia would be wiped out as an independent state. Caught, as often, between these two ideologues, the pragmatic Alec Cadogan noted in his diary, 'Nevile H is completely bewitched by his German friends' while Van 'out Cassandras Cassandra in a kind of spirit of pantomime'.[14] He could not decide whether to recommend Halifax rebuke Vansittart for alarmism or recall Henderson for incompetence – or perhaps both.

To protect his and Christie's German sources, whose lives were at risk, Conwell-Evans asked Vansittart to redact his identity in all government papers except those reserved for the foreign secretary, Cadogan and one other senior official. Emphasising the 'state of terrorism' in Berlin, Vansittart supplied Halifax with a list of Conwell-Evans's informants and confirmed they were also known to him.[15] Although confusion within the Foreign Office is still vivid from any reading of its files, the warnings from the Vansittart camp were finally gaining an audience.[16] Cadogan read and annotated the February report carefully, particularly endorsing the criticisms of the meddling and misguided Brocket. A few days later, he prepared a minute accepting Hitler's intentions as 'strictly dishonourable' but worried the Germans might be duping Conwell-Evans to spread misinformation. He queried the wider value of the intelligence given Hitler's frequent changes of mind, for example around the rumoured invasion of Holland.[17] Other voices in the Office were less convinced. Frank Roberts, a junior official in the Central Department, added a minute encouraging colleagues to read Brocket's different account of the views expressed by Ribbentrop at that fateful last lunch.

Brocket followed up his report to Chamberlain with a letter to *The Times* berating other newspapers for publishing 'alarming reports' about foreign affairs, including 'inaccurate, unconfirmed or even false news'. He suggested this had triggered the May Crisis and generated needless heat between Britain and Germany. Telling readers he had left Berlin impressed by the Germans' 'obvious desire for a period of consolidation and peace with other countries, particularly with England', he ended by explaining:

World peace and world trade are built up on friendship and confidence.
The circulations of some newspapers depend on scares and crises. But war
would affect all alike. Why cannot the press take a longer, wiser, and, may
I say, more Christian, view, and work actively with those who are striving
to promote prosperity, friendship, and peace in the world?

Preferring this far sunnier interpretation, Chamberlain shared its sentiments
with the parliamentary press lobby, without clearance from the foreign
secretary or his office. When press reports duly appeared the next day
painting the picture as 'brighter than it had been for some time', Cadogan
dismissed this 'rainbow story' as too optimistic, while the 'quite nettled'
Halifax rebuked the prime minister for raising hopes of disarmament when
rearmament would be the only way forward. Chamberlain replied with a
grovelling apology, explaining that he had never intended to be quoted and
had only given the journalists 'background'.[18]

Now barred from Germany since February, Conwell-Evans had
abandoned hope of persuading the National Socialists to negotiate with
Britain, but Ernest Tennant continued his own shuttle diplomacy well
into the summer. In March, he attended a banquet given by Cologne's
Bürgermeister to mark the opening of its branch of the Deutsch-Englische
Gesellschaft. Frank Tiarks, a Fellowship founder and leading banker,
was the keynote speaker and guests included the British ambassador
and the German finance minister. Tiarks's speech (delivered in German
and then printed in English) celebrated the long-standing connections
between Germany, especially the Hanseatic cities, and the City of London,
echoing the economic appeasement advocated by the sister societies
back in the Baldwin years. Given the abject failure of Chamberlain's
diplomatic appeasement at and since Munich, this approach must have
seemed worthy of revival. But Henderson showed no new thinking,
merely repeating his pacific theme by stressing that British rearmament
was defensive, with no question of it being deployed 'aggressively, or
to attack Germany'. At a time when both the Cabinet and the British
public were fast losing faith in Chamberlain's foreign policy, this was
his second such conciliatory speech to the DEG in only weeks and they
were covered by the press of both countries. Conwell-Evans had made
it quite clear that the sister societies did not share the ambassador's

views, but by giving him such a prominent platform, unsurprisingly many assumed they did so.

Three days later and back in London, the Anglo-German Fellowship welcomed Frau Gertrud Scholtz-Klink at a dinner at Claridge's. Labelled Hitler's 'perfect Nazi woman' by the press, the thirty-four-year-old *Reichsfrauenführerin* headed the National Socialist Women's League and various other women's organisations, putting her nominally in charge of thirty million German women. The British newspapermen waiting excitedly at Croydon to greet this paragon of Nazi womanhood as she stepped out of her aeroplane were sorely disappointed. Her austere wardrobe of 'black shoes, dark stockings, a black cape of a silky material, a black tailored suit, with a white shirt and tartan tie' intimidated the correspondent from the *Evening Standard*, who was also disappointed by her freckles, lack of make-up and unplucked eyebrows.

This bizarre and controversial visit by one of Hitler's least-remembered acolytes was the Fellowship's last major social event. It cemented the reputational damage done by the resignations of Mount Temple and so many members. Lady David Douglas-Hamilton, formerly Prunella Stack, had invited Scholtz-Klink to London. Stack headed the Women's League of Health and Beauty and had recently married the younger brother of the Everest-conquering Marquess of Clydesdale. His family were enthusiastic supporters of the Fellowship and their connections with the National Socialists would come under worldwide scrutiny two years later when Rudolf Hess, the deputy führer, parachuted onto their Scottish estate.

The timing of Scholtz-Klink's trip and her effusive welcome seem tone-deaf, as Hitler's army was days away from invading Prague and relations between Britain and Germany were in crisis. Historians have rightly questioned Conwell-Evans and the Council's support for her visit, and the motives of the German authorities in sponsoring it, given they had lost faith in the Fellowship, and such soft propaganda in Britain was now a low priority.[19] Commentators have assumed her invitation dated from the previous December, two months after Kristallnacht, but it has now emerged that the dinner had been originally scheduled for early 1938, well before Munich, when Anglo-German relations had been far rosier.[20]

Lady Halifax welcomed Scholtz-Klink, whom the ambassador's wife and the Kordts had escorted from the embassy. Given the low ebb of

Anglo-German relations, the prestige of the British guests and the organisations they represented (which later played critical roles in Britain's wartime civil defence) is noteworthy. The Marchioness of Reading, widow of an earlier foreign secretary, chaired the Women's Voluntary Services for Civil Defence, Lady Violet Astor served as controller of the County of London Auxiliary Territorial Service, while Dame Beryl Oliver represented the British Red Cross and Dorothy Peto, Britain's first female police superintendent, the Metropolitan Police. A host of other women's organisations, ranging from the Women's Gas Council to the Association for Moral and Social Hygiene, sent representatives.

Scholtz-Klink opened her speech on 'Women's Work in Germany', delivered in German, with a pointed attack on international journalists. Introducing herself sarcastically as the 'leader of the most oppressed women in the world', her themes were soundly Nazi and the dinner gave her views a prominent platform in central London in front of this distinguished audience only six months before the outbreak of war.[21] Having extolled the healthy virtues and employment of German womanhood under National Socialism, she attacked the evils of both Bolshevism and the Weimar Republic. Florence Horsbrugh, the Chamberlain-supporting, pro-appeasement MP (later minister of education), commended the work of Britain's women's organisations, while Lady David spoke of those devoted to physical fitness.

In the weeks following the awkward Scholtz-Klink dinner, a series of events redefined Anglo-German relations, shaping the deteriorating global situation for the rest of the year and setting the scene for the Second World War. Back in February, Christie had warned the Foreign Office that 'our incalculable Führer is now planning to strike nearer home, viz., a punitive expedition to Prague.'[22] On Friday, 10 March, an assistant secretary in the German war ministry warned him that the army would occupy Bohemia and Moravia some time in the next ten days. Unwilling to risk an intercepted telephone call or telegram, he hurried back to London over the weekend. Drily, he explained to Van that the alleged mistreatment by the Czechs of the Slovaks had provoked 'tender emotions' from the Führer even faster than his 'remarkable personal solicitude' for the Sudeten Germans the previous year.[23] Over the weekend, MI5 and SIS confirmed the rumours of a planned occupation. But Nevile Henderson still recommended Alec

Cadogan ignore these 'wild stories of attacks', reassuring London that the German government was 'not contemplating action' and advising Halifax against any reaction as Hitler was yet to make up his mind.[24]

On that Wednesday (the Ides of March), the Munich Agreement, and with it Henderson's last shreds of credibility, suffered their mortal blow when the Wehrmacht marched into Prague and took control of the rump of Czechoslovakia. The Reich absorbed eight million non-Germans and a delighted Hitler issued an official proclamation confirming the country had ceased to exist. The rarely ruffled Halifax summoned the German ambassador for a dressing-down, recalled Henderson from his embassy and postponed the visit to Berlin by the president of the Board of Trade which had been planned for the next day. Despite all the intelligence warnings, the news still stunned Chamberlain, and in the House of Commons the next day, as Hitler's forces reached Prague, he maintained a tone of only 'moderate disappointment and regret' and continued to defend his Munich Agreement.[25] On Friday, following criticism from all quarters, he sharpened his response in a speech broadcast from Birmingham chastising Hitler for forcing non-Germans into the Reich and mistreating Jews.

The German ambassador reported to Berlin that the occupation had 'stiffened' the mood in London and led to a 'sharper line' in the Cabinet, especially by Halifax. As the Munich Agreement had been 'fundamentally repudiated', Hitler's word would now not be trusted, as people asked whether Germany aspired to hegemony over Europe or even 'world dominion'.[26] While unlikely to trigger a war, the repercussions, he concluded, would be deeper and longer-lasting than following the *Anschluss*, the September crisis or Kristallnacht.

Both supporters and opponents of the embattled prime minister agreed his credibility had been hard hit, especially given his optimism to the press and his hopes for the trade minister's visit. Winston Churchill's own constituency party had, only weeks before, tried to deselect him for insisting the Munich Agreement had 'sealed the ruin' of Czechoslovakia. Now, as German forces massed on its borders, he warned his constituents that the Czechoslovak Republic was being 'broken up before our eyes' as the Nazis stole its gold, 'blotted out' its freedoms and eviscerated its army so that it had now lost 'all symbols of an independent democratic state'.[27] Two days later, a similarly vindicated Anthony Eden asked fellow MPs, 'Is there any member... now who believes that after these events we shall have more than another brief respite, perhaps briefer than the last, before further demands are made, before another victim is arraigned and before that victim is again faced with the alternative of resistance or surrender?'[28]

Lothian now agreed with Churchill and Eden, admitting that before Prague it had been possible to believe Germany only sought 'normal rights of a great power', but now Hitler was a 'fanatical gangster who will stop at nothing to beat down all possibility of resistance'.[29] That weekend, an emotional Conwell-Evans wrote to the foreign secretary applauding the prime minister's tougher line but admitted to feeling 'rather hurt' at how in recent speeches both Halifax and Chamberlain had condemned rumours of German aggression as being alarmist. Halifax replied at once to assure him he should not take it personally and insisting how much they appreciated *his* intelligence and hard work.[30] But despite Henderson's litany of bad advice, the British government still supported its hapless envoy, at least publicly. In the House of Commons, the Chancellor of the Exchequer defended the failure of 'our very competent ambassador' to predict Hitler's action on the absurd grounds it had been dependent on the 'decision of a single man'.[31] Cadogan privately admitted that Vansittart, whom only a month before he had considered dismissing, had been right all along.[32]

The march into Prague was the second existential shock for the Anglo-German Fellowship following Kristallnacht. It was also a disaster for Chamberlain's policy of appeasement. MPs asked hostile questions in the House of Commons about both his policy and the continuing role of the Fellowship, which were reported in the national newspapers. William Gallacher, the only British communist MP, accused the government of betraying the Czechs and called for its removal before drawing the attention of his colleagues to the list of MPs, bankers and insurance company directors associated with the 'so-called Anglo-German Fellowship'.[33] A month later, Geoffrey Mander, a Liberal MP and vocal anti-appeaser, asked Samuel Hoare, the Home Secretary, about the extent of German support for such 'pro-Nazi' organisations and demanded a committee of inquiry.[34] Hoare dismissed the request and defended the Fellowship's promotion of Anglo-German understanding. But accepting the risk of it being used for 'other purposes', he did reassure Mander it would be watched closely. Unconvinced, Mander asked whether it promoted Nazi propaganda and anti-Semitism, provoking angry responses from the two MPs who served on its Council. The next day, the Conservative MP Vyvyan Adams asked the Home Secretary whether the Fellowship offered a 'channel for Nazi propaganda' and, four days later, demanded its 'surviving members' be 'vigilantly encircled'.[35] Despite the vigorous defences voiced by its supporters in the House, there is no doubt this mud stuck.

Against this avalanche of hostility, Conwell-Evans had asked in his letter to the foreign secretary for guidance on what to do with the now moribund Fellowship. Elegantly gentle in his advice, Halifax wanted to avoid anything that might 'break down all the bridges between the two peoples' and hoped to retain 'such means as we can of showing that the British people have no quarrel with the German people'. Rather than order its closure (as some have claimed) he therefore suggested deferring any meetings for a 'month or two' until the situation was clearer.[36]

Despite the Führer's triumphant return to Berlin from Prague on 19 March, the rape of Czechoslovakia faced a mixed reception domestically. Unlike Hitler's three earlier military excursions, this returned neither German territory nor German speakers to the Reich, and many Germans had taken on trust his assurances that the Sudetenland would be his last such adventure. Therefore, Joseph Goebbels designed the elaborate celebrations of Hitler's fiftieth birthday the next month as a 'mammoth display of the might and power of the Third Reich, calculated to show the Western powers what faced them if they should tangle with the new Germany'.[37] The military parade through Berlin lasted for five hours, leaving the audience, but apparently not Hitler, exhausted.

The attendance by any British guests at Hitler's birthday was provocative, even for his most forgiving admirers within and without the Anglo-German Fellowship. The French, British and American ambassadors remained withdrawn in protest at the invasion of Prague. The Poles refused to attend. Lord Halifax had ordered the chargé d'affaires not to contribute to a birthday present for the Führer, while Cadogan had arranged for the King to send congratulations but pointedly exclude the 'happy returns'.[38] Having accepted the foreign secretary's guidance to soft-pedal the Fellowship and Vansittart's warning not to travel to Germany, neither Conwell-Evans nor any member of the Council attended. But two members did go as Hitler's private guests: the irrepressible Lord Brocket and the eccentric Major General J. F. C. Fuller, a well-known military strategist, historian, occultist and noted pro-Nazi. Brocket had wilfully ignored Alec Cadogan who, having consulted the prime minister, instructed him not to 'junket with Hitler on his birthday'. He flew out with the eighth Duke of Buccleuch, the owner of vast estates in Scotland, whose enthusiasm for Hitler had so embarrassed King George VI. Clearly furious, Cadogan noted in his diary: 'Ye Gods and little fishes! Is the world upside down? ... those 2... must make it perfectly clear that they have no sort of official approval of any kind.'[39]

Reporting on the birthday celebrations, the *Manchester Guardian* implied wrongly that Brocket was attending on behalf of the Anglo-German Fellowship when the organisation had already been suspended under Halifax's direction.[40] With hostile questions echoing around the chamber of the Commons, this mistaken association between Brocket's attendance and the Fellowship, so soon after the disastrously timed dinner for Frau Scholtz-Klink, permanently damaged the organisation's reputation, undermining the Council's careful efforts over so many years to position itself as Germanophile rather than Hitlerite.

On their return from Berlin, Brocket and Buccleuch energetically briefed anyone who would listen with their wildly optimistic report of the political atmosphere in Berlin. Chips Channon, the arch-appeasing junior minister in the Foreign Office and famous diarist, arranged for Buccleuch to have separate meetings with Rab Butler and the prime minister, following which the duke was 'ticked off' by a clearly furious Alec Hardinge, the King's private secretary, for these unhelpful 'interventions'.[41] In similar vein, Brocket told Chamberlain how warmly they had been welcomed by their 'cheerful and calm' hosts, who had claimed to be astonished by the 'tension and anxiety elsewhere'. Hitler, he promised, still considered himself bound by the piece of paper signed with the prime minister and did not think he had broken the Munich Agreement. Even Chamberlain struggled to swallow this obvious German propaganda but hoped nonetheless Hitler had now 'touched the limit and has decided to put the best face on it'.[42]

Two weeks after the invasion of Prague, hoping to seize back the initiative in foreign policy, Chamberlain announced to the Commons that Britain and France would guarantee protection to Poland despite having no plan as to how to do so were it ever needed. This was exactly the sort of guarantee that might have protected the Czechs and which he had worked so hard to avoid. Lloyd George warned him privately that Britain needed the support of Russia to give such a guarantee any teeth.[43] Chamberlain hoped this bold move would dissuade Hitler from any further bellicose outrages. Instead, the German leader reacted with fury, thumping his desk and screaming, 'I'll brew them a devil's potion.'[44] Just as the May Crisis had accelerated the implementation of Case Green (the dismembering of Czechoslovakia), so with horrible symmetry this triggered Case White, the planned conquest of Poland – exactly what Chamberlain hoped to avoid.

On Good Friday, Mussolini caused the second continental European crisis when his forces invaded Albania. Chamberlain felt obliged to recall parliament from their Easter holidays and cancel his own yearned-for fishing holiday at Castle Forbes in Aberdeenshire. In mid-April, against all his instincts as a committed anti-communist, he started desultory negotiations with the USSR, which dragged on throughout the summer. At the end of the month, Britain announced the Military Service Bill, introducing a limited form of conscription for men in their early twenties.

That same fateful summer, the Left Book Club published *Tory MP* (more provocatively titled *England's Money Lords* in the US), and this slim volume has shaped the historiography of the Fellowship ever since. Founded by Victor Gollancz, the campaigning publisher, pacifist and humanitarian, in the same year as the Fellowship, the important and immediately successful Left Book Club made no secret of its politically evangelical purpose. With a list of distinguished left-wing authors, including George Orwell, Conwell-Evans's mentor Philip Noel-Baker, Stafford Cripps, Arthur Koestler, and Sidney and Beatrice Webb, its prolific output has been credited with helping the Labour Party win the 1945 general election.[45]

Offered by the club in July, affordably priced at 7s 6d and authored pseudonymously by 'Simon Haxey', *Tory MP* was an immediate bestseller. A political polemic attacking the Conservative Party, it set out a detailed and (at least as far as it went) meticulously researched critique of the 'economic affiliations of the "hard-faced men" who compose the ranks of the Government's supporters'.[46] The chapter entitled 'The Tory Right Wing' includes a dozen pages analysing those Conservative MPs connected with the Fellowship. Consistent with the book's wider purpose, Haxey looked to interpret these links with Germany as explicit support for National Socialism and, in doing so, attacked the organisation aggressively and effectively.

Tory MP was the first published critique of the Anglo-German Fellowship, following what might now be seen as a comfortable ride from the British media. Up to that point, coverage of its aims and activities in *The Times*, *Daily Telegraph*, *Manchester Guardian* and *Evening Standard* had been generally uncritical and limited to reports of its events including extracts from speeches and lists of guests attending. Most scholars and other commentators assessing the Fellowship since the Second World War have relied on data and analysis from this book. But contemporary reviewers were less accepting of its objectivity. *The Times* saw it as 'propaganda as remarkable for its tireless research as for its fanatical one-sidedness'.[47] The *Manchester Guardian* recognised it as a useful handbook for critics of the parliamentary elite, but thought far-fetched the allegations of fascist tendencies within the Fellowship, pointing out that its members had 'long since slunk away with their tails between their legs and, apart from a few cranky incorrigibles, are now as anti-Hitler as Mr Haxey'.[48] Similarly, the *Times Literary Supplement* approved of the book's aims but regretted its 'narrowly partisan… spirit'.[49] Apparently, only one historian, Robert Caputi, has ever questioned *Tory MP*'s suitability as a primary source, pointing out that its 'venomous tone and accusatory content had the flavour of class warfare, from an overly bitter and cynical perspective'.[50]

Recently, it has transpired that these allegations of extreme political bias were well justified. Simon Haxey had been a pseudonym for a husband-and-wife team, Arthur and Margaret (née Moxon) Wynn.[51] Arthur's 2001 obituary in the *Guardian* paints a cosily benign portrait of a leading light on the left of British politics who, during a 'long and astonishingly productive life', had championed mine safety and free school meals. The couple were acknowledged as 'lifelong Labour supporters' and compared to 'Sydney [*sic*] and Beatrice Webb', albeit reputedly 'more fun'.[52] Eight years after his death, it emerged that Arthur had leaned quite a lot further to the left. Exposed as Agent SCOTT, a Soviet spy recruited like Kim Philby by Russian recruiters targeting leading universities, he has been credited with building the Oxford spy ring, that university's less prominent but similarly treasonous counterpart to the Cambridge Five.

German troops in Prague, 1939.

22

GANGSTER POLITICS

THE SEIZURE OF PRAGUE COULD NOT BE IGNORED. EVEN THOSE who had taken coffee with Hitler over the previous five years, including Lloyd George, Halifax, Lothian and Londonderry, had now abandoned appeasement as a cogent foreign policy and found themselves less hostile to the warnings of Winston Churchill and Robert Vansittart. All the Fellowship's social activities went into abeyance. Only the prime minister, his chief adviser and his ambassador in Berlin clung to the lingering hope that Hitler might somehow honour the spirit of the Munich Agreement. Increasingly, Britain's topmost foreign policy priority would be to enlist the support (ideally), or the benign neutrality (at least) of the two major powers still standing aloof from the ructions in Continental Europe. The Soviet Union and the United States of America would of course determine the outcome of the upcoming war and go on to define the geopolitics of the rest of the twentieth century. As the incoming British ambassador to Washington, the Marquess of Lothian, Conwell-Evans's friend and mentor, had cemented his promotion from the ranks of the ambulant amateurs to a professional in a pivotal role. For him there was now no question of appeasing Germany.

During that spring and summer of 1939, the tensions building between Germany and Poland, centred on the status of the free city of Danzig, would require the full attention of the foreign ministries of Europe. Though predominantly German-speaking, Danzig (now Gdańsk) had been set up following the Great War as a semi-autonomous state to give Poland access to a port on the Baltic Sea. Grahame Christie had warned back in May that the Germans were staffing a garrison of over twenty thousand SS troops in the territory. The pace of activity now required him to file reports to London as often as twice a week, while Conwell-Evans boasted to Lloyd George that, in that last year of peace, he had been in almost daily contact with the British Foreign Office about their jointly sourced intelligence.[1] At the same time, Ernest Tennant was agonising over how he might be of help.

In late April, Lothian's appointment as ambassador, agreed a full eight months earlier, had finally been announced, to mixed reviews. Due to reach Washington in late August, he was replacing Sir Ronald Lindsay, a career diplomat who, though liked and respected, was notably shy and reluctant to schmooze the American cousins. The career mandarins in the Foreign Office, led by Alec Cadogan, were surprised and frustrated by Lothian's selection, considering him an amateur compromised by his past sympathies towards Germany and his association with the Cliveden Set, the political salon hosted by his friend Nancy Astor and entangled with the failed policy of appeasement. But in the House of Commons, only William Gallacher, the token communist, sounded a caustic note, attacking the appointment as a signal to Hitler that 'his friends are still in power.'[2] The British newspapers were supportive, seeing the advantages of a gregarious politician over a career civil servant in this pivotal post at such a fraught time.

Whatever his judgement on Germany, Lothian was expert on the United States, with experience as both a journalist and secretary of the Rhodes Trust. He had made friends easily there, touring the country over fourteen visits covering forty-four of the forty-eight states. Appreciating his easy charm and commitment to Atlanticism, the American papers courteously welcomed his promotion. Though tainted by his association with the Third Reich, by appointing Lothian (as the historian James Fox has perceptively summarised) Halifax had shrewdly calculated that 'someone who had gone the last mile trying to get on with Hitler would be the right person to persuade an insuperably cautious, neutral America, entrenched in isolationism, that it was in its own vital interest to support Britain.'[3]

Lothian had been arguing since the twenties that Great Britain and the US shared a duty to preserve world peace. In a speech given to the Scottish Liberal Federation, which he chaired, he laid out his updated Atlantic manifesto two days after the announcement of his appointment. The aggression of the dictators, he argued, undermined individual and national freedoms, those pillars of western civilisation, and so threatened injustices on others far worse than anything inflicted by the Treaty of Versailles on them. Calling for a 'solid and irresistible grand alliance against military aggression', he rejected the glib comparisons made by the dictators (especially Hitler) between their allegedly modest territorial ambitions and the vast British Empire. Turning to the 'great opportunity and… great responsibility' offered by his posting, he expressed delight at going to America, whose people, great leaders and institutions he had long admired. Calling for a reimagined successor to the League of Nations with real powers to keep the global peace, he insisted it would be vital for liberal civilisations such as the US and Great Britain to 'stand together if liberalism was really going to prevail in the world'.[4]

In June, his upcoming mission received a fillip when King George VI, accompanied by Queen Elizabeth, became the first reigning British monarch to visit the US, hoping to help President Roosevelt win popular support for American aid to Great Britain. Meanwhile, Lothian had been engaged with both his political opponents and his allies. He had admitted to his friend but stern critic, Vansittart, that his judgement on Hitler had been right all along. They agreed that if appeasement had been deployed during the Weimar Republic there 'might never have been a Hitler at all'.[5] Lothian wrote to his friend Halifax urging him to challenge Hitler to abandon his 'gangster politics'.[6] He also asked Winston Churchill for a meeting to discuss the US, clearly anticipating his return from the backbenches to any wartime Cabinet.

Ever more alarming intelligence from Germany set the background to the royal visit, deliberately limited to only five days. Between April and September, Christie's network of informants in the country continued to supply convincing intelligence on Hitler's plans and their progress. While not always accurate and vulnerable to deliberate German misinformation, these reiterated three main themes: the Germans were convinced Britain would be too weak to risk war by honouring her commitments in Eastern Europe; Hitler planned to attack Poland in the late summer before the weather worsened; and there were talks ongoing between Germany and Russia. Hitler, he explained, believed an alliance with Russia would allow him to deliver the 'decisive blow' against the British Empire. Then he could subjugate Poland, Romania and the Balkans before throwing the 'full power of Germany' westwards. To this end the German General Staff had been working up plans for operations against Belgium, Holland and Denmark.[7]

Notwithstanding the recent anti-Bolshevik rhetoric from the Nazi leadership, Vansittart had been harassing the Foreign Office to take seriously the threat of a Soviet-German alliance and to improve Britain's relations with the USSR instead. On 18 May he sent Halifax a forceful memorandum with intelligence gathered by Christie from the German General Staff evidencing Hitler's negotiations with Stalin through the acting Czech president, General Syrový. Not all his colleagues were convinced. Ivone Kirkpatrick (Halifax's escort to Berchtesgaden, now back in London) damned the report as 'unreliable for a variety of reasons which it would be otiose to set forth', before asserting he did 'not believe that Germany, so long as Hitler rules, will compound with Stalin'.[8] Less than a week later, Christie reported that Werner von Tippelskirch (the German chargé d'affaires in Moscow who served under three ambassadors) had been quietly but effectively improving relations and calming Russian concerns around the invasion of Bohemia and Moravia. The German press had been ordered to moderate any reporting on the USSR and avoid 'unfriendly references' to Joseph Stalin.

The fissures opening in policy, tactics and style between the British prime minister and his foreign secretary were widening into a gulf. With war feared imminent, the Cabinet pushed Neville Chamberlain to announce the introduction of a limited military conscription. Halifax had been notably more hawkish, pressing for a state of emergency to be declared and military reservists called up. By June, the foreign secretary was lunching, discreetly but often, with Winston Churchill and Anthony Eden and enjoying walks in the park with those younger MPs similarly lining up against the prime minister.

That June, the German opposition renewed their efforts to persuade Britain to put on a show of strength, sending several envoys to lobby the government. Again, Conwell-Evans played the role of facilitator. Erich Kordt arrived back in London, ostensibly en route to Scotland for a week's holiday with his brother Theo, but in truth with a mission to derail the Hitler-Stalin pact. Before the brothers, now two of Germany's most senior diplomats, headed north, Conwell-Evans hosted a meeting at his Kensington flat for them to reconnect with Vansittart. Held in the strictest secrecy, the meeting had the blessing of both the foreign secretary and Ernst von Weizsäcker, Ribbentrop's ever more frustrated and despondent secretary of state. Uncharacteristically on edge, the chief diplomatic adviser arrived incognito in Cornwall Gardens by taxi with a Special Branch detective to keep watch from the far side of the road.

The brothers made clear they were speaking under authority from military and civilian opposition leaders, including Generals Beck and Halder and Hjalmar Schacht. Together, they feared the guarantees given by Britain and France to Poland and others would inflame Hitler's paranoia of Germany being encircled by her enemies. Erich confided that the Führer sought a friendship treaty with the Soviet Union to secure his eastern flank. The opposition feared (correctly as would turn out) that the negotiations between Britain and the Soviets were stalling. Hitler had told his inner circle, 'If Chamberlain makes a pact with Stalin, this autumn I will not do anything – except call my congress at Nuremberg "the *Parteitag* of peace"… but if Chamberlain fails, I will move in and smash the Poles, because the West will not be able to make contact with them and my rear will be safe.'[9]

Vansittart reassured the brothers that the British government was close to an accord with the Soviets and, believing him, a newly optimistic Erich returned to Germany to brief his fellow conspirators.[10] Within weeks, it seemed Van had either been lying or out of touch. Erich assumed the former and when interviewed after the war admitted 'to this day [he] does not know why'.[11] Van's biographer thought the Kordts had been naïve in their optimism and he had not been 'privy to the exact stage the negotiations had reached and was simply expressing his own view of what should happen'.[12]

Colonel Oster, the Abwehr officer behind the aborted 1938 plot, was still bruised by Chamberlain's Plan Z scuppering the coup and alarmed by the muted British response to the invasion of Prague. That week, he sent a second emissary to represent General Beck and Admiral Canaris to the British government. Lieutenant Colonel Gerhard von Schwerin oversaw the British and US intelligence sections in the ministry of war, so had been encouraged to explore his countries of interest on his six-week holiday, but his covert mission was to urge the British government to take a stronger line with Hitler. His visit was closely monitored by the Security Service, who noted that his busy itinerary included meetings with former Berchtesgaden coffee drinkers such as Lothian, Londonderry and Paul Rykens of Unilever (an established intelligence source for the Foreign Office), as well as twelve MPs, including Rab Butler. He also saw Lord Trenchard, head of the RAF, Rear Admiral John Godfrey, the director of naval intelligence (and inspiration for Ian Fleming's 'M'), and his military counterpart. Von Schwerin also met with Germans in London sympathetic to the opposition's cause, including the ambassador, whom he met with far from the bug-ridden embassy.[13] The Foreign Office was defensively cynical about his spirited mission to embolden the British government; Frank Roberts minuted the file: 'As usual the German army trusts us to save them from the Nazi regime.'[14]

During the early summer, further bridges were built between the previously dissenting camps, Lord Halifax and his Foreign Office on one hand and the anti-appeasers calling for rearmament on the other. Winston Churchill gave a barnstorming speech to a club dinner at the Dorchester Hotel, toasting the health of Halifax in front of six hundred guests, with Lord Londonderry in the chair. While accepting their past differences, he praised Halifax's 'sterling qualities as an Englishman, a fox hunter and a friend' before explaining how the 'flagrant and brutal manner in which the Munich Agreement has been torn to pieces' by the Nazis had brought them together. In similar vein, he noted that he and his cousin, Charley Londonderry, had not always seen 'eye to eye' but the 'villainy of the Nazi outrage upon Bohemia and Moravia' had engendered 'cordial and resolute agreement tonight'. While all agreed that a 'prosperous, honoured and contented Germany' should be 'one of the first, permanent interests of the British Empire', Hitler's recent actions meant Great Britain and her Empire would deploy their 'united strength' against any unprovoked aggression. Knowing the Nazis studied his speeches closely, he then painted a rosy picture of British military readiness: 'Our Air Force has been equipped with the best machines... our air defences are not only far better armed but constantly manned... the Army is stronger... the Navy is ready and relatively far stronger than in 1914.'

Meanwhile, Christie reported that Hitler had postponed his attack on Poland till September, with reservists called up and mobilised in August so that all German military forces would be on a 'full war basis' by the end of the month. Two days later Halifax gave a major speech at the annual dinner of the Royal Institute of International Affairs with 'The Choice for Germany' as his theme. The six hundred guests included the high commissioners of Canada, Southern Rhodesia and South Africa, senior Foreign Office staff as well as Conwell-Evans and Christie, both long-standing members of the Institute. Broadcast in the UK, the US and elsewhere, the speech underpinned the foreign secretary's divergence from Chamberlain's caution and prevarication and signalled Halifax's willingness to countenance war. Prompted by Vansittart, Cadogan had at the last minute added two pages to 'put teeth' into the text to make it clear Britain was 'neither bluffing nor willing to put up with further blackmail'.[15] To noisy cheers, Halifax reminded his audience that, within the last year, Britain had made agreements for mutual defence with Poland and Turkey, guaranteed assistance against aggression to Greece and Romania, and were in negotiations with the Soviet government to get their support. Echoing Churchill's themes from the week before, he highlighted Britain's unprecedented rearmament at sea, in the air and on land and insisted there would be no 'yielding to force'. Germany, he argued, had isolated herself 'economically by her policy of autarky, politically by a policy that causes constant anxiety to other nations, and culturally by her policy of racialism'.[16]

Soon the grumblings from the press and the public against Chamberlain's refusal to bring Churchill into the Cabinet escalated to a clamour, with leading newspaper editors calling for his return as an essential member of any War Cabinet. Meanwhile, mounting tensions around the status of Danzig seemed the likely trigger for war on the Continent. By early July, widespread rumours in Paris suggesting Germany planned to seize the city were traced to belligerent statements from Otto Abetz (Ribbentrop's agent in France), who was then expelled by the authorities. A German press campaign had whipped up indignation about Danzig. Chamberlain told the House of Commons he had reliable reports of military disturbances there and, within days, there were Nazi rallies calling for the German army to 'liberate' the city. The Polish government, emboldened by the guarantees from France and Britain, threatened war if the Germans moved on their cherished port. By now, preparations for war were being accelerated in earnest around Europe. In southern England, there were full-blown air raid blackout practices. A contingent of British troops accompanied by RAF planes was dispatched to France for the 150th anniversary Bastille Day celebrations in a joint show of strength. Reluctantly, the British government extended its Polish guarantee formally to include Danzig.

Meanwhile, rather than organising or attending social events, Conwell-Evans, Christie and, more clumsily, Tennant were focused on continuing to supply prompt and mostly accurate intelligence to the heart of the British government from credible German sources, especially arch-rivals Ribbentrop and Göring and their respective entourages. Between them, Christie and Conwell-Evans correctly predicted, to within days, Hitler's two greatest initiatives of 1939 – the invasions of Czechoslovakia in March and Poland in September – while also warning the British government of Germany's diplomatic outreach to Japan and then Russia. There were, of course, other noises off who were predicting Hitler's next steps, but none seems to have been so accurate nor offered the background analysis and colour on the National Socialist regime. In parallel, the two friends were keeping close to the struggling German resistance to Hitler and exploring opportunities with them to avoid a total war. Given the Fellowship's crumbling reputation, what is surprising is the currency this intelligence had with the British and US governments, up to and including President Roosevelt and the extent to which Conwell-Evans, Christie and Tennant remained in the thick of things right up to the outbreak of war.

Schloss Fuschl, Salzkammergut, Austria, Joachim Ribbentrop's holiday home, where he entertained Ernest Tennant in July 1939.

23

THE TENNANT MISSION

THOUGH WARY OF THE PRECARIOUS OPPOSITION WATERS IN which Conwell-Evans and Christie were now swimming, Ernest Tennant remained eager to deploy his skills as an ambulant amateur diplomat and sometime professional intelligence officer. In July 1939, he undertook a bizarre, secret, government-sanctioned mission to Germany. This last throw of the dice to secure a lasting peace had been built on his hope that Hitler and Ribbentrop were still 'anxious for friendship with this country', a claim even Sir Horace Wilson, the doyen of appeasement, found improbable.[1] Tennant had last seen Ribbentrop in Berlin earlier that summer, when the foreign minister had pompously expressed his and Hitler's irritation with facetious letters from the British public asking them to defer any war until after the horseracing at Ascot and the Eton-Harrow cricket match at Lord's. But as the crisis developed, Tennant had been 'bombarded' with less flippant letters from friends in both England and Germany urging him to intervene with Ribbentrop. And so he wrote unsolicited to the prime minister, flattering him and Halifax for their efforts to halt the worsening relations between the two countries. Enclosing a twenty-three-page chronicle of his relationship with Ribbentrop, whom he ventured he knew 'better than any other Englishman', he offered to fly to Germany at his own expense to try to guide the German foreign minister 'away from his present feeling of hostility to Britain and back nearer to his state of mind of seeking friendship with this country which existed until the beginning of 1937'.[2]

A junior civil servant in Downing Street reviewed Tennant's letter and memorandum sceptically but admitted he knew too little to judge.[3] The prime minister, who liked such cloak and dagger operations, read both and was more excited so asked Horace Wilson to meet the author that week. Wilson agreed Tennant should seek an audience with Ribbentrop but insisted he travel under the cover of his business interests and make no mention of Downing Street. (Tennant's mission would be one of three such back-channel approaches that month; the others involved a Swedish businessman contacting Hermann Göring, and Arthur Bryant, the Nazi-sympathising popular historian, also heading over to Germany.) Relishing the intrigue, Chamberlain told the King he hoped to use these ambulant amateurs to 'bring home to Hitler that we mean business this time'.[4]

Tennant wrote at once to Ribbentrop explaining he had booked an August family holiday in the South of France but would visit Germany on business first so hoped to see him in late July. Coyly suggesting that visiting the foreign minister in his 'magnificence in the Wilhelmstrasse' would be intimidating, he asked if instead they might 'dine quietly together one night and have a real talk as we used to in earlier days'.[5] Already ensconced in his Austrian summer holiday home, Ribbentrop offered to receive Tennant any day the following week and to book his accommodation in Salzburg.

Arriving the next day at Wilson's office in Downing Street to discuss tactics, Tennant offered to postpone, given an unexpected scandal around an unauthorised meeting that week between Robert Hudson, a junior trade minister, and a representative of Göring, at which they had discussed a 'peace loan'. Hudson had exceeded his brief and leaked to the press, requiring Chamberlain to make a statement in the Commons. Though furious with Hudson, the prime minister reassured his sister there were still 'other and discreeter [sic] channels' by which contact could be maintained.[6] Wilson agreed the trip should go ahead, since Tennant had already accepted the invitation and could 'talk freely' to Ribbentrop. Ever the businessman, Tennant asked if he could offer Germany a variant of Hudson's loan concept in return for a definitive peace. This could be pegged to the inevitable stock market recovery triggered by any agreed peace. He had previously discussed conventional inter-governmental loans with Hitler, who disliked foreign exchange interest commitments. Unconvinced, Wilson argued that the restoration of international confidence should be reward enough in itself.

On landing at Salzburg, a car sent by Ribbentrop met Tennant and drove him to Schloss Fuschl in time for afternoon tea. Encircled by pine-clad mountains and situated on the beautiful Lake Fuschl, twenty-five kilometres from the Nazi summer capital at Berchtesgaden, the castle had been built by the Salzburg prince-archbishops in the fifteenth century as a hunting lodge. Tennant understood the Führer had provided the property, which included an estate and the neighbouring village, when in truth Ribbentrop had unlawfully confiscated it from Austrian family friends of his wife, who had been imprisoned in Dachau concentration camp for resisting the *Anschluss*.

His host, recently reported as ill, now looked 'well and alert' in his white cotton knickerbocker suit and brown stockings as he welcomed his old friend. His good humour dispelled Tennant's concerns, based on rumours circulating in London, that he was out of favour with Hitler. Conversation remained light until six o'clock, when Ribbentrop launched into a four-hour diatribe against the duplicity and ingratitude of the Poles and the British and their refusal to recognise the benevolent intentions of the Third Reich. The inferiority complex diagnosed by Conwell-Evans soon bubbled to the surface as Ribbentrop ventured that the British were 'perhaps too snobby, after centuries of world domination and Oxford and Cambridge tradition, to admit that Germany or anyone else should exist on terms of complete equality and with important spheres of influence of their own'. Despite no British statesman taking the trouble to understand him, Hitler still offered 'peace and prosperity for a thousand years' if Germany, having guaranteed the frontiers of France, Holland and Belgium, could 'look after Britain's interests on the Continent in exchange for Britain looking after Germany's interests overseas'.

Ribbentrop admitted Chamberlain's guarantee to Poland had blindsided the German leadership and was frustrated at how the Poles had rebuffed the Führer's settlement offers earlier that year. As all Germans despised the Poles (even small children), he claimed that nothing would 'rally the whole German nation' better than threats from a Poland emboldened by the British guarantee. Rising to his theme, he insisted they were 'insects who could be crushed by a small portion of the German army in a few days', before theatrically demonstrating his point by stamping on imaginary spiders in the room. He then painted a bathetic picture of Hitler sitting in Berchtesgaden 'constantly receiving reports about British interference, about the hostility of the British Press and about the repeated unpardonable Polish insults to Germany and of the ill-treatment of the German minority in Poland'. Assuring Tennant that he could prove the British had tried to thwart the annexation of Austria and the march into Prague, he insisted they were doing the same with Poland. Echoing his diatribe to Conwell-Evans about the Czechs a year before, he promised that in the case of war, 'everything would be all over with Poland in a few days and that country would cease to exist.' But he had dropped his earlier ideas of a short, localised campaign, agreeing any war would be the 'most terrible and ruthless in the history of the world', leading to the 'end of the German Reich and the destruction of the German race or the end of the British Empire and the destruction of the British race'.

When Tennant reminded his host that Britain was stronger than Germany at sea and her equal in the air, he shook his head and said, 'Britain's strength or weakness never enters into our calculations because Britain could never get at us. For one Maginot Line we have seven or eight impregnable Siegfried lines... if France tried to storm the Siegfried lines, then within a year she would have two million dead... and Hitler is prepared for a war lasting ten years.' Ribbentrop's ambassadors, Lord Rothermere, and the foreign ministers of Italy and Hungary, had each similarly confirmed that Britain and France would fight, but tragically he chose to ignore this consistent advice. Erich Kordt noted he had even threatened 'to shoot any official who... presumed to argue that Britain would fight'.[7]

Keen to make mischief between the Allies, Ribbentrop told Tennant how Hitler preferred the French and had grown close to Georges Bonnet, their foreign minister and an appeaser. Smugly cynical, he argued that Britain's support for Poland and negotiations with Moscow had united the German nation together 'in a way that not even the Führer could have done'. For war to be avoided, Polish insults to Germany and to Danzig should stop, the 'battle of words and ink' in the press should cease, and Poland be persuaded that war would result in her being 'wiped out and finished as a nation within a few days'.

Now badly shaken, Ernest Tennant left the castle believing war to be almost certain. His companion in the car back to Salzburg, Professor Fritz Berber, Ribbentrop's English-educated adviser, ventured that Britain should pressure the Poles to concede Danzig. Tennant questioned what else Germany would then demand of Poland, to which Berber suggested Britain's guarantee would protect her from any further encroachment.

The following day, Tennant joined Ribbentrop, now changed from his knickerbockers into his custom-designed foreign ministerial uniform, for the eleven-hour train journey to Berlin. Two special coaches had been provided for the minister's entourage and Tennant was given his own compartment. Their party included Walther Hewel, who had been at Conwell-Evans's final lunch back in February. One of the handful of paladins genuinely close to the Führer, Tennant rated him as the 'best friend Britain has amongst Hitler's immediate entourage' and took him to one side for a private chat. Another Anglophile, urbane and widely liked, Hewel had been at the signing of the Munich Agreement. He reassured the Englishman that August would be 'quiet' but predicted a 'stormy autumn unless the Poles come to their senses'. He admitted a bad harvest that year would be disastrous for Germany, as she lacked self-sufficiency in cereals. Hitler still hoped for friendship with England but remained insistent on reaching a settlement on Poland and needed former German colonies returned. When Tennant pressed him on why the British should trust Hitler following Prague, Hewel insisted the Cabinet had overreacted. It should have been of no interest to Britain, the Führer believed he was still honouring Munich, and Chamberlain had provoked him by announcing rearmament.

Tennant joined the party for lunch in the dining car at the far end of the train. As he walked through the carriages, he was struck by the warm welcome and fascination for the foreign minister from fellow passengers and the crowds of bystanders on the platforms as they passed through the stations. At dinner served in his private saloon, Ribbentrop, having unburdened his vitriol against Britain the evening before, was now in a reflective mood. He introduced Tennant to their fellow diners as an 'old English friend with whom he had worked for Anglo-German understanding', crediting him for introducing him to the British government and remembering their disappointment when Stanley Baldwin's positive speech in the Commons soon after had not led to detente. As they travelled past new factories in industrial Saxony (including one making wool out of potato peelings), conversation turned to economics. Ribbentrop boasted of two secret power plants, one looking to split the atom and another to develop perpetual motion. He chastised the British Board of Trade for rebuffing Germany's offers of cooperation in 1934, which could have made Germany's Four-Year Plan unnecessary. Here Tennant agreed, having himself been patronised and rebuffed by the British civil servants. When pushed on recent British resistance to German demands, Tennant cited the pace of rearmament and the scale of his army as signifying Hitler's objectives were 'far more important' than the conquest of the 'little countries near his frontiers'. Many believed the Führer wanted world domination, he explained, including the conquest of the British Empire, a notion Ribbentrop and Hewel dismissed as 'utterly fantastic'.

Tennant's expedition had been a poignant swansong for the two friends' shared vision in founding the Anglo-German Fellowship to promote peace and understanding between the two countries. As they bid their last fare-wells on the platform in Berlin, Ribbentrop's parting words were, 'Goodbye and let us remember your English proverb, "it is never too late to mend".'

Safely back in his country house in rural Essex that weekend, Tennant wrote at once to Horace Wilson promising detailed notes which confirmed a 'serious state of affairs'. On Monday, he sent a fourteen-page report, copied to Vansittart at the Foreign Office, apologising for anything that might raise hackles. Wilson summoned him to Downing Street that evening, where Tennant justified his failure to challenge Ribbentrop's wilder excesses on the grounds it was better to listen than argue. Both Ribbentrop and Hewel had been parroting Hitler rather than sharing their own views, he explained, but neither expected 'serious trouble' that autumn. In conclusion, Tennant advised the prime minister that the 'misunderstanding' between the two countries was a 'clash between the traditions of the nineteenth century and the new ideas of the twentieth, comparable in art to a clash of ideas between the school of Gainsborough and that of the post-impressionists'. The remilitarisation of the Rhineland had been the last chance to check the rise of the Nazis; the British now had no choice but to make better efforts 'to understand it, work with it and accept it'.[8]

How useful the British government found this intelligence is hard to judge and Tennant makes no comment in his memoir. Despite the esca-lating risk of European war, like most of the British Cabinet, civil service and the military chiefs, he went on holiday. Reassured war would not break out within weeks, he left by car with his children for one week on the Loire followed by two at the seaside near Bordeaux. He left his contact details with Downing Street, promising he could return by air within five or six hours if there were anything useful he could do.[9]

By 20 August, the newspaper reports on the worsening state of inter-national affairs had sufficiently alarmed Tennant for him to write to Rab Butler, the Foreign Office minister, offering to intercept Walther Hewel at the upcoming *Parteitag* at Nuremberg. Hewel wanted peace, he explained, and they were old friends and so offered a discreet conduit to Ribbentrop and Hitler. Tennant modestly admitted his offer was unlikely to be of the 'slightest use at this late stage'; Butler seemed to agree, passing the letter to Wilson should he wish to follow up.[10]

Though Tennant sensed his influence in Downing Street was fading, Conwell-Evans and Christie remained amid the Foreign Office maelstrom and so at the centre of events up to and beyond the declaration of war. While Tennant was with Ribbentrop in Salzburg, Conwell-Evans had been tracking the Germans in London. Still *persona grata* at the embassy, he attended a music recital in late July hosted by General Wenninger, the air attaché. Having much enjoyed the performance, ruefully he reflected 'how delightful everybody was to everyone, and why couldn't we always be like this?' He met the 'rather tough' second assistant attaché, Herr Schwencke, who asserted that his government would never be satisfied with just Danzig and spoke of a partition of all Poland. Incensed, Conwell-Evans said that would mean war, but the German thought Britain not strong enough to get her forces past the Siegfried Line, dismissing British aircraft production at no more than five hundred planes per month. Conwell-Evans then posited that Germany yearned to restore the Holy Roman Empire and bring Holland and Switzerland into the Reich. This was met with stony silence.

Conwell-Evans asked Vansittart to brief the foreign secretary on this alarming conversation, made more so by increased Gestapo surveillance at the embassy, with a man sporting the 'golden badge of the party' closely watching Ambassador von Dirksen. Conwell-Evans stressed the 'extraordinary difficulties under which our friends work, and the *terrible ruthlessness* of the German government' before insisting '*only overwhelming force* can stop them.' Vansittart passed it to Halifax, labelling it 'foam straight from the horse's mouth – and a horse with a red bow in its tail too!'[11]

The historian Richard Griffiths has neatly highlighted the full irony of the situation in these final months before war. Conwell-Evans, he explained, 'who had been ignored by Baldwin when he had put forward pro-German views' was then ignored by Chamberlain when he changed his views. Meanwhile, it is 'equally ironic that the Foreign Office, which opposed him in 1933–5, had been trusted by Baldwin, but that the same Foreign Office, backing [Conwell-Evans's] views in 1938, should have been mistrusted by Chamberlain.'[12]

'Leave Hitler to me sonny', Ministry of Health poster encouraging the evacuation of London. 1940.

24

IF THE WORLD
SHOULD FALL AND BREAK

The middle of August 1939 found Sir Alec Cadogan left
in charge of Britain's foreign policy and grumbling gently to his diary how
difficult it had been 'to conduct affairs of this kind with Halifax in Yorkshire
and the PM in Scotland!'[1] Coyly, he hoped their trust in him should not
be misplaced. As the crisis mounted, almost everyone who mattered had
been away from London relishing the unusually sunny late August weather.
Neville Chamberlain was six hundred miles north of Downing Street fishing for salmon at the Duke of Westminster's shooting lodge in Sutherland.
There he had caught three fish within an hour and felt 'wonderfully well'.[2]
The public were holidaying too. *Country Life* reported that, despite the
circumstances, most Britons were taking their holidays, 'relaxing on moor
and seashore'.[3] Cadogan's temper improved when the prime minister sent
him one of the salmon. His spirits lifted further when 'C' (head of the
Secret Intelligence Service) reported that the German railway chief had
just briefed Hitler he could arrange mass transport either for the *Parteitag*
that September or for the rumoured German military mobilisation, but
not both. According to the intelligence, the Führer had plumped for the
former, so the threat of military action had receded.

But within hours, any comfort Cadogan might have enjoyed evaporated
when Vansittart, close to 'nervous collapse', arrived at his house after dinner
to spoil both their weekends. Christie's source in Germany had reported
Hitler planned to launch his war against Poland between 25 and 28 August.[4]
It was no accident this coincided with the first weeks of the grouse shooting
season. As a keen student of the English ruling classes, Hitler understood

well the inviolability of their summer holidays just as he did the sanctity of their weekends. While cautious about its reliability, Cadogan realised he could not ignore such intelligence, and so recalled the foreign secretary from his beloved Yorkshire, but they agreed to let the prime minister continue his fishing. Exhausted, Cadogan noted in his diary: 'These crises are really too tiresome... we can't go on living like this in Europe. There is no point in it.'[5]

The next day, Saturday, Cadogan drafted a long briefing letter for Halifax to send to Chamberlain. Now the intelligence about the Nuremberg trains was dismissed as misinformation, as the rally was only 'symbolic' and troop transport would always take priority. Hitler still believed Britain would not fight, or in any event he could 'crush' Poland before her allies could respond. Recognising that the German leader had ignored all earlier warnings, Halifax nonetheless agreed they should spare no effort and advised the prime minister to send him a personal letter appealing for calm.

Chamberlain received Halifax's briefing en route to London by train. British intelligence reported a request from Hermann Göring to fly to London for secret negotiations, so made plans for him to land at a small airfield at Bovingdon in Hertfordshire for a discreet meeting with the prime minister at Chequers, where the Security Service would substitute for the regular staff. Somehow, Guy Burgess learned of the proposed visit and alerted Moscow, a tip-off believed to have encouraged the Russians to welcome Ribbentrop with his proposed non-aggression pact later that week. Cadogan recalled the chief of the Air Staff, the first sea lord and the Cabinet secretary, all of whom he noted with indignant relish in his diary were still on holiday.

Following Ribbentrop's Herculean efforts to ingratiate himself with the previously reviled Soviets, news reached London of his planned treaty of non-aggression between the USSR and Germany. Despite repeated warnings from Christie and others over the spring and summer, as one Cabinet minister admitted in his diary, this still came as a 'complete bombshell' to the British government.[6] Chamberlain admitted to the House of Commons the next day that it was indeed an unpleasant surprise, just like the march into Prague that spring. Downing Street summoned Vansittart to help in the escalating crisis for the first time since Cadogan had replaced him. This return into the prime ministerial fold effectively acknowledged that his advice and Christie's intelligence had been broadly right for months. That evening, Cadogan dined with Lothian ahead of his departure by sea to take up his post as ambassador in Washington. Frequent telephone calls interrupted their dinner.

On Tuesday, 22 August, Chamberlain recalled parliament from its summer holidays, without consulting the King. There was now clear intelligence the foreign ministers of Germany and the Soviet Union would sign their pact the next day, allowing Hitler and Stalin to launch a joint attack on their mutual neighbour Poland and robbing Britain and France of any ally in the Kremlin. Having accepted Halifax's advice, the prime minister sent a personal letter to Hitler via the ambassador in Berlin stressing that Britain would fight if Poland were attacked. Cadogan recalled all Foreign Office staff from leave and returned all overseas diplomats to their posts. By Thursday, the King had returned to London furious with the German dictator for obliging him to cut short a successful grouse shooting party at his Scottish estate, leaving the Queen and the young princesses to look after their guests. That day, the recalled parliament passed the Emergency Powers (Defence) Act giving the British government broad authority to prepare the country for war. The fleet was ordered to its war stations. In Germany, the upcoming *Parteitag* (the 'Rally of peace') was postponed indefinitely.

Meanwhile, Conwell-Evans had been in the alpine resort of St Cergue sur Nyon in Switzerland (presumably on a mountaineering holiday but perhaps also meeting his German contacts on neutral territory) when he received a cable from Vansittart:

RETURN AT ONCE. VAN.[7]

He reached London by Friday afternoon just as Hitler ordered the invasion of Poland for four-thirty the next morning. Christie sent Vansittart the German operational plans, noting that their generals were confident of overwhelming the Polish forces within less than three weeks.

But three events in quick succession caused Hitler to blink.

In London, Lord Halifax signed the Anglo-Polish agreement of mutual assistance, cementing the British guarantee agreed back in March. In the afternoon, Mussolini, nervous of his fellow dictator dragging Italy into a reckless European war, telegrammed to confirm Italy would remain neutral if Germany invaded Poland. On the same day, the French ambassador confirmed his country would come to Poland's aid if it were attacked. This news from Britain, Italy and France shocked Hitler into the realisation that the Allies may not have been bluffing, and he ordered that the invasion of Poland be delayed.

Meanwhile, world leaders appealed for calm. President Roosevelt called for civilian populations to be protected from air attack. His Holiness Pope Pius XII warned his flock 'nothing is lost with peace; all may be with war.'[8] The Duke of Windsor sent a telegram to Hitler imploring him to 'find a peaceful solution of the present problems'.[9] His brother the King offered to make a similar personal approach but was dissuaded by his prime minister.

London moved towards a war footing. The civilian population was being prepared for enemy attack by air, and especially for the use of poison gas, with systems for warning of air raids installed and explained to the public. Plans were being finalised to evacuate over a third of the population of London, especially young children and their mothers. For those who planned to remain in the cities, including the royal family in Buckingham Palace, over one million steel air raid shelters had been delivered. (While the fragile peace prevailed, the newspapers reported their widespread use for storing garden tools; for one man in Leyton, his shelter proved ideal for housing pet rabbits.) Street lights and road signs were covered, sandbags filled and tree trunks painted with white paint to aid motorists. An 'attractive velour material' was advertised in the newspapers to prepare all houses, offices and shops for the blackout.[10] Alongside the capital's children and their mothers, art treasures, including the stained-glass windows from Westminster Abbey, were carefully packed up into lorries and trains for removal to commandeered stately homes and abandoned Welsh slate mines.

Arrangements for feeding Londoners in wartime were put under the charge of a committee comprising a public-school bursar, the retired commissioner of Buganda, the former secretary of the Law Society and a senior manager from Pickfords, the celebrated removals company. A special tribunal was set up to consider applications from conscientious objectors. German residents in Britain left en masse from Southampton on liners bound for Germany.

In the City, the international situation was understandably making investors nervous, with share prices slumping and the Bank of England doubling its interest rate to four percent. Reports circulated of the Germans buying up commodities essential for the military, including copper, rubber and nickel.

Even the inmates of London Zoo were organised for war. With limited space in rural zoos, the public was reassured a bomb strike would kill most before they could escape and attack passers-by. The black widow spiders and some reptiles would be destroyed following any declaration of war and six riflemen stationed around the Zoo to dispatch any larger beasts escaping. Otherwise, *The Times* assured its readers, it would be business as usual in Regent's Park and London remained 'calm and cheerful'.[11]

It was the issuance of gas masks to each civilian that brought home the new realities. The terrible effects of gas in the Great War were still widely remembered, and now civilians faced the chilling prospect of poison gas being delivered to British cities by German bombers. Therefore, all adults and children had to carry these alarming objects in their cardboard boxes at all times. *The Times* chronicled Mrs Miniver, a semi-fictionalised middle-class housewife, as she took her young family to be fitted for their gas masks. Ruefully she sensed they had 'said good-bye to something' of the comforting norms of pre-war everyday life. Was it for this she had 'boiled the milk for their bottles, and washed their hands before lunch, and not let them eat with a spoon which had been dropped on the floor?'[12]

In that last week of peace, while Chamberlain still resisted a full military mobilisation for fear of antagonising the so-called Rome-Berlin Axis, anti-aircraft and coastal defences were made ready. Public interest in the mounting crisis was intense, with almost hourly editions of the newspapers rushed from Fleet Street. With little enthusiasm for fighting and the hope Chamberlain could again prevent hostilities, crowds gathered each day in Downing Street, Parliament Square and outside the Foreign Office to watch the back and forth of ministers, civil servants and military chiefs arriving for daily Cabinet and other crisis meetings.

Although excluded from a Cabinet still struggling to appease Hitler, Winston Churchill believed he should be at the heart of events. He met with Lloyd George and Harold Nicolson, another noted anti-appeaser, in the smoking room of the House of Commons, where Lloyd George argued for a secret session of parliament to 'tell the PM that he must go'.[13] Churchill then dined at the Savoy with other rebels, including Anthony Eden and

Duff Cooper, who had both resigned from the Cabinet in frustration with Chamberlain's foreign policies, and (as the latter recorded in his diary) they were all 'very gloomy'.[14] On Monday, 28 August, the Territorial Army called up 35,000 reserves. On the same day, Conwell-Evans was called into the Commons to brief Lloyd George, Churchill and Eden on any lingering chance of preventing hostilities.[15] That night, the border between France and Germany was closed and panic buying emptied the Berlin shops of food. By Thursday, the Royal Navy was being mobilised and the evacuation of cities begun. Hitler ordered the attack on Poland for just before dawn on the first day of September 1939.

That same day Theo Kordt arrived in Cornwall Gardens for his final secret meeting with Vansittart and Conwell-Evans, bringing a document detailing Germany's apparently sensible proposals for an agreed settlement with Poland. These included Danzig returning to Germany, a plebiscite deciding the sovereignty of the Polish Corridor, and arrangements to allow access across each other's territory. But a telephone call from Theo's wife interrupted the meeting to relay radio reports confirming any chance of compromise between Germany and Poland had been sabotaged and war was now days away. When the furious Vansittart had calmed down, the three men agreed to keep open a channel of covert communication for peace negotiations even after the outbreak of hostilities. Van suggested that, by brokering a future peace, they might ensure a war resulting in the deaths of only 'thousands instead of millions'. They decided that Kordt would send them a postcard from neutral Switzerland inscribed, '*Si fractus illabatur orbis impavidum ferient ruinae*', a line from the Roman poet, Horace, roughly translated as 'Yea, if the world should fall and break, he [the just man] will stand serene amidst the crash.'[16] The postmark would indicate the location where Conwell-Evans should rendezvous with Kordt precisely two weeks after the date stamp.

In Germany, the net closed on suspected British agents. Alice Schuster (daughter of Marie, Grahame Christie's beloved godmother) was summoned to meet Field Marshal Göring in Berlin. Notwithstanding their distant kinship, with the international situation in crisis, the Nazi leadership in fevered preparation for war, and her two passions being promoting artists the Nazis condemned as 'degenerate' and smuggling Jews into Holland, this understandably alarmed her. Having arrived at his offices, she waited anxiously in a room until Göring himself appeared, asking if she knew Christie's whereabouts. If so, she should warn him to leave the country at once. Within an hour, he had escaped by taxi for a nearby airfield, from where he flew back to London. Fifteen minutes after his departure, the Gestapo arrived at his Berlin flat to arrest him.

Meanwhile in Washington, Lord Lothian had no time to ease into his new job. Having left England to the news of the Molotov-Ribbentrop Pact, he arrived three days before the invasion of Poland. At his meeting the next day with President Roosevelt, he eschewed the dress uniform of gold lace in favour of his customary crumpled suit and broad smile. One journalist noted approvingly that he looked 'more like an American businessman than a British aristocrat'. Unlike at their rumbustious encounter eight months previously, the two men were now in furious agreement, with Roosevelt sympathising with 'every fibre' with Britain and France, but admitting he was hidebound by the US Neutrality Acts. The new ambassador needed to persuade the American public that Britain and France deserved practical US support in their new war with Germany; only such a swing in public opinion could pressurise Congress to amend the law to allow the export of munitions to the democracies in Europe.

As Lothian emerged from the White House, giving the expectant crowd of newspapermen his customary friendly smile, something so trivial happened as to seem almost flippant in the telling, yet which helped tip the balance of American sentiment towards his home country. A small black kitten (quickly nicknamed 'Crisis' by the media) appeared at his feet. Deftly and unselfconsciously, he scooped up the feline and put it onto his shoulders while chatting with the journalists, a spontaneous gesture captured by the photographers and syndicated in newspapers across the country. As he later told his friend Nancy Astor, he was as a result 'voted human'.[17]

As dawn broke through the Berlin skies on Sunday, 3 September, Sir Nevile Henderson awoke to receive the text of the ultimatum he had to deliver to his hosts. Unless, by eleven o'clock, Germany had delivered assurances she would withdraw her forces from Poland, then Great Britain and Germany would be at war. The ambassador duly arrived, in full dress uniform, at the foreign ministry on Wilhelmstrasse for a nine o'clock appointment. Astonishingly, Ribbentrop was 'unavailable' and so deputised to Paul-Otto Schmidt, the exhausted interpreter, who had himself overslept.

Rushing to the ministry in a taxi, Schmidt spotted Henderson entering the building and only just made it through a side entrance to Ribbentrop's office in time. Handing over the ultimatum, the embarrassed British envoy said, 'I am sincerely sorry that I must hand such a document to you in particular, as you have always been most anxious to help.' Schmidt hurried round to the Führer's office at the Chancellery, where Hitler sat at his desk with Ribbentrop standing by the window. After he had read the translation to the assembled company listening in stunned silence, a coldly furious Hitler turned towards his foreign minister and with a 'savage look' asked, 'What now?' As he escaped into the anteroom, Schmidt briefed those waiting, including Hermann Göring, who snapped, 'If we lose this war, then God have mercy on us.'[18]

The declaration of war had been delivered simultaneously to the German government in both Berlin and London that Sunday morning. With poignant irony, the two foreign ministry civil servants who took delivery of this grim missive in each city were both Anglophiles who had done what they could to champion peace. Ribbentrop had detained the ambassador in Germany following his holiday, so Theo Kordt was once again the senior German diplomat at Carlton House Terrace. Theo telephoned his brother in Berlin to relay the three notes, each signed with absurd diplomatic courtesy, 'I have the honour to be with high consideration, Your obedient servant, HALIFAX.' The first confirmed that the British government now considered itself in a state of war with Germany. The second dealt with the departure of German diplomats under passes, subject to reciprocal arrangements for their British counterparts in Berlin. The third promised to limit bombing outside the area of hostilities to prevent civilian casualties and to abide by the Geneva protocol prohibiting 'asphyxiating or poisonous or other gases and of bacteriological methods of warfare'. It asked whether the Germans would do the same.

Meanwhile, the Commons met in emergency session, the first time on a Sunday in over a century. Neville Chamberlain admitted to a packed House, 'Everything that I have worked for, everything that I have hoped for, everything that I have believed in during my public life, has crashed into ruins.'[19] As he shepherded his fellow diplomats and staff back to Germany through Holland the next day, Theo Kordt carried with him a letter from Grahame Christie acknowledging his efforts to avoid a war. Written on

Travellers Club writing paper, it opened, 'Dear Friend, I hope you do not mind my addressing you thus, for friend you have been and are to your own great people, to us Britons, and to all who are struggling to restore the conception of honour and integrity amongst nations.' After wishing the German a 'deeply felt "Auf Wiedersehen"', it went on to say, 'if you must leave us soon, ours is the loss: if a miracle should keep you here, ours is to rejoice,' before concluding, 'thank you a thousand times for all your noble work: Come what may, we shall regard you always as a great gentleman and a great Christian.'[20]

*Dr Theo Kordt, the German chargé d'affaires, leaving
10 Downing Street, 1 September 1939.*

25

THE POLITICAL AND MORAL SCUM OF THE EARTH

PHILIP CONWELL-EVANS HAD SUSPENDED THE ANGLO-GERMAN Fellowship on the day Germany invaded Poland. At its last meeting, held a month later in the Unilever boardroom, the Council agreed to keep the register of members in the hope the organisation might rise, phoenix-like, 'when peace comes'. While Lord Lothian had found his métier in Washington, the outbreak of war did little for the employment prospects of the Fellowship's champions. Those first eight months of hostilities were dubbed the Bore War by British wits, as the *Sitzkrieg* (sitting war) by their German counterparts and the *Drôle de Guerre* (joke of a war) by the French. Only later did American journalists coin the now prevailing term – the Phoney War – during which the Fellowship's alumni and other former appeasers struggled to adjust to the grim prospect of armed conflict. Now unemployed and anxious to find a wartime role, Conwell-Evans asked Lloyd George to recommend him to Winston Churchill as a political secretary, expert on contemporary Germany.[1] Ernest Tennant also later petitioned Churchill for a job through his eccentric cousin, Margot, Lady Oxford, widow of the former prime minister, Herbert Asquith.[2]

The Fellowship was not legally dissolved until 1949, but unlike the openly pro-Nazi organisations that had also lobbied for closer relations with Germany, it did not go underground. Despite continuing insinuations in parliament and elsewhere, it was never credibly accused of treachery, disloyalty to the Crown, nor of harbouring a fifth column. But in those lethargic early months of war, those arguing for peace continued to argue, those supporting the Nazi cause continued to support, and those conspiring with the German resistance to unseat Hitler continued to conspire. Only the businessmen who had originally sponsored the Fellowship adapted quickly to the new realities of war. How and why each group reacted proved crucial to the Fellowship's wartime and indeed post-war reputation.

In the House of Lords, an aristocratic peace lobby, centred on the Duke of Westminster, pressed their fellow peer, Lord Halifax, to sue for a negotiated peace with Germany. Several ennobled Fellowship alumni, including Lords Londonderry, Arnold, Brocket, Noel-Buxton, Mottistone and Sempill, attended meetings in September 1939 at Bourdon House, the duke's Mayfair home. Londonderry tried to persuade the retired Stanley Baldwin to travel to Berlin to propose peace terms to Adolf Hitler. While far-fetched, the suggestion (ignored by Baldwin as before) seems less eccentric than it might, given the Führer's fascination with the former British prime minister and the repeated attempts over the previous seven years to arrange a meeting between the two statesmen.

In parallel to these peace-mongering lords, the other group campaigning for the cessation of hostilities were the fellow-travelling sharks. In a frantic round of secret meetings and furtive communications being watched intently by MI5, they tried to bring together the relics of the most prominent pro-Nazi and anti-Semitic groups, including Sir Oswald Mosley's British Union of Fascists (BUF), Admiral Sir Barry Domvile's The Link, and Captain Archibald Ramsay's Right Club. These at best unpatriotic and at worst treasonous activities ended abruptly in May 1940 with the widespread arrests under Defence Regulation 18B, the emergency powers allowing the suspension of habeas corpus and the indefinite detention of those suspected of sympathy with National Socialism. Nearly two thousand individuals were interned without trial, most commonly members of the BUF.[3]

Associating with the Fellowship was not in itself grounds for detention, but some prominent members, whose pro-Nazi activities had taken them far beyond the mainstream, were indeed detained. Domvile and his wife's arrest was well publicised; he was the only former Council member to be locked up. C. E. Carroll, the secretary of The Link and editor of the *Anglo-German Review*, was incarcerated for three years. The authorities also rounded up the troublemakers who had plotted against the Fellowship's Council two years before, including George Pitt-Rivers and Elwyn Wright, its hate-fuelled former secretary. Pitt-Rivers's girlfriend (and Conwell-Evans's scourge), Catherine Sharpe, abandoned her lover and escaped by boat to South Africa while Margaret Bothamley and her friend Dorothy Eckersley, two other ardent disciples of Hitler, fled to Germany. There were other prominent Fellowship members, including Viscountess Downe, Queen Mary's former lady-in-waiting, General Fuller, and Sir Jocelyn Lucas MP, who fell into a grey area where they may have deserved incarceration but seem to have avoided it, perhaps because of their Establishment connections.

In the House of Lords there were even rumours the Security Service might detain Lord Londonderry. Any past appeasement of the Third Reich – especially if it had involved taking coffee with Hitler – was an intense humiliation. As his biographer concluded, Londonderry was left 'exposed to public ignominy and without political friends'.[4] The opprobrium heaped on the once cocksure Lord Brocket triggered a nervous breakdown; unfit for military service, he spent the war on his estates. Unity Mitford's father, Lord Redesdale, was so irked by the publicity around his daughter's tragic obsession with Hitler, which had led to letters of abuse and government restrictions on his movements, that he wrote to *The Times* insisting he really did want Britain to win the war and had never been, nor was likely to become, a fascist.[5]

The Fellowship's financial sponsors had an altogether better war. While the Great War had caught the nation unawares, the scares of the previous eighteen months had given alert businessmen time to prepare and many were already vitally engaged with Britain's rearmament programme. Their pre-war championing of economic appeasement and the Fellowship provoked no hesitation in enlisting their support for the war effort. Unilever, Dunlop, ICI and Morris Motors each played critical roles in arming, equipping, transporting, feeding, washing and clothing the military and its citizenry. Having hosted all of the Fellowship's Council meetings in open support for the preservation of peace, Unilever quickly moved on to a war footing by standardising its branded products for wartime use. Its Lifebuoy vans, equipped with hot showers, soap and towels offered mobile washing facilities to bombed out Londoners during the Blitz. The government asked its chairman, Francis D'Arcy Cooper (whom Tennant had introduced to Hitler) to chair the committee reorganising Britain's export trade. Later it sent him to the US on a mysterious mission which earned him a baronetcy.

His fellow director, Paul Rykens (who had also joined the meeting with Hitler), advised the Dutch government during the war and chaired its post-war reconstruction committee.

Dunlop had been manufacturing military supplies for many years and, given the threat of aerial attack, moved its headquarters to a country house, where a flock of carrier pigeons helped maintain contact if modern means were disrupted. As well as Winston Churchill's mattress, it made most of the country's vehicle and cycle tyres and military kit, ranging from dinghies, barrage balloons, wetsuits, refuelling hoses and infantrymen's boots to the rubber decoy tanks and field guns used as a diversion during the Normandy landings. ICI, the Fellowship's most generous funder, played a similarly vital role by developing novel technologies to defeat the Axis Powers. These varied from penicillin, anti-malarials, anaesthetics and beta blockers to radar and the atomic bomb. Lord Nuffield, the founder and chairman of Morris Motors (proposed as Fellowship chairman after Mount Temple's resignation), had been an early advocate of rearmament, expanding into aeroengines in 1929. The Air Ministry had rebuffed his offer to supply these until war became inevitable, when he adapted his Cowley works to repair over eighty thousand planes, while another of his subsidiaries manufactured more than a quarter of Britain's tanks.

The government similarly deployed the skills of the senior financiers who had supported the Fellowship from the outset to buttress Britain's wartime economy. As president of the National Savings Committee (which he had founded in the previous war), the leading banker Robert Kindersley persuaded the British public to save nine billion pounds (over £430 billion in current prices). Neville Chamberlain appointed Josiah Stamp (by now Lord Stamp) as chief adviser on economic coordination and proposed him as Chancellor of the Exchequer in January 1940. His contribution to the war effort ended tragically, a year later, when a bomb hit his Kent home, killing him, his wife and his eldest son, robbing the country of one of its most talented businessmen and public servants.

Conwell-Evans, Grahame Christie and their patron and spymaster, Robert Vansittart, had little sympathy with either the aristocratic peace initiatives floating around the Lords or the treasonous manoeuvrings of the so-called patriotic societies. With all the conviction of a convert, Conwell-Evans wrote furiously to his old boss, Lord Noel-Buxton: 'how anybody can talk of negotiating with Hitler passes… comprehension', before insisting any negotiated peace would give the Germans, who are 'bullies in victory, and whine in defeat', the respite to invade Great Britain.[6] Writing in similar vein to Lloyd George, who had just called for a negotiated peace in the Commons, Conwell-Evans was adamant Hitler wanted to 'bring down the British Empire', and the attitude of the former prime minister would only help the German leader to undermine the 'resolution of the British and French peoples to defeat him'.[7]

But Conwell-Evans reserved his particular wrath for the now seriously ill and discredited Nevile Henderson, who published his memoir, *Failure of a Mission*, in the spring of 1940. Although it offered some degree of apology, the former ambassador still justified appeasement as the only option during his posting. Reviewing it for *The Nineteenth Century and After*, a well-respected literary periodical, Conwell-Evans lambasted Henderson for his lethal mix of naivety and over-caution in dealing with the National Socialists. He damned him for being ignorant of German history, for being suckered by Göring, and for ignoring the wisdom of his two predecessors. In June, just days after German troops had marched into Paris, Henderson wrote privately to Conwell-Evans in response to the review. He accepted grimly how 'France is on the verge of collapse and surrender, and it is Britain alone at last', but he claimed it had been 'by turning German eyes eastward we should keep her from turning them westward'. He insisted he hated Nazism but offered the hope that 'one day (though not now in our lifetime) Germany will become a reformed character, otherwise we had better shut up the shutters in Europe'. He offered to meet his critic, saying he would 'rather talk than write'.[8]

Conwell-Evans's fury with his former clients underscores his transition from Britain's 'most ardent Germanophil' [*sic*] to passionate proponent of 'Vansittartism'.[9] Defined by Van's biographer as an 'extreme and obsessive anti-Germanism', this novel dogma blamed the new war not just on National Socialism and Hitler's leadership, but on an innate German and more precisely Prussian bellicosity dating back over centuries.[10] Increasingly embittered, Vansittart was now convinced 'eighty percent of the German race are the political and moral scum of the earth' and so it was crucial to 'eradicate not only Hitlerism, but Prussianism'.[11] Despite having lived part of each year in Germany since the 1920s and made many German friends,

Christie made the same connection, now damning National Socialism as the 'last and most hideous manifestation of the Prussian Militarism'.

Vansittartism soon reached a wider audience when Duff Cooper, now minister of information, invited the chief diplomatic adviser to broadcast lectures on the BBC (later published as *Black Record: Germans Past and Present* and serialised in the *Sunday Times*). Though this both reflected and fuelled popular anti-German sentiment, even in the heat of war his splenetic tone and unapologetic racism disturbed some listeners, who suggested its invective would unify German public opinion against Great Britain and feed Joseph Goebbels's propaganda machine. Hostile questions were asked in the Commons and pamphlets issued both condemning the post-war implications of Van's ideology and the propriety of a senior civil servant making such charged broadcasts.[12] Conwell-Evans remembered his shock when he had asked to buy a copy in a shop and the assistant had warned him, 'Oh, it's very extreme.'[13]

Anxious to salvage something from the ashes of the German intelligence networks nurtured by the three friends, Christie drafted a memorandum for Vansittart in late September proposing the establishment of a 'German advisory committee'. Tasked with designing propaganda, 'tuned flawlessly to the different moods and mentalities of all classes in Germany', this would pool their expertise and intelligence to support the British war effort and work in complete secrecy. He suggested it could be housed in the Fellowship's now empty offices in Chelsea, with Conwell-Evans as secretary, Vansittart as chairman, and staffed by Germans overseen by a committee of both nationalities. He recommended Dr Hermann Rauschning and Dr Otto Strasser, two former Nazis who had fallen out with the regime early on. Although the scheme never went past the planning stage, the newly minted Ministry of Information adopted its concepts and the two Germans became prolific propagandists, with Rauschning authoring *Hitler Speaks: A Series of Political Conversations with Adolf Hitler on his Real Aims* in 1939, and Strasser publishing *The Gangsters Around Hitler* in 1942.

The outbreak of war galvanised the still fragmented and ill-coordinated German resistance. General Halder ordered Colonel Oster to dust down and update their 1938 plans for a coup, which Neville Chamberlain had so clumsily thwarted with his quixotic flight to Munich. Separately, some of Christie's informants were contemplating installing Hermann Göring as a less bellicose alternative to Hitler. What all the resisters now needed most, and at once, was support from outside Germany to legitimise any replacement German government. Klemens von Klemperer, the distinguished historian and himself an anti-Nazi student leader in pre-war Vienna, expertly analysed this quest in *German Resistance Against Hitler: The Search for Allies Abroad, 1938–1945*. He is one of the few historians to have recognised the contribution to the opposition made by Grahame Christie and Philip Conwell-Evans, whom he eulogised as 'men of extraordinary enterprise and ingenuity'.[14]

As during the Munich crisis, the means of overthrowing Hitler's regime was to be key units of the German army supported by the Berlin police force. The main obstacle was the moral grappling this required of the senior soldiers, who were hidebound by both traditional military codes of honour and the 'soldier's oath' each had sworn to Hitler. Erich Kordt co-authored a memorandum titled 'The Imminent Disaster' to address this and distributed it to the commander-in-chief of the army, his chief of staff and other senior officers. Its thesis was pragmatic rather than ideological: Hitler's reckless military strategy excused soldiers from their oath on the grounds that, by overthrowing him, they could preserve their beloved army, protect Germany's traditional borders and secure 'peace with honour'.

Having avoided arrest in Germany thanks to Göring's tip-off, Christie now made his wartime base the Travellers Club. Still struggling with his health, he grumbled that he felt in poor shape for long journeys. Nonetheless, he and Conwell-Evans stepped up their cloak and dagger liaisons with the German resistance. They continued to report to Vansittart, whose star had risen now that his warnings had proven justified, and their German networks became conduits for overtures about an alternative German leadership with whom the Allies might agree an honourable peace. These discussions had the prime minister's blessing and, unlike before the war, His Majesty's Government covered their substantial travel expenses, albeit with grumblings from the civil servants.

Having left London to debrief State Secretary von Weizsäcker and Colonel Oster in Berlin, Theo Kordt had secured a posting to Bern in neutral Switzerland, barely a week after the declaration of war. While his official duties were to coordinate the handling of prisoners of war with the International Red Cross, his covert mandate was to secure British government support for an internal coup against Hitler. He and his colleagues respected and trusted Conwell-Evans, to whom they had given the codename 'Philipos'. Downing Street, and more cautiously the Foreign Office, shone a brighter light on such intrigues than they had in the months leading up to war. Jock Colville, Chamberlain's private secretary, noted in his diary that these offered the enticing prospect of 'getting rid of Hitler and coming to terms with an anti-Nazi government under Goering on the basis of restoring independence to Poland and Bohemia, disarming all round, and agreeing to leave inviolate the unity and boundaries of Germany proper'.[15]

Following the protocol agreed with his British friends at their last meeting at Cornwall Gardens, Theo's wife had sent Lady Vansittart a postcard depicting the Zum Weissen Kreuz, a picturesque hotel in Interlaken, bearing the line of Latin verse. This was the signal for the two Britons to find their way to Switzerland for the first in a series of clandestine meetings during those early months of the Phoney War. Conwell-Evans met with Theo Kordt while Christie reconnected with his 'South German group', which had fed him valuable and mostly accurate intelligence over many years and had now found refuge in neutral Switzerland. This included Prince Max Egon zu Hohenlohe-Langenburg, a wealthy Bohemian nobleman; Dr Joseph Wirth, the former German chancellor; Fritz Thyssen, the steel and mining magnate, who had fallen out with the Nazis; Hermann Rauschning, whom he had proposed for the German advisory committee; and his most valued informant, the aviation expert Hans Ritter.

The outbreak of hostilities had a different flavour to the previous war, when public anger had erupted, German-sounding businesses had been vandalised and dachshunds stoned to death. From the outset, Neville Chamberlain set the tone publicly for a possible reconciliation with Germany through the offices of 'good Germans'. In speeches he emphasised he had no quarrel with the people, while Halifax told Lothian it would be helpful if they could 'formulate objectives that would be acceptable to any "moderate" section in Germany that might have any chance of overthrowing the present regime'.[16] Alec Cadogan confirmed the first aim of the British war effort should be to 'get rid of Hitler'.[17]

In response to the postcard, in late October, Conwell-Evans and Christie made their first attempt to reach Switzerland, only to be frustrated by Police Sergeant Ashwell-Cooke, who prevented their boarding the Air France flight to Paris on the grounds they lacked security clearance. Having detained them and confiscated their documents, he reported sceptically to MI5 that their supposed mission was to discuss 'some sort of *coup d'état* in Germany which would result in the setting up of a government from which the leading Nazis would be excluded'.[18] Furious at this interference, Robert Vansittart quickly intervened to ensure the pair were granted permission to leave the next day for the three-day trip.

Conwell-Evans eventually reached Lausanne for a covert meeting with Theo Kordt, who asked the British government for a *Stillhatezusage*, a standstill commitment, to assure the plotters it would not exploit any attempted coup for military advantage. Vansittart had made clear, on behalf of Chamberlain and Halifax, that the British government refused to negotiate with 'Hitler or his like', so the onus would be on the opposition to engineer a replacement government whose word could be trusted.[19] Conwell-Evans had brought with him a note extracted from a speech given by the prime minister in response to Hitler's half-hearted peace proposals made in the Reichstag. This was significantly the first time the government had taken such initiative, indicating that it and probably its electorate were not yet reconciled to an all-out European war.[20] The text had been hurriedly copied by Conwell-Evans from the prime minister's handwritten original in Van's room at the Foreign Office. Its peace-signalling themes purportedly offered an olive branch to the 'good Germans' in the resistance: 'no effective remedy can be found for the world's ills that does not take account of the just claims and needs of all nations… we desire nothing from the German people which should offend their self respect… we are not aiming only at victory but… a foundation of a better international system which will mean that war is not the inevitable lot of every generation.'[21]

Despite Vansittart assuring him these words had been 'specially written' with the conspirators 'in mind', Conwell-Evans worried it was still too vague.[22] Nonetheless, Theo accepted it as evidence Downing Street would negotiate peace terms with a future German government led by moderates. Convinced of the personal prime ministerial blessing, he arranged for his wife to smuggle the note to his excited brother in Berlin. Erich saw it as a 'trump card' to embolden the General Staff to launch a coup and so shared it with Colonel Oster and General Beck.[23] But though re-energised by these overtures from London, Erich Kordt nonetheless felt frustrated by the continued dithering of his co-conspirators. He decided the only way of 'liberating our generals from their scruples' was to assassinate the Führer.[24] What's more, he decided to do so himself.

Of the many assassination attempts on Adolf Hitler, this ranks among the least hare-brained. Unquestionably brave, Kordt had the means, the motive and the opportunity. Notwithstanding the tight security around the increasingly paranoid Führer and the unpredictability of his schedule, Kordt's plan, as Patricia Meehan concluded, had 'every chance of succeeding'.[25] Oster volunteered to source the explosives and the detonator from Major Erwin von Lahousen, his fellow conspirator and subordinate. An Austrian aristocrat close to Admiral Canaris, von Lahousen headed Section II (Sabotage) of the Abwehr, which included an explosives laboratory, and he would be involved with several later attempts to blow up Adolf Hitler. As the foreign minister's long-standing *chef de cabinet*, Kordt was no longer subject to identity checks and had easy and frequent access to the inner sanctums of the Reich Chancellery. A mild-mannered, bespectacled civil servant, familiar and unthreatening to the sentries protecting the Führer, he made an improbable assassin.

Conscious that his chances of survival were low, Erich sent a letter to his brother and informed his cousin Simone and two other co-conspirators of his plans. He also arranged for senior diplomats at the American embassy and the Swiss legation to be briefed on the conspiracy at the right moment, recognising that a prompt and supportive international response to any coup would be critical to its sustained success. But three days before the planned assassination, Georg Elser, a factory worker apparently acting on his own initiative, detonated a bomb at the Bürgerbräukeller in Munich where Hitler had been celebrating the anniversary of the 1923 putsch with other prominent National Socialists. The explosion brought down the roof and an external wall of the building, killing eight and injuring many more. The Führer escaped only because a change of travel arrangements had led to his giving a shortened speech and leaving early along with other senior colleagues. This near miss resulted in a tightening of his security detail and closer scrutiny of the explosives laboratory. And so, when Kordt arrived at Oster's house to collect their bomb on the afternoon of 11 November, he was met by the devastating news that, despite his seniority and security clearance, his host had been unable to secure the necessary equipment from the laboratory. Kordt was so frustrated by this turn of events that he volunteered to complete the assassination with a pistol, but Oster persuaded him it would be madness.

The second shattering blow to both the opposition's cause and any chance of it securing British government support followed, with horrible coincidence, on the day after the cellar bomb. Undercover SS officers duped two inept British SIS agents operating in neutral Holland into believing they were negotiating with senior German army officers working with the resistance. They framed the discussions on similar lines to the various peace-feelers emanating from the Kordt circle, the Vatican and several businessmen in neutral Sweden. Following a series of inconsequential meetings, German soldiers waiting five metres inside the German border ambushed the hapless British agents in Venlo, a town just in Holland. Following a shoot-out in which a Dutch colleague was killed, they were handcuffed, bundled into a truck and abducted into Germany, where they spent the rest of the war imprisoned. Astonishingly, they carried documents compromising most of the network of British agents across central and western Europe and gave up further information on SIS's operations under interrogation. Despite Georg Elser insisting to his captors that he had acted alone and had no British connections, Hitler seized the opportunity to conflate the two incidents to foment anti-British sentiment in Germany and later used both as justification for the invasion of the Netherlands.

While his friend Conwell-Evans had been meeting Theo Kordt in Switzerland, Grahame Christie had been seeing Prince Max Hohenlohe. Codenamed 'Vanloo', Hohenlohe had hosted Lord Runciman, the British prime minister's envoy, and Konrad Henlein, the head of the Sudeten party, at his castle in the former Czechoslovakia during the Sudeten crisis. He was well known to Vansittart and Churchill, while Christie considered him a friend, but in time he would prove no more trustworthy than Henlein. The prince suggested to Christie that Hermann Göring would offer himself as a credible, peaceable alternative head of state. Christie was intrigued but knew (as von Klemperer recognised) that, 'despite all his rakish charm', his former whisky-drinking companion was as ruthless as Hitler. Despite such reservations, Downing Street remained enthusiastic about the chance of a conciliatory Göring replacing the bellicose Hitler, with Colville noting that this showed the 'upper classes and high military authorities in Germany were anxious to avoid the outbreak of real war, since they believe that bolshevism would be the final and inevitable outcome'.[26]

At some point in early 1940, Christie received word from Göring that he wished to meet his old friend in person. With British government blessing, he travelled over to the Continent for the weekend and the two men met at a property straddling the Dutch-German border (quite possibly Wylerberg). Göring gave him a signed portrait commemorating their 'long and happy friendship', but no record survives of anything else resulting from the meeting.[27] Christie's discussions with Hohenlohe rumbled on till Christmas, with another meeting in Holland, but soon he advised Vansittart and Halifax not to negotiate further with Göring, who was playing both sides against the middle. By the spring, Vansittart had to admit to Halifax that, despite early promise, best intentions and considerable ingenuity, these 'manoeuvres' – whether the 'will-o'-the-wisp dances in the name of phantom generals' or of a 'fat field-marshal with neutral go-betweens' – had failed to gain traction.[28] Now all agreed they had little to no chance of bringing the war to an early conclusion.

In March 1940, Conwell-Evans and Christie were back in Lausanne for further meetings, this time with Joseph Wirth and Hans Ritter. Wirth had written to Neville Chamberlain four months earlier, urging him to announce publicly that the British did not want to vanquish the German people. As a former German chancellor, Wirth had a high profile and good connections with other resisters (both among the generals and the industrialists surrounding Robert Bosch) but he was also unreliable and an alcoholic. At what would be their last meeting, Christie brought a document confirming that the British government would not attack from the west if the opposition moved against Hitler and would cooperate with a new German government. But again, this initiative fizzled out, just as had the Kordts', for reasons von Klemperer found 'all the more puzzling' given the 'omens seemed most auspicious'.[29]

Ernest Tennant admitted in his memoirs that he had kept a dignified distance from such 'conspiratorial negotiations'. Before the war, he had played his part by hosting Erich Kordt for the weekend at his Essex country house and had loaned his bedroom at the Grand Hotel in Nuremberg for meetings with the opposition. But, in October 1939, he too had to dust down his Great War intelligence skills when the Ministry of Supply sent him to still neutral Norway to report on the ferro-alloy industry, on which Britain depended for the manufacture of armaments and in which he was expert. Travelling out by sea, he spent time in Oslo with George Ogilvie-Forbes, now councillor at the British Legation and previously at the Berlin embassy (where he had briefed Halifax on Kristallnacht). Ogilvie-Forbes warned Tennant that the German legation had learned of his mission, so on his return journey he travelled under a Norwegian alias, only to struggle to convince the Newcastle passport officials to let him back into the country. The ministry sent him back to Scandinavia four months later to update his report. Returning home through neutral Sweden and Denmark, he visited the British legations. His cousin Peter Tennant was nominally the press attaché in Stockholm, but (according to a family member) worked with SIS at the time. Presumably briefed by Peter, Ernest had been shocked at the underfunded and understaffed legations struggling to counter the effective German propaganda, so he reported it angrily in a letter to the *Daily Telegraph*.

Conwell-Evans and Theo Kordt were due to meet again in Switzerland that April, but the German invasion of Denmark and Norway on 9 April 1940 stymied both that meeting and any further visits to Scandinavia by Tennant. This was the start of the infamous Norwegian campaign, the disastrous Allied military engagement that ended Neville Chamberlain's premiership and heralded in Winston Churchill as wartime prime minister.

Between them, our three sometime 'ambulant amateurs', Tennant, Christie and Conwell-Evans, had made at least half a dozen clandestine trips over to Continental Europe during the Phoney War. Having previously been suspected of harbouring dubious intentions by MI5 and Special Branch, now they travelled on official British government business to explore any opportunities, however remote, of finding alternative outcomes to armed conflict and alternative regimes to Adolf Hitler's. But the Führer's fraudulent but skilful conflation of Georg Elser's lone bomb attack with the spectacularly bungled Venlo incident had marked the end of any patience the Foreign Office and SIS might have with such Continental adventures. Nothing more could be done to civilise the Nazis.

Philip Kerr, Lord Lothian, photographed reading Hitler's Mein Kampf *in his office in London, following the announcement of his appointment as the new British ambassador to the United States, 25 April 1939.*

26

BRITAIN'S BROKE;
IT'S YOUR MONEY WE WANT

FOLLOWING THE THREE-DAY DEBATE IN THE HOUSE OF COMMONS
on the Norway campaign, Winston Churchill replaced Neville Chamberlain
as prime minister on 10 May 1940, the day the German army launched its
invasion of Holland, Belgium and Luxembourg. Lord Halifax had been the
candidate favoured by most of the Conservative Party, as well as the King and
Queen, the House of Lords, the Labour Party and the BBC. But in a pivotal
meeting between him, Chamberlain, Churchill and David Margesson, the
chief whip, Halifax had famously and controversially demurred, while an
uncharacteristically coy First Lord of the Admiralty agreed to take on the
premiership. Within just over a fortnight, the new prime minister oversaw
the evacuation of the British Expeditionary Force from Dunkirk following
the fall of France. By the summer, he would be coordinating the aerial
defence of England itself – the Battle of Britain – and preparing to defend
her from a full-scale German invasion. The Phoney War was over.

Generously and shrewdly, Churchill was magnanimous in political victory. Ignoring the many voices clamouring for Chamberlain's dismissal from
government, he kept him in the five-man War Cabinet, with responsibility
for the domestic economy as lord president of the Council. He also let him
continue as leader of the Conservatives, bringing the divided and suspicious
party behind the new National Government. The Labour leaders were
brought into the War Cabinet and Halifax continued as foreign secretary.

But July 1940 brought Neville Chamberlain two devastating blows.
The first was the disease that would end his life. He was suffering with
stomach pains, for which his doctors performed an operation confirming

terminal bowel cancer. They hid the fatal prognosis from him and the disease progressed fast. In late September, Churchill reluctantly accepted his resignation from the Cabinet, and within a month the King and Queen were visiting him at his home to say goodbye. On 9 November 1940, aged seventy-one, Chamberlain died. Churchill gave generous eulogies in the House of Commons and at his funeral.

The second tragedy for Chamberlain was the publication by Victor Gollancz, in the wake of the ignominious retreat from Dunkirk, of *Guilty Men*. Authored under the pseudonym 'Cato' by a trio of journalists – Michael Foot (later leader of the Labour Party), Frank Owen and Peter Howard – who each worked for newspapers owned by Churchill's friend, Lord Beaverbrook, it was written in just four days. They identified MacDonald, Chamberlain, Baldwin, Simon, Hoare, Halifax and nine other British politicians as the architects of interwar appeasement and, as one historian summarised, damned them as 'cowardly, traitorous crypto-Fascists' whose failures had led to the outbreak of war.[1] Though issued by the same publisher and in a similar format to *Tory MP*, it had benefitted from none of the Wynns' meticulous evidence-gathering nor calm analysis. It is a wildly unbalanced polemic, not least because it ignored the widespread support for appeasement and disarmament from the Labour Party, most newspapers, their publishers, especially Beaverbrook himself, and most of the electorate. Venomous, vicious and vindictive, it was an instant success, reprinted seventeen times in its first two months and going on to sell over 200,000 copies. Immodestly, but quite possibly correctly, Gollancz claimed it to be 'probably the most famous British pamphlet for a hundred years', while Foot admitted it had sold like a pornographic classic.[2]

While yet to be defined as 'special', the relationship between American president and British premier during the 1930s was unsurprisingly important, but in case of a war it would be crucial. Churchill had inherited Philip Lothian as his ambassador in Washington and, while the two men had known and liked each other for decades, they had vehemently disagreed on both independence for India and, certainly before Munich, the appeasement of Germany. Despite Churchill's American parentage and enthusiasm for his mother's country, President Roosevelt distrusted him as an aristocrat, imperialist and alcoholic. Churchill had been looking to correct these negative impressions directly with the president in a series of telephone calls and letters (using the moniker 'naval person') since the start of the war, and quickly enlisted the ambassador's support in his charm offensive. But their shared vision for Anglo-American cooperation had been hampered by the extreme views of Lothian's opposite number in London, the isolationist, anti-Semitic US ambassador, Joseph Kennedy. The father of the future US president thought Great Britain bound to lose the war, so advised the president against giving support, urging instead a negotiated peace settlement with Hitler, even offering to intermediate himself.

Having arrived in Washington four days before the outbreak of war, Lothian served as ambassador for just sixteen months, but in that short time, against the headwinds of the US Neutrality Acts and the 1940 presidential election, he played a vital role in building American public support for the British war effort. His diplomatic task would be as delicate as it was critical. He recognised that, while most Americans were anti-Hitler, they had little enthusiasm to intervene in a second European war and were, like the president, suspicious of the British Empire. Avoiding obvious propaganda, he deployed his quiet persuasive charm to change political and public opinion across the country in Great Britain's favour. His series of carefully crafted speeches, syndicated to newspapers across the country, gave an unvarnished picture of the challenges faced by the Allies, while focusing on the naval threat to the US: 'the outcome of the grim struggle will affect you almost as much as it will affect us… for if Hitler gets our fleet, or destroys it, the whole foundation on which the security of both our countries has rested for 120 years will have disappeared.'[3]

Lothian's first breakthrough was the Destroyers-for-Bases agreement, signed in September 1940, whereby fifty elderly US Navy destroyers were transferred to the Royal Navy, in exchange for ninety-nine-year leases setting up US naval and air bases on British Overseas Territories from Newfoundland to Antigua. Recognising this as the first but 'long step' towards bringing the US into the war, Winston Churchill advised the King to appoint Lothian to the Order of the Thistle, the highest Scottish honour.[4] In November, the US government repealed the embargo on the export of munitions, allowing 'cash and carry' purchases whereby Great Britain could buy American armaments if she paid in cash and arranged for collection.

But cash was now the main issue. Despite her empire, industrial base and the financial clout of the City of London, Britain's finances were increasingly precarious. In October, Lothian returned by sea to Britain to spend two days cloistered in the Oxfordshire countryside with the prime minister, whom he urged to make this hidden predicament plain to Roosevelt in a long letter they drafted together. Arriving back into New York, tired through overwork and increasingly ill, the British ambassador was met by American journalists on the dockside. Controversially eschewing diplomatic niceties, he succinctly summarised the prognosis: 'Well boys, Britain's broke; it's your money we want.'

A month later, Roosevelt conclusively beat the Republican presidential candidate, Wendell Willkie, to be re-elected for an unprecedented third term. Writing a fortnight later to George VI, the president reassured him that this victory offered a 'definite benefit to your nation', while admitting there had been 'absolutely no question that the appeasement element, the pro-Germans, the communists, and the total isolationists did their best for my defeat'. Promising 'literally everything that we can spare', he paid tribute to the British war effort and to the King and Queen, who had 'deepened the respect and affectionate regard in which you are held in this country by the great majority of Americans'.[5]

In a speech given two weeks later to the American Farm Bureau Federation, written by the ailing ambassador but delivered by his deputy, Lothian had ended with a characteristically blunt and honest appeal:

> I have endeavoured to give you some idea of our present position, of the dangers and problems of 1941, of our hopes for the future. It is for you to decide whether you share our hopes and what support you will give us in realising them. We are, I believe, doing all we can. Since May there is no challenge we have evaded, no challenge refused. If you back us you won't be backing a quitter. The issue now depends largely on what you decide to do. Nobody can share that responsibility with you. It is the great strength of democracy that it brings responsibility down squarely to every citizen and every nation. And before the Judgement Seat of God each must answer for his own actions.[6]

The next morning, having refused medical treatment as a Christian Scientist, and after asking how the speech had gone down with its audience, Philip Lothian died of blood poisoning. His unexpected death provoked an emotional outpouring of admiration on both sides of the Atlantic. Honoured with a state funeral, his coffin draped in a union flag was carried from Washington's National Cathedral to the National Cemetery in Arlington on a horse-drawn gun carriage with a cavalry escort. Churchill eulogised him to Roosevelt as 'our greatest ambassador to the United States'. The president cabled his shock and horror 'beyond measure' to the King at the loss of his 'old friend'.[7] Having dismissed him as an 'incurably superficial Johnny know-all' and considered his appointment 'disastrous', both on the grounds of his amateurism and his involvement with appeasement, Robert Vansittart now called him the 'greatest of all our ambassadors'.[8] Lord Halifax called his truncated period in office 'one of the outstanding achievements of British diplomatic history'.[9] Lothian's junior, the historian John Wheeler-Bennett, who like many in the Foreign Office had bitterly opposed his appointment, now concluded that 'his was the hand who laid the foundation for the "Special Relationship"'.[10] Lloyd George explained to the House of Commons that Lothian could talk to Americans in a 'language which no other man of British birth could dare'.[11] Jay Moffat, the US ambassador to Canada, noted that if Joseph Kennedy said 'something is black and Lothian says it is white, we believe Lord Lothian'.[12] The *New York Times* credited him with considerable success, concluding: 'American sentiment [in September 1939] was generally favourable to the cause he advocated, yet without Lothian's earnestness and ability, the confidences he won and the energy he expended tirelessly, America's contribution might have been substantially less.'[13]

Lothian did not live to see either signed, but his hard work had laid the foundations for both the Lend-Lease Act and the Atlantic Charter. Under the first, passed in March 1941, the US could, under generous payment terms, supply the UK with military hardware, food, clothing and other provisions in vast quantities while nominally retaining its neutral status on the grounds it would be essential for its own security. By the end of the war, it had shipped supplies to the value of approximately fifty billion pounds to its allies under the Act. The Atlantic Charter, signed in August 1941, set out the basis for the post-war Anglo-Saxon world order, including the establishment of NATO and the dismantling of the British Empire.

Philip Lothian's sudden death ended his career at its peak. Despite the pivotal importance of his short time in the Washington embassy, he is now far from a household name. Historians of Anglo-American diplomacy agree on his sterling contribution, assessing him as a sophisticated and effective diplomat at the top of his game. Meanwhile, critics of appeasement have overlooked his prompt and honest volte-face on Nazi Germany and ignored his US triumphs to paint an alternative picture of a naïve, gullible and almost idiotic amateur duped by Hitler. In one recent survey of appeasement, while noting his intelligence and ability, the author damns the 'portly' Lothian for having an 'ostentatious sense of morality' combined with an 'irritating sense of mission', both made worse by a 'lack of judgement'.[14] Only a year or so separate these two phases of his career, so it is clearly not a question of maturity. Though less well remembered, he has been lumped in with the guilty men of Munich. Surely, he deserves better.

Remains of the Messerschmitt twin-engine fighter which crashed in a field twelve miles from Dungavel House, home of the Duke of Hamilton, and from which Rudolf Hess had parachuted having flown from Augsburg, Germany. 11 May 1941.

27

THE FLYING VISIT

AT THE HEIGHT OF THE PHONEY WAR, DURING A WEEK'S SICK leave suffering, appropriately enough, with German measles, the writer Peter Fleming (elder brother to James Bond's creator Ian) authored a short humorous novel. With delightful illustrations by the cartoonist David Low, *The Flying Visit* was published in July 1940. The story imagines the German Führer, accompanied by fawning journalists and cameramen, flying in a bomber at thirty thousand feet to reconnoitre England as part of a wartime propaganda stunt. The explosion of a time bomb secreted in a thermos flask destroys the plane and all of its occupants except, miraculously, for Hitler, who parachutes into a muddy horse pond in the Oxfordshire countryside. After a night in the woods sustained only by a turnip, he determines to connect with Neville Chamberlain or Horace Wilson, on the hastily concocted premise that his visit had been a peace mission rather than a reconnaissance.[1] Predating as it does the worst horrors of the Second World War, the book is both a comic attack on Hitler and a gentle satire on the English aristocrats and politicians who had promoted Anglo-German amity. Astonishingly, it also anticipated one of the war's most bizarre – and still far from fully explained – causes célèbre.

Unable to speak a word of English and with his only knowledge of England gleaned from maps, the German leader gathers he is tantalisingly close to Hymper Hall, the stately home of the second Lord Scunner. Attracted by the 'informal, free-for-all swashbuckling of the peace-time Nazis', this pink-faced and half-witted peer had met Hitler at a Nuremberg rally. The son of a war-profiteering manufacturer of collapsible greenhouses, Marcus Scunner offers one of the first fictional stereotypes of the pre-war Englishmen who travelled to Germany to take coffee with Hitler.

With no chance of reaching London incognito, the parachutist engages with the locals to find Hymper Hall, where he hopes Scunner will pass him into the 'embrace of the Prime Minister'.[2] Splendid comedy follows as the muddied Hitler, clad in field marshal's uniform under a heavy greatcoat, tackles the English countryside, drunk partygoers and fierce terriers. Having stumbled into a village fancy-dress party, his pitch-perfect rendition of the Nazi leader wins him the first prize, a pound of butter done up in pale blue ribbon. The book's satirical twist – and prescient insight – develops as, having been locked in a country house lavatory, he is handed over to the authorities. Despite enlisting help from Winston Churchill, the British government struggles with the propaganda dilemma as to what on earth to do with the captured German leader, not least because he has been replaced by a doppelgänger in Germany and his status as a prisoner of war in England means he has no legal authority to negotiate a peace.

Exactly one year since he had been appointed prime minister, on Saturday, 10 May 1941, the real Winston Churchill had been enjoying a weekend away from London in a genuine stately home near Charlbury, also in Oxfordshire. Hitler's army had by now overrun the Continent and the Luftwaffe was devastating London and other British cities. Russia and the US were still sitting on the sidelines, leaving Great Britain standing alone. In Germany, military priorities were shifting away from Operation Sea Lion, the long-planned invasion of Great Britain, to Operation Barbarossa, the soon-to-be-launched attack on the Soviet Union.

Churchill's hosts, Nancy Lancaster, the American interior decorator, and her husband Ronald Tree, a noted anti-appeasing MP, had rescued and restored Ditchley Park, an exquisite Palladian masterpiece designed by James Gibbs, with interiors by William Kent. It offered the prime minister a welcome refuge from the struggles of leadership, where pre-war standards of entertainment were kept up and the risk of bombing less than at Chequers, the prime ministerial country retreat, or nearby Blenheim Palace, his ancestral home. At nine minutes past eleven that Saturday night, in a bizarre but significant postscript to the fading story of the Anglo-German Fellowship, a German Messerschmitt Bf 110E fighter crashed into a field just south of Glasgow in Scotland and burst into flames. The plane had been adapted to carry the extra fuel needed to cover the over eight hundred miles from the manufacturer's airfield in southern Germany, from where it had taken off about five hours earlier. Having failed to find the small private airfield he was targeting, the solo pilot turned the plane onto its back, wriggled out of the cockpit and parachuted to the ground where, with an injured ankle, he blacked out. He was quickly apprehended by David McLean, the farm's head ploughman, whose mother promptly made a pot of tea. The pilot introduced himself as Hauptmann Alfred Horn, explaining he had an important message for the Duke of Hamilton and asked to be taken to Dungavel House, his nearby stately home. His captors noted his well-cut captain's uniform, gold watch and handmade flying boots.

The duke had succeeded his father in 1940 to become Scotland's most senior peer. As Marquess of Clydesdale he had visited Berlin for the Olympics, toured Luftwaffe bases and kept a close eye on Nazi Germany ever since. Now serving as the wing commander in charge of a fighter station near Edinburgh, he had not been at home. That night he had been monitoring the progress of the lone Messerschmitt and attempts by the RAF to intercept it, before retiring to bed exhausted. Meanwhile, five hundred German planes were engaged in the Luftwaffe's last major bombing raid on London, ending the lives of 1,212 Londoners, destroying the chamber of the House of Commons, damaging Big Ben and flattening the offices of Ernest Tennant's family business.

In the early hours of Sunday morning, a telephone call woke Hamilton, summoning him to interrogate the German pilot, who quickly identified himself as Rudolf Hess, Germany's deputy führer. Almost as improbably as in Fleming's comedy and in a staggering exemplar of life imitating art, Hess explained that his crash-landing had been intentional and he wanted to negotiate a peace settlement between Germany and Great Britain. Quickly grasping the enormity of the situation, Hamilton inspected the wrecked plane before telephoning the Foreign Office and asking to speak to its head, Alec Cadogan. While he remonstrated with a recalcitrant civil servant, the prime minister's private secretary, Jock Colville, hurried over from Downing Street to join the call. He authorised the duke to fly south in a Hurricane fighter plane to RAF Northolt in north-west London, which he reached within half an hour, to be given a second plane to fly on to RAF Kidlington near Oxford. A car was waiting to take him to Ditchley Park, where he arrived, tired, hungry and in need of a wash, just in time to join the house party for dinner. After the meal, having briefed the astonished prime minister on Hess's odyssey, the exhausted Hamilton fell asleep while the rest of the guests settled down to watch *Go West*, the Marx Brothers' latest film.

The next day, Churchill and Hamilton returned to Downing Street to brief the foreign secretary and Cadogan, after which the duke flew Ivone Kirkpatrick (who had known Hess when first secretary at the Berlin embassy) up to Scotland to confirm the prisoner's identity. More than forty-eight hours after his departure, German radio finally claimed that the mentally ill deputy führer, ignoring a flying ban from Hitler, had left Germany by plane, had failed to return, and so was assumed to have crashed. A furious Hitler ordered the arrest of Hess's staff and the abolition of the post of deputy führer. Later that evening, Downing Street issued a press release, drafted by Churchill and Eden, allowing the BBC and British newspapers to report the basic facts of this scarcely believable story to an astonished public. Reading the news, Ernest Tennant, who had befriended Hess back in 1933, contacted a friend in Downing Street and volunteered to be imprisoned (on what charge is not recorded) alongside his old friend on the basis he might glean more than the official interrogators. He noted drily in his memoir that the authorities ignored his offer.

With neither the German nor British authorities willing or indeed able to explain Hess's eccentric pilgrimage, international press interest mushroomed into full-blown conspiracy theorising, which over eight decades later still rumbles on. Thousands of newspaper articles and hundreds of books have proposed dozens of theories: Hitler secretly sent Hess to negotiate a peace; a covert British peace party had invited him; the British security services had fabricated a fake peace party to lure him over; he was a doppelgänger; the RAF deliberately let his plane enter Scottish airspace; the Luftwaffe intentionally let him leave German airspace; the bombing of London that night had been a planned diversion; he refuelled in France or Belgium; he was accompanied by Reinhard Heydrich in another plane; and that many years later, desperate to cover up one or more of these conspiracies, British security agents had murdered Hess. Richard Evans, the former Cambridge Regius professor of history, has convincingly argued in a very recent study that there is no reliable evidence to support any of these fantasies.[3]

Rudolf Hess's motives in coming to Scotland were personal and peculiar – needing no connivance from either the German or British governments.

Marginalised within the Nazi hierarchy during the war and isolated from his beloved Führer, his mental health would remain fragile for the rest of his long but pathetic life. Scribe and proof-reader for *Mein Kampf* and Hitler's most constant companion, Hess was nominally third in the NSDAP hierarchy after Hitler and Göring. A loyal and enthusiastic friend to the Anglo-German Fellowship since its inception, he had led the party into dinner as guest of honour at the opening ceremony of the Deutsch-Englische Gesellschaft alongside the Duke of Coburg and the British ambassador. As Tennant recognised, unlike most of the senior Nazis, he was not so 'completely lacking in knowledge of conditions outside of Germany', having been born and raised in Egypt.[4] Many British visitors, amateur and professional, who had come to take coffee with Hitler, also went on for afternoon tea with the deputy leader, including Lloyd George, Londonderry, Lothian and the Duchess of Windsor. Now Hess hoped his past hospitality might be reciprocated.

A persistent question, distinct from the wilder conspiracy theories, is why, from all the impeccably connected Britons the Anglophile Hess had met, he chose to crash-land onto the estate of this particular duke, whom he had not met. If, as had been suggested at the time, he had wanted to meet those disgruntled British peers hostile to Churchill, he could have parachuted onto at least four other ducal estates, each closer to Augsburg than Dungavel – Stratfield Saye in Hampshire (Wellington), Eaton Hall in Cheshire (Westminster), Drumlanrig Castle in Dumfriesshire (Buccleuch) or Alnwick Castle in Northumberland (Northumberland). If he had wanted to parley with Lady Astor's Cliveden Set, he could have targeted her Thameside mansion near Windsor. If he had wanted to negotiate with the Nazi apologists, he could have aimed at Brocket Hall in Hertfordshire for Lord Brocket, at Hinton St Mary in Dorset for George Pitt-Rivers, or at Swinbrook in Oxfordshire for the Mitfords.

The answers lie in the elite social networks the Anglo-German Fellowship had cultivated during its glory years in the mid-thirties. The King had recently appointed Hamilton to replace the disgraced eighth Duke of Buccleuch as lord steward of the royal household and hereditary keeper of Holyroodhouse, the monarch's official residence in Scotland. The Douglas-Hamilton family were enthusiastic Germanophiles, and while his father-in-law and sister-in-law had expressed admiration for National Socialism, there is no evidence of the duke sharing such enthusiasms. Nonetheless, on hearing of Hess's arrival, George VI had warily noted the irony in his diary: 'Perhaps the post of Lord Steward is bewitched or is it Germanised? ... Hess might have landed two miles from Drumlanrig [Buccleuch's castle] instead.'[5]

Fevered rumours surfaced in the newspapers about what linked the duke to Hess. MPs asked questions in the House of Commons. Forced to defend his reputation, Hamilton clarified that, while their paths had crossed at the Olympics, they had never formally met. Indeed, Hess carried with him visiting cards of their mutual friends, Karl and Albrecht Haushofer, to prove his bona fides with the duke. But, far from quelling speculation, Hamilton's clarification only further fuelled the mystery, with insinuations about his Nazi sympathies rumbling on for years.

Within days, the dots between Hess, the duke and the now defunct Anglo-German Fellowship were being better joined in both the US and Soviet Russia. Under the delighted headline, 'Hess Taken by Scottish Farmer with Pitchfork', the *New York Times* explained that the 'young Duke of Hamilton, on whose Scottish estate Herr Hess landed, had belonged to the now condemned Anglo-German Fellowship Association [*sic*]', before caveating that, while the two men were 'understood to have been acquainted', there was no indication the duke was 'connected in any way with a peace movement'.[6] That same day, Kim Philby (by now working for both MI6 and Soviet intelligence) had been the first to brief the Russian authorities with the exactly opposite interpretation. Linking the two men with a supposed peace party, he reported that Hess had written to the duke only weeks before. His source, Tom Dupree, a friend who served as deputy head of the Foreign Office press department, had confirmed that the German deputy leader proposed a compromise peace and believed there remained a 'powerful anti-Churchill party'. Philby prodded his Soviet masters that Dupree had suggested Hess might become the 'centre of an intrigue' to negotiate a peace that might morph into an Anglo-German alliance against the USSR.[7] Back during his days working in the Fellowship's publicity department, Philby's reportage about the organisation had stoked similar fears with his Soviet handlers. None of which speculation helped Anglo-Soviet relations at this pivotal phase in the war.

Hess believed that by navigating towards the Duke of Hamilton he would find the Anglo-German Fellowship and that it could serve as a forum for peace settlement between the two countries. Though defunct for nearly two years, its legacy still resonated in Hitler's Germany, Stalin's Russia and Roosevelt's United States. But in Great Britain any past association with Anglo-German friendship initiatives was deeply embarrassing, so while Hess had been suitably sure of the duke's involvement with the organisation, Hamilton doggedly played it down. A year after the crash landing, he successfully sued for libel several British communists who had published a pamphlet alleging he was both a 'Quisling' and a friend of Hess, and that their connection was the Fellowship. By insisting in his lawsuit – probably truthfully, but certainly disingenuously – that he had never been a signed-up member, the duke has misdirected historians looking to cut through the conspiracy theories ever since.[8] While on none of the lists of members, an application form survives in his archive alongside a receipt from the Fellowship for a guinea, which may have been payment either for membership or a dinner ticket. Actively involved with Nazi Germany and the Fellowship for at least five years, Lord Londonderry had introduced him to the Ribbentrops and Hamilton had invited the couple to his own wedding. He and his family attended Anglo-German events in London, including the von Blomberg reception at the coronation and the infamous dinner for Gertrud Scholtz-Klink hosted by his sister-in-law. In early 1939, the Fellowship, with support from the British Council, had asked Hamilton to give a series of lectures in Germany on aviation and his flight over Everest, for which he had received enthusiastic approval from the chief of the Air Staff. Though cancelled due to diplomatic tensions, it is intriguing how the RAF and the British Council still rated the Fellowship as a conduit for such a propaganda play and Hamilton as the person to deliver it.

Five years previously, while at the Olympics in Berlin, Hamilton had befriended Albrecht Haushofer, one of Hess's most trusted advisers and a family friend, who had then introduced him to Hermann Göring. An ardent Anglophile, whom MI5 assessed as the 'greatest authority in Germany on the British Empire', Haushofer had been wary of Hitler from the outset and had used the Olympics to recruit sympathetic British friends. When he visited England, he stayed chez Hamilton and the suspicious British intelligence services monitored their friendship over several years, during which Hamilton introduced his friend to the foreign secretary, who enlisted him as a Foreign Office intelligence asset. Hoping to avert hostilities, in July

1939, Haushofer had sent Hamilton a letter warning war could break out at any date after the middle of August. He was convinced Germany 'cannot win a short war and… cannot stand a long one'. Bravely, over a year before he had told Ribbentrop and Hitler that the British government suspected a 'new imperialism' in Germany and would get public support for a 'crusade' to liberate Europe from 'German militarism'.[9] Hamilton had shown the letter first to Winston Churchill before passing it to the foreign secretary and the prime minister.

A month after the outbreak of war, Hamilton published his own analysis of the situation in a letter to *The Times*, broadcast on German radio that same night. Speaking on behalf of his generation (he was only thirty-six), he opened firmly, 'If Hitler is right when he claims that the whole of the German nation is with him in his cruelties and treacheries… then this war must be fought to the bitter end.' But echoing Chamberlain's speeches, he acknowledged the injustices of the Treaty of Versailles and proposed a 'just and comprehensive' peace. This could include territorial concessions so long as '*Lebensraum* is not made the grave of other nations' and 'no race will be exposed to being treated as Hitler treated the Jews on November 9 of last year'.[10] It has been suggested that Halifax advised on its drafting but, either way, even the duke's sympathetic biographer concluded, for all its good intentions, it betrays a 'certain naivety' which led to him being associated with the supposed peace party.[11]

So, while Rudolf Hess's quixotic peace mission had been doomed to fail, his choice of landing site was far from foolish. The Duke of Hamilton had been committed to Anglo-German amity, his social and political ties were impeccable, and they shared a friend in Albrecht Haushofer, who had first suggested Hess approach him with peace feelers before the war. Although historians rightly consider the duke a marginal figure politically and Haushofer had underestimated (as did Hitler and Ribbentrop) the limitations of the British constitutional monarchy, the events of that week prove Hamilton had exactly the level of access the two Germans wanted. Within twenty-four hours of Hess pulling the ripcord, Hamilton was seated at dinner with the prime minister at his weekend hideaway. Just five days later, he briefed the King at a private lunch. That neither prime minister nor king took the peace offer seriously was the fault of the message, not the messenger.

Joseph Stalin's reaction to the whole sorry affair further draws together these loose threads. As one historian has summarised, the 'outstanding and lasting feature of Soviet foreign policy' had been a 'pathological suspicion that Germany and Britain might close ranks and mount a crusade against Russia'.[12] The *New York Times* stoked these suspicions when it reported that British sources had 'intimated that Herr Hess, in deciding to fly to the enemy, felt that Germany should make peace with Britain rather than cooperate with the Bolsheviks'.[13] Another historian concluded that, 'all too conscious that perfidious Albion was perpetually up to no good, Stalin became obsessed with uncovering the truth behind the Hess affair', while a third has argued that the Russian leader 'could not quite persuade himself that Hitler should have been so stupid as to attack the Soviet Union without a prior agreement with Britain.'[14] Intentionally or not, the Germans also helped to promote this bogey of an Anglo-German alliance even after war had been declared. Valentin Berezhkov, the Soviet first secretary in Berlin, had been astonished to see pre-war pamphlets promoting 'German-British Friendship' in the waiting room at the German foreign ministry.[15]

From such mischief-making are myths built. Winston Churchill, during his visit to Russia in 1944, confessed his astonishment at finding Stalin still 'convinced that Hess had been involved in organising a joint British-German crusade against Russia which had "miscarried"'.[16] Back in Britain, as the historian Jo Fox has revealed, the Communist Party used these Soviet-inspired conspiracy theories to accuse the British aristocracy of 'close association with the Nazis, contending that they were united by the forces of imperialism, plutocratic governments, and capitalism'.[17] Taken in tandem with the Churchillian and Gollancz interpretations, these at best partial truths underline how a substantially left-wing interpretation of the Fellowship took hold. When stirred into the orthodoxies and conspiracy theories surrounding appeasement, the Guilty Men, the Cliveden Set, Rudolf Hess and the Trinity Spies, such biases and distortions have dominated its ongoing historical interpretation. Just as damagingly, this cloud of suspicion has overhung the personal reputations of all those individuals associated with the Fellowship ever since.

Rudolf Hess would be sentenced to life imprisonment at the Nuremberg trials after the war and incarcerated at Spandau Prison in West Berlin under the joint control of the UK, France, the US and the Soviet Union. By 1966, all the other prisoners had left Spandau, but the Soviet Russians refused to release Hess, still convinced of German and British collusion. Prisoner number seven was detained for a further twenty-one years until, aged ninety-three, he ended his life by hanging himself in the summer house in the prison garden he had used for many years as a reading room.

Hermann Göring, Rudolf Hess and Joachim Ribbentrop in the dock at the Nuremberg Trial, waiting for the morning session to start, 1946.

EPILOGUE

NONE SO BLIND AS
THOSE WHO WILL NOT SEE

THE DEPUTY FÜHRER HAD SEALED HIS FATE WHEN HE LANDED in Scotland. A triumphant return with a peace treaty to Berlin had never been a realistic concept. Six weeks later, Adolf Hitler decided to abandon Operation Sea Lion, his long-planned invasion of Britain, and shift his attentions eastwards to Russia – Operation Barbarossa. This pivot sealed the fate of the thousand-year Third Reich as it fought a global conflict on multiple fronts. Following the Japanese attack on Pearl Harbor and Germany's declaration of war on the US in December 1941, the Americans joined the war as a full belligerent, but, as Conwell-Evans summed up, 'not before three further years of all-out effort had been undertaken could the German armies be driven back into their own territory and forced into final surrender.'[1]

The Soviet army, having swept across Poland into Germany, then reached Berlin; Russian troops were only yards away when, on the afternoon of 30 April 1945, Hitler took his own life. Closeted for over three months in the Führerbunker and riven by paranoid megalomania, he had convinced himself Heinrich Himmler and Hermann Göring had betrayed him, so ordered their arrests. Ten days earlier, on his fifty-sixth birthday, he had grudgingly granted his devoted acolyte, Joachim Ribbentrop, a ten-minute audience for what would be their last encounter. The Führer's confidence in his foreign minister had waned during the war, much to the relief of his rivals. When asked why he had never replaced him, he countered that he was 'just a stubborn man I set against the stubborn English'.[2] The failed 'Bomb Plot' of July 1944 (Operation Valkyrie) led by Lieutenant Colonel Claus von Stauffenberg, having come tantalisingly close to ending the Führer's life, further weakened Ribbentrop's standing. More than seven thousand Germans implicated in the plot, however tenuously, were arrested, and nearly five thousand executed, including senior military figures led by Admiral Wilhelm Canaris, the head of the Abwehr, and Field Marshal Erwin von Witzleben. Damagingly for Ribbentrop, several of his senior diplomats, along with more junior officials from his foreign ministry, were arrested, including the former ambassadors to Moscow and Rome.

Göring also saw the German leader for the last time on his birthday, before escaping Berlin to a castle near Salzburg, where he surrendered to the US army. Himmler, travelling under a false identity, had been captured and interrogated by British military intelligence, before taking his own life with a cyanide pill hidden in his tooth. Meanwhile, Ribbentrop, also under an assumed name, had found his way to the bombed and chaotic Hamburg. Here, he lay low in the suburbs, until he was betrayed to the British authorities and arrested while sleeping. The doctor who examined him removed a small tin of poison taped to his nether regions under his pink and white pyjamas.

Ribbentrop was sent to the Grand Hotel at Mondorf-les-Bains in Luxembourg, a former spa hastily converted into a prison (codenamed ASHCAN) to accommodate the most senior captured Nazis. Foremost among these prisoners was Göring, who had arrived with a valet, sixteen monogrammed suitcases, a red hat box, and twenty thousand paracodeine tablets, which he consumed at the rate of forty a day. From there, the twenty major German war criminals were flown to the bomb-shattered ruins of Nuremberg for the first of the series of trials held before the International Military Tribunal, jointly convened by the British, French, Americans and Russians. Nuremberg had been chosen for its potent and poignant associations with the glory days of National Socialism. Rudolf Hess, who had been imprisoned in England for four years, joined them for the eleven-month trial. Each defendant had been charged under all four counts available to the prosecution: crimes against peace, war crimes, crimes against humanity, and conspiracy.

Locked up in his damp cell, Ribbentrop responded badly to captivity. Now 'bewildered and dejected', with uncombed hair, far from the castles, embassies and ministries that had been his milieu for a decade, he looked much older than his fifty-two years.[3] Previously immaculate in appearance if not behaviour, he neglected the hygiene of both his cell and his person and was deemed a high suicide risk. In the courtroom, the prosecution argued convincingly that Ribbentrop had, from the outset of the conflict, been complicit with any number of Nazi atrocities, far beyond the usual brutalities of war. He had embraced anti-Semitism with vigour and promoted anti-Jewish propaganda campaigns abroad, urging foreign politicians to exterminate their own Jews, whom he dismissed as 'pickpockets, murderers and thieves'.[4] Fully cognisant of the rounding-up, deportation to Auschwitz, and extermination of thousands of Hungarian Jews in the spring of 1944, he had also encouraged the lynching of captured Allied bomber crews and recommended the execution of partisans, including women and children.

Rather than evoking any sympathy, the wretched former foreign minister managed to alienate, irritate and infuriate his gaolers, prosecutors and co-defendants. The witnesses called by both prosecution and his defence offered no effective mitigation. His long-suffering secretary portrayed him as a friendless workaholic, even now still slavishly in thrall to Hitler, while his predecessor, Konstantin von Neurath, revealed how disliked he was in the foreign ministry and how hard he had tried to block his promotion. In a muddled and contradictory defence, the former ambassador to London highlighted his friendly pre-war diplomatic overtures to London and Moscow, asking permission to call defence witnesses including King George VI, Nancy Astor, Winston Churchill, the Dukes of Windsor and Buccleuch, and Lords Derby, Dawson, Vansittart, Londonderry, Beaverbrook and Kemsley. Lower on the list were his two former friends, Ernest Tennant and Philip Conwell-Evans, with whom he had launched the Anglo-German Fellowship a decade before. Asked to confirm he had indeed introduced Ribbentrop to Stanley Baldwin and Ramsay MacDonald in the search for an Anglo-German alliance, Tennant had been relieved when Sir David Maxwell Fyfe, the British chief prosecutor, disallowed him as a character witness as he was a 'gentleman of no official position', whose evidence would be the 'acme of irrelevance'.[5] With even greater disdain, the patrician Maxwell Fyfe (later to serve as Attorney General, Home Secretary and Lord Chancellor) dismissed Conwell-Evans's suitability as a witness on the grounds that he was 'not even in *Who's Who*'.[6]

Deprived of whatever support his pre-war British associates might have offered, Ribbentrop crumbled into hysterics under Maxwell Fyfe's cross-examination. The summary judgment by Lord Justice Lawrence, the British presiding judge, left no room to doubt he had indeed participated in 'all of the Nazis' aggressions' from the *Anschluss* to the invasion of Russia, had been involved in the extermination of Jews, and 'in complete sympathy' with National Socialism.[7]

In startling contrast, Hermann Göring thrived in captivity, cutting an altogether finer figure in the courtroom, having lost twenty-seven kilograms and weaned himself off the painkillers. Appalled by Ribbentrop's feeble performance on the witness stand, he insisted that, had he been foreign minister, he would have held the line that 'this was my foreign policy and I stick to it'. Eloquent, detailed and persuasive, his barnstorming performance, with no hint of mea culpa, demolished the arguments of the American prosecutor, Robert Jackson, so effectively that the poor man suffered a nervous collapse days later. Maxwell Fyfe's cross-examination saved the prosecution and, though impressed by his bravura, the judges remained unconvinced by Göring's arguments, concluding his guilt had been 'unique in its enormity' and the 'record discloses no excuses for the man.'[8]

Rudolf Hess failed to engage with the proceedings of the court. Having made two suicide attempts while captive in England, he claimed amnesia and appeared detached and distracted throughout the trial. Following his intrepid solo flight, British popular opinion had inclined to be forgiving and, like Göring, he earned some respect as an ex-officer and pilot – almost a gentleman. Insisting on wearing the flying boots in which he had landed in Scotland, he stood out from his fellow defendants, who shuffled into court in prison-issued carpet slippers. Having left Germany early in the war to fly to Scotland, the tribunal accepted that he had missed many of the worst war crimes, while his secretary confirmed his sincerity in seeking peace. But his record was far from clean; openly anti-Semitic, he had signed the Nuremberg Laws and had helped Göring arrange the murderous butchery during the Night of the Long Knives.

The tribunal found all three – the most senior defendants in the trial – guilty. Prominent sponsors of the Anglo-German Fellowship and its sister society, they had been at various times, and in diverse ways, the three most ardent seekers of peace with Great Britain: Ribbentrop, in the early days, before his failure as ambassador to London put his nose permanently out of joint with the English; the self-serving Göring, recognising the strategic advantage in avoiding a fight with the British and their Empire, who had schemed for peace right up to the last minute; and Hess, whose pilgrimage to Scotland never made sense but attracted some public admiration for its sheer absurdity. Each had served with distinction in the Great War and aspired to the military codes of honour so precious to the German Imperial army. Each saw themselves as 'gentlemen' with an understanding of European high culture. Admiring the Empire and appreciating the social and sporting pursuits enjoyed by the English elite, they had cultivated British friends in Londonderry, Lothian, Mount Temple, Conwell-Evans, Christie and Tennant, and warmly welcomed the wider stream of notables who had journeyed from London to Berlin, Nuremberg and Bavaria before the war.

But despite the efforts of the British amateurs and professionals who came over to Germany to drink coffee, tea, whisky, wine or champagne with them, they had in no way been civilised by their Anglophile encounters. None of this had lessened their wholehearted embrace of the unforgivable evil of National Socialism. Nothing in their admiration of the English nor their internationalism could overturn the Faustian pact each had made with Adolf Hitler. As the German peacetime state apparatus metamorphosed into the Nazi war machine, their pathway into hell would be irreversible.

There was no glimpse of redemption nor sliver of clemency for Göring and Ribbentrop. Found guilty on all four counts, they were sentenced to death by hanging. Hess was found guilty of crimes against peace and war crimes, but not guilty of crimes against humanity and conspiracy and so sentenced to life imprisonment. Denied his request to be shot by a military firing squad, Göring cheated the hangman by taking his own life the night before his scheduled execution. Quite how remains mysterious, but Jock Colville suspected an 'anally secreted cyanide pill'.[9] Having coped so badly during his incarceration and trial, Ribbentrop pulled himself together sufficiently to lead, with some dignity, the ten condemned prisoners into the gymnasium for their hanging on 16 October 1946. According to the author and journalist Rebecca West, who covered the trials for the *New Yorker*, his execution was bungled; his death took twenty minutes while he 'struggled for air'.[10]

Despite his battles with literacy, depression and poor health, Ribbentrop had been drafting what he called his 'beautiful memoirs', in which he insisted he had always been a man of peace. His widow, Annelies, completed these after his death and published them in 1953. But their shared social anxieties and absurdly skewed priorities had not died with him. In one footnote, she sought to clarify the pre-war furore surrounding her husband's infamous social gaffes – the Hitler salute to King George VI and a separate breach of etiquette when he had failed to remove his hat in the royal presence at a garden party. Notwithstanding six years of war; the devastation of Europe; maybe 75 million people dead; the total collapse of the Third Reich; and the execution of her husband as a war criminal, she still felt it a priority to counter the brickbats she and Joachim had suffered from London society a decade before.

Like his friend Ribbentrop, with whom he had championed the Deutsch-Englische Gesellschaft, the Duke of Saxe-Coburg and Gotha had never wavered in his devotion to the Führer, even when Hitler issued a 'Nero decree' ordering he should be executed rather than fall into enemy hands. When arrested by the Americans in April 1945, the former Eton schoolboy quickly remembered his kinship with the House of Windsor and switched back to being an Englishman, swapping his cherished SS uniform for old tweed hunting clothes. Stubbornly insisting that no German could be guilty of any war crimes, he avoided detailed interrogation about the crimes against humanity perpetrated by the German Red Cross of which he was the president. Following lobbying from his English sister, Princess Alice, and her husband, the Earl of Athlone, he would be released early the next year. He survived a de-Nazification trial, having whitewashed the worst excesses of his Nazi past. But having paid substantial fines and lost his estates to the Russians, he spent his remaining life as a rural recluse in a gamekeeper's cottage outside Coburg. The year before his death, he visited the local cinema to watch the coronation of Queen Elizabeth II, his first cousin's granddaughter.

While the trial of the major German war criminals had offered no mitigation for their pre-war dealings with the British, a later and lesser trial, *The USA vs. Ernst von Weizsäcker, et al.* (also known as the 'Ministries' or 'Wilhelmstrasse' trial) raised more nuanced questions of guilt and innocence. Von Weizsäcker, who served as German ambassador to the Vatican for the last years of the war, had been arrested in July 1947. While historians of German diplomacy continue to debate the extent of any 'good' Germans actively opposing Hitler's policies within the foreign ministry (and Weizsäcker's role in particular), Patricia Meehan has catalogued how the civil servants in the British Foreign Office energetically downplayed their pre-war contacts with such Germans – good or bad – as they were anxious to avoid any suggestion the war might have been prevented, or at least shortened, had their engagement been less grudging.[11]

Robert – now Lord – Vansittart's behaviour in this regard does him no credit. Von Weizsäcker's supporters, led by Theo and Erich Kordt, had asked Van, as well as Lord Halifax and other prominent Englishmen, to confirm that their former chief had worked to restrain and even undermine Ribbentrop's disastrous foreign policies. The now retired chief diplomatic adviser refused, instead damning von Weizsäcker as the 'chief executant of Ribbentrop's policy'. While grudgingly recognising that the Kordts were 'anti-Nazi', he then wrote 'neither of them, so far as I know, ever did anything to demonstrate the fact'. Theo, he even suggested, would have shown true bravery by staying in London at the outbreak of war, despite he himself having encouraged the move to Switzerland and devised and sponsored the Horace-quoting postcard routine that dispatched Conwell-Evans to Bern. Given the mortal risks the brothers had taken to supply him intelligence, their secret meetings at his Mayfair home, in Downing Street and Cornwall Gardens, and their wartime assignations with his agents in Switzerland, this was shockingly disingenuous, even an outright lie.

Lord Halifax's response to the same request puts him in a far better light. Now retired to his estates in Yorkshire, the former viceroy of India, foreign secretary and ambassador to Washington supplied an affidavit explicitly contradicting Vansittart's testimony. He confirmed that von Weizsäcker had been a 'convinced opponent of Nazi ideals and policies', using his position to obstruct Ribbentrop by supplying relevant intelligence to Britain through intermediaries such as the Kordts and Conwell-Evans.[12] Despite Halifax's support, von Weizsäcker was nonetheless found guilty in July 1949 and sentenced to seven years' imprisonment, albeit released after three years following a legal review.

Grahame Christie had no doubts about the integrity and conviction of his German friends who had worked with the resistance, writing of how, 'at great risk, throughout the years, they gathered very valuable information revealing Hitler's preparations and intentions' in order to 'liberate their own country from the blight of Nazi rule and to help to save Europe from the devastation of another war'.[13]

Many of his contacts and most of those involved with the 1938 Oster conspiracy had been caught up in the later Bomb Plot. At the heart of both had been General Ludwig Beck, whom Conwell-Evans so admired and who had sent a stream of clandestine emissaries to lobby the British government. He had been chosen to lead the interim government should Operation Valkyrie have succeeded. Arrested immediately, he had been allowed to shoot himself with his own pistol. His ever-loyal co-conspirator, Hans Oster, was afforded no such dignity. Having been imprisoned at Flossenbürg, he was found guilty of treason, forced to strip naked and hanged just two weeks before the US army would liberate the concentration camp. Albrecht Haushofer, the Duke of Hamilton's friend, who had advised both Hess and Ribbentrop, was shot by a firing squad in a Gestapo prison just two weeks before Germany surrendered. His parents, also arrested in July 1944, took their own lives when they heard of their son's murder.

The Kordt brothers survived the war. Having been posted to Japan and Shanghai, Erich avoided implication in the Bomb Plot and would be appointed professor of international law at the University of Cologne after the war. Theo had survived by remaining in Switzerland and later served the new Federal Republic of Germany as ambassador to Greece. Neither was prosecuted for war crimes but, infuriated by the attitudes of Vansittart and others, in 1950 Erich published their version of events as *Nicht aus den Akten* ('Not from the files').

Few of the senior German businessmen who had sponsored the Deutsch-Englische Gesellschaft at the outset and seen Anglo-German trade as a worthy alternative to hostilities survived the war. Robert Bosch, Christie's trusted friend and valued intelligence source for over thirty years, died in 1942, aged eighty. The Third Reich, which he so despised, insisted on honouring this national hero with a state funeral. His nephew Carl had never given up his criticism of the regime, openly challenging Nazi economic policy and questioning the Führer's infallibility. His failure to sway the regime led to his withdrawal from public life, alcoholism and death in 1940 aged sixty-five. Carl Friedrich von Siemens died in September 1941. Hermann Bücher had been implicated in the 1944 plot and only saved from execution by the intervention of his friend Albert Speer, Hitler's architect.

Edward Halifax was exceptional, as his former subordinates ignored or denigrated the pre-war efforts of their German counterparts to mitigate Hitler and Ribbentrop's foreign policy. There remains a wealth of documentation in the Foreign Office files to testify to the efforts of the resisters, but Alec Cadogan and Ivone Kirkpatrick refused to share them with the courts, to a degree one later commentator claimed would have qualified them as 'competent prefects of Judea in the reign of Tiberius'.[14] Leading historians of the day shared this selective memory, quick to rubbish any suggestion that the opposition to Hitler (and by implication their British friends) might have deserved better support. Seemingly inspired by Vansittart, they argued that the German resistance was a chimera devised by the post-war survivors to obfuscate their own war crimes. Hugh Trevor-Roper dismissed it as a 'creature as fabulous as the Centaur and the hippogriff', while Lewis Namier damned the Kordts as 'resisters after the event'.[15] The diplomat and historian John Wheeler-Bennett, then working in the Foreign Office's Political Intelligence Department, cruelly articulated the Office's dismissive assessment of the resistance after the Valkyrie executions when he wrote that 'the Gestapo and the SS have done us an appreciable service in removing a selection of those who would undoubtedly have posed as "good Germans" after the defeat of a Nazi Germany.'[16]

Such mean-spirited orthodoxy prevailed until the groundbreaking work of Peter Hoffmann, Klemens von Klemperer and others from the 1970s. In *The Unnecessary War*, Patricia Meehan goes as far as to argue that this vilification by retired diplomats and historians implies a guilty conscience; had the resisters been 'responded to with goodwill, and their warnings acted upon then the consequences for the benefit of all might have been immeasurable'.[17]

Vansittart hammered the last nails into the legacy of the Anglo-German Fellowship in a House of Lords debate in February 1945, when, to Ernest Tennant's fury, he disparaged it as a 'dangerous organisation', all of whose

membership 'should come under suspicion', despite his own eager attendance at its receptions.[18] Stung by this assertion, Tennant wrote to *The
Times* insisting that the continued existence of the Fellowship had been
discussed with the British government after Munich, but claimed wrongly
that Vansittart had advised against closure when in fact it had been Halifax,
as foreign secretary, who had given the stay of execution. While factually
correct, Van's tone and posturing seems pusillanimous given how closely
he had worked with the Fellowship's leaders, particularly between Munich
and the invasion of Poland, to leverage its networks to gather intelligence
on the German regime.

Tennant felt the need to put his side of the story in print following the end of the war. His first marriage to the challenging and capri-
cious Eleonora, whom he had wed when she was just seventeen, had
collapsed and they separated in 1945. She had embraced far-right and
anti-Semitic causes, leading two extreme nationalist groups, the Never
Again Association and the Face the Facts Association, the second gaining
notoriety for campaigning against post-war bread rationing. Ernest having
sued for divorce on the grounds of her desertion, she had vindictively
counterclaimed her issues with him centred on his 'Nazi sympathies'.
Having avoided the awkwardness of appearing as Ribbentrop's character
witness and now remarried, he used his comfortable retirement in his
Essex country house to write *True Account* (1957). These firmly titled
memoirs detail his dealings with Germany and chart the rise and fade
of the Anglo-German Fellowship. According to his grandson, Tennant
had been prompted to publish this mea culpa clarifying his engagement
with the Third Reich because of Eleonora's threats of embarrassment and
ever more extreme politics.[19]

Rightly treated warily as a revisionist apologia by an old man embarrassed by his past enthusiasm for Hitler, *True Account* is nonetheless an
important published primary source and ruefully honest.[20] Tennant based it
on his contemporary notes, especially his July 1939 briefing memorandum
to Neville Chamberlain, which are available for cross-referencing. It was
well reviewed on publication, with Muriel Spark, the novelist and wartime
intelligence officer (whose best-known novel, *The Prime of Miss Jean Brodie*,
explored British fascination with fascism), praising it as 'delightfully rich,
recounted with humorous and modest charm'.[21]

Soon after the outbreak of war, demoralised by the state of Europe, Grahame Christie began to destroy his extensive papers, convinced all his work had been 'in vain'.[22] Thankfully for historians, Conwell-Evans interceded and persuaded his friend to let him, a published author, collate his archives and their joint recollections into what would be his last book, a memoir, *None So Blind: A study of the crisis years, 1930–1939, based on the private papers of Group-Captain M. G. Christie*. Harshly critical of the British government's failure to act on their intelligence, it had been written in 1941, a year after *Guilty Men*. Agreeing it would have been unhelpful to raise such 'contentious' issues during the war, the two friends waited six years to have the book privately printed by Harrison & Sons, printers to His Majesty the King, better known for producing banknotes, passports and postage stamps, and for publishing *The London Gazette* and *Burke's Peerage*. Despite post-war shortages, the book is elegantly typeset, nicely printed on watermarked laid paper, and case-bound in blue cloth with gilt lettering to the spine. Most unusually, and for reasons unclear, the print run was limited to only one hundred numbered and signed copies, following which the type was distributed (or 'dissed' in printer's jargon) so no reprint would ever be possible. Again mysteriously, Conwell-Evans and Christie agreed that these few copies should be distributed only when both men were dead, and then only to carefully selected libraries and individuals on both sides of the Atlantic.

None So Blind is now, despite its rarity, well regarded and well referenced by most historians publishing on the subject. To date, twenty-six surviving copies have been identified. In Britain, they were sent to the British Library, the Imperial War Museum and the university libraries at Brunel, Cardiff, Cambridge, Edinburgh, Glasgow, Leeds and Oxford. There is a copy at Trinity College Dublin and another at McGill University in Canada. In the US, the Library of Congress, Columbia University, Harvard College Library, Princeton University and Yale University each have copies.

Why the two friends, having gone to the significant expense of having their book printed by the King's printer, should have kept the copies languishing in the vaults of the Midland Bank for a quarter of a century, we can only speculate. Shortly before he died, Christie told his great-nephew, Nicholas Blain, he was still worried there could be adverse consequences for any of his surviving German informants. This may partially explain the delay in release but not the limited distribution. Writing thirty years ago, Patricia Meehan recognised that its publication must have 'filled the Foreign Office with horror'. Pointing a finger firmly at the Office, she insisted, 'somebody, somewhere, must have embargoed the book.'[23] But on what legal basis is unclear. The material belonged to them; neither had been paid to gather it; they had done so patriotically; they had quoted no official documents; and, as a former attaché, Christie had been scrupulous to avoid breaking the Official Secrets Act.

Although none of their intelligence missions in the first year of war had borne fruit, Conwell-Evans and Christie remained in close touch with their sometime spymaster, Vansittart. Following the very public controversy surrounding the publication of *Black Record*, he suffered emotional strain, depression and felt isolated and ignored. Having agreed to retire fully from government service after nearly forty years of public service in the spring of 1941, he was elevated to the House of Lords and appointed a Privy Councillor. Reflective ahead of his retirement, he wrote to Conwell-Evans to celebrate his becoming a 'free man, able to speak and to write… without the handicap which officialdom necessarily imposes'. Admitting that having his 'advice rejected for eight years and neglected for three' had been 'hard to bear', he insisted he would continue 'more than ever' to need Conwell-Evans and Christie's collaboration, before signing off tenderly, 'with my love to you both'.[24]

The German Advisory Committee having failed to take off, Grahame Christie did some wartime radio broadcasts on military aviation for the BBC. After the war, he rejoined the Otto Group, with responsibility for its overseas companies, and lectured on engineering at Leeds University. Having helped his German godmother recover her estate from the Canadian troops who had commandeered it, he continued to visit Wylerberg, now in Holland, well into the 1960s. In London, he lived comfortably in a flat in the fashionable Cranmer Court in Chelsea, the building that had housed the offices of the Anglo-German Fellowship on the ground floor. Enjoying the arts, he sponsored and encouraged promising young musicians and artists, including a young Nigerian sculptor. He became a friend and patron to the painter, L. S. Lowry, providing him with a regular stipend and buying several of his pictures. His great-nephew remembers an iconic large industrial scene hung in the flat, where he had been looked after by his devoted housekeeper, Mrs Enid Scott, known to all as 'Scottie', who always referred to her employer as 'the Colonel'.

Vansittart had recommended Conwell-Evans to his friend Hugh Dalton, the Labour minister of economic warfare, for a job in propaganda, but had been rebuffed, which Conwell-Evans ascribed to bad blood dating back to his friendship with Ramsay MacDonald. Having drafted *None So Blind* but failed to find war work, Conwell-Evans appears to have eked a living by authoring articles, reviewing books, giving occasional lectures, proof reading and translating from French and German. At the end of the war, he left Cornwall Gardens, the scene of his meetings between the British government and the German resistance, to move a mile and a half north to a flat in 26 Pembridge Crescent in the then run-down Notting Hill. There, he established himself in a large, high-ceilinged bedsit and took in lodgers at four pounds per week to supplement his limited income. Increasingly reclusive, he resigned his cherished membership of the Travellers Club, perhaps through shame or as an economy, or both, leaving no forwarding address. The Kordts tried and failed to track him down in the late forties to give evidence supporting von Weizsäcker in the Wilhelmstrasse Trial. Apart from giving a lecture series on International Relations at the Hampstead Centre in the early fifties, he then disappears for the rest of that decade. Like his friend, he found comfort in music and art, playing the piano, especially Bach and Beethoven, having been taught by the village schoolmistress at the age of nine. He developed a talent for drawing in pastels, including portraits of Lloyd George and Christie, which he hung on the walls of his bedsit.

In the early sixties, two young Oxford historians, Martin Gilbert and Richard Gott, became intrigued by appeasement and the activities of the Anglo-German Fellowship and its supporters. During their research they stumbled on the name T. P. Conwell-Evans and featured him in their ground-breaking book, *The Appeasers*, written in just six months and published in 1963. Taking a forensic approach to investigating those now vilified politicians who had supported Munich, they persuaded Sir Horace Wilson to be interviewed for the first time and met others including R. A. Butler and Sir Alec Cadogan. Broadly taking a traditional 'Guilty Men' line, they were brutal in their condemnation of Neville Chamberlain and his supporters. The book re-energised historical debate about appeasement, not least because its authors, both born in the thirties, were the first generation of historians too young to have served in the war. Though commercially successful and translated into several languages, *The Appeasers* received some criticism for failing to appreciate the full context of appeasement, especially from Gilbert's former tutor, the celebrated historian, A. J. P. Taylor, and Lord Strang, the diplomat who had followed Vansittart and Cadogan as head of the Foreign Office.

Gilbert and Gott were the first historians to give Conwell-Evans more than a footnote in the story of appeasement. They included a short but accurate biographical sketch and highlighted his shepherding both Philip Lothian and David Lloyd George to take coffee with Hitler. Having failed to track him down in person, they conceded he remained an 'elusive figure'.[25] Recalling their search over half a century later, Richard Gott remembered how 'intrigued' they had been by his appearance in their story.[26] Just as *The Appeasers* came out, Lady Diana Cooper recommended Martin Gilbert to Randolph Churchill as his research assistant on the gargantuan official biography of his (then still alive) father, Winston. Gott having moved into journalism, Gilbert persisted in the quest for Conwell-Evans, convinced he would be a rich source of better understanding about appeasement. The helpful assistant secretary at the Travellers Club regretted he had no forwarding address but did, at least, confirm that the club's hall porter had been sure he was still alive. Finally, Gilbert managed to meet Grahame Christie, still a club member, who introduced him to his close friend, the elusive Conwell-Evans.

Taking the criticism of his first book to heart and, notwithstanding the challenges of the Churchill biography and the workload imposed by his son, Gilbert followed it only three years later with *The Roots of Appeasement* (1966). Dramatically different in tone, this acknowledged the honourable intentions behind appeasement, its long history at the heart of British foreign policy, and its having been the default position of most politicians, even Churchill and Eden, right up to 1938. Appeasement, Gilbert now argued, was 'not a silly or treacherous idea in the minds of stubborn, gullible men, but a noble idea, rooted in Christianity, courage and common sense'. Vehemently he asserted, 'the "Guilty Men" tradition in English historical writing has flourished for over a century, and ought now to fade away.'[27]

The rediscovery of Conwell-Evans's papers in the Gilbert archive and the two men's correspondence reveals how well they cooperated in the last six years of the older historian's life. Gilbert interviewed him for *The Roots of Appeasement* and included his verbatim account of Lloyd George's meeting with Hitler as an appendix. He was the only historian allowed to read *None So Blind* prior to the 1970s, and then only by signing a non-disclosure agreement. Conwell-Evans helped Gilbert with several books, reviewing drafts of *Germany Between the Wars*, his biography of Horace Rumbold, and *The Roots of Appeasement*, which he applauded as his best work to date. Critics agreed and the book stimulated the breadth and vigour of debate enduring to this day. The two of them also discussed a possible biography of Vansittart, with Conwell-Evans urging haste while Christie, by then in his eighties, and who had known Van so well, was still alive and alert.

Conwell-Evans's spirits were lifted by this kindly attention from a revisionist historian of the post-war generation looking at appeasement through a new lens, thanking him for his 'kind words of appreciation in regard to the difficult past'.[28] Admitting seeing his account of the famous alpine meeting in print had provoked 'nostalgia of what might have been, if Hitler had not gone berserk', he concluded that, if the German leader had listened to Lloyd George, he might 'not have met such a horrible end'.[29] Despite their forty-five-year age gap, the two men became friends. Supported by Helen Robinson, his girlfriend and later first wife, Martin gently coaxed Conwell-Evans out of seclusion, visiting him in London and hosting day trips to Oxford, their shared alma mater. Conwell-Evans took an avuncular interest in the Gilberts' baby daughter Natalie and Helen remembers him bringing her a doll clad in traditional Welsh costume complete with large black hat.

Philip Conwell-Evans died in his sleep in the early hours of Monday, 11 November 1968, a fortnight short of his seventy-seventh birthday. That day was the fiftieth anniversary of the signing of the Armistice, ending the Great War to which he had so conscientiously objected, and which had driven his obsession with Anglo-German amity as Europe careered towards its second great conflagration. He had been so anxious about a planned move downstairs within his building that the Gilberts offered to host him in Oxford while his cherished piano and books were moved, a worry it seems hastened his end. Writing, only days later, to Conwell-Evans's niece Pamela Turner, Gilbert remembered how her uncle had served as a mentor before volunteering his assessment as a historian:

TP played an important part in our history – and sooner or later it will be recognised. He suffered more than anyone I knew from the sneers and accusations of those who did not know his true achievements. When I first met him, I was one of those who believed that he had betrayed his country: over the years I have collected evidence absolutely refuting these charges. To the contrary, he did things for our country of which no man need be ashamed – and few could parallel.

Signing off with how he had been a 'wonderful man in my own life', he begged that his papers be saved, as they were 'part of our national story', explaining that her uncle knew he planned to write something about him.[30] The completion of *Churchill* and so many other books intervened so that the memoir never advanced. Now, over fifty years later, it has been possible to include this primary material in such a study for the first time. This is thanks to the kind initiative of Esther Goldberg, the Holocaust historian and Sir Martin's widow, who, having found the Conwell-Evans papers in her late husband's archive, remembered a two-year-old enquiry and tracked down the author.

Christie and Conwell-Evans had sustained their close friendship and shared their Christmases. Having decided (or perhaps been officially coerced) not to distribute *None So Blind* until after their deaths, Christie avoided discussion of his work in pre-war Germany. Although ill health dogged the last forty years of his life, family photographs show him in well-cut suits with immaculate bow ties, trim and alert, eyes still twinkling with kindly intelligence under a generous head of greying hair. The widow of one of his nephews, who knew him for his last twenty years, remembered an 'upright and handsome old man with beautiful manners and consideration for everyone, an interesting conversationalist with a wide knowledge of the arts and a devotion to opera and ballet'.[31] As he reached his ninety-first year, feeling he would be of 'little further use to mankind' and distressed by the indignities of old age and his illness, he took his life on the evening of 3 November 1971. Scottie, his housekeeper, came into his room to see his feet disappearing through the window of his sixth-floor flat. He was pronounced dead on arrival at St Stephen's Hospital.[32]

Characteristically keen to evade public recognition even in death, Christie had stipulated cremation in his will, with his ashes scattered, and had forbidden anyone from wearing any 'sign of mourning'. Typically unpompous, he asked for 'John Brown's Body' to be played at his funeral. Scottie deposited his surviving papers at Churchill College, Cambridge, where they have intrigued curious historians ever since, and donated his personal copy of *None So Blind* to the London Library in St James's Square in his memory. A small brass plaque commemorates his life in the Chapel of St Michael and St George at St Paul's Cathedral in London.

*Winston Churchill and Joseph Stalin at the Kremlin
in Moscow, 11 September 1942.*

CONCLUSION

WHEN HE DIED ON A CHELSEA PAVEMENT CONVINCED HE WAS A burden on others, Grahame Christie concluded a brave and extraordinary life. As the last of our three protagonists to die, he closed the final chapter of the untidy story of their ultimate failure to civilise the Nazis. Though cherished by family and a handful of friends, he, Ernest Tennant and Philip Conwell-Evans died largely forgotten, and still embarrassed by their pre-war engagement with Hitler's Germany as ambassadors of peace. The distribution of one hundred copies of *None So Blind* would only very slowly and partially start to restore their reputations. Having published and circulated his own mea culpa to a somewhat wider but still sceptical readership, Tennant had died nine years earlier, peacefully in his sleep.

Readers should – of course – come to their own conclusions as to whether history has treated these men unfairly. My own thesis is that they and the Anglo-German Fellowship have, in George W. Bush's unmatchable term, been *misunderestimated* by commentators over the last eighty years. However total the failure of their mission to prevent war, theirs had been a significant and wholehearted enterprise. Neither 'Fellow Travellers of the Right' nor 'Guilty Men', they were decent individuals caught up in the mercilessly cruel whirlwind of the rising Third Reich. Though guilty early on, to varying degrees, of naivety and gullibility about the National Socialist regime, they were better men doing better jobs for better reasons than has been assumed.

As agents of intelligence and persuasion they were much more successful. Realising both the evil intentions and alarming momentum of Adolf Hitler's regime well before the much-publicised horrors of Kristallnacht, they had striven to re-educate the main actors in the British government on the urgency of the global situation – first Edward Halifax and Alec Cadogan, followed, months later, by Neville Chamberlain, Horace Wilson and Nevile Henderson, who had each so gravely misread the Führer. The lynchpin of all this was Robert Vansittart. His influence over the government had recovered following Munich, to an extent overlooked by many commentators, including his own biographer. As the historian John Ferris has shown through careful analysis, Van had helped 'change minds' about Hitler and to do so had used the Fellowship's leadership, network and credibility.[1] All of this was backed by the intelligence so bravely and painstakingly gathered by Christie and Conwell-Evans. That Chamberlain's government was still so misguided on its strategy and so ill-prepared for war with Germany was not for their want of trying. And thanks to their efforts it was better prepared than it otherwise might have been. Most critically, Philip Lothian, the first prominent Englishman to take coffee with Hitler (whose very public Pauline conversion exposed him to derision that continues today), won the American president's trust and proved his authority on the German threat. This helped persuade the reluctant United States into the European conflict.

The coterie around the Fellowship played a bigger role in the diplomatic crises of the late 1930s than the British have tended to remember, and the organisation attracted a breadth of support from their Establishment elites which they then preferred to forget. Even Winston Churchill, traditionally the arch anti-appeaser, was exploring alternatives to war only days before it was declared. In Britain, the Fellowship was taken seriously by government, parliament, the intelligence services, the press, business and the military in its time. At home, it fell from both grace and relevance almost as soon as war was declared (even when a negotiated peace with either Hitler or a replacement seemed a real prospect). Surprisingly, the Fellowship's reputation overseas fared better: its legacy lingered longer among the Germans, the Russians and the Americans. Rudolf Hess hoped to find the Fellowship in Scotland. With the Machiavellian Philby and the *New York Times* stoking Soviet paranoia about an Anglo-German alliance, Joseph Stalin's worst fear was that Hitler's deputy would indeed find it there.

Though the Fellowship was a child of business and finance, where the profit motive was king, its supporters were capable of higher motives in arguing for peace. They secured wide engagement from both veterans and serving British military, who like their counterparts across the North Sea looked at the prospect of a second European war with dread. And contrary to its popular reputation, the Fellowship was a poor place for the promotion of those venomous ideologies around race and religion that defined the

Third Reich, and still rightly preoccupy commentators. Yes, the Fellowship promulgated Nazi propaganda in its publications, but its leadership was from the outset notably courageous in criticising National Socialist policy, including the abuse of German Jews. That such criticism riled the NSDAP leadership and its British champions, resulting in both losing faith in the organisation as a propaganda tool, proves it does not deserve its casual reputation as pro-Nazi and anti-Semitic. While around one in twenty of its members expressed views that chimed with the worst ideologies of National Socialism, we should not let that distract us from the other nineteen motivated by a desire for peace and a hope for a civilised Germany.

Understanding Anglo-German cooperation before 1939 matters, if only to put Anglo-German conflict in its proper context. Not least, given the cultural links between the British and Germans, a peaceful modus vivendi between Europe's two most powerful economies was a credible and moral diplomatic strategy in the first half of the twentieth century – despite nine years of war. Prestigious organisations such as the Fellowship had a role to play in promoting Anglo-German friendship before, between and after both wars. By targeting the socially anxious, gauche and instinctively Anglophile Nazis with their 'civilising missions' they really had picked an important and valid target for their amateur diplomacy.

Germanophile myopia should not be confused with bright-eyed Nazi fanaticism fuelled by rabid anti-Semitism. Despite progress in setting pro-German sentiment in the 1930s within a subtler context (in for example Ian Kershaw's masterly reappraisal of Londonderry), the popular association between the Fellowship and the far right has survived well into the twenty-first century. Richard Ingrams, the former editor of *Private Eye*, was forced to defend his late father against allegations of anti-Semitism, purely for being a member.[2] Similarly, the eighth Duke of Wellington (an MC-awarded veteran of El Alamein), when in his late eighties was ambushed by a journalist who questioned why his uncle, the fifth Duke, had joined the Fellowship.[3]

In the wider debate over appeasement, defenders of Neville Chamberlain's reputation have argued it is easy to criticise him from the sidelines, but far harder to suggest a 'constructive, coherent alternative that he could have pursued'.[4] But, as the record shows, the leadership of the Fellowship did propose alternatives to the British government throughout its short life – specifically, more energetic and professional diplomacy in the earlier years (1935–6), underpinned by economic appeasement that would weave together the two economies. In parallel, they encouraged rearmament at home and firmer responses to each of Hitler's expansionist military forays, especially through better alliances with France, Czechoslovakia, the US and Russia. Their contacts within the German opposition to Hitler had offered tantalising intelligence, showing that his regime was more fragile, chaotic and opportunistic than realised. While certainly still classifiable as appeasement, this was at odds with the strategies adopted by each of the three pre-war British prime ministers, and was widely divergent from Chamberlain's personal brand of appeasement culminating in Plan Z. This, they correctly advised, was a step too far, undermining British credibility within the German government. It was Plan Z that convinced Conwell-Evans and Christie that Chamberlain, Wilson and Henderson were together the 'guilty men'. While there is a respectable body of scholarship looking to defend them, I cannot help but agree with their guilty verdicts, given how dangerously late Chamberlain and company were in understanding Hitler's determined intentions and their stubborn resistance to any contradictory advice.

Wherever one sits on the appeasement debate there is little doubt those few turbulent years leading up to the Second World War offered a series of missed opportunities to derail the far from inevitable rise of the Nazis. What is extraordinary, significant and interesting is how this intrepid and diverse group of amateurs came together to take on the challenge the professionals had so vigorously ducked. The degree of access and influence they so quickly achieved with both German and British governments seems without parallel.

Hindsight has shown not only their intelligence, but also their guidance, to have been correct. British foreign policy should be strategically cogent, competently executed, backed by Cabinet, and supported by parliament and the electorate. A diplomatic strategy that requires charming people you may neither like nor trust may serve you better than staying isolated on the moral high ground. Trade, commerce and finance between countries should ease cooperation and discourage conflict. Communication with allies is essential. Dictators and other political scoundrels – like small children – respond better to firm boundaries and consistent discipline. Bad ambassadors are a needlessly high risk. Statesmen should listen to historians.

Dehumanising the enemy is rarely helpful. And despite his reputation as a warmonger, Winston Churchill agreed, recognising that 'meeting jaw to jaw is better than war', echoing his distant cousin John Adams, second president of the United States, who reminded us that 'great is the guilt of an unnecessary war'.[5]

In the end, they were shouting into winds even stronger than they realised, as great swirling historical forces overwhelmed their personal beliefs around pacifism and Anglo-German amity. Sometimes the narrative of history becomes merciless: a torrent of events that overwhelms everything in its path, and in which the individual vessel becomes helpless flotsam, despite every good intention, or noble instinct.

ACKNOWLEDGEMENTS

THE TEAM AT ONEWORLD IN LONDON, LED BY THE INESTIMABLE Sam Carter, deserves boundless credit for taking on a neophyte author and guiding him through the complex process of making a book. Sam took the risk and directed the orchestra; Rida Vaquas hunted down the best illustrations; Holly Knox untangled my grammar; Tom Feltham calmly copyedited the manuscript; while Paul Nash, Laura McFarlane and Hannah Haseloff expertly guided it through production.

None of which would have started without my agent, Katie Fulford of Bell Lomax Moreton, championing the book when it was just a thought. Parallel transatlantic thanks to Helen Edwards, who introduced me to Claiborne Hancock and Jessica Case at Pegasus Books in New York, who have brought *Coffee with Hitler* to a North American audience.

Most of these pages are inspired by overlooked primary sources unearthed over the last ten years. As much a test of sleuthing as historical research, this has required tracking down evidence, informants and witnesses. Sifting through archives is a pleasure made possible by the patient and learned archivists at the key collections. The Churchill College Archives in Cambridge contribute to the world's better understanding of the 1930s. The cloistered calm is a delight, and the college kitchens supply excellent fish and chips to the hungry researcher. Helpful welcomes were also extended by the custodians of the Mount Temple papers in the Hartley Library at the University of Southampton; the Lothian and Duke of Hamilton papers at the National Records of Scotland in Edinburgh; the Lloyd George and Davidson papers at the UK Parliamentary Archives in the House of Lords; the Halifax papers at the Borthwick Institute at the University of York; the Hamilton papers at the Liddell Hart Military Archives at King's College London and the Wiener Holocaust Library. Many happy days were passed sifting through the National Archives in Kew, which hold the crucial Foreign Office, prime ministerial and security services files.

Serendipity played its part with each discovery. Many people helped to unearth vital clues and deserve my fullest thanks. Early in the investigation, Caterina Anrecht, of the Herzogin Anna Amalia Bibliothek in Weimar, found the previously lost 1937 annual report and membership list for the Anglo-German Fellowship, which unlocked a fuller understanding of its place in British society. Meanwhile, the enigmatic Conwell-Evans had eluded historians for decades, so pursuing him became a preoccupation. Given he was a bachelor with no descendants, the search seemed almost fruitless until the late Christopher Jeens, archivist at Jesus College, Oxford, found the undergraduate file of a Thomas Pugh Evans who later rebadged himself as Philip Conwell-Evans. This sent me to the London School of Economics, where Sue Donnelly dug out his thick graduate file stuffed with gems including letters from progressive liberals such as Lord Beveridge.

From there a long-shot enquiry led me to a terraced house in north London, home of the late Sir Martin Gilbert, the renowned Holocaust historian and Churchill biographer. His widow and fellow historian Esther (née Goldberg) had discovered Conwell-Evans's personal papers. As these included his notes of Lloyd George's infamous meeting with Hitler and unseen correspondence with prime ministers and foreign secretaries, this was my Sutton Hoo. My debt to Esther for her kindness in encouraging me to pick up this loose strand of her husband's research is hard to exaggerate. She also introduced me to Helen Gilbert and Richard Gott, who had supported Martin in his quest for Conwell-Evans in the early 1960s. Helen remembered meeting this diffident Welshman and empathising with his social awkwardness as a working-class student at Edwardian Oxford and their shared admiration for Lloyd George. Richard Gott offered kindly encouragement and reminisced about co-authoring *The Appeasers* over an engaging lunch.

Grahame Christie, another publicity-shy bachelor, had left historians few clues as to his personal life and character. Here a lucky connection led me to David Denton and Sarah Evans, who introduced me to the extended Christie family around the world. Nicholas Blain was generous in sharing his recollections of his great-uncle, whom he had got to know as a young student in 1960s London. Margaret Christie took me to tea with her wonderful mother, the late Enid Christie, whose fond reminiscences of her husband's uncle were enlightening. Suni Christie shared happy childhood memories of her great-uncle, guided me on his artistic pursuits and dug out a trove of photographs. Tim Christie added colour and encouragement. Heartfelt thanks to them all and I hope these pages have done justice to their fascinating relation.

Ernest Tennant's story was less opaque, as he published his memoir, but it was fascinating to meet his grandson Mungo Tennant for coffee and background on the family. My close friend Hamish McLean introduced me to Sarah Barclay, who has written about Nancy Tennant, Ernest's sister, and who generously shared her insights and introduced me to her uncle, John Tennant, whose recollections of working for Cousin Ernest in the 1950s helped round out his character. Other descendants of Fellowship alumni have been generous with time and sources, especially Julie Wheelwright about her grandfather Major Charles Ball, Victoria and Henry Maxton-Livesey on her father and his grandfather Gerald le Blount Kidd, and Nick Stamp on his great-grandfather Lord Stamp of Shortlands. Sophie Mallinckrodt helped me better understand the Schroder family and their bank, introducing me to the ever-helpful Caroline Shaw at the fascinating Schroder Archive. Other custodians of corporate archives were similarly responsive, especially Josette Reeves at the Unilever Archives.

After the people came the places. Our dear friend Alan Higgs gave me an expert architectural tour of the Travellers Club, Charles Barry's exquisite early masterpiece, and provided lunch in the very room where Lothian, Christie and Conwell-Evans had plotted their missions to Germany while Stanley Baldwin ate alone nearby. Alan introduced me to Sheila Markham, the archivist who outlined the club's unique history. Thanks are also due to the staff at Broadlands in Hampshire, Lord Mount Temple's elegant English estate, and Blickling Hall in Norfolk, Lothian's Jacobean mansion. Julia Record, Rosanna Fishbourne and Sara Mirza kindly investigated the archives of The Dorchester to illuminate the glamour of the hotel between the wars. Huis Wylerberg, Christie's headquarters on the Dutch-German border near Nijmegen, is a German expressionist architectural gem. Now in the custody of the Vereniging Nederlands Cultuurlandschap (Association for Dutch Cultural Landscapes), its director Jaap Dirkmaat was generous in sharing his knowledge of Marie Schuster-Hiby and her daughter Alice. Many thanks also to Tim Leenders, who sought out evocative pictures, and to him and Leon Otten, who showed me round the house.

Most of the secondary sources consulted can be found in the cast iron stacks of the London Library in St James's Square, the *ne plus ultra* of lending libraries. Without this unique facility neither my book nor doctoral thesis would have seen the light of day, so credit to Philip Marshall and his team for maintaining that unique environment and for cherishing us members.

History writing can be a lonely job and the path to publication far from smooth. Experienced historians and authors have been unflinchingly generous with their time and guidance. Robert McCrum volunteered early in the process to demystify the business of book writing and bravely read the first full draft. With his novelist's eye, editor's rigour and deep learning, his critical input and editorial suggestions have been invaluable. A thousand thanks, Robert.

Ben Macintyre also offered early reassurance that the Fellowship deserved a book. Michael Bloch, whose biography of Ribbentrop sets the standard for such lives, kindly took me to lunch and offered wise counsel. Bradley Hart's biography of George Pitt-Rivers unlocked the plot to radicalise the Fellowship. His enthusiasm for the era is infectious and *Hitler's American Friends* an inspiration. Sharing notes on Edward and Wallis with Anna Pasternak has likewise been intriguing, while her husband, Andrew Wallas, was right to urge me to get on with it. Julia Blackburn and our class at the Faber Academy helped to humanise my prose. Other inspiring historians and authors who have compared notes and offered encouragement include Andrew Adonis, Richard Bassett, Sacha Bonsor, Philip Boobbyer, Chris Bryant, Bernard Casey, Susan Goodman, Geordie Greig, Robert Hardman, Henry Hemming, Tony Lentin, Andrew Lownie, Patricia Meehan, Rudolf Muhs, Darren O'Byrne, Effie Pedaliu, Matthew Stibbe, Peter Watson, Steven Webbe, Geoffrey Wheatcroft and Anna Wyatt. Special thanks to Jane St Aubyn for unearthing the Savoy menu and to Hellmer Schmidt for alerting me to the Cornish swastika cake.

Several friends and family valiantly read early drafts. Jeremy Adams skilfully critiqued each chapter as it came off the printer. Julian Sainty thoughtfully reviewed the first full manuscript while Lily Spicer, Rupert Stonehill, Adrian Harley and Joshua Mendelson all commented on various chapters, and Christopher Spicer spotted a vital typo. Of course, all remaining errors are my own. Other brave souls helped this monoglot to understand important French and German sources including Aidan Friedberg, Céline Buckens, Ina De, John Banes and Molly Banes.

Coffee with Hitler builds on research for a doctorate undertaken at the Institute of Historical Research. First thanks must go to Vivian Bickford-Smith and John Sainty, both alumni, who supported my application. The Institute proved the perfect place for an old dog to learn new tricks. I owe a huge debt to the then director, Miles Taylor, who took me on as his student. Having enlisted the support of the indefatigable Karina Urbach as second supervisor, they together offered expert guidance with patience and good humour while insisting on the highest of standards. Miles persuaded Richard Overy, David Cannadine and Julie Gottlieb, each acclaimed experts in the field, to examine me for the PhD and each offered rigorous review leavened by generous encouragement. Jo Fox, Miles's successor as director, urged me to plan a book and recruited James Stourton, who cooked a lunch at which he explained how to write a proposal. Thanks to all the other patient IHR staff, especially Elena Aliferi, Elaine Walters and Simon Trafford, who supported the process and to John and Frances Sainty, Louisa Hellier and Alastair Winter who bravely read the thesis for sense, style and syntax.

Plaudits are also due to those exceptional historians who guided me through my first degree at the delightful Selwyn College, Cambridge, especially John Morrill, Gordon Johnson, Mark Thompson, David Smith and (again, a small world) David Cannadine. Equally, I must pay tribute to the inspirational teachers at Hitler's favourite English school who sowed the seeds, particularly Nigel Goodman, Henry Proctor, the late Nick Welsh, Tim Connor and Robert Franklin.

I am eternally grateful to all my extended family, friends and colleagues for indulging this quixotic project, particularly my best man, Tim Harvey-Samuel, who keeps me sane with excellent claret, novels and bicycle rides. Others who have supported me in body and soul over the last decade include Zacc Bingham, Beni Bitter, Zsofi Foldvari, Ray Goldsmith, Timea Tünde Gomes, Jillian Lavender, Michael Miller, François Moutou, Charlotte Murray, and Paul and Debbie Webster.

My bright, beautiful and loving daughters, Lily and Grace, have endured their father's strange obsession with wry amusement for a decade. Despite obvious paternal neglect, they have quietly fledged from promising teenagers into extraordinary women carving their way in the twenty-first century. I could not be prouder. Finally, unending thanks and love to the first of 'We Four', their mother, my darling wife, Vic, who makes all things possible.

DRAMATIS PERSONAE

GREAT BRITAIN

BALDWIN, STANLEY (LATER EARL BALDWIN), 1867–1947

Conservative politician. Educated at Harrow and Trinity College, Cambridge. Prime minister, 1935–7 and twice previously. Lord president of the Council, 1931–5. Member of Travellers Club.

BROCKET, LORD (RONALD), 1904–1967

Conservative politician and landowner. Educated at Eton and Magdalen College, Oxford. Fellowship member. Previously Member of Parliament and barrister.

CADOGAN, SIR ALEXANDER, 1884–1968

Diplomat, civil servant and diarist. Educated at Eton and Balliol College, Oxford. Permanent undersecretary of state for foreign affairs, 1938–46. Previously ambassador to Peking.

CHAMBERLAIN, NEVILLE, 1869–1940

Conservative politician. Educated at Rugby and Mason College, Birmingham. Prime minister, 1937–40. Previously Chancellor of the Exchequer.

CHURCHILL, SIR WINSTON, 1874–1965

Liberal and Conservative politician, soldier, writer, historian and painter. Prime minister, 1940–5 and 1951–5. Previously First Lord of the Admiralty, Chancellor of the Exchequer and Home Secretary.

CHRISTIE, GROUP CAPTAIN MALCOLM GRAHAME, 1881–1971

Aviator, diplomat and intelligence agent. Educated at Malvern College and the University of Aachen. Fellowship Council member. Previously

air attaché in Berlin and Washington. Member of Travellers Club and
Chatham House.

CLYDESDALE, MARQUESS OF (LATER DUKE OF HAMILTON), 1903–1973

Boxer, aviator and Conservative politician. Educated at Eton and Balliol
College, Oxford. Hereditary keeper of Holyroodhouse and lord steward
of the royal household. Member of parliament, 1930–40.

CONWELL-EVANS, DR THOMAS PHILIP, 1892–1968

Historian, political secretary and intelligence agent. Educated at
Carmarthen Grammar School, Jesus College, Oxford and the LSE. Secretary
of the Fellowship. Visiting lecturer at Königsberg University, East Prussia,
1932–4. Previously secretary to the British Armenian Committee and
the Balkan Committee. Member of Travellers Club and Chatham House.

EDEN, ANTHONY (LATER EARL OF AVON), 1897–1977

Conservative politician. Educated at Eton and Christ Church, Oxford.
Foreign secretary, 1935–8 and 1940–5. Previously Lord Privy Seal. Later
prime minister.

GAERTNER, FRIEDL, BORN 1911

Austrian model and MI5 intelligence agent from 1938. Codenamed
Gelatine or M/G. Later a double agent with MI6's XX programme
sending misinformation to contacts in Germany.

HALIFAX, EARL OF (EDWARD FREDERICK LINDLEY WOOD), 1881–1959

Politician and diplomat. Educated at Eton, Christ Church and All Souls,
Oxford. Foreign secretary, 1938–40. Previously leader of the House of Lords,
Lord Privy Seal and viceroy of India. Chancellor of Oxford University.
Master of the Middleton Foxhounds. Later ambassador to Washington.

HENDERSON, SIR NEVILE, 1882–1942

Diplomat. Educated at Eton and abroad. Ambassador to Berlin, 1937–9.
Previously ambassador to Buenos Aires. Honorary member of the DEG.

LLOYD GEORGE, DAVID (LATER EARL LLOYD GEORGE), 1863–1945
Liberal politician. Educated at Llanystumdwy Church School. Father of the House of Commons, 1929–45. Previously leader of the Liberal Party, prime minister and Chancellor of the Exchequer.

LONDONDERRY, MARQUESS OF, 1878–1949
Conservative politician and aristocrat. Educated at Eton and Sandhurst. Fellowship member. Previously secretary of state for air, Lord Privy Seal and leader of the House of Lords.

LOTHIAN, MARQUESS OF (PHILIP KERR), 1882–1940
Writer, Liberal politician and diplomat. Educated at Oratory School and New College, Oxford. Fellowship member. Ambassador to Washington, 1939–40. Secretary of the Rhodes Trust. Previously secretary to Lloyd George as prime minister. Member of Travellers Club and Chatham House.

MACDONALD, RAMSAY, 1866–1937
Labour politician. Educated at Drainie parish school. Prime minister, 1924 and 1929–35. Lord president of the Council, 1935–7.

MOUNT TEMPLE, LORD (FORMERLY COLONEL WILFRID WILLIAM ASHLEY), 1867–1939
Soldier and Conservative politician. Educated at Harrow and Magdalen College, Oxford. Chairman of the Fellowship, 1935–8. Chairman of the Anti-Socialist Union, the Navy League and the Comrades of the Great War. Previously Member of Parliament, minister of transport and undersecretary of state for war.

PHILBY, H. A. R. ('KIM'), 1912–1988
Journalist, intelligence agent and traitor. Educated at Westminster and Trinity College, Cambridge. Member and employee of the Fellowship. Soviet agent from 1934. Later correspondent for *The Times* and SIS (MI6) officer.

PHIPPS, SIR ERIC, 1875–1945

Diplomat. Educated at King's College, Cambridge and University of Paris. Ambassador to Berlin, 1933–7, and to Paris, 1937–9.

TENNANT, ERNEST, 1887–1962

Industrialist and businessman. Educated at Eton. Director of C. Tennant and Sons. Served in Intelligence Corps in Great War.

VANSITTART, SIR ROBERT (LATER LORD VANSITTART), 1881–1957

Diplomat, author and dramatist. Educated at Eton. Permanent under-secretary of state for foreign affairs, 1930–8, chief diplomatic adviser to the government, 1938–41. Previously private secretary to two prime ministers.

WILSON, SIR HORACE, 1882–1972

Civil servant. Educated at Kurnella School and the LSE. Chief industrial adviser to the government, 1930–9, seconded to the prime minister, 1935. Permanent secretary of HM Treasury, 1939–42.

WRIGHT, ELWYN

Travel agent and anti-Semite. Salaried secretary of the Fellowship, 1935–7. Employed by Thomas Cook & Sons. Later a member of the Nordic League.

GERMANY

BLOMBERG, FIELD MARSHAL WERNER VON, 1878–1946

Minister of war, 1935–8. Represented Hitler at George VI's coronation.

BRUNSWICK, DUKE OF (ERNST AUGUST), 1887–1953

Aristocrat and soldier. Founder member of DEG. First cousin of George V. Married Princess Viktoria Luise of Prussia, daughter of Kaiser Wilhelm II. Honorary member of the Royal British Legion.

DIRKSEN, HERBERT VON, 1882–1955

Diplomat. Ambassador to the Court of St James's, 1938–9. Previously ambassador to Tokyo and Moscow.

GÖRING, FIELD MARSHAL HERMANN, 1893–1946

Pilot, politician and art collector. Commander-in-chief of the Luftwaffe, president of the Reichstag, and prime minister of Prussia. *Reichsjägermeister* (Game Warden of the Reich).

HESS, RUDOLF, 1894–1987

Politician. Educated at the University of Munich. Deputy leader of the NSDAP, 1933–41.

HEWEL, WALTHER, 1904–1945

Diplomat. Educated at the Technical University of Munich. Council member of the DEG. Liaison officer between Ribbentrop and Hitler from 1938.

HIMMLER, HEINRICH, 1900–1945

Reichsführer of the SS, 1929–45, and head of the Gestapo. Main architect of the Holocaust. Former agronomist and poultry farmer.

HITLER, ADOLF, 1889–1945

Austrian-born politician and dictator. NSDAP leader, 1921–45. Chancellor of Germany, 1933–45.

HOESCH, DR LEOPOLD VON, 1881–1936

Diplomat. Educated at universities of Geneva, Heidelberg, Munich and Leipzig. Ambassador to the Court of St James's, 1932–6.

KORDT, DR ERICH, 1903–1969

Diplomat and member of the resistance. Rhodes scholar at Oxford University. *Chef de cabinet* to the foreign minister, 1938–40. Previously first secretary at the embassy in London. Founder member of the DEG.

KORDT, DR THEODOR ('THEO'), 1893–1962

Diplomat and member of the resistance. Chargé d'affaires in the London embassy. Previously *chef de cabinet* to the state secretary, von Bülow.

NEURATH, KONSTANTIN VON, 1873–1956

Diplomat. Educated in Tübingen and Berlin. Foreign minister, 1932–8. Thereafter, Reichsprotektor of occupied Bohemia and Moravia.

OSTER, COLONEL HANS, 1888–1945

Soldier and resistance leader. Chief of staff to Admiral Canaris, chief of the Abwehr (military intelligence).

RIBBENTROP, JOACHIM, 1893–1946

Wine merchant, amateur diplomat and politician. Ambassador to the Court of St. James's, 1936–8. Foreign minister, 1938–45. Founder of the DEG.

SAXE-COBURG-GOTHA, DUKE OF (PRINCE CHARLES EDWARD, DUKE OF ALBANY), 1884–1954

Anglo-German royal prince. Educated at Eton and Bonn University. Grandson of Queen Victoria. Founder member and president of the DEG. President of the German Red Cross and NSDAP member.

SCHUSTER-HIBY, MARIE, 1867–1949

Owner of Huis Wylerberg, patron of the arts and member of the resistance. Formerly nanny to Grahame Christie and his brother. Distant relation of Hermann Göring.

BIBLIOGRAPHY

PRIMARY SOURCES

Personal archives

Christie, Group Captain Malcolm Grahame, Churchill College, Cambridge (CHRS)

Churchill, Sir Winston, The Sir Winston Churchill Archive Trust (CHAR)

Conwell-Evans, Thomas Philip, Lady Gilbert private collection (CONWELL)

Davidson, J. C. C., MP (later Viscount Davidson), UK Parliamentary Archives (DAV)

Gilbert, Sir Martin, Lady Gilbert private collection (GILB)

Halifax, 1st Earl of (Edward Wood), Borthwick Institute for Archives, University of York (HALIFAX)

Hamilton, General Sir Ian, Liddell Hart Military Archives, King's College London (HAMILTON/KCL)

Hamilton, 14th Duke of (previously Marquess of Clydesdale), National Records of Scotland (HAMILTON/NRS)

Inskip, Thomas (later Viscount Caldecote), Churchill College Archives, Cambridge (INKP)

Lloyd George, David (later Earl Lloyd George), UK Parliamentary Archives (LG)

Lothian, 11th Marquess of (previously Philip Kerr), National Records of Scotland (KERR/NRS)

Mount Temple, 1st Baron (previously Wilfrid Ashley), Broadlands Archives, Hartley Library, University of Southampton (BR)

Pitt-Rivers, George, Churchill College Archives, Cambridge (PIRI)

Vansittart, Sir Robert (later Lord Vansittart), Churchill College Archives, Cambridge (VNST)

The National Archives, Kew, Richmond, Surrey

BT Series, Records of the Board of Trade and of successor and related bodies

CAB Series, Records of the Cabinet Office

FCO Series, Records of the Foreign and Commonwealth Office and predecessors
FO Series, Records of the Foreign Office
KV Series, Records of the Security Service
LASP Series, Lascelles Papers
PREM1 Series, Prime Minister's Office records

Other archives

Jesus College Oxford, The College Archives
London Metropolitan Archives, Records of the Board of Deputies of British Jews, London (ACC)
London School of Economics and Political Science, the Archives and Special Collections, London
Herzogin Anna Amalia Bibliothek, Klassik Stiftung Weimar, Germany
The British Library Manuscript Collections, London (BL)
The Schroder Archive, Papers of J. Henry Schroder & Co., London (SCHROD)
The Unilever Archive, Unilever plc, Port Sunlight, Cheshire
The Weiner Library for the Study of the Holocaust & Genocide, London

Printed Primary Sources

Allen, Reginald Clifford, (ed. Martin Gilbert), *Plough My Own Furrow: The story of Lord Allen of Hurtwood as told through his writings and correspondence* (London, 1965)
Athlone, HRH Princess Alice Countess of, *For My Grandchildren: Some Reminiscences* (London, 1980)
Baldwin, Stanley, *Service of Our Lives: Last speeches as Prime Minister* (London, 1937)
Barsley, Michael, *Ritzkrieg: The old guard's private war* (London, 1940)
—*The Intimate Papers of Colonel Bogus* (London, 1943)
Baxter, Richard, *Guilty Women* (London, 1941)
Bruce Lockhart, Sir Robert, (ed. Kenneth Young), *The Diaries of Sir Robert Bruce Lockhart, Vol. 1, 1915–1938* (London, 1973)
Bryant, Arthur (ed.), *The Man and the Hour: Studies of Six Great Men of Our Time* (London, 1934)
Burge, Gordon C., *The Annals of 100 Squadron* (London, 1919)
Burn, Michael, *Turned Towards the Sun: An autobiography* (Norwich, 2003)
Cadogan, Alexander, (ed. David Dilks), *The Diaries of Sir Alexander Cadogan, 1938–1945* (London, 1971)
Cassius, *The Trial of Mussolini* (London, 1943)
Cato, *Guilty Men* (London, 1940)

Chamberlain, Sir Neville, (ed. Robert Self), *The Neville Chamberlain Diary Letters: The Downing Street Years, 1934–1940: Volume 4* (Aldershot, 2005)

Channon, Henry 'Chips', (ed. Simon Heffer), *The Diaries (Volume 1): 1918–38* (London, 2021)

— (ed. Robert Rhodes James), *Chips: The Diaries of Sir Henry Channon* (London, 1967)

Churchill, Winston S., *Great Contemporaries* (London, 1937)

— *The Second World War* (London, 1948–53)

Cockburn, Claud, *Cockburn Sums Up: An autobiography* (London, 1981)

Colville, John, *Footprints in Time* (London, 1979)

— *The Fringes of Power: Downing Street Diaries 1939–1955* (London, 1985)

Conwell-Evans, T. P., 'Between Berlin and London', *Nineteenth Century and After*, vol. 119, p. 57 (1936)

— 'Germany in July–August', *Nineteenth Century and After*, vol. 120, p. 416 (1936)

— 'Impressions of Germany', *Nineteenth Century and After*, vol. 115, p. 72 (1934)

— 'Sir Horace Rumbold on Germany', *Nineteenth Century and After*, vol. 128, p. 144 (1940)

— 'Sir Nevile Henderson's Apologia', *Nineteenth Century and After*, vol. 128, p. 28 (1940)

— 'The Foreign Policy of Lord Halifax', *Nineteenth Century and After*, vol. 128, p. 427 (1940)

— 'The Statesmanship of Mr Churchill', *Nineteenth Century and After*, vol. 129, p. 45 (1941)

— *Foreign policy from a back bench, 1904–1918: a study based on the papers of Lord Noel-Buxton* (Oxford, 1932)

— *None So Blind: A study of the crisis years, 1930–1939, based on the private papers of Group-Captain M. G. Christie* (London, 1947)

— *The League Council in Action: a study in the methods employed by the council of the League of Nations to prevent war and to settle international disputes* (Oxford, 1929)

Cowles, Virginia, *Looking for Trouble* (London, 1941)

D'Arcy Cooper, Francis, 'Germany's Economic Policy: An attempt at an Interpretation', *Progress* (published by Lever Brothers Limited), vol. 35, no. 203 (January 1935)

Diplomaticus, (Zilliacus K.), *Can the Tories Win the Peace? And How They Lost the Last One* (London, 1945)

Dodd, William, (ed. W. and M. Dodd), *Ambassador Dodd's Diary 1933–1938* (New York, 1941)

Domvile, Barry, *From Admiral to Cabin Boy* (London, 1947)

Duhamel, Georges, (trans. T. P. Conwell-Evans), *Civilisation* (London, 1919)

Eden, Anthony, *The Eden Memoirs: Facing the Dictators* (London, 1962)

Einzig, Paul, *Appeasement: Before, During and After the War* (London, 1941)

Fellowes, P. F. M. et al., *First Over Everest: The Houston-Mount Everest Expedition 1933* (London, 1935)

Fleming, Peter, *The Flying Visit* (London, 1940)

Fraenkel, Heinrich, Fabian Society, *Vansittart's Gift for Goebbels: A German Exile's Answer to Black Record* (London, 1941)

Fromm, Bella, *Blood and Banquets: A Berlin social diary* (London, 1943)

Gibbs, Philip, *Ordeal in England* (London, 1937)

Gisevius, Hans Bernd, (trans. Richard and Clara Winstone), *To the Bitter End* (London, 1948)

Gladwyn, Lord (Gladwyn Jebb), *The Memoirs of Lord Gladwyn* (London, 1972)

Gollancz, Victor, *Shall our Children Live or Die? A Reply to Lord Vansittart on the German Problem* (London, 1942)

Gracchus, *Your M.P.* (London, 1944)

Halifax, Edward Frederick Lindley Wood, Earl of, *Fullness of Days* (London, 1957)

Harvey, Oliver, (ed. John Harvey), *Diplomatic Diaries, 1937–40* (London, 1970)

Hassell, Ulrich von, *The Ulrich von Hassell Diaries, 1938–1944* (London, 2011)

Haxey, Simon, *Tory MP* (London, 1939)

Hazlehurst, Cameron; Whitehead, Sally, *A Guide to the Papers of British Cabinet Ministers 1900–1964* (Cambridge, 1996)

Henderson, Sir Nevile, *Failure of a Mission: Berlin 1937–1939* (London, 1940)

—*Water Under the Bridges* (London, 1945)

Her Majesty's Stationery Office, (ed. W. N. Medlicott, Douglas Dakin, et al.), *Documents on British Foreign Policy 1919–1939* (London, 1946–86)

—*Documents on German Foreign Policy 1918–1945* (London, 1951–83)

Hesse, Fritz, (ed. and trans. F. A. Voigt), *Hitler and the English* (London, 1954)

Hogg, Quintin, *A Sparrow's Flight: Memoirs* (London, 1990)

—*The Left Was Never Right* (London, 1945)

Jones, Henry, *The War in the Air; being the story of the part played in the Great War by the Royal Air Force* (Oxford, 1928)

Jones, Thomas, *A Diary with Letters 1931–1950* (Oxford, 1954)

Kennedy, A. L., (ed. Gordon Martel), *The Times and Appeasement: The Journals of A. L. Kennedy, 1932–1939* (Cambridge, 2009)

Kessler, Harry, *The Diaries of a Cosmopolitan 1918–1937* (London, 1971)

Keynes, John Maynard, *The Economic Consequences of the Peace* (London, 1919)

King-Hall, Stephen, *Total Victory* (London, 1941)

Kirkpatrick, Ivone, *The Inner Circle: Memoirs of Ivone Kirkpatrick* (London, 1959)

Kordt, Erich, *Nicht aus den Akten* (Stuttgart, 1950)

Lambert, Richard. S., *Propaganda* (London, 1938)

Liddell, Guy, (ed. Nigel West), *The Guy Liddell Diaries, Volume I: 1939–1942* (Abingdon, 2005)

Londonderry, Marquess of, *Ourselves and Germany* (London, 1938)

Lothian, Philip, *The American Speeches of Lord Lothian, July 1939 to December 1940* (Oxford, 1941)

Luise, Viktoria, Duchess of Brunswick and Luneburg, *The Kaiser's Daughter* (London, 1977)

Macnamara, J. R. J., *The Whistle Blows* (London, 1938)

Maisky, Ivan, (ed. Gabriel Gorodetsky), *The Maisky Diaries: Red Ambassador to the Court of St James's, 1932–1943*, 3 volumes (New Haven, CT, 2017)

Mander, Geoffrey Le Mesurier, *We Were Not All Wrong* (London, 1944)

Meinertzhagen, Colonel Richard, *Diary of a Black Sheep* (Edinburgh, 1964)

Miller, Joan, *One Girl's War: Personal Exploits in MI5's Most Secret Station* (Dublin, 1986)

Mitford, Nancy, *The Pursuit of Love* (London, 1945)

Moskowitz, Moses, *The American Jewish Year Book*, vol. 41 (Philadelphia, 1939–40)

Mosley, Leonard, *Down Stream* (London, 1939)

Namier, Lewis, *Diplomatic Prelude, 1938–9* (London, 1948)

—*In the Nazi Era* (London, 1952)

Neave, Airey, *Nuremberg* (London, 1978)

Nichols, Beverley, *Men Do Not Weep* (London, 1941)

Nicolson, Harold, (ed. Nigel Nicolson), *Diaries and Letters, 1907–1964* (London, 2004)

Parliamentary Peace Aims Group, *Germany's Record: A reply to Lord Vansittart* (London, ND)

Philby, Kim, *My Silent War* (London, 1968)

Phipps, Sir Eric, (ed. Gaynor Johnson), *Our Man in Berlin: The Diary of Sir Eric Phipps, 1933–1937* (Basingstoke, 2008)

Price, G. Ward, *I Know These Dictators* (London, 1937)

Pride, Emrys, *Why Lloyd George Met Hitler* (Risca, 1981)

Rauschning, Hermann, *Hitler Wants the World* (London, 1941)

Rees, Goronwy, *Chapter of Accidents* (London, 1971)

Ribbentrop, Joachim, (ed. Alan Bullock), *The Ribbentrop Memoirs* (London, 1954)

Rothfels, Hans, (trans. Lawrence Wilson), *The German Opposition to Hitler: An Appraisal* (Chicago, 1948)

Rowse, A. L., *All Souls and Appeasement: A Contribution to Contemporary History* (London, 1961)

Schmidt, Paul, *Hitler's Interpreter* (London, 1951)

Schwartz, Paul, *This Man Ribbentrop: His Life and Times* (New York, 1943)

Schweppenburg, Leo Geyr von, *The Critical Years* (London, 1952)

Shirer, William L, *Berlin Diary: The journal of a foreign correspondent, 1934–1941* (London, 1942)

Siemens, Georg, *The History of the House of Siemens* (Freiburg, 1957)

Silex, Karl, *John Bull at Home* (Leipzig, 1931)

Simon, Lord, *Retrospect: The memoirs of the Rt. Hon. Viscount Simon* (London, 1952)

Smith, Thomas F. A., *Schrag's Handy Guide to Nuremberg*

Spitzy, Reinhard, (trans. G. T. Waddington), *How We Squandered the Reich* (Norwich, 1997)

Straight, Michael, *After Long Silence* (London, 1983)

Strang, Lord, *Home and Abroad* (London, 1956)

Struther, Jan, *Mrs Miniver* (London, 1939)

Sylvester, A. J., *Life with Lloyd George: The Diary of A. J. Sylvester* (New York, 1975)

—*The Real Lloyd George* (London, 1947)

Templewood, Viscount, *Nine Troubled Years* (London, 1954)

Tennant, Eleonora, *Spanish Journey: Personal Experiences of the Civil War* (London, 1936)

Tennant, Ernest W. D., *True Account* (London, 1957)

Uhl, Matthias and Eberle, Henrik, *The Hitler Book: The Secret Report by His Two Closest Aides* (New York, 2005)

Ustinov, Peter, *Dear Me* (Boston, 1977)

Vansittart, Peter, *A Verdict of Treason* (London, 1952)

Vansittart, Robert, *Black Record: Germans Past and Present* (London, 1941)

—*Lessons of My Life* (London, 1943)

—*The Mist Procession: The Autobiography of Lord Vansittart* (London, 1958)

Weizsäcker, Ernst von, *Memoirs* (London, 1951)

West, Rebecca, *A Train of Powder* (London, 1955)

Wheeler-Bennett, John, *Knaves, Fools & Heroes* (London, 1974)

—*Munich: Prologue to Tragedy* (London, 1948)

—*The Nemesis of Power: The German Army in Politics, 1918–1945* (London, 1953)

Williamson, Henry, *Goodbye West Country* (London, 1937)

Williamson, Philip; Baldwin, Edward, (ed.), *Baldwin Papers: A conservative statesman, 1908–1947* (Cambridge, 2004)

Windsor, Duchess of, *The Heart Has Its Reasons* (London, 1956)

Windsor, Duke of, *A King's Story: The Memoirs of HRH the Duke of Windsor* (London, 1951)

Woolf, Leonard, *Barbarians at the Gate* (London, 1939)

Young, A. P., (ed. Sidney Aster), *The 'X' Documents* (London, 1974)

zu Putlitz, Wolfgang, *The Putlitz Dossier* (London, 1957)

Newspapers and periodicals

American Mercury

Anglo-German Fellowship Monthly Journal

Anglo-German Review

Australian Women's Weekly

Bristol Times and Mirror

Country Life

Daily Express

Daily Herald

Daily Mail

Daily Telegraph

Economist

Evening Standard

Financial News
Homes and Gardens
Jewish Chronicle
London Gazette
Manchester Guardian
New York Times
News Chronicle
News Review
Observer
Pittsburgh Press
Saturday Review of Literature
Spectator
Sunday Times
Tatler & Bystander
The Times
Time and Tide
Times Literary Supplement
Tribune
Western Morning News and Daily Gazette

SECONDARY SOURCES

Books

Adams, R. J. Q., *British Politics and Foreign Policy in the Age of Appeasement, 1935–39* (London, 1993)

Allport, Alan, *Britain at Bay: The Epic Story of the Second World War: 1938–1941* (London, 2020)

Anderson, Mosa, *Noel Buxton, a Life* (London, 1952)

Andrew, Christopher, *Secret Service: The Making of the British Intelligence Community* (London, 1985)

— *The Defence of the Realm: The Authorized History of MI5* (London, 2009)

Andrew, Christopher and Mitrokhin, Vasili, *The Mitrokhin Archive: The KGB in Europe and the West* (London, 1999)

Andrews, P. W. S.; Brunner, E., *The Life of Lord Nuffield* (Oxford, 1955)

Annan, Noel Gilroy, *Changing Enemies: Defeat and Regeneration of Germany* (London, 1995)

Aronson, Theo, *Princess Alice: Countess of Athlone* (Littlehampton, 1981)

Aster, Sidney (ed.), *Appeasement and All Souls: A Portrait with Documents, 1937–1939* (Cambridge, 2004)

Bailey, Catherine, *The Lost Boys: A Family Ripped Apart by War* (London, 2019)

Baker, Anne, *The Pilgrims of Great Britain: A Centennial History* (London, 2002)

Balfour, Michael, *Propaganda in War 1939–1945: Organisations, Policies and Publics in Britain and Germany* (London, 1979)

Barnes, James; Barnes, Patience, *Nazis in Pre-War London 1930–1939* (Eastbourne, 2005)

Barr, Niall, *The Lion and the Poppy: British Veterans, Politics, and Society, 1921–1939* (London, 2004)

Billington, David P., *Lothian: Philip Kerr and the Quest for World Order* (London, 2006)

Birkenhead, Frederick, *Halifax: The Life of Lord Halifax* (London, 1965)

Blakeway, Denys, *The Last Dance 1936: The Year of Change* (London, 2010)

Bloch, Michael, *Closet Queens* (London, 2015)

—*Operation Willi: The Plot to Capture the Duke of Windsor July 1940* (London, 1984)

—*Ribbentrop* (London, 1992)

Blow, Simon, *Broken Blood: The Rise and Fall of the Tennant Family* (London, 1987)

Blythe, Dr Ronald, *The Age of Illusion: Glimpses of Britain Between the Wars, 1919–40* (Oxford, 1963)

Bosco, Andrea; Navari, Cornelia, *Chatham House and British Foreign Policy 1919–1945: The Royal Institute of International Affairs during the inter-war period* (London, 1994)

Bouverie, Tim, *Appeasing Hitler: Chamberlain, Churchill and the Road to War* (London, 2019)

Bowd, Gavin, *Fascist Scotland: Caledonia and the Far Right* (Edinburgh, 2013)

Boyd, Julia, *Travellers in the Third Reich: The rise of Fascism through the eyes of everyday people* (London, 2017)

Boyle, Andrew, *Montagu Norman* (London, 1967)

—*The Climate of Treason* (London, 1979)

Bradford, Sarah, *King George VI* (London, 1989)

Bruegel, J. W., *Czechoslovakia before Munich* (Cambridge, 1973)

Bryant, Chris, *The Glamour Boys: The Secret Story of the Rebels who Fought for Britain to Defeat Hitler* (London, 2020)

Burden, Hamilton T., *The Nürnberg Party Rallies: 1923–1939* (New York, 1967)

Burn, Duncan, *Economic History of Steelmaking 1867–1939: A Study in Competition* (Cambridge, 1961)

Butler, J. R. M., *Lord Lothian (Philip Kerr)* (London, 1960)

Cadbury, Deborah, *Princes at War: The British Royal Family's Private Battle in the Second World War* (London, 2015)

Calder, Angus, *The People's War: Britain 1939–45* (London, 1969)

Cannadine, David, *Aspects of Aristocracy: Grandeur and Decline in Modern Britain* (New Haven, 1994)

—*In Churchill's Shadow: Confronting the Past in Modern Britain* (London, 2002)

—*Pleasures of the Past* (New York, 1989)

—*The Decline and Fall of the British Aristocracy* (New Haven, CT, 1990)

Caputi, Robert J., *Neville Chamberlain and Appeasement* (Selinsgrove, PA, 2000)

Carley, Michael Jabara, *1939: The Alliance That Never Was and the Coming of World War II* (Chicago, 1999)

Cave Brown, Anthony; MacDonald, Charles B., *On a Field of Red: The Communist International and the Coming of World War II* (New York, 1981)

Ceadel, Martin, *Pacifism in Britain, 1914–1945: The Defining of a Faith* (Oxford, 1980)

—*Semi-Detached Idealists: The British peace movement and international relations, 1854–1945* (Oxford, 2000)

Charmley, John, *Chamberlain and the Lost Peace* (London, 1989)

—*Churchill: The End of Glory – A Political Biography* (London, 1993)

Cockburn, Patricia, *The Years of The Week* (London, 1968)

Cockett, Richard, *Twilight of Truth: Chamberlain, Appeasement and the Manipulation of the Press* (London, 1989)

Colvin, Ian, *Vansittart in Office: An Historical Survey of the Second World War based on the papers of Sir Robert Vansittart* (London, 1965)

Connell, Brian, *Manifest Destiny: A study in five profiles of the rise and influence of the Mountbatten family* (London, 1953)

Conyers Nesbit, Roy and Acker, Georges van, *The Flight of Rudolf Hess: Myths and Reality* (Cheltenham, 2007)

Conze, Eckart; Frei, Norbert; Hayes, Peter and Zimmermann, Moshe, *Das Amt und die Vergangenheit: Deutsche Diplomaten im Dritten Reich und in der Bundesrepublik* (Munich, 2010).

Costello, John, *Mask of Treachery* (London, 1988)

Costello, John and Tsarev, Oleg, *Deadly Illusions: The KGB Orlov Dossier Reveals Stalin's Master Spy* (London, 1993)

Cowling, Maurice, *The Impact of Hitler: British Politics and British Policy, 1933–1940* (Cambridge, 1975)

Craigie, Emma, *Chocolate Cake with Hitler: A Nazi Childhood* (London, 2010)

Crowson, N. J., *Facing Fascism: The Conservative Party and the European Dictators 1935–1940* (Abingdon, 1997)

Curry, John, *The Security Service 1908–1945: The Official History* (Kew, 1999)

D'Almeida, Fabrice, *High Society in the Third Reich* (Cambridge, 2008)

Davenport-Hines, Richard, *Enemies Within: Communists, the Cambridge Spies and the Making of Modern Britain* (London, 2018)

De Courcy, Anne, *Diana Mosley* (London, 2003)

Deutsch, Harold C., *The Conspiracy Against Hitler in the Twilight War* (Minnesota, 1968)

Donaldson, Frances, *Edward VIII* (London, 1986)

Dorril, Stephen, *Blackshirt: Sir Oswald Mosley and British Fascism* (London, 2006)

—*MI6: Fifty Years of Special Operations* (London, 2000)

Douglas-Hamilton, James, *Motive for a Mission: The story behind Rudolf Hess's flight to Britain* (Edinburgh, 1971)

—*The Truth about Rudolf Hess* (Edinburgh, 1993)

Driberg, Tom, *Guy Burgess* (London, 1956)

Du Bois, Josiah E.; Johnson, Edward, *Generals in Grey Suits: The directors of the international 'I. G. Farben' cartel, their conspiracy and trial at Nuremberg* (London, 1953)

Duff, William E., *A Time for Spies: Theodore Stephanovich Mally and the Era of the Great Illegals* (London, 1999)

Dutton, David, *Neville Chamberlain* (London, 2001)

Eckert, Astrid M., *The Struggle for the Files: The Western Allies and the Return of German Archives after the Second World War* (Cambridge, 2012)

Edgerton, David, *England and the Aeroplane: An Essay on a Militant and Technological Nation* (London, 1991)

Edwards, Ruth Dudley, *Victor Gollancz: A biography* (London, 1987)

Egremont, Max, *Forgotten Land: Journeys Among the Ghosts of East Prussia* (London, 2011)

Evans, Richard J., *The Hitler Conspiracies: The Third Reich and the Paranoid Imagination* (London, 2020)

—*The Third Reich in Power, 1933–1939: How the Nazis Won Over the Hearts and Minds of a Nation* (London, 2005)

Faber, David, *Munich: The 1938 Appeasement Crisis* (London, 2008)

Fairfax, Ernest, *Calling All Arms: The story of how a loyal company of British men and women lived through six historic years* (London, 1945)

Farnham, Barbara Rearden, *Roosevelt and the Munich Crisis: A Study of Political Decision-Making* (Princeton, 1997)

Feldenkirchen, Wilfried; Posner, Eberhard, *The Siemens Entrepreneurs, Continuity and Change, 1847–2005, Ten Portraits* (Munich, 2005)

Ferris, John, *Intelligence and Strategy: Selected Essays* (Abingdon, 2005)

Fielding, Steven; Schwarz, Bill and Toye, Richard, *The Churchill Myths* (London, 2020)

Fleming, N. C., *The Marquess of Londonderry: Aristocracy, Power and Politics in Britain and Ireland* (London, 2005)

Foley, Michael, *Pioneers of Aerial Combat: Air Battles of the First World War* (Barnsley, 2013)

Forbes, Neil, *Doing Business with the Nazis: Britain's Economic and Financial Relations with Germany 1931–39* (London, 2000)

Fox, James, *The Langhorne Sisters* (London, 1998)

Garfield, Brian, *The Meinertzhagen Mystery: The life and legend of a colossal fraud* (Washington, 2007)

Gilbert, Martin, *Britain and Germany Between the Wars* (London, 1964)

—*In Search of Churchill: A historian's journey* (London, 1994)

—*Kristallnacht: Prelude to Destruction* (London, 2006)

—*Sir Horace Rumbold: Portrait of a Diplomat* (London, 1973)

—*The Roots of Appeasement* (London, 1966)

—*Winston S. Churchill: Prophet of Truth 1922–1939* (London, 1979)

—*Winston S. Churchill: The Coming of War, 1936–1939*, Documents (London, 1982)

Gilbert, Martin and Gott, Richard, *The Appeasers* (London, 1963)

Gill, Anton, *A Dance Between Flames: Berlin Between the Wars* (London, 1994)

Gottlieb, Julie V., *Feminine Fascism: Women in Britain's Fascist Movement, 1923–1945* (London, 2000)

—*'Guilty women', Foreign Policy, and Appeasement in Inter-War Britain* (London, 2015)

Gottlieb, Julie V.; Hucker, Daniel; Toye, Richard (eds), *The Munich Crisis, politics and the people: International, transnational and comparative perspectives* (Manchester, 2021)

Greig, Geordie, *Louis and the Prince* (London, 1999)

Griffiths, Richard, *Fellow Travellers of the Right: British Enthusiasts for Nazi Germany 1933–1939* (London, 1980)

—*Patriotism Perverted: Captain Ramsay, the Right Club and British Anti-Semitism 1939–40* (London, 1998)

—*What Did You Do During the War? The Last Throes of the British Pro-Nazi Right, 1940–45* (London, 2017)

Hancock, Peter, *Cornwall at War, 1939–1945* (Wellington, 2009)

Hannah, Leslie, *Rise of the Corporate Economy* (London, 1976)

Harding, Brian, *Keeping Faith: The History of the Royal British Legion* (London, 2001)

Harris, John; Trow, M. J., *Hess: The British Conspiracy* (London, 2011)

Harris, Robert, *Munich* (London, 2017)

Hart Bradley, W., *Hitler's American Friends: The Third Reich's Supporters in the United States* (New York, 2018)

—*George Pitt-Rivers and the Nazis* (London, 2015)

Hart-Davis, Duff, *Hitler's Games* (London, 1986)

—*Peter Fleming* (London, 1974)

Haslam, Jonathan, *Near and Distant Neighbours: A New History of Soviet Intelligence* (Oxford, 2015)

—*The Spectre of War: International Communism and the Origins of World War II* (Princeton, 2020)

Hattersley, Roy, *David Lloyd George – the Great Outsider* (London, 2010)

Hauner, Milan, *Hitler: A Chronology of his Life and Time* (London, 2008)

Hayes, Peter, *Industry and Ideology: IG Farben in the Nazi Era* (Cambridge, 1987)

Heideking, Jurgen and Mauch, Christof, *American Intelligence and the German Resistance to Hitler: A Documentary History* (London, 1996)

Hemming, Henry, *M: Maxwell Knight, MI5's Greatest Spymaster* (London, 2017)

—*Our Man in New York: The British Plot to Bring America into the Second World War* (London, 2019)

Heuss, Theodor, (trans. Susan Gillespie), *Robert Bosch: His Life and Achievements* (New York, 1994)

Higham, Charles, *Wallis: Secret Lives of the Duchess of Windsor* (London, 1998)

Hilton, Christopher, *Hitler's Olympics: The 1936 Berlin Olympic Games* (London, 2006)

Hoffmann, Peter, *The History of the German Resistance, 1933–1945* (London, 1977)

—*Behind Valkyrie: German Resistance to Hitler, Documents* (Montreal, 2011)

Hopkins, Michael F.; Kelly, Saul; Young, John W. (ed.), *The Washington Embassy: British Ambassadors to the United States, 1939–77* (London, 2009)

Inglis, Brian, *Abdication* (London, 1966)

Inglis, Ruth, *Evacuation: The Children's War 1939–1945* (London, 1989)

Ishiguro, Kazuo, *The Remains of the Day* (London, 1989)

Jackson, Robert, *The Nuffield Story* (London, 1964)

Jacobsen, Hans-Adolf, *Nationalsozialistische Aussen Politik 1933–38* (Berlin, 1968)

James, Lawrence, *Aristocrats: Power, Grace and Decadence* (London, 2009)

Jeffrey, Keith, *MI6: The History of the Secret Intelligence Service 1909–1949* (London, 2010)

Jones, Edgar, *True and Fair: A History of Price Waterhouse* (London, 1995)

Jones, J. Harry, *Josiah Stamp, Public Servant: The Life of the First Baron Stamp of Shortlands* (London, 1964)

Jones, Thomas, *Lloyd George* (London, 1951)

Kavanagh, Dennis; Seldon, Anthony, *The Powers Behind the Prime Minister: The Hidden Influence of Number Ten* (London, 1999)

Kenny, Antony (ed.), *The History of the Rhodes Trust: 1902–1999* (Oxford, 2001)

Kershaw, Ian, *Hitler, 1889–1936: Hubris* (London, 1998)

—*Hitler, 1936–1945: Nemesis* (London, 2000)

—*Making Friends with Hitler: Lord Londonderry and Britain's Road to War* (London, 2004)

Kirsch, Jonathan, *The Short, Strange Life of Herschel Grynszpan: A Boy Avenger, a Nazi Diplomat, and a Murder in Paris* (London, 2013)

Klemperer, Klemens von, *German Resistance Against Hitler: The Search for Allies Abroad, 1938–1945* (Oxford, 1992)

Knightly, Phillip, *Philby: KGB Masterspy* (London, 1998)

Kynaston, David, *The City of London: Illusions of Gold, 1914–1945* (London, 1994)

—*Till Time's Last Sand: A History of the Bank of England 1694–2013* (London, 2017)

Laity, Paul, *The British Peace Movement 1870–1914* (Oxford, 2002)

Lamb, Richard, *The Drift to War, 1922–1939* (London, 1989)

—*The Ghosts of Peace 1935–1945* (Wilton, 1987)

Lanyon, Andrew, *Von Ribbentrop in St Ives: Art and War in the Last Resort* (Thatcham, 2011)

Large, David Clay, *Nazi Games: The Olympics of 1936* (New York, 2007)

Leasor, James, *Rudolf Hess: The Uninvited Envoy* (London, 1962)

Lehrman, Lewis E., *Churchill, Roosevelt & Company* (Guildford, CT, 2017)

Lentin, Anthony, *Lloyd George and the Lost Peace: From Versailles to Hitler 1919–1940* (Basingstoke, 2001)

Lewis, John, *The Left Book Club: An Historical Record* (London, 1970)

Lloyd George, Robert, *David & Winston: How a Friendship Changed History* (London, 2005)

Lovell, Mary S., *The Mitford Girls: The Biography of an Extraordinary Family* (London, 2001)

Lownie, Andrew, *Stalin's Englishman: The Lives of Guy Burgess* (London, 2015)

—*The Mountbattens: Their Lives & Loves* (London, 2019)

MacDonagh, Giles, *A Good German* (London, 1994)

Macintyre, Ben, *A Spy Among Friends: Kim Philby and the Great Betrayal* (London, 2014)

—*Double Cross: The True Story of the D-Day Spies* (London, 2012)

MacMillan, Margaret, *Peacemakers: The Paris Peace Conference of 1919* (London, 2001)

Malinowski, Stephan, (trans. Jon Andrews), *Nazis and Nobles: The History of a Misalliance* (Oxford, 2020)

Mandell, Richard D., *The Nazi Olympics* (Illinois, 1971)

Marwick, Arthur, *Clifford Allen: The Open Conspirator* (Edinburgh, 1964)

Masterman, J. C., *Double-cross System in the War of 1939 to 1945* (New Haven, CT, 1972)

Masters, Anthony, *The Man Who Was M: The Life of Charles Henry Maxwell Knight* (Oxford, 1984)

McCarthy, Helen, *The British People and the League of Nations: Democracy, Citizenship and Internationalism, c.1918–45* (Manchester, 2011)

McDonough, Frank, *Neville Chamberlain, Appeasement and the British Road to War* (Manchester, 2010)

—*The Conservative Party and Anglo-German Relations, 1905–1914* (Basingstoke, 2007)

—*The Hitler Years: Triumph 1933–1939* (London, 2019)

McMillan, James, *The Dunlop Story* (London, 1989)

Meehan, Patricia, *The Unnecessary War* (London, 1992)

Middlemas, Keith, *Diplomacy of Illusion: The British Government and Germany, 1937–39* (London, 1972)

Milne, Tim, *Kim Philby: The Unknown Story of the KGB's Master Spy* (London, 2014)

Modin, Juri, (trans. Anthony Roberts), *My Five Cambridge Friends* (London, 1994)

Morgan, Austen, *J. Ramsay MacDonald* (Manchester, 1987)

Morgan, Kenneth, *Lloyd George* (Worthing, 1974)

Mosley, Leonard, *On Borrowed Time: How World War Two Began* (London, 1969)

—*The Reich Marshal: A Biography of Hermann Goering* (London, 1974)

Mowat, C. L., *Britain Between the Wars 1918–1940* (London, 1955)

Murphy, Sean, *Letting the Side Down: British traitors of the Second World War* (Stroud, 2003)

Neville, Peter, *Hitler and Appeasement: The British Attempt to Prevent the Second World War* (London, 2006)

—*Appeasing Hitler: The diplomacy of Sir Nevile Henderson, 1937–39* (Basingstoke, 2000)

Newton, Scott, *Profits of Peace: The Political Economy of Anglo-German Appeasement* (Oxford, 1996)

Oldfield, Sybil, *The Black Book: The Britons on the Nazi Hitlist* (London, 2020)

Olson, Lynne, *Those Angry Days: Roosevelt, Lindberg and America's Fight over World War II, 1939–1941* (New York, 2013)

Osborne, Eric W., *Britain's Economic Blockade of Germany, 1914–1919* (Abingdon, 2004)

Overy, Richard, *1939: Countdown to War* (London, 2009)

—*Göring: The Iron Man* (London, 1984)

—*The Morbid Age: Britain Between the Wars* (London, 2009)

—*William Morris, Viscount Nuffield* (London, 1976)

Owen, Frank, *Tempestuous Journey: Lloyd George, His Life and Times* (London, 1954)

Owens, Edward, *The Family Firm: Monarchy, Mass Media and the British Public, 1932–53* (London, 2019)

Padfield, Peter, *Hess, Hitler and Churchill: The Real Turning Point of the Second World War – A Secret History* (London, 2013)

—*Hess: The Fuhrer's Disciple* (London, 1991)

Page, Bruce; Leitch, David; Knightley, Philip, *Philby: The Spy Who Betrayed a Generation* (London, 1968)

Panayi, Panikos (ed.), *Germans in Britain Since 1500* (London, 1996)

Parker, R. A. C., *Churchill and Appeasement* (London, 2000)

—*Chamberlain and Appeasement* (Basingstoke, 1993)

Parssinen, Terry, *The Oster Conspiracy Of 1938: The Unknown Story of the Military Plot to Kill Hitler and Avert World War II* (London, 2004)

Pedersen, Susan, *The Guardians: The League of Nations and the Crisis of Empire* (Oxford, 2015)

Peel, Mark, *The Patriotic Duke: The Life of the 14th Duke of Hamilton* (London, 2013)

Petropoulos, Jonathan, *Royals and the Reich: The Princes von Hessen in Nazi Germany* (Oxford, 2006)

Phillips, Adrian, *Fighting Churchill, Appeasing Hitler: How a British Civil Servant Helped Cause the Second World War* (London, 2019)

Picknett, Lynn; Prince, Clive; Prior, Stephen, *Double Standards: The Rudolf Hess Cover-up* (London, 2001)

Pryce-Jones, David, *Unity Mitford: A Quest* (London, 1976)

Pugh, Martin, *'Hurrah for the Blackshirts': Fascists and Fascism in Britain Between the Wars* (London, 2005)

—*We Danced All Night: A Social History of Britain Between the Wars* (London, 2008)

Rawson, Andrew, *Showcasing the Third Reich: The Nuremberg Rallies* (Staplehurst, 2012)

Reader, W. J., *Fifty Years of Unilever* (London, 1980)

—*Imperial Chemical Industries: A History* (Oxford, 1970–5)

Reynolds, David, *In Command of History: Churchill Fighting and Writing the Second World War* (London, 2004)

—*The creation of the Anglo-American alliance, 1937–41* (London, 1981)

Reynolds, Nicholas, *Treason Was No Crime: Ludwig Beck, Chief of the German General Staff* (London, 1976)

Rhodes James, Robert, *Anthony Eden* (London, 1986)

Roberts, Andrew, *Churchill: Walking with Destiny* (London, 2018)

—*Eminent Churchillians* (London, 1994)

— *'The Holy Fox': A Biography of Lord Halifax* (London, 1991)

Roberts, Richard W., *Schroders: Merchants and Bankers* (Basingstoke, 1992)

Robinson, John Martin, *The Travellers Club: A Bicentennial History 1819–2019* (Marlborough, 2018)

Rock, William R., *British Appeasement in the 1930s* (London, 1977)

Rose, Norman, *Harold Nicolson* (London, 2005)

— *The Cliveden Set: Portrait of an Exclusive Fraternity* (London, 2000)

— *Vansittart: Study of a Diplomat* (London, 1978)

Rudman, Stella, *Lloyd George and the Appeasement of Germany, 1919–1945* (Cambridge, 2011)

Saika, Robin, *The Red Book: The Membership List of the Right Club – 1939* (London, 2010)

Sandner, Harald, *Hitlers Herzog: Carl Eduard von Sachsen-Coburg und Gotha* (Aachen, 2010)

Sansom, C. J., *Dominion* (London, 2012)

Schwartz, Paul, *This Man Ribbentrop, His Life and Times* (New York, 1943)

Seabury, Paul, *The Wilhelmstrasse: Study of German Diplomats Under the Nazi Regime* (Westport, CT, 1954)

Seale, Patrick; McConville, Maureen, *Philby: The Long Road to Moscow* (London, 1973)

Sebba, Anne, *Battling for News: The Rise of the Woman Reporter* (London, 1994)

— *That Woman: The Life of Wallis Simpson, Duchess of Windsor* (London, 2011)

Self, Robert, *Neville Chamberlain: A Biography* (Vermont, 2006)

Sereny, Gitta, *Albert Speer – His Battle With Truth* (London, 1995)

Shakespeare, Nicholas, *Six Minutes in May: How Churchill Unexpectedly Became Prime Minister* (London, 2017)

Shepherd, Naomi, *Wilfred Israel: German Jewry's Secret Ambassador* (London, 1984)

Shepherd, Robert, *A Class Divided: Appeasement and the Road to Munich 1938* (London, 1988)

Sherwood Harris, *First to Fly: Aviation's Pioneer Days* (London, 1970)

Shirer, William L., *The Rise and Fall of the Third Reich* (London, 1961)

Simpson, A. W. Brian, *In the Highest Degree Odious: Detention Without Trial in Wartime Britain* (Oxford, 1992)

Smil, Vaclav, *Enriching the Earth: Fritz Haber, Carl Bosch, and the Transformation of World Food Production* (Cambridge, MA, 2001)

Stafford, David (ed.), *Flight from Reality: Rudolf Hess and His Mission to Scotland, 1941* (London, 2002)

Stapleton, Julia, *Sir Arthur Bryant and National History in Twentieth-Century Britain* (Lanham, MD, 2005)

Stedman, Andrew David, *Alternatives to Appeasement: Neville Chamberlain and Hitler's Germany* (London, 2011)

Steiner, Zara, *The Triumph of the Dark: European International History, 1933–1939* (Oxford, 2011)

Stewart, Graham, *Burying Caesar: Churchill, Chamberlain and the Battle for the Tory Party* (London, 1999)

Stone, Dan, *Responses to Nazism in Britain, 1933–1939: Before War and Holocaust* (Basingstoke, 2003)

Storrs, Ronald, *Dunlop in War and Peace* (London, 1946)

Stratigakos, Despina, *Hitler at Home* (New Haven, CT, 2015)

Strobl, Gerwin, *The Germanic Isle: Nazi Perceptions of Britain* (Cambridge, 2000)

Sweet, Matthew, *The West End Front: The Wartime Secrets of London's Grand Hotels* (London, 2011)

Taylor, A. J. P., *The Origins of the Second World War* (London, 1961)

Taylor, S. J., *The Great Outsiders: Northcliffe, Rothermere and the Daily Mail* (London, 1996)

Thompson, Laura, *Take Six Girls: The Lives of the Mitford Sisters* (London, 2015)

Thurlow, Richard, *Fascism in Britain: A History, 1918–85* (Oxford, 1987)

Times, The, *The History of The Times* (London, 1952)

Tinniswood, Adrian, *The Long Weekend* (London, 2016)

Tooze, Adam, *The Wages of Destruction: The Making and Breaking of the Nazi Economy* (London, 2006)

Trevor-Roper, Hugh, *The Last Days of Hitler* (London, 1947)

Tsarev, Oleg; Costello, John, *Deadly Illusions* (London, 1993)

Turner Jr., Henry Ashby, *German Big Business and the Rise of Hitler* (New York, 1985)

Tusa, Ann and John, *The Nuremberg Trial* (London, 1983)

Urbach, Karina (ed.), *European Aristocracies and the Radical Right 1918–1939* (Oxford, 2007)

—*Go-Betweens for Hitler* (Oxford, 2015)

Urban, Markus, *The Nuremberg Trials: A Short Guide* (Nuremberg, 2017)

Vincent, Paul, *The Politics of Hunger: The Allied Blockade of Germany, 1915–1919* (Ohio, 1985)

Waller, John H., *The Unseen War in Europe: Espionage and Conspiracy in the Second World War* (London, 2016)

Walters, Guy, *Berlin Games: How Hitler Stole the Olympic Dream* (London, 2006)

Wark, Wesley K., *The Ultimate Enemy: British Intelligence and Nazi Germany, 1933–1939* (Oxford, 1985)

Watson, Francis, *Dawson of Penn* (London, 1950)

Watson, Peter, *The German Genius: Europe's Third Renaissance, the Second Scientific Revolution, and the Twentieth Century* (London, 2010)

Watt, Donald Cameron, *How War Came: The Immediate Origins of the Second World War, 1938–1939* (London, 1989)

Weijers, Wouter and Manheim, Ron, et al., *Huis Wylerberg: Een expressionistisch landhuis van Otto Bartning* (Nijmegen, 1988)

Weinberg, Gerhard L., *Hitler's Foreign Policy 1933–1939: The Road to World War II* (New York, 2005)

Weitz, John, *Joachim von Ribbentrop: Hitler's diplomat* (London, 1992)

Wheeler-Bennett, John, *Special Relationships: America in Peace and War* (New York, 1975)

Whitman, James Q., *Hitler's American Model: The United States and the Making of Nazi Race Law* (Princeton, 2017)

Wilkerson, Isabel, *Caste: The Lies That Divide Us* (London, 2020)

Williamson, Philip, *Stanley Baldwin: Conservative Leadership and National Values* (Cambridge, 1999)

Wilson, Charles, *A History of Unilever: A Study in Economic Growth* (London, 1954)

Wolfers, Arnold, *Britain and France Between Two Wars: Conflicting Strategies of Peace from Versailles to World War II* (New York, 1966)

Wootton, Graham, *The Official History of the British Legion* (London, 1956)

Worsthorne, Peregrine, *In Defence of Aristocracy* (London, 2013)

Wyllie, James, *Nazi Wives: The Women at the Top of Hitler's Germany* (Cheltenham, 2019)

Ziegler, Philip, *King Edward VIII: The Official Biography* (London, 1990)

—*Legacy: Cecil Rhodes, the Rhodes Trust and Rhodes Scholarships* (New Haven, CT, 2008)

Published articles and reviews

Aster, Sidney, 'Appeasement: Before and After Revisionism', *Diplomacy and Statecraft*, vol. 19, no. 3 (September 2008), p. 443

—'Guilty Men: The Case of Neville Chamberlain', in Robert Boyce and Esmonde Robertson, (ed.), *Paths to War* (London, 1989), p. 235

Bruegel, J. W.; Stern, J. P., 'Defending the State against the Nations: The Work of J. W. Bruegel', *The Historical Journal*, vol. 28, no. 4 (December 1985), pp. 1023–7

Cannadine, David, 'Historians as Diplomats?: Roger B. Merriman, George M. Trevelyan, and Anglo-American Relations', *The New England Quarterly*, vol. 72, no. 2 (June 1999), pp. 207–31

Carr, Richard; Hart, Bradley W., 'Old Etonians, Great War demographics and the interpretations of British eugenics, c.1914–1939', *First World War Studies*, vol. 3, no. 2 (2012), pp. 217–39

Cook, Colin, 'A fascist memory: Oswald Mosley and the myth of the airman', *European Review of History*, vol. 4 (1997), pp. 147–61

Cullen, Stephen M., 'Strange Journey: The life of Dorothy Eckersley', *The Historian* (Autumn 2013)

Douglas-Hamilton, James, 'Ribbentrop and War', *Journal of Contemporary History*, vol. 5, no. 4 (1970), pp. 45–63

Ferris, John R, '"Now that the Milk is Spilt": Appeasement and the Archive on Intelligence', *Diplomacy and Statecraft*, vol. 19, no. 3 (September 2008), p. 527

Finney, Patrick, 'The romance of decline: the historiography of appeasement and British national identity', *Electronic Journal of International History* (2000)

Fleming, N. C., 'Aristocratic appeasement: Lord Londonderry, Nazi Germany, and the promotion of Anglo-German misunderstanding', *Cardiff Historical Papers* (April 2007)

Fox, Jo, 'Propaganda and the Flight of Rudolf Hess, 1941–45', *The Journal of Modern History*, vol. 83 (March 2011), pp. 78–110

Gilbert, Martin, 'Horace Wilson: Man of Munich?', *History Today*, no. 32, issue 10 (1982)

Goldman, Aaron L., 'Defence Regulation 18B: Emergency Internment of Aliens and Political Dissenters in Great Britain during World War II', *Journal of British Studies*, vol. 12, no. 2 (May 1973), pp. 120–36

—'Two Views of Germany: Neville Henderson vs. Vansittart and the Foreign Office, 1937–1939', *British Journal of International Studies*, vol. 6, no. 3 (October 1980), pp. 247–77

Gorodetsky, Gabriel, 'The Hess Affair and Anglo-Soviet Relations on the Eve of "Barbarossa"', *The English Historical Review*, vol. 101, no. 399 (April 1986), pp. 405–20

Gottlieb, Julie V.; Stibbe, Matthew, 'Peace at any Price: The Visit of Nazi Women's Leader Gertrud Scholtz-Klink to London in March 1939 and the Response of British Women Activists', *Women's History Review* (2016)

Haase, Christian, 'In Search of a European Settlement: Chatham House and British-German Relations, 1920–55', *European History Quarterly*, vol. 37, no. 3 (2007), pp. 371–97

Hayes, Peter, 'Carl Bosch and Carl Krauch: Chemistry and the Political Economy of Germany, 1925–1945', *The Journal of Economic History*, vol. 47, no. 2 (1987), pp. 353–63

Hinton, James, 'Militant Housewives: the British Housewives' League and the Attlee Government', *History Workshop Journal*, issue 38, no. 47 (1994)

Hitchens, Christopher, 'Lucky Kim', *London Review of Books*, vol. 17, no. 4 (February 1995)

Hoffmann, Peter, 'The Question of Western Allied Co-Operation with the German Anti-Nazi Conspiracy, 1938–1944', *The Historical Journal*, vol. 34, no. 2 (June 1991), pp. 437–64

Holman, Brett, 'The Air Panic of 1935: British Press Opinion between Disarmament and Rearmament', *Journal of Contemporary History*, vol. 46, no. 2 (April 2011), pp. 288–307

Howard, N. P., 'The Social and Political Consequences of the Allied Food Blockade of Germany, 1918–19', *German History*, vol. 11, no. 2 (June 1993), pp. 161–88

Jones, Geoffrey, 'The growth and performance of British multinational firms before 1939: the case of Dunlop', *The Economic History Review*, vol. 37, no. 1 (February 1984), p. 48

Jones, Stephen G., 'State Intervention in Sport and Leisure in Britain between the Wars', *Journal of Contemporary History*, vol. 22, no. 1 (January 1987), pp. 163–82

Jupp, Peter, review of N. C. Fleming, *The Marquess of Londonderry. Aristocracy, Power and Politics in Britain and Ireland*, Institute of Historical Research, www.history.ac.uk

Klemperer, Klemens von, 'Adam von Trott zu Solz and Resistance Foreign', *Central European History*, vol. 14, no. 4 (December 1981), pp. 351–61

—'Hans Rothfels, 1891–1976', *Central European History*, vol. IX, no. 4 (December 1976)

—review of Joachim Scholtyseck, *Robert Bosch und der lierale Wilderstand gegen Hitler, 1933 bis 1945* (Munich, 1999), *Central European History*, vol. 34, no. 3 (2001), p. 450

Marks, Sally, 'Mistakes and Myths: The Allies, Germany, and the Versailles Treaty, 1918–1921', *The Journal of Modern History*, vol. 85, no. 3 (September 2013), pp. 632–59

McIvor, Arthur, 'A Crusade for Capitalism: The Economic League, 1919–1939', *Journal of Contemporary History*, vol. 23, no. 4 (October 1988), pp. 631–55

Morgan, Kenneth O., 'Lloyd George and Germany', *The Historical Journal*, vol. 39, no. 3 (September 1996), pp. 755–66

Namier, L. B., 'Erich and Theo Kordt: Resisters after the Event', *History Today*, vol. 1 (1951)

Neville, Peter, 'The Appointment of Sir Nevile Henderson, 1937: Design or Blunder?', *Journal of Contemporary History*, vol. 33, no. 4 (October 1998), pp. 609–19

Newton, Scott, 'The Anglo-German connection and the political economy of appeasement', *Diplomacy & Statecraft*, vol. 2, no. 3 (1991), pp. 178–207

Orwell, George, 'Who are the War Criminals?', *Tribune* (October 1943)

Peden, G. C., 'Sir Horace Wilson and Appeasement', *The Historical Journal*, vol. 53, issue 4 (December 2010), pp. 983–1014

Reader, W. J., 'Imperial Chemical Industries and the State 1926–1945', in Barry Supple (ed.), *Essays in British Business History* (Oxford, 1977)

Reynolds, David, 'FDR on the British: a Postscript', *Proceedings of the Massachusetts Historical Society*, series 3, vol. 90 (1978), pp. 106–10

—'Lord Lothian and Anglo-American relations, 1939–40', *Transactions of the American Philosophical Society*, vol. 73, part 2 (1983), pp. 1–65

Ritter, Ernst, 'Die erste Deutsch-Englische Gesellschaft (1935–1939)', in *Aus der Arbeit der Archive* (Boppard, 1989)

Roberts, Priscilla, 'Lord Lothian and the Atlantic World', *The Historian*, vol. 66, no. 1 (2004), pp. 97–127

Rofe, J. Simon, 'Lord Lothian, 1939–1940' in Michael F. Hopkins, Saul Kelly and John W. Young (ed.), *The Washington Embassy: British Ambassadors to the United States, 1939–77* (London, 2009)

Rüger, Jan, 'Revisiting the Anglo-German Antagonism', *The Journal of Modern History*, vol. 83, no. 3 (September 2011), pp. 579–617

Stafford, Paul, 'Political Autobiography and the Art of the Plausible: R. A. Butler at the Foreign Office, 1938–1939', *The Historical Journal*, vol. 28, no. 4 (December 1985), pp. 901–22

Stone, Lawrence, 'Prosopography', Daedalus, vol. 100, no. 1, *Historical Studies Today* (Winter, 1971), pp. 46–79

Strang, G. Bruce, 'The Spirit of Ulysses? Ideology and British Appeasement in the 1930s', *Diplomacy and Statecraft*, vol. 19, no. 3 (September 2008), p. 481

Thomas, Donald E., Jr., 'Diesel, Father and Son: Social Philosophies of Technology', *Technology and Culture*, vol. 19, no. 3 (July 1978), pp. 376–93

Waddington, G. T., '"An idyllic and unruffled atmosphere of complete Anglo-German misunderstanding": Aspects of the Operations of the Dienststelle Ribbentrop in Great Britain, 1934–1938', *History*, vol. 82, no. 265 (January 1997), pp. 44–72

Wark, Wesley K., 'British Intelligence on the German Air Force and Aircraft Industry, 1933–1939', *The Historical Journal*, vol. 25, no. 3 (September 1982), pp. 627–48

Watt, Donald Cameron, 'Appeasement: The Rise of a Revisionist School?', *Political Quarterly*, vol. 36, issue 2 (1965), pp. 191–213

—'Chamberlain's Ambassadors' in M. L. Dockrill and B. J. C. McKercher (ed.), *Diplomacy and World Power* (Cambridge, 1996)

Webber, G. C., 'Patterns of Membership and Support for the British Union of Fascists', *Journal of Contemporary History*, vol. 19, no. 4 (October 1984)

Williamson, Philip, 'The Conservative Party, Fascism and Anti-Fascism 1918–1939', in *Varieties of anti-fascism: Britain in the inter-war period* (Basingstoke, 2010)

Wubs, Ben, 'Guns and margarine. Or how the Nazis disliked margarine, but could not afford to attack the Dutch Margarine Trust', *14th Annual Conference EBHA* (August 2010)

Unpublished Ph.D. theses

Glenn Zander, Patrick, 'Right Modern Technology, Nation, and Britain's Extreme Right in the Interwar Period (1919–1940)', Georgia Institute of Technology (2009)

May, Alex, 'The Round Table, 1910–66', University of Oxford (1995)

Spicer, Charles, '"Ambulant Amateurs": the rise and fade of the Anglo-German Fellowship', University of London (2018)

Stewart, N. M., 'Fellow travellers of the right and foreign policy debate in Scotland 1935–39', University of Edinburgh (1995)

Reference works

British Electoral Facts: 1832–1987, compiled and edited by F. W. S. Craig, Parliamentary Research Services (Dartmouth, 1989)

Crockfords Clerical Directory 1935, published by Horace Cox (London, 1860–)

Dictionary of Business Biography, edited by David J. Jeremy and published by Butterworths in five volumes (London, 1984–6)

Hansard, hansard.parliament.uk

Oxford Dictionary of National Biography, published by Oxford University Press (Oxford, 1900–), available online at www.oxforddnb.com

The Times House of Commons Guide 1935, The Times Office (London, 1880–)

Who Was Who, published by A. & C. Black, available online at www.ukwhoswho.com

Who's Who, published by A. & C. Black (London, 1936)

Who's Who in Nazi Germany, Robert S. Wistrich (London, 2001)

NOTES

INTRODUCTION

1 Camus, Albert, 'Create Dangerously' lecture, 14 December 1957, University of Uppsala, Sweden, in *Resistance, Rebellion, and Death*, trans. Justin O'Brien (New York, 1995).

2 James, *Aristocrats: Power, Grace and Decadence*, p. 371.

3 Knightly, *Philby: KGB Master Spy*, p. 51.

4 E.g. the film adaptation of *The Remains of the Day* (1993), *Six Minutes to Midnight* (2020), Stephen Poliakoff's film *Glorious 39* (2009), television series such as *Cambridge Spies* (2003), *Upstairs Downstairs* (2010–12) and *The Halcyon* (2017) and historical novels such as William Boyd's *Any Human Heart* (2002), C. J. Sansom's *Dominion* (2012) and Ken Follett's *Winter of the World* (2012).

PROLOGUE: LLOYD GEORGE'S NAZI

1 Conwell-Evans, Memoir, CONWELL.

2 Griffiths, *Fellow Travellers*, p. 112; Morgan, K., 'Lloyd George and Germany', pp. 755–66; Kershaw, *Making Friends*, p. 62; Roberts, *Eminent Churchillians*, p. 300.

3 Bouverie, *Appeasing Hitler*, pp. 49, 113.

4 Gilbert to Pamela Turner, 22 November 1968, CONWELL.

5 Urbach, *Go-Betweens for Hitler*, p. 300.

6 Gilbert, *Churchill*, vol. V companion, part 3, p. 1592.

7 Conwell-Evans, *None So Blind*, p. 154.

8 Meehan, *The Unnecessary* War, p. 2.

9 Conwell-Evans, Memoir, CONWELL.

10 Inglis, *The Children's War*, p. 3.

11 Cowles, *Looking for Trouble*, p. 268.

12 Rhodes James, *Chips*, p. 209.

13 Nicolson, *Diaries and Letters*, p. 415.

14 Conwell-Evans, *None So Blind*, p. 197.

15 Conwell-Evans to Lloyd George, 7 September 1939, LG.

1. DINNER ON THE TERRACE WITH HIMMLER

1   Jones, *Diary with Letters*, p. 198.
2   Tennant, *True Account*, p. 175.
3   Gisevius, *To the Bitter End*, p. 158.
4   Tennant, *True Account*, p. 176.
5   Ibid., p. 151.
6   Tennant to Davidson, 13 November 1933, DAV.
7   *Time and Tide*, 1 February 1958.
8   Tennant, 'Confidential report to prime minister on E. W. D. Tennant's Relations with Herr von Ribbentrop', 4 July 1939, PREM 1/335 C497340, TNA.
9   Tennant, *True Account*, p. 74.
10 See Carr and Hart, 'Old Etonians, Great War demographics and the interpretations of British eugenics'.
11 War Cabinet, *Combined Report on Food Conditions in Germany during the period 12 January–12 February 1919*, 16 February 1919, FO 608/222/18, TNA.
12 Tennant, 'Confidential report to prime minister on E. W. D. Tennant's Relations with Herr von Ribbentrop', 4 July 1939, PREM 1/335 C497340, TNA.
13 Tennant, *True Account*, pp. 153–9.
14 Davidson report on lunch, 20 November 1933, DAV.
15 Tennant, *True Account*, p. 164.
16 *The Times*, 28 November 1933.
17 Tennant, *True Account*, p. 169.

2. ROAST CHICKEN AT THE CHANCELLERY

1   Stratigakos, *Hitler at Home*, p. 25.
2   Tennant, *True Account*, pp. 185–6.
3   Tennant to Davidson, 13 November 1933, DAV.
4   Ward Price, *I Knew these Dictators*, p. 30.
5   Bryant, *The Man and the Hour*, p. 130.
6   Tennant, *True Account*, pp. 186–8.
7   Martin Gilbert, handwritten note, 26 December 1962, CONWELL.
8   Lothian to Conwell-Evans, 17 December 1934, KERR/NRS.
9   Lothian to Conwell-Evans, 24 December 1934, KERR/NRS.
10 Lothian to Conwell-Evans, 17 December 1934; Conwell-Evans to Lothian, 8 January 1935, KERR/NRS.
11 *The Times*, 11 April 1936.
12 Tennant, *True Account*, p. 194.
13 Simon, *Retrospect*, p. 197; Salomon to Isidore Warski, 29 April 1937, ACC.
14 *DGFP*, Series C, vol. III, no. 445, p. 837.
15 Butler, *Lothian*, p. 197.

16 Lothian to Allen, 18 October 1935, KERR/NRS.

17 Conwell-Evans to Lothian, 8 January 1935, KERR/NRS.

18 Martin Robinson, *The Travellers Club*, p. 232.

19 Conwell-Evans, Note of interview with Herr Hitler, 29 January 1935, CONWELL.

20 Conwell-Evans to Lothian, 10 August 1935, KERR/NRS.

21 *The Times*, 31 January and 1 February 1935.

22 Conwell-Evans to Lothian, 23 June 1935, CONWELL.

23 Lothian to Simon, 17 February 1935, KERR/NRS.

24 Tennant report, 17 February 1935, DAV.

25 Conwell-Evans to Lothian, 1 March 1935, KERR/NRS.

26 Kennedy, *Journals*, p. 177.

27 Simon, *Retrospect*, p. 201.

28 Schweppenburg, *Critical Years*, pp. 33–4

29 Conwell-Evans, *None So Blind*, p. 36.

30 Simon, *Retrospect*, p. 202.

31 Conwell-Evans, *None So Blind*, p. 31.

32 Tennant to Lloyd George, 3 April 1935, LG.

33 Tennant to Lloyd George, 12 May 1935, LG.

3. MARGARINE, RUBBER AND GOLD

1 Newton, *Profits*, p. 9.

2 D'Arcy Cooper, 'Germany's economic policy: an attempt at an interpretation', *Progress*, vol. 35, no. 203, pp. 1–6.

3 Conwell-Evans to Lothian, 13 March 1935, CONWELL.

4 The Anglo-German Fellowship launch brochure, KV5/3 C 440756, TNA.

5 For more on the predecessors see Spicer, Charles, 'Ambulant Amateurs', pp. 28–34.

6 Conwell-Evans to Lothian, 13 March 1935, CONWELL.

7 Reader, 'ICI and the State', pp. 237–8.

8 See Tooze, *Wages*, p. 133.

9 Roberts, *Schroders*, pp. 155–6.

10 The Anglo-German Fellowship launch brochure, KV5/3 C 440756, TNA.

11 Urbach, *Go-Betweens*, p. 203.

12 Heuss, *Robert Bosch*, p. 542.

13 Hayes, *Industry and Ideology*, pp. 90–2.

14 Report on Anglo-German Fellowship, Special Branch, Metropolitan Police, 5 April 1935, KV5/3 C 440756, TNA.

4. THE PRINCE AND THE POPPY

1 *The Times*, 1 June 1935.

2 Ibid., 4 June 1935.

3   MacDonald letter to Conwell-Evans, 10 June 1935, CONWELL.

4   Conwell-Evans, *None So Blind*, p. 36.

5   Halifax, *Fullness of Days*, p. 181.

6   Allport, *Britain at Bay*, p. 44.

7   Gibbs, *Ordeal in England*, p. 25.

8   *DGFP*, Series C, vol. IV, no. 27, p. 49.

9   *The Times*, 12 June 1935.

10 Harding, *Keeping Faith*, p. 149.

11 *The Times*, 13 June 1935.

12 *Hansard*, HC Deb, 19 June 1935, vol. 303, col. 340.

13 Windsor, *A King's Story*, p. 236.

14 Conwell-Evans to Lothian, 23 June 1935, CONWELL.

15 Kershaw, *Hubris*, p. 558.

16 *The Times*, 15 July 1935.

17 Schmidt, *Hitler's Interpreter*, p. 37.

18 Connell, *Manifest Destiny*, p. 90.

19 Mount Temple draft speech, 1 April 1933, BR 81.

5. BEER AND SAUSAGE AT NUREMBERG

1   Bloch, *Ribbentrop*, p. 76.

2   Williamson, *Goodbye*, p. 234.

3   Tennant to Christie, 23 August 1935, CHRS/01/02.

4   Tennant to Ribbentrop, 7 September 1935, BR 81.

5   Williamson, *Goodbye*, p. 239; Burn, *Turned Towards the Sun*, p. 74.

6   Conwell-Evans to Lothian, 25 September 1935, KERR/NRS.

7   See Whitman, *Hitler's American Model* and Wilkerson, *Caste*.

8   Tennant report to Mount Temple, September 1935, BR 81.

9   Tennant, *True Account*, p. 173.

10 Conwell-Evans to Lothian, 25 September 1935, KERR/NRS.

11 Tennant, *Nuremberg Report*, September 1935, BR 81.

12 Conwell-Evans, 'Report of an address on impressions of Germany given at a private gathering in London', October 1933, KERR/NRS.

13 Kennedy to Dawson, 12 March 1936, CONWELL.

14 *Pittsburgh Press*, 27 July 1930.

15 Conwell-Evans to Rosenberg, September 1933, PREM1.

16 Conwell-Evans to Rosenberg, 22 April 1934, PREM1 (emphasis in the original).

17 Rosenberg to Conwell-Evans, 24 April 1934, PREM1.

18 Tennant to Mount Temple, 24 September 1935, BR 81.

19 Conwell-Evans, *None So Blind*, p. 42.

6. WHISKY WITH GÖRING

1 *The Times*, 24 November 1971.
2 Michael Christie, 'Obituary for MG Christie', privately printed, Christie family.
3 Jones, *The War in the Air*, vol. 2, pp. 124–132.
4 Burge, *Annals of 100 Squadron*, p. 6.
5 Ibid., p. 68.
6 Ferris, *Intelligence and Strategy*, p. 61.
7 Christie to Newall, 17 November 1928, CHRS/01/01.
8 Conwell-Evans, *None So Blind*, p. ix and pp. 5–6.
9 Ibid., p. 19.
10 Ibid., pp. 16–7.
11 Conwell-Evans, *None So Blind*, introduction, p. x; Ferris, *Intelligence and Strategy*, p. 64.

7. SWASTIKAS OVER WHITE HART LANE

1 *Hansard*, HC Deb, 24 October 1935, vol. 305, col. 357.
2 Tennant to Lloyd George, 25 October 1935, LG.
3 Wright to Budding, 25 May 1937, GBR/0014/PIRI 1/4.
4 Waddington, 'Aspects', p. 64.
5 Harding, J. (2017), 'The Nazis at Tottenham: Why did the swastika fly at White Hart Lane?' *FourFourTwo* [online], http://www.fourfourtwo.com/features/nazis-tottenham-why-did-swastika-fly-white-hart-lane (accessed 26 January 2022).
6 *Manchester Guardian*, 5 December 1935.
7 *The Times*, 6 December 1935.
8 Ibid., 13 January 1936.
9 Gilbert, *Rumbold*, p. 452.
10 *DBFP*, Second Series, vol. XII, no. 440, pp. 511–2.
11 Phipps to the King, 8 January 1936, PHPP.
12 *The Observer*, 29 December 1935.
13 Wootton, *British Legion*, p. 194.
14 Windsor, *A King's Story*, p. 178.
15 Ziegler, *Edward VIII*, p. 267.
16 Donaldson, *Edward VIII*, p. 198.

8. VISTAS OF UNLIMITED AGGRESSION

1 *DBFP*, Second Series, vol. XVI, no. 363, p. 502.
2 *Hansard*, HC Deb, 30 July 1934, vol. 292, col. 2340.
3 Conwell-Evans, Memoir, CONWELL.
4 Conwell-Evans to Lothian, 17 March 1935, CONWELL.
5 Tennant, Memorandum, 2 February 1936, PREM 1/335 C497340, TNA.

6   Kershaw, *Nemesis*, p. xxxvi.

7   Shirer, *Berlin Diary*, p. 49.

8   Conwell-Evans, *None So Blind*, p.52; Kershaw, *Hubris*, p. 588.

9   Maisky, *The Maisky Diaries*, vol. 1, p. 162.

10 Wright to Budding, 25 May 1937, GBR/0014/PIRI 1/4.

11 *DGFP*, Series C, vol. V, no. 66, p. 92.

12 Conwell-Evans, *None So Blind*, p. 54.

13 Ribbentrop, Memoirs, p. 58.

14 *New York Times*, 12 April 1936.

9. MAYFAIR RUSHING HITLERWARDS

1   Bruce Lockhart, *Diaries*, 15 July 1936.

2   *Sunday Times*, 31 May 1936.

3   Viktoria Luise, *Kaiser's daughter*, p. 127.

4   Conwell-Evans to Lothian, 25 June 1936, KERR/SNR.

5   James Douglas-Hamilton, 'Hess and the Haushofers', in Stafford, *Flight*, p. 81.

6   *The Times*, 15 July 1936.

7   *The Tatler*, 19 July 1936.

8   *DBFP*, Second Series, vol. XVII, no. 365, p. 531.

9   Colvin, *Vansittart in Office*, p. 109.

10 Rhodes James, *Chips*, pp. 108–11.

11 *DBFP*, Second Series, vol. XVII, p. 758.

12 *The Times*, 27 August 1936.

13 Ibid., 19 August 1936.

14 *DBFP*, Second Series, vol. XVII, p. 769.

15 Hart-Davis, *Hitler's Games*, p. 203.

10. COFFEE WITH HITLER

1   Conwell-Evans, *None So Blind*, p. 162.

2   *Daily Express*, 17 September 1936; *News Chronicle*, 21 September 1936.

3   Sylvester, *The Real Lloyd George*, p. 192.

4   Conwell-Evans to Lothian, 22 July 1936, KERR/NRS.

5   Sylvester, *The Real Lloyd George*, pp. 192–3.

6   Conwell-Evans, 'Notes of a conversation between Mr Lloyd George & Herr Hitler', CONWELL.

7   *Country Life*, 28 March 1936.

8   Watson, *Dawson of Penn*, p. 289.

9   Morgan, *Lloyd George*, p. 188.

10 Conwell-Evans, 'Notes of a conversation between Mr Lloyd George & Herr Hitler', CONWELL.

11 Maisky, *The Maisky Diaries*, vol. 1, p. 206.

12 Conwell-Evans, 'Notes of a conversation between Mr Lloyd George & Herr Hitler', CONWELL.

13 Jones, *Diary with Letters*, p. 246.

14 Sylvester, *Life with Lloyd George*, p. 148.

15 Schmidt, *Hitler's Interpreter*, p. 66.

16 Maisky, *The Maisky Diaries*, vol. 1, p. 206.

17 *The Times*, 5 September 1936.

18 Schmidt, *Hitler's Interpreter*, pp. 64–5.

19 Jones, *Diary with Letters*, p. 249.

20 Ibid., p. 258.

21 Conwell-Evans, 'Notes of a conversation between Mr Lloyd George & Herr Hitler', CONWELL.

22 Jones, *Diary with Letters*, p. 20.

23 Ibid., p. 254.

24 Pride, *Why Lloyd George met Hitler*, pp. 21, 34.

25 Lentin, *Lloyd George*, p. 103.

26 Schmidt, *Hitler's Interpreter*, p. 64.

27 *Daily Express*, 17 September 1936.

28 Tennant to Lloyd George, 17 September 1936, LG.

29 Conwell-Evans to Sylvester, 21 October 1936, LG. The Lloyd George family hung Hitler's signed photograph in their downstairs lavatory. Author's 2013 interview with Lloyd George's great-grandson.

30 Bloch, *Ribbentrop*, p. 105; Morgan, 'Lloyd George and Germany', p. 764.

31 Churchill, *The Gathering Storm*, pp. 224–5.

32 Kenneth Morgan, *Lloyd George*, p. 188.

33 Parker, *Chamberlain*, p. 316; Lentin, *Lloyd George*, p. 99.

34 Maisky, *The Maisky Diaries*, vol. 1, p. 292.

35 Statement issued by Churchill to the press responding to remarks made by Hitler about Churchill, 6 November 1938, 9/133/18-19, CHAR.

11. PREACHING BROTHERLY LOVE TO A ROGUE ELEPHANT

1 https://www.presidency.ucsb.edu/documents/address-chautauqua-ny.

2 Bloch, *Ribbentrop*, p. 110.

3 *DBFP*, Second Series, vol. XVII, no. 365.

4 Ibid., p. 767.

5 Ibid., no. 317.

6 Bloch, *Ribbentrop*, p. 101.

7 Ustinov, *Dear Me*, p. 59.

8 Rose, *Vansittart*, p. 77 fn.

9   Eden, *Facing the Dictators*, p. 140.

10 Cowles, *Looking for Trouble*, p. 247.

11 Wilkinson, *Baldwin*, p. 2; Eden, *Facing the Dictators*, p. 410.

12 Wright to Budding, 25 May 1937, GBR/0014/PIRI 1/4.

13 *The Times*, 16 December 1936.

14 Pitt-Rivers to Wright, 6 April 1937, GBR/0014/PIRI 1/4.

15 Wright signed statement, 11 May 1938, GBR/0014/PIRI 1/4.

16 *Hansard*, HL Deb, 24 February 1937, vol. 104, col. 309.

17 AGF, *1935–36 Annual Report*, p. 3, KV5/3 C440756, TNA.

18 Conwell-Evans, *None So Blind*, p. 31.

19 Conwell-Evans to Mount Temple, 18 May 1937, BR 81.

20 Henderson, *Water under the Bridges*, p. 212.

21 Conwell-Evans, *None So Blind*, p. 93.

22 *The Times*, 2 June 1937.

23 Henderson, *Failure of a Mission*, pp. 19–20.

24 Maisky, *The Maisky Diaries*, vol. 1, p. 197.

25 AGF, *Monthly Journal*, June 1937. KV5/3 C440756, TNA.

26 Harvey, *Diplomatic Diaries*, p. 41.

27 Vansittart minute, 2 June 1937, C4047/4047/18, TNA.

28 Kershaw, *Nemesis*, p. 27.

29 Conwell-Evans, *None So Blind*, pp. 68–81.

12. THE BRICKENDROP CIRCUS

1   AGF, *Monthly Journal*, June 1937.

2   Chamberlain, *Diary Letters*, vol. 4, p. 249.

3   Tennant to Chamberlain, 1 July 1939, TNA.

4   *Western Morning News and Daily Gazette*, 5 April 1937.

5   Spitzy, *How We Squandered The Reich*, p. 102.

6   Channon (ed. Heffer), *Chips*, p. 699.

7   *News Chronicle*, 15 May 1937; *Sunday Times*, 16 May 1937.

8   Putlitz, *The Putlitz Dossier*, p. 130.

9   *Sunday Times*, 16 May 1937.

10 Channon (ed. Heffer), *Chips*, p. 678.

11 *DBFP*, Second Series, vol. XVIII, no. 495, pp. 747–50.

12 Conwell-Evans to Mount Temple, 18 May 1937, BR 81.

13 *DGFP*, Series C, vol. VI, no. 370, pp. 757–8.

14 Butler, *Lothian*, p. 218.

15 Maisky, *The Maisky Diaries*, vol. 1, pp. 182, 194.

16 Conwell-Evans to Mount Temple, 18 May 1937, BR 81.

17 Conwell-Evans, Memoir, CONWELL.

18 Bloch, *Ribbentrop*, p. 131.

19 Weinberg, *Hitler's Foreign Policy*, p. 335.

20 Chamberlain, *Diary Letters*, vol. 4, p.255; *Hansard*, HC Deb, 19 July 1937, vol. 326, col. 1783; *The Times*, 22 June 1937.

21 Conwell-Evans, *None So Blind*, p. 82.

22 *DBFP*, Second Series, vol. XIX, no. 92, pp. 173–5.

13. SHARKS, STALIN AND INSPECTOR MORSE

1   Paul Einzig, *Appeasement Before, During and After the War*, p. 18.

2   Wright to Conwell-Evans, 10 May 1937, GBR/0014/PIRI 1/4.

3   Wright to le Blount Kidd, 7 May 1937; GBR/0014/PIRI 1/4.

4   Wright to Budding, 25 May 1937, GBR/0014/PIRI 1/4.

5   Griffiths, *Fellow Travellers*, pp. 185–6 and *What did...*, p. 3. Griffiths, *Patriotism Perverted*, p. 35.

6   Pitt-Rivers to Beazley, 28 September 1937, GBR/0014/PIRI 1/4.

7   Philby, *My Silent War*, p. 14.

8   Davenport-Hines, *Enemies Within*, p. 210.

9   Philby, *Silent War*, p. 14.

10 Andrew, *MI5*, p. 169.

11 Borovik, *Philby Files*, p. 59.

12 MI5 report on AGF, 16 August 1937, KV5/3 C440756, TNA.

13 Report following Home Office Warrant on the Dienststelle Ribbentrop, 16 October 1937, KV5/6 C492109, TNA.

14 For more on Dickson see Hemming, *M: Maxwell Knight*, p. 229.

15 MI5 report on AGF, 22 November 1937, KV5/3 C440756, TNA.

16 MI5 report, 30 May 1938, KV2/1280 C503281, TNA.

14. SENDING A CURATE TO VISIT A TIGER

1   *DBFP*, Second Series, vol. XIX, no. 160, pp. 275–83.

2   *The Times*, 3 December 1937.

3   Kirkpatrick, *The Inner Circle*, pp. 96–8.

4   Birkenhead, *Halifax*, p. 372.

5   Kirkpatrick, *The Inner Circle*, pp. 100–1.

6   Conwell-Evans, *None So Blind*, p. 103.

7   Kirkpatrick, *The Inner Circle*, p. 102.

8   Birkenhead, *Halifax*, p. 372.

9   Churchill, *Gathering Storm*, p. 224.

10 R. Lloyd George, *David & Winston*, p. 220.

11 Schmidt, *Hitler's Interpreter*, p. 76.

12 Roberts, *Holy Fox*, pp. 67–74.

13 AGF, *Monthly Journal*, December 1937.

14   *Country Life*, 11 December 1937.

15   *Manchester Guardian*, 3 December 1937.

16   *The Times*, 3 December 1937.

17   Halifax to Conwell-Evans, 6 December 1937, CONWELL.

18   AGF, *Monthly Journal*, December 1937.

15. CLEARING THE DECKS

1   Conwell-Evans, *None So Blind*, p. 111.

2   Gilbert, *Churchill*, vol. V companion, part 3, p. 882.

3   Phillips, *Fighting Churchill, Appeasing Hitler*, p. 51.

4   Conwell-Evans, *None So Blind*, p. 114.

5   Bloch, *Ribbentrop*, pp. 146–8.

6   Christie report, early 1938, CHRS.

7   Cadogan, *Diaries*, p. 59.

8   Conwell-Evans, *None So Blind*, p. 121.

9   Christie report, March 1938, CHRS.

10   *The Times*, 11 March 1938.

11   Churchill, *Gathering Storm*, p. 243.

12   *DBFP*, Third Series, vol. I, no. 44, p. 21.

13   Chamberlain, *Diary Letters*, vol. 4, p. 304.

14   Cowles, *Looking for Trouble*, p. 117.

15   Christie report, March 1938, CHRS.

16   Conwell-Evans, *None So Blind*, p. 123.

17   Mosley, *Downstream*, p. 175.

18   Gilbert, *Churchill*, vol. v (companion), p. 1032.

19   Roberts, *Holy Fox*, pp. 104–5.

20   Henderson, *Failure of a Mission*, p. 48.

21   Vansittart to Halifax, 8 July 1938, FO C7007/1180/18, TNA.

22   Faber, *Munich*, p. 185.

23   Cabinet Minutes, 22 June 1938, p. 7, CAB/23/94, TNA.

24   Tennant, *True Account*, p. 206.

16. THE OSTER CONSPIRACY

1   For more on the Oster conspiracy and the German resistance to Hitler see: Parssinen, *Oster*; Reynolds, *Treason Was No Crime*; Klemperer, *German Resistance*; Meehan, *Unnecessary War*; Rothfels, *The German Opposition to Hitler*; Hoffmann, *History of the German Resistance*; Young, *The 'X' Documents*.

2   Conwell-Evans, Memoir, CONWELL.

3   See Ibid.

4   Conwell-Evans, *None So Blind*, p. 139.

5   Christie to Vansittart, 10 August 1938, and 19 August 1938, CHRS.
6   Butler, *Lothian*, p. 237 fn.
7   Chamberlain, *Diary Letters*, vol. 4, p. 338.
8   Harvey, *Diplomatic Diaries*, p. 168.
9   Peden, 'Sir Horace Wilson and Appeasement', p. 996.
10   Vansittart memorandum to Halifax, 30 August 1938, VNST.
11   Conwell-Evans to Halifax, 31 August 1938, HALIFAX.
12   For detailed chronologies of the Munich crisis see Faber, *Munich*; Roberts, *Holy Fox*; Cadogan, *Diaries*; Harvey, *Diaries*; Middlemas, *Diplomacy*.
13   Chamberlain, *Diary Letters*, vol. 4, p. 342.
14   Thomas Inskip diary, 7 September 1938, INKP; Cadogan, *Diaries*, p. 95.

17. TEA AT NUREMBERG

1   Cowles, *Looking for Trouble*, p. 147.
2   Mitford, *The Pursuit of Love*, p. 113.
3   Cowles, *Looking for Trouble*, p. 155.
4   See *DGFP*, Series D, vol. II, no. 482, pp. 765–80.
5   Conwell-Evans, *None So Blind*, p. 141.
6   *DBFP*, Third Series, vol. II, no. 839, pp. 298–300.
7   *DGFP*, Series D, vol. II, no. 482, p. 766.
8   Cited in Parssinen, *The Oster Conspiracy*, p. 101 (emphasis added).
9   Hoffmann, *The German Resistance*, p. 65.
10   Cadogan, *Diaries*, pp. 94–5.
11   Faber, *Munich*, p. 238.
12   Hoffmann, *The German Resistance*, p. 67.
13   Cadogan, *Diaries*, p. 96; *DBFP*, Third Series, vol. II, no. 815, pp. 277–8.
14   *Daily Mail*, 10 September 1938.
15   *DBFP*, Third Series, vol. II, no. 818, p. 279.
16   Ibid., p. 280.
17   Cowles, *Looking for Trouble*, p. 156.
18   Brocket report to Wilson, 10 September 1938, PREM 1/249/65-70, TNA; Cowles, *Looking for Trouble*, p. 157.
19   Brocket report to Wilson, 10 September 1938, PREM 1/249/65-70, TNA.
20   Tennant, *True Account*, p. 206.
21   Conwell-Evans handwritten notes, CONWELL.
22   Conwell-Evans memorandum to Vansittart, Halifax and Chamberlain, 14 September 1938, CONWELL.
23   Conwell-Evans, *None So Blind*, p. 144.
24   Harvey, *Diplomatic Diaries*, p. 179.
25   Chamberlain, *Diary Letters*, vol. 4, p. 344.
26   Meehan, *Unnecessary War*, p. 14.

27 DBFP, Third Series, vol. II, no. 849, p. 306.
28 DBFP, Third Series, vol. II, no. 862, p. 314.

18. PLAN Z

1   Butler, *Lothian*, p. 225.
2   Maisky, *The Maisky Diaries*, vol. 1, p. 328.
3   Harvey, *Diplomatic Diaries*, p. 180.
4   Chamberlain, *Diary Letters*, vol. 4, pp. 346–8.
5   Faber, *Munich*, p. 325.
6   Cadogan, *Diaries*, p. 105.
7   Roberts, *Holy Fox*, p. 117.
8   Harvey, *Diplomatic Diaries*, 29 September 1938.
9   Conwell-Evans, *None So Blind*, p. 148.
10 *The Times*, 28 September 1938.
11 Tennant, *True Account*, pp. 207–8.
12 Faber, *Munich*, p. 419.
13 Chamberlain, *Diary Letters*, vol. 4, p. 351.
14 McDonough, *Hitler Years, Triumph 1933–1939*, p. 325.
15 Conwell-Evans, *None So Blind*, p. 162.
16 Parssinen, *Oster*, p. 172; Hoffmann, *German Resistance*, p. 96.
17 Hoffmann, *German Resistance*, p. 96; Parssinen, *Oster*, p. xvi.
18 Ferris, *Intelligence and Strategy*, p. 83.
19 Conwell-Evans, *None So Blind*, p. 149.
20 Vansittart memorandum to Halifax, 19 October 1938, FO C12655, TNA; Conwell-Evans, *None So Blind*, p. 157.
21 Conwell-Evans, *None So Blind*, p. 149.
22 Conwell-Evans, Memoir, CONWELL.
23 Curry, John, *The Security Service*, p. 121 fn.

19. THE NIGHT OF BROKEN GLASS

1   *The Times*, 20 October 1938.
2   MI5 report on AGF dinner at Claridge's, 24 October 1938, KV 5/3 C440756, TNA.
3   *DBFP*, Third Series, vol. III, no. 313., pp. 275–7.
4   Gilbert, *Kristallnacht*, p. 16.
5   Vansittart to Halifax, 4 January 1939, TNA.
6   *DBFP*, Third Series, vol. III, no. 313., pp. 275–7.
7   Steiner, *The Triumph of the Dark*, p. 679.
8   Conwell-Evans, *None So Blind*, p. 157.
9   *DBFP*, Third Series, vol. III, no. 306, pp. 270–1.

10 Self, *Chamberlain*, p. 345.

11 Report by Gaertner on the AGF, 23 November 1938, KV5/3, TNA.

12 *Daily Telegraph*, 19 November 1938.

13 *The Times*, 22 November 1938; AGF letter to membership, 18 November 1938, KV5/3, TNA.

14 Bruce Lockhart, *Diaries*, 5 October 1935.

15 *Evening Standard*, 19 November 1938.

16 Moskowitz, *The American Jewish Year Book*, vol. 41, pp. 233–7.

17 Bloomfield to Mount Temple, 19 November 1938, BR 81.

18 *The Times*, 13 November 1938.

19 Carroll to Pitt-Rivers, 10 December 1938, GBR/0014/PIRI 1/4.

20 See Griffiths, *Travellers*, p. 340 and *Patriotism Perverted*, p. 37; *Evening Standard*, 13 January 1939; Haxey, *Tory MP*, p. 198; Kershaw is however spot on, see: *Making Friends with Hitler*, p. 263 and p. 428 n. 36.

21 Report by Gaertner on the Anglo-German Fellowship, 23 November 1938, MI5 files, KV5/3, TNA.

22 MI5 note, 17 February 1939, KV5/3, TNA.

23 *DGFP*, Series D, vol. IV, no. 269, pp. 332–4.

24 Tennant, *True Account*, p. 210.

20. THE TWO ENGLISHMEN WHO KNOW GERMANY BEST

1 See e.g. Griffiths, *Patriotism Perverted*, pp. 37–8.

2 Conwell-Evans, Memoir, CONWELL.

3 For more on Eugen Diesel see Thomas, 'Diesel, Father and Son', pp. 376–93; Conwell-Evans, *None So Blind*, pp. 160–1.

4 M/G Memorandum, 'Anglo-German Fellowship meeting', 13 December 1938, KV 5/3 C440756, TNA.

5 Mosley, *Downstream*, p. 77.

6 Reynolds, 'Lord Lothian and Anglo-German relations', p. 7.

7 Reynolds, 'FDR on the British: A Postscript', p. 109.

8 Farnham, *Roosevelt*, pp. 152–62.

9 Tennant, *True Account*, p. 200.

10 Cabinet memorandum by the Secretary of State for Foreign Affairs, 'British Propaganda in Germany', 8 December 1938, pp. 3, CP 284, TNA.

11 Vansittart to Halifax, 21 February 1939, FO 371/23006, TNA.

12 Christie to Vansittart, 10 April 1938, CHRS. Vansittart memorandum to Halifax, 4 January 1939, CONWELL.

13 Vansittart memorandum to Halifax, 4 January 1939, CONWELL.

14 Minutes of 35th Meeting of the Cabinet Committee on Foreign Policy, 23 January 1939, CAB 27/624, TNA.

15 D. Cameron Watt, 'Christie, Malcolm Grahame (1881–1971)', *ODNB*.
16 Cadogan, *Diaries*, pp. 140–1.

21. NO HAPPY RETURNS FOR THE FÜHRER

1 Conwell-Evans, Memoir, CONWELL and *None So Blind*, p. 173. For more on German suspicions of Conwell-Evans see Ritter, '*Die erste DEG*'.
2 See Conwell-Evans, *None So Blind*, p. 72.
3 *The Times*, 16 February 1939.
4 Henderson, *Failure of a Mission*, pp. 185–6.
5 Vansittart to Halifax, 21 February 1939, FO 371/23006, TNA.
6 Conwell-Evans Memorandum, 21 February 1939, C2762/53/18 TNA.
7 Chamberlain, *Diary Letters*, vol. 4, pp. 381–5.
8 Self, *Chamberlain*, p. 347.
9 Conwell-Evans memorandum, 21 February 1939, C2762/53/18 TNA.
10 Conwell-Evans, *None So Blind*, p. 173.
11 Conwell-Evans memorandum, 21 February 1939, C2762/53/18 TNA.
12 Henderson telegram no. 64, 18 February 1939, FO371/23006, TNA.
13 Vansittart to Halifax 21 February 1939, FO 371/23006, TNA; Conwell-Evans, *None So Blind*, p. 173.
14 Cadogan, *Diaries*, p. 151.
15 Vansittart to Halifax, 24 February 1939, FO 371/23006, TNA.
16 Ferris, *Intelligence and Strategy*, p. 97.
17 Cadogan Minute, 26 February 1939, FO 371/23697, TNA.
18 Cadogan, *Diaries*, p. 155; Roberts, *Holy Fox*, p. 141; *The Times*, 8 March 1939; *DBFP*, Third Series, vol. IV, no. 229, p. 237.
19 Gottlieb and Stibbe, 'Peace at any Price'; see also Gottlieb, '*Guilty Women*', pp. 61–3.
20 See Sharpe to Conwell-Evans, 8 June 1938, GBR/0014/PIRI 1/4.
21 Scholtz-Klink speech at AGF Dinner, 7 March 1939, translation by Anglo-German Information Service, March 1939, Wiener Library.
22 Conwell-Evans, *None So Blind*, p. 176.
23 Ibid., p. 182.
24 Cadogan, *Diaries*, p. 155.
25 Chamberlain, *Diary Letters*, vol. 4, p. 393.
26 *DGFP*, Series D. vol. VI, no.35, pp. 36–9.
27 Gilbert, *Churchill*, vol. v (companion), pp. 1389–90.
28 Rhodes James, *Eden*, p. 215.
29 Butler, Lothian, p. 227.
30 Conwell-Evans to Halifax (rough draft), 18 March 1919; Halifax to Conwell-Evans, 19 March 1939. CONWELL.
31 Conwell-Evans, *None So Blind*, p. 183.
32 Cadogan, *Diaries*, p. 163.

33 *Hansard*, HC Deb, 15 March 1939, vol. 345, col. 562.

34 *Hansard*, HC Deb, 19 April 1939, vol. 346, col. 356.

35 *The Times*, 21 April, 25 May 1939; *Manchester Guardian*, 25 April 1939.

36 Roberts, *Holy Fox*, p. 145; Halifax to Conwell-Evans, 19 March 1939, CONWELL.

37 Kershaw, *Nemesis*, p. 184.

38 Cadogan, *Diaries*, pp. 175–6.

39 Ibid., p. 174.

40 *Manchester Guardian*, 20 April 1939.

41 Heffer, *Chips*, vol. 2, p. 115.

42 Chamberlain, *Diary Letters*, vol. 4, p. 409.

43 Conwell-Evans, *None So Blind*, p. 185.

44 Kershaw, *Nemesis*, p. 178.

45 Edwards, *Victor Gollancz*, p. 399; see also Lewis, *The Left Book Club* and Stone, *Responses to Nazism*.

46 *Manchester Guardian*, 28 July 1939.

47 *The Times*, 21 July 1939.

48 *Manchester Guardian*, 28 July 1939.

49 *Times Literary Supplement*, 29 July 1939.

50 Caputi, *Chamberlain*, p. 18.

51 And not for Foot, Owen and Howard as assumed by Cowling, in *The Impact of Hitler*, pp. 539–40.

52 The *Guardian*, 29 September 2001.

22. *GANGSTER POLITICS*

1   Conwell-Evans to Lloyd George, 7 September 1939, LG.

2   *Hansard*, HC Deb, 25 April 1939, vol. 346, col. 1087.

3   Fox, *Langhorne Sisters*, pp. 507–8.

4   *The Times*, 27 April 1939.

5   Butler, *Lothian*, p. 228.

6   Ibid., p. 232.

7   Conwell-Evans, *None So Blind*, pp. 192–8.

8   Meehan, *Unnecessary War*, p. 223.

9   Mosley, *Downstream*, p. 256.

10 See Kordt, *Nicht aus den Akten*, pp. 313–6.

11 Mosley, *Downstream*, p. 257.

12 Rose, *Vansittart*, p. 237.

13 For more on the Schwerin Mission see Klemperer, *Search*, pp. 120–2 and Meehan, *Unnecessary War*, pp. 205–6.

14 Kershaw, *Nemesis*, p. 906.

15 Cadogan, *Diaries*, p. 190.

16 Roberts, *Holy Fox*, p. 164.

23. THE TENNANT MISSION

1   See Wilson minute, 10 July 1939, PREM 1/335 C497340, TNA.
2   Tennant to Chamberlain, 4 July 1939, PREM 1/335 C497340, TNA.
3   Memorandum to Wilson, 5 July 1939, PREM 1/335 C497340, TNA.
4   Self, *Chamberlain*, p. 372.
5   Tennant to Ribbentrop, 10 July 1939, PREM 1/335 C497340, TNA.
6   Chamberlain, *Diary Letters*, vol. 4, p. 435.
7   Bloch, *Ribbentrop*, p. 220.
8   Tennant Report to Wilson, 31 July 1939, PREM 1/335 C497340, TNA.
9   See Tennant to Wilson, 1 August 1939, PREM 1/335 C497340, TNA.
10 Tennant to Butler, 20 August 1939, PREM 1/335 C497340, TNA.
11 Conwell-Evans to Vansittart, 27 July 1939 (emphasis in the original), C10644/415/18, TNA.
12 Griffiths, *Travellers*, p. 302.

24. IF THE WORLD SHOULD FALL AND BREAK

1   Cadogan, *Diaries*, p. 194.
2   Self, *Chamberlain*, p. 374.
3   *Country Life*, 26 August 1939.
4   This intelligence was, at the time, accurate to within hours. See Kershaw, *Nemesis*, pp. 205–15 and Rose, *Vansittart*, pp. 237–8.
5   Cadogan, *Diaries*, p. 200.
6   Self, *Chamberlain*, p. 374.
7   Telegram Vansittart to Conwell-Evans, 24 August 1939, CONWELL.
8   Radio message of His Holiness Pope Pius XII to the Heads of State and Peoples of the World, 24 August 1939, https://web.archive.org/web/20151221130810/http://w2.vatican.va/content/pius-xii/it/speeches/1939/documents/hf_p-xii_spe_19390824_ora-grave.html.
9   Ziegler, *Edward VIII*, p. 400.
10 *The Times*, 25 August 1939.
11 Ibid., 29 August 1939.
12 Struther, *Mrs Miniver*, p. 63.
13 Gilbert, *Churchill*, vol. V, companion part 3, p. 1596.
14 Gilbert *Churchill*, vol. V, p. 1105.
15 Conwell-Evans was unsure of the exact date, estimated 'about 28 August' in his memoir.
16 Horace, *Odes*, Book III, Ode iii, l. 7.
17 Butler, *Lothian*, p. 261.
18 Schmidt, *Hitler's Interpreter*, p. 172.
19 Self, *Chamberlain*, p. 382.
20 Meehan, *Unnecessary War*, p. 246.

25. THE POLITICAL AND MORAL SCUM OF THE EARTH

1   Conwell-Evans to Lloyd George, 7 September 1939 (emphasis in the original), LG.
2   Lady Oxford to Churchill, 25 May 1940, CHAR.
3   For more on 18B see Simpson, *Odious;* Goldman, 'Defence Regulation 18B'.
4   Kershaw, *Making Friends*, p. 302.
5   *The Times*, 6 March 1940.
6   Conwell-Evans to Buxton, 13 October 1939, CONWELL.
7   Conwell-Evans to Lloyd George, 14 October 1939, LG.
8   Henderson to Conwell-Evans, 16 June 1940, CONWELL.
9   Vansittart memorandum to Halifax, 30 August 1938, VNST.
10 Rose, *Vansittart*, p. 247.
11 Christie note, 26 September 1939, CHRS; Rose, *Vansittart*, pp. 240–2.
12 E.g. Parliamentary Peace Aims Group, *Germany's Record: A reply to Lord Vansittart;* and Fraenkel, *Vansittart's Gift for Goebbels*.
13 Conwell-Evans, Memoir, CONWELL.
14 Klemperer, *German Resistance Against Hitler*, p. 90.
15 Colville, *Diaries*, 25 October 1939.
16 Meehan, *Unnecessary War*, p. 263.
17 Cadogan, *Diaries*, pp. 219–22.
18 Memorandum by P. M. Burke, 23 January 1943, KV2 3289, TNA.
19 Hoffmann, *German Resistance*, p. 120.
20 Klemperer, *German Resistance Against Hitler*, p. 158.
21 Kordt, *Nicht aus den Akten*, p. 442. For full speech see *Hansard*, HC Deb, 12 October 1939, vol. 352, col. 564.
22 Conwell-Evans, Memoir, CONWELL.
23 See Meehan, *Unnecessary War*, pp. 256–8.
24 Hoffmann, *German Resistance*, p. 256.
25 Meehan, *Unnecessary War*, p. 259. See also Hoffmann, *German Resistance*, p. 136 and pp. 255–7.
26 Colville, *Diaries*, p. 50.
27 Michael Christie, Obituary of M. G. Christie, privately printed, Christie family.
28 Vansittart to Halifax, 11 March 1940, FO371/24389/c 3439/6/18, TNA.
29 Klemperer, *German Resistance Against Hitler*, p. 166.

26. BRITAIN'S BROKE; IT'S YOUR MONEY WE WANT

1   Caputi, *Chamberlain*, p. 230.
2   Ibid., p. 17.
3   Lothian, *The American Speeches*, pp. 104–9.
4   Gilbert, *Finest Hour*, p. 733.

5   President Roosevelt to King George VI, 22 November 1940, http://docs.fdrlibrary. marist.edu.

6   Lothian, *The American Speeches*, p. 144.

7   Butler, *Lothian*, p. 318.

8   Minute by Creswell, 1 February 1935, FO 371/18824, TNA; Wheeler-Bennett, *Special Relationships*, p. 66; Vansittart, *The Mist Procession*, p. 255.

9   Lothian, *The American Speeches*, p. ix

10 Wheeler-Bennett, *Special Relationships*, pp. 115–6.

11 Butler, *Lothian*, p. 313.

12 Rofe, 'Lord Lothian, 1939–1940', p. 28.

13 *New York Times*, 13 December 1940.

14 Bouverie, *Appeasing Hitler*, pp. 48–9.

27. THE FLYING VISIT

1   Fleming, *Flying Visit*, p. 47.

2   Ibid., p. 71.

3   Richard Evans, *The Hitler Conspiracies*.

4   Tennant, *True Account*, p. 235.

5   Cadbury, *Princes at War*, p. 195.

6   *New York Times*, 14 May 1941.

7   Urbach, *Go-Betweens*, p. 202; Stafford, *Flight*, pp. 41–2.

8   E.g. Evans, *The Hitler Conspiracies*, p. 128.

9   James Douglas-Hamilton, 'Hess and the Haushofers', in Stafford, *Flight*, p. 81.

10 *The Times*, 6 October 1939.

11 Peel, *The Patriotic Duke*, p. xiv.

12 Gorodetsky, 'The Hess affair and Anglo Soviet relations on the eve of "Barbarossa"', p. 405.

13 *New York Times*, 14 May 1941.

14 Haslam, *Near and Distant Neighbours*, p. 113; Lothar Kettenackert, 'Mishandling a Spectacular Event', in Stafford, *Flight*, p. 30.

15 Gorodetsky, 'The Hess affair and Anglo Soviet relations on the eve of "Barbarossa"', pp. 413–4.

16 Churchill, *Second World War*, vol. 3, p. 49.

17 Fox, 'Propaganda', pp. 104–5.

EPILOGUE: NONE SO BLIND AS THOSE WHO WILL NOT SEE

1   Conwell-Evans, *None So Blind*, p. 198.

2   Bloch, *Ribbentrop*, p. 424.

3   Neave, *Nuremberg*, p. 74.

4   Ibid., p. 77.

5   Tennant, *True Account*, pp. 243–4.

6   Conwell-Evans, Memoir, CONWELL.

7   Bloch, *Ribbentrop*, p. 454.

8   Tusa, *The Nuremberg Trials*, p. 468.

9   Colville, *Diaries*, p. 55.

10 West, *A Train of Powder*, p. 72.

11 Especially Conze, Frei, Hayes and Zimmermann, *Das Amt und die Vergangenheit*.

12 Meehan, *Unnecessary War*, pp. 370, 347, 363.

13 Conwell-Evans, *None So Blind*, p. 211.

14 *The Independent*, 23 October 2011.

15 Trevor-Roper, *The Last Days of Hitler*, p. 262.

16 Meehan, *Unnecessary War*, p. 8. See Trevor-Roper, *The Last Days of Hitler*; Namier, *In the Nazi Era* and 'Erich and Theo Kordt: Resisters after the Event'; Wheeler-Bennett, *The Nemesis of Power*.

17 Meehan, *Unnecessary War*, p. 403.

18 *The Times*, 28 February 1945.

19 Author's conversation with Mungo Tennant, 25 February 2015.

20 See e.g. Urbach, *Go-Betweens*, pp. 204–6.

21 *Time and Tide*, 1 February 1958.

22 Conwell-Evans, *None So Blind*, p. x.

23 Meehan, *Unnecessary War*, p. 94.

24 Vansittart to Conwell-Evans, 29 May 1941, CONWELL.

25 Gilbert and Gott, *The Appeasers*, p. 367.

26 Correspondence Richard Gott to Author, 4 December 2012.

27 Gilbert, *Roots of Appeasement*, pp. xi–xiii.

28 Conwell-Evans to Gilbert, 21 May 1962, CONWELL.

29 Conwell-Evans to Gilbert, 13 November 1966, CONWELL.

30 Gilbert to Pamela Turner, 22 November 1968, CONWELL.

31 Enid Christie, 'Brief Notes of what I know of the Christie side', Author's collection.

32 Michael Christie, Obituary of M. G. Christie, privately printed, Christie family.

CONCLUSION

1   Ferris, *Intelligence and Strategy*, p. 98.

2   Harris and Trow, *Hess: The British Conspiracy*, p. 134.

3   *The Times*, 6 June 2002.

4   Stedman, *Alternatives to Appeasement*, p. 232.

5   Packwood, A., 'What would Winston Churchill have thought of COP26?' Churchill College Cambridge Archives Centre [online], https://www.chu.cam. ac.uk/news/2021/nov/5/wsc-cop26/ (accessed 26 January 2022); Letter from John Adams to Abigail Adams, 19 May 1794, https://www.masshist.org/digitaladams/ archive/doc?id=L17940519jasecond (accessed 26 January 2022).

INDEX

References to images are in *italics*.

Göring, Hermann (*cont.*)
  and Schuster 268–9
  and surrender 308
  and Tennant 256
Gott, Richard: *The Appeasers* 319–20
Great Britain 2–3, 57, 60, 127–8, 163, 232
  and Czechoslovakia 179–80, 188, 197–9, 200–2
  and finances 289–90
  and Germany 13, 24–6, 37–8, 40–1
  and Göring 138–9
  and Himmler 19
  and Hitler 23, 39
  and industry 46–9
  and Jews 70
  and Poland 241–2, 269–70
  and Rhineland 98–100
  and Ribbentrop 20–1, 55, 56, 142–4, 170–1, 257–8, 259
  and USA 224–5, 228–9, 246–7
  and war declaration 270–1
  see also Anglo-German Fellowship; British Empire; Chamberlain, Neville; Churchill, Winston; England; Plan Z; Scotland; War Cabinet
Great War, *see* First World War
Greece 251
Greig, Wing Cmdr Sir Louis 106
Griffiths, Richard 9, 154, 261
Grynszpan, Berta 213, 215
Grynszpan, Herschel 215
Guilty Men (Foot/Owen/Howard) 288

Haber, Fritz 51
Halder, Franz 192, 249, 278
Halifax, Edward, Lord 9, 57, 147, 164–7, 274, 288
  and Anglo-German Fellowship 240, 316
  and Blomberg 146
  and Chamberlain 193
  and 'Choice for Germany' speech 250–1
  and Christie 189
  and Churchill 287
  and conscription 248
  and coronation 145
  and Czechoslovakia 180, 181, 191, 192, 202, 238, 239
  and foreign secretary 173, 174
  and Göring 284
  and Hamilton 302
  and Henderson 199
  and Hitler 160, 163–4
  and hunting exhibition 161–2
  and intelligence 226–7, 234, 235, 264
  and Kordt 197, 198

and Kristallnacht 217
  and Lothian 246, 247, 291
  and Plan Z 205, 206, 207, 208, 209, 211
  and Poland 265
  and Rhineland 99
  and Ribbentrop 176
  and Weizsäcker 313
Hamilton, Duke of 105, 108, 109, 297–8, 299–302
Harmsworth, Esmond 30
Harvey, Oliver 136–7, 173–4, 191, 202, 207
Haushofer, Albrecht 108–9, 300, 301–2, 314
Haushofer, Karl 108, 157, 300
Hawes, Captain Melville 60
Hawke, Justice 131
Henderson, Sir Nevile 88, *126*, 135–7, 193, 234, 277
  and Czechoslovakia 180, 181, 191, 198, 199, 201–2, 237–8, 239
  and DEG 231–2, 235–6
  and Göring 233
  and Halifax 162
  and hunting exhibition 161
  and Neurath 149–50
  and Nuremberg rally 196, 197
  and Plan Z 205, 210
  and Poland 269–70
Henlein, Konrad 179–80, 186, 187, 200
Hess, Rudolf 2, 7, 36, 40, 80, 120
  and Berlin Olympics 87–8, 107
  and Edward VIII 58
  and Haushofers 108–9
  and imprisonment 303–4
  and Nuremberg rally 200
  and Nuremberg Trial *306*, 308, 310–11
  and Scotland 236, *294*, 296–301, 302–3, 326
Hewel, Walther 232, 259, 260–1
Heydrich, Reinhard 298
Himmler, Heinrich 2, 60, 67, 142, 171, 177
  and Czechoslovakia 201
  and Dahlem 17, 18–20
  and Hitler 187, 307
  and suicide 308
Hindenburg, Paul von 23, 29
Hitler, Adolf 1, 2, 80–1, 147–8, 185–7, 197
  and Anglo-German Fellowship 10, 154–5, 214
  and Austria 162–3, *168*, 174, 175, 176, 177, 178
  and Baldwin 24, 25–6, 274
  and Berlin Olympics 85, 107–8
  and birthday *230*, 240–1
  and Blomberg 146–7
  and Britain 13, 134